Foundations of Economic Thought

B

Foundations of Economic Thought

Edited by

John Creedy

BLACKWELL
Oxford UK & Cambridge USA

Copyright © Blackwell Publishers 1990

First published 1990
Reprinted 1991

Blackwell Publishers
108 Cowley Road, Oxford, OX4 1JF, UK

3 Cambridge Center
Cambridge, Massachusetts 02142, USA

British Library Cataloguing in Publication Data
A CIP catalogue record for this book is available from the British Library.

Library of Congress Cataloging in Publication Data
Foundations of economic thought/edited by John Creedy.
p.   cm.
Includes bibliographical references.
ISBN 0–631–15642–9
1. Economics.   I. Creedy, John, 1949–
HB171.F618   1991
330—dc20   90–35175
CIP

Typeset in 10 on 12pt Times
by Vera-Reyes, Inc., Philippines
Printed and bound in Great Britain by
Billings, Hylton Rd., Worcester

Contents

Contributors

JOHN CREEDY was educated at Bristol University and Balliol College, Oxford. He has been the Truby Williams Professor of Economics at the University of Melbourne since December 1987. He was previously Professor of Economics at Durham University, England (1978–86), and the Pennsylvania State University, USA (1986–7). His major research interests are in the areas of labour economics, public finance and the history of economic analysis. He is the author of *State Pensions in Britain* (Cambridge University Press, 1982), *Dynamics of Income Distribution* (Blackwell, 1985) and *Edgeworth and the Development of Neoclassical Economics* (Blackwell, 1986), and joint author (with Richard Disney) of *Social Insurance in Transition: An Economic Analysis* (Oxford University Press, 1985). He is also the major author of *Economics: An Integrated Approach* (Prentice Hall, 1984), and has edited several volumes of contributed papers.

MARK C. CASSON is Professor of Economics and Head of the Department of Economics at the University of Reading. Born in 1945, he was educated at Manchester Grammar School, Bristol University and Churchill College, Cambridge. He has taught at the University of Reading since 1969. His principal research interests are entrepreneurship, the economics of the multinational enterprise and the theory and policy of unemployment. He has also published in econometric theory, business history and transport studies. His most recent book is *The Firm and the Market: Studies in Multinational Enterprise and the Scope of the Firm* (1987). He has delivered seminars and public lectures on entrepreneurship in many countries and is a contributor on this subject to the *International Encyclopaedia of Social Sciences* and the *New Palgrave Dictionary of Economics*.

D. A. REISMAN is Senior Lecturer in the Department of Economics, University of Surrey. His books include *Adam Smith's Sociological Economics*, *Richard Titmuss: Welfare and Society*, *Galbraith and Market Capitalism*, *State and Welfare: Tawney, Galbraith and Adam Smith*, *The Economics of Alfred Marshall*, *Alfred Marshall: Progress and Politics*, *The*

Political Economy of James Buchanan and *Theories of Collective Action: Downs, Olson and Hirsch*.

ROGER E. BACKHOUSE was born in 1951. He studied economics and economic history at Bristol University after which he completed a Ph.D. on the theory of economic growth at Birmingham University. He has taught economics at University College London and at Keele University and is now a Senior Lecturer in Economics at Birmingham University. His main interests lie in the fields of macroeconomics and late-nineteenth-century and twentieth-century history of economic thought and methodology. Books he has written include *Macroeconomics and the British Economy* (Martin Robertson, 1983), *A History of Modern Economic Analysis* (Blackwell, 1986; Spanish edition, Allianza Editorial, 1988) and *Economists and the Economy* (Blackwell, 1988). Since October 1989 he has been Book Review Editor of the *Economic Journal*.

LYNN MAINWARING is lecturer in Economics at the University College of Swansea, Wales. He has also taught at University College, Cardiff, and at the University of Reading. His main interests are the theories of capital and distribution deriving from the work of Sraffa and Leontief, and the application of those theories to international trade and investment. He is the author of *Value and Distribution in Capitalist Economies* (Cambridge University Press, 1984) and co-editor (with K. D. George) of *The Welsh Economy* (University of Wales Press, 1988). He is currently preparing a book entitled *Dynamics of Uneven Development: An Analysis of the Global Accumulation of Capital* (to be published by Edward Elgar).

PETER C. DOOLEY is Professor of Economics at the University of Saskatchewan, Canada, where he teaches economic theory and its history. He was educated at Grinnell College and received his doctorate from Cornell University. His main area of research is the conceptual foundations and historical development of the theories of value, distribution and welfare from the time of Adam Smith to the present day. In addition to articles on the history of classical and neoclassical theory, he has published *Elementary Price Theory*, *Introductory Macroeconomics* and *Retail Oligopoly*.

RANDALL G. HOLCOMBE is a Professor of Economics at Florida State University. He received his Ph.D. in economics in 1976 from Virginia Polytechnic Institute, and taught at Texas A & M University and Auburn University before joining the Florida State faculty in 1988. He is the author of *Public Finance and the Political Process* (1983), *An Economic Analysis of Democracy* (1985) and *Public Sector Economics* (1988). His main research interests are in the areas of public finance and public choice, where he has written extensively on the implication of using majority rule political institutions to determine resource allocation.

GEOFF HARCOURT is a University Lecturer in Economics and Politics at the University of Cambridge and the President and a Fellow of Jesus College, Cambridge. In December 1988 he became Professor Emeritus of the University of Adelaide and in November 1988 was awarded the Degree of Doctor of Letters by the University of Cambridge. His major interests are in economic theory, especially the approaches taken to it under the broad rubric of post-Keynesian economics, and its application to policy. He has also become more and more interested in the history of economic thought and in the intellectual biographies of leading economists, trying through these channels to make the subject more alive and humane. His major books include *Some Cambridge Controversies in the Theory of Capital* (Cambridge University Press, 1972), *The Social Science Imperialists. Selected Essays* (ed. Prue Kerr; Routledge & Kegan Paul, 1982) and *Controversies in Political Economy. Selected Essays of G. C. Harcourt* (ed. O. F. Hamouda; Wheatsheaf, 1986), and he is the editor of *The Microeconomic Foundations of Macroeconomics* (Macmillan, 1977) and *Keynes and his Contemporaries* (Macmillan, 1985).

GEOFFREY WHITTINGTON is currently Price Waterhouse Professor of Financial Accounting in the Faculty of Economics and Politics, University of Cambridge, having previously held Chairs in the Universities of Bristol (1975–88) and Edinburgh (1972–5). He is also a part-time member of the Monopolies and Mergers Commission and of the Technical Committee of the Institute of Chartered Accountants in England and Wales. He is a Fellow of the Institute of Chartered Accountants in England and Wales and holds a Ph.D. in Economics from Cambridge. His research interests in recent years have been centrally concerned with accounting for price changes and he has published *Inflation Accounting, an Introduction to the Debate* (1983) and (with D. P. Tweedie) *The Debate on Inflation Accounting* (1984). He was also co-editor (with R. H. Parker and G. C. Harcourt) of *Readings in the Concept and Measurement of Income* (second edition, 1986).

BRIAN LOASBY was born in 1930, and read economics at the University of Cambridge. He held appointments at the Universities of Aberdeen, Birmingham and Bristol (spending a year from Bristol as Arthur D. Little Management Fellow in Cambridge, Massachusetts) before joining the new University of Stirling in 1967. He was Professor of Management Economics at Stirling from 1972 to 1984, when he took early retirement. He retains a base in the Stirling Economics Department, and still teaches part-time. His interest in theories of the firm is linked both to the history of economic theory and method and to organizational behaviour; he attempts to find common principles in the development of economic ideas. His publications include *The Swindon Project* (Pitman, 1973), *Choice, Complexity and Ignorance* (Cambridge University Press, 1976) and *The Mind and Method of the Economist* (Edward Elgar, 1989).

DAVID F. HEATHFIELD is a Senior Lecturer in Economics at the University of Southampton. He is a graduate of University College Cardiff having previously worked in industry as a controls engineer. He has published widely on various aspects of production and on econometric modelling. He has taught in England and in America and is Chairman of the European Production Study Group which he founded with Derek Bosworth in 1976. His books include (with S. Wibe) *An Introduction to Cost and Production Functions* (Macmillan, 1987) and *Modern Economics* (Philip Allan, 1987) and he is co-editor (with D. Bosworth) of *Working Below Capacity* (Macmillan, 1987).

BRIAN HILLIER is a lecturer at the University of York. He has also taught at Durham University, Trent University and Sunderland Polytechnic. His research interest is macroeconomics. He has published in several leading journals and is the author of *Macroeconomics: Models, Debates and Developments* and Assistant Editor of the *Bulletin of Economic Research*.

M. TERESA LUNATI is a lecturer at the University College of Wales, Aberystwyth. Her special research interest in macroeconomics concerns the effects of financing the public sector, which formed the topic for her D.Phil. thesis at the University of York.

MERVYN K. LEWIS is Midland Bank Professor of Money and Banking at the University of Nottingham and visiting professor in economics at Flinders University of South Australia. Recently he has been visiting scholar at the Bank of England, consultant to Australian Financial System Inquiry, and visiting professor at the University of Cambridge and the Business University of Vienna. He holds a bachelor's degree and a Ph.D. from the University of Adelaide and is a Fellow of the Academy of Social Sciences in Australia. He has published six books and numerous articles on monetary economics.

DAVID COLLARD was educated at Cambridge University. He is Professor of Economics at Bath University and Review Editor of the *Economic Journal*. His principal interests are in welfare economics (including the economics of cooperative action) and in the history of economics. He has published material on Walras, Edgeworth, Pigou and Marshall. The most influential of his books has been *Altruism and Economy* (Martin Robertson, 1978, 1981). His recent books include (with D. Pearce and D. Ulph) *Economics, Growth and Sustainable Environments* (Macmillan, 1988).

HUW DIXON was born in 1958 and educated at Balliol College, Oxford, and Nuffield College, Oxford. He is Reader in Economics at Essex University, and is on the editorial board of the *Review of Economic Studies* and an associate editor of the *Journal of Industrial Economics*. He has also lectured at Birkbeck College, London. His prime research interest is the study of imperfect competition and its implications at both the microeconomic and macroeconomic level. He has studied the incentives of oligopolists to precommit themselves (by investment, delegation) and the consequences of such behaviour for oligopolistic equilibrium. His current interest is focused on the implications of the presence of unionized labour markets and concentrated product markets for the nature of macroeconomic equilibrium and the effectiveness of fiscal and monetary policy.

Introduction

A very cursory glance at the literature of economics reveals that economists are much more comfortable when manipulating models than when examining the foundations of the subject. The typical journal article begins by making an appeal to various authorities for the adoption of a framework, or set of assumptions, before quickly getting down to the business of 'cranking the handle', or investigating minor variations as part of a taxonomic analysis. This statement is intended to be descriptive rather than critical; indeed, this type of activity is a necessary and very important part of the research process. But, without doubt, it is occasionally useful to pause in order to assay the value and significance of research programmes. Such an examination of basics can really only come *after* a great deal of preliminary work has been carried out; paradoxical though it may appear, it is not usually feasible to begin with the foundations.

The same process is true of the teaching of economics. Only after students have had some exposure to, and experience in handling, some simple models and techniques of analysis, and have familiarity with the special language used in the subject, can the fundamentals be tackled. Any attempt to begin with first principles generally leads to confusion, created by the need to deal with difficult conceptual issues without a clear context. But good students inevitably reach a stage where they need to 'go back to the beginning' and attempt to place what they have learnt into a clearer perspective.

These comments do not of course apply only to economics, but seem to be true of most subjects. The following remarks, made by J. S. Mill over 145 years ago, are still well worth reading today:

> If we open any book, even of mathematics or natural philosophy, it is impossible not to be struck with the mistiness of what we find represented as preliminary and fundamental notions, and the very insufficient manner in which the propositions which are palmed upon us as first principles seem to be made out, contrasted with the lucidity of the explanations and the conclusiveness of the proofs as soon as the writer enters upon the details of his subject. Whence comes this anomaly?

Why is the admitted certainty of the results of those sciences in no way prejudiced by the want of solidity in their premises? How happens it that a firm superstructure has been erected upon an unstable foundation? The solution for the paradox is, that what are called first principles, are, in truth, *last* principles. Instead of being the fixed point from whence the chain of proof which supports all the rest of the science hangs suspended, they are themselves the remotest link of the chain. (*Essays on Some Unsettled Questions of Political Economy*, 1844, London: J. W. Parker, p. 122)

The purpose of this book is therefore to examine the foundations of a number of areas of economics. It is not directly concerned with methodological issues, nor does it set out to review the historical development of the subject. The exercise involved asking a variety of economists to examine the basics of central and reasonably well-defined, though sometimes broad, topics. Each author was particularly asked to examine the nature of the concepts involved. An important requirement was that they should not only have a thorough familiarity with the area, but should be capable of 'standing back' and forming an independent view of their subject. Authors were not constrained, or chosen, to follow any particular point of view or to follow a specified format. It was felt that to constrain the authors in that way would produce a uniformity that is really not necessary in this type of volume. No attempt to be exhaustive could possibly be made in a volume of this kind, but it is hoped that the serious reader, whether student, teacher or experienced researcher, will find the following essays both informative and stimulating.

John Creedy
The University of Melbourne

1

Economic man

Mark C. Casson

1.1 The Search for a More Relevant Alternative

Economists fall into two main groups: those who believe that there is a crisis in their subject, and those who believe that there is not. The crisis school typically alleges that conventional economic theory is irrelevant to major real world problems (Wiles and Routh, 1984). Such problems do not occur neatly packaged as 'economic', they claim, but rather their economic aspects are intertwined with social and political aspects too. When we look at the intellectual division of labour within the social sciences, economics seems to be isolated from other disciplines. Economists fail to collaborate effectively with sociologists and political scientists: the different disciplines seem to produce conflicting analyses of similar aspects of a problem, rather than complementary analyses of different aspects, as they should.

One reason for its isolation, the critics allege, is that conventional economic theory does not do full justice to the cultural and historical dimensions of its subject. The accusing finger is pointed at the way that economics substitutes for a realistic account of human nature the artificial construct of economic man (Hollis and Nell, 1975; Leibenstein, 1976). Economic man – or 'economic person', as some prefer to call him – is the representative individual who appears in many economic models, particularly the so-called 'neoclassical' ones. He is usually assumed to be optimizing, selfish and materialistic (these terms are defined later). Because of these assumptions, explanations of behaviour couched in terms of economic man often conflict with the evidence of introspection, and appear repugnant in terms of conventional moral values (Sen, 1985). (It is worth noting that most economists do not describe their own motivations in terms of economic man; they speak instead of the fearless pursuit of truth and of dedication to the advancement of learning. If economists *really* believe in economic man then their professional rhetoric is essentially hypocritical.)

I am grateful to Peter Buckley, John Creedy, Jim Pemberton and Alan Roberts for their comments on an earlier draft.

Defenders of orthodoxy (for example, Friedman, 1953) claim that criticism of economic man in terms of the realism of the assumptions is misplaced. The relevant comparison is not between theory and reality, but between one theory and another. Economics should focus on explaining the behaviour of the system as a whole. It cannot expect to explain every act of every single individual within it. Individuals exist only as typical elements which can be aggregated to form a profile of the population as a whole. The system is so complex that there is room for only a very simple account of individual behaviour within it. Economic man merely personifies a parsimonious set of assumptions about human motivation that generate a mutually consistent set of testable hypotheses about system behaviour. The onus is on the critics, it is suggested, to propose an alternative set of assumptions which can perform better in terms of this criterion. It is by no means obvious, however, what this alternative should be.

1.2 Optimization and Comparative Statics

An appraisal of economic man must inevitably range widely, because the concept of economic man is inseparable from the nature of economic theory as a whole. Conventional economics is committed to methodological individualism (Boland, 1982, ch. 2): the economist accepts an obligation to explain social processes as a result of the interplay of separate individual decisions. Economic theorizing cannot therefore begin until the fundamentals of human motivation have been established.

Economic man is essentially man the decision-maker. Decisions imply choice, and choice implies the existence of alternatives. Conventional economics is an applied theory of choice. To explain why someone acted in the way they did is to explain why they chose not to act in some other way.

Three main presuppositions underpin the theory of choice. The first is that in identical situations a given person will make the same choice. Since the same person does not make different choices in the same situation, this suggests that behaviour is systematic rather than erratic. This rules out schizophrenic personality, for example. The second is that a given person may, in different situations, make different choices. Since the person does not resolutely adhere to the same action, this suggests that he is adaptable. Behaviour is not governed by a simple rule which ignores the characteristics of the environment. The third is that there is a discernible pattern in the response to the environment which is compatible with purposeful and intelligent behaviour.

A purposeful agent distinguishes between ends and means. An intelligent agent pursues his ends by selecting appropriate means. He selects the means by constructing a mental model of the environment which is consistent with the information at his disposal.

The most powerful forms of explanation address themselves to comparative evidence obtained under controlled conditions. Because economic
conditions are difficult to control, explanation is usually conducted on
ceteris paribus assumptions. Much of the comparative evidence used in
conventional economics relates to how people's behaviour varies across
different market or fiscal environments (see below). Given this emphasis
on cross-section variation, the theory of choice highlights the margin at
which one course of action is substituted for another.

Emphasis on the margin has implications both for the nature of the
individual's preferences and for his perception of constraints. An individual who has a very strong preference for acting in one particular way
may never act otherwise. To rule out such cases, it is useful to distinguish
between a high-order objective such as utility, to which the individual is
invariably committed, and lower-order objectives which are instrumental
in generating utility, such as the consumption of particular goods. It is
assumed that no single lower-order objective dominates. There are instead
several conflicting lower-order objectives which much be traded off against
each other.

Failure to perceive alternatives could also lead to invariant behaviour.
To rule this out, it is assumed that the individual can perceive all available
alternatives, because his mental model of the environment accurately
reflects the options available.

The handling of the trade-off is considerably simplified if only marginal
alternatives need to be considered. A sufficient condition for this involves
quasi-concavity of the utility function and convexity of the feasible set. If
an option can be identified for which no marginal variation yields a utility
improvement, then, under these conditions, no extra-marginal alternative
will yield an improvement either.

When the utility function and the relevant boundary of the feasible set
can be represented in simple mathematical terms (using, for example,
continuous and differentiable functional forms) then the condition relating to
marginal variations can be expressed in equation form (or some variant,
such as a system of inequalities). Decision-making then reduces to calculation, and intelligence implies optimization. This view of decision-making
based on the calculation of an optimum reflects the standard conception of
economic man.

Using this approach, variations in behaviour are induced by implementing an exogenous parameter shift in the model of environmental constraints. Comparative statics analysis examines the change in behaviour in
terms of the substitution of a new best-response to the environment. Under
suitable assumptions (of the kind indicated above) continuity of response is
guaranteed. An arbitrarily small change in the parameter generates an
arbitrarily small change in behaviour. The direction of response can often
be identified as well without any knowledge of the preference function

other than its quasi-concavity. The classic example is the proof, using revealed preference theory, that a non-zero substitution effect is always negative. According to the Samuelson–Le Châtelier correspondence principle, such qualitative results are also associated with important dynamic properties of the system.

All conventional comparative statics analysis – whether qualitative or quantitative – is predicated on the assumption that preferences are fixed. Changes in individual behaviour are explained by changes in the alternatives available to the decision-maker, and not by changes in his preferences. The autonomy of individual preferences is widely regarded as crucial (Becker, 1976; Becker and Stigler, 1977). This is presumably because changes in alternatives are related to changes in the environment which are easily measurable, whereas changes in preferences might be related to psychological characteristics which cannot be objectively measured. Allowing for the presence of such changes, it is suggested, would undermine the ability to identify the impact of measurable environmental change on individual choice.

This argument, however, is spurious. While the psychological characteristics themselves may not be measurable, there are measurable factors which govern psychological characteristics in a determinate way. It is therefore possible to develop a predictive theory showing how changes in these factors combine with other changes in the environment to affect choice.

1.3 The Conceptualization of Alternatives

Critics of economic man typically take a different view of economic explanation. Their emphasis is on explaining the initial position rather than the response to change. Although conventional economics restricts preferences to a quasi-concave function, it does not provide a unique specification of preferences. (Whilst applied econometricians often select specific functional forms, their criteria concern the identification of parameters and the computability of estimators and often result in choices that appear *ad hoc* from a strictly economic point of view.) The non-uniqueness of the postulated preference structure leaves conventional economics powerless to account for the initial position.

Explanations of the initial position attempt to circumvent the difficulty in three main ways. The first is to postulate a single dominant objective which encourages people to act persistently in a particular way. This view is characteristic of those who explain behaviour in terms of what people want to do rather than in terms of the constraints upon them.

The second is to argue that in practice people have few alternatives. This approach is typical of those who see individuals as victims of some kind of class conspiracy. All the alternatives to the chosen course may be so unpleasant that they are not worth detailed consideration. This suggests that the constraints do not afford the decision-maker a continuum of choices, but present a small discrete set in which one is much more preferable than the others.

The third approach is to deny that people can perceive alternatives even when they exist. It may be claimed, for example, that individuals cannot visualize hypothetical alternatives that they have never tried (or seen others try) before. Another possibility is that people are so busy that they have no time to investigate alternatives and so continue, through inertia or habit, to repeat the choices they have made before. A more extreme approach argues that people can be conditioned to ignore alternatives. The Stalinist view of human nature, for example, suggests that people's minds are like blank sheets of paper on which preferences can be stamped through propaganda or brainwashing. A leader can therefore persuade his followers that there is no alternative to the choice he wants them to make.

It is worth noting that all these approaches provide a simple account of the initial position by implicitly denying the possibility of adjustment to incremental change. These accounts work by denying that there is a margin around which minor modifications of behaviour will occur. The more extreme accounts deny that any kind of adaptation will occur, whilst the more moderate ones suggest that adaptation will occur only through discrete jumps triggered by very major changes in the environment.

Scholars who adopt this alternative perspective on choice frequently talk about 'power'. Power has little significance for an economic man preoccupied with marginal choices between many correctly perceived alternatives, but it does have considerable significance where perceived alternatives are few and the margin is normally remote. The power of the leader of an organization, for example, stems from his capacity to punish those who do not conform and obey the rules – either by exacting penalties or withholding rewards. The near-certainty of unavoidable punishment removes disobedience from marginal consideration. The power of a leader also stems from his ability to mould followers' preferences so that they dedicate themselves to a single course of action (see below). The leader may also control their knowledge of alternatives by encouraging the conservative inward-looking attitude that there is no feasible alternative to doing things the way they are already done within the group.

1.4 General Equilibrium Theory

The single most important factor explaining the influence of economic man on the thinking of professional economists is his role in the neoclassical general equilibrium (GE) model. Economic man provides remarkably parsimonious microfoundations for this model. Some of the assumptions about economic man are, in fact, finely tuned to the specific needs of the GE model.

The high profile of the GE model stems partly from the fact that it tackles an important issue relating to the resolution of human conflict which goes back to antiquity. The issue is whether paternalism and hierarchical organization are necessary to maintain social order (Myers, 1983; Goldsmith, 1985). The movement towards individualism at the end of the Middle Ages revived intellectual interest in this issue, whilst the trend towards individuals holding property absolutely and in their own right, rather than as members of a family, made it of practical political concern (Macfarlane, 1978).

The Newtonian revolution in physics drew yet more attention to this issue. Newton showed how harmony in the heavens was maintained by an equilibrium of gravitational forces. If there is harmony in the heavens, it may be asked, why is there so much conflict on earth? This question directs attention to the search for social and economic forces which have similar equilibrating tendencies. Adam Smith (1776) identified these forces with the invisible hand. He showed how the balance between supply and demand sustained a harmonious division of labour which evolved naturally in a progressive fashion. This revealed market forces as the providentially ordained forces of a self-adjusting social system. A precise correspondence with Newtonian mechanics could not be achieved, however, until this theory had been placed upon secure mathematical foundations.

The development of Benthamite utilitarianism provided a philosophical framework with which individual preferences could be given a simple mathematical form (Steintrager, 1977). It seems doubtful whether the economists who developed applications of utilitarianism appreciated the full impact of modelling human behaviour in these terms, though there is no doubt that the philosophical standpoint appealed to the Whiggish rationalism of many nineteenth-century intellectuals. The harnessing of utilitarianism was a crucial element in the marginalist revolution of the 1870s (Stigler, 1982; Barrientos, 1988), which narrowed the focus of economics to the study of decentralized decision-making within a market system. The broader concerns of the classical economists were largely abandoned. Not surprisingly, the tightly focused research agenda attracted many able mathematicians to the study of economics and, following important work by Walras, Marshall, Cassel, Hicks and Samuelson, the application of topological fixed-point theorems led to the classic formulation of GE theory by Arrow and Debreu (1954).

In the GE model individual preferences are specified in a very particular way. The low-level objectives which appear as arguments of the utility function are confined exclusively to the individual's own consumption of tangible goods and services, whilst the quasi-concavity assumption implies, amongst other things, that the individual is never satiated by the consumption of any of these goods. The individual is also assumed to have perfect information about market prices.

These assumptions impose crucial restrictions on the individual's supplies and demands in each market. These restrictions ensure that, when supplies and demands are aggregated, the excess demand schedules in the various markets have the properties needed to guarantee the efficiency of the market system. It can therefore be seen that both the preference structure and the information set associated with economic man are finely tuned to supporting the efficiency results obtained in GE theory.

To appreciate the logical steps involved in this argument, it is useful to begin by noting that for a GE to prevail, the total value of supplies must equal the total value of demands. Otherwise, it would be impossible to have simultaneous equilibrium in all markets. Whilst this requirement is always satisfied *ex post*, in the sense of accounting for realized outcomes, equilibrium requires that it applies *ex ante* too. A simple way of meeting this requirement is to postulate that each individual's demands and supplies exactly satisfy his budget constraint. Since profit is defined as a residual, the firm's budget constraint is the profit identity and so is always satisfied.

In a GE system the burden of maintaining budgetary discipline therefore falls upon the household. The householder must correctly perceive all prices and also correctly anticipate the profit of each firm in which he holds shares. He therefore requires perfect information on prices and on the profit implications of firms' production plans. To determine firms' production plans, he must know factor prices and their technological parameters too. He must also have sufficient calculating ability to ensure that his demands and supplies are consistent with budgetary balance. Under these conditions, the aggregation of demands and supplies across all firms and households leads to Walras's law. There is overall budgetary balance, so that equilibrium in all markets except one ensures that there is equilibrium in the last market too.

To guide the system to equilibrium it is sufficient that market excess demands are uniquely defined as continuous functions of prices. Optimization provides a convenient framework within which to derive this result. Since the budget constraint determines a bounded and weakly convex feasible set, quasi-concave household preferences of the usual type guarantee a unique optimum which exactly satisfies the constraint. This optimum responds smoothly to changes in prices.

For GE to be efficient it is necessary that all the coordination that needs to be done is done through markets. This imposes exceptionally strong conditions – namely that no one interacts with others except through markets and that the markets that handle these interactions work perfectly. If these conditions are not satisfied then externalities arise. One individual's actions affect another's welfare and there is no way that the victim of the action can influence it. In the absence of such influences, a Pareto-inefficient decision may be made.

The need to avoid externalities helps to explain the focus of GE theory on private rather than public goods. For a given level of production of a private good, an additional unit of consumption by one person denies a unit of consumption to someone else. This does not apply to public goods. Any individual procuring the production of a public good indirectly benefits other people. This encourages selfish people to wait for others to provide the good and so generates a 'free-rider' problem.

Most pure public goods are intangible – tangible goods usually have some capacity limit which, once reached, means that each user precludes another, as with a private good. Information is a good example of an intangible public good. The fact that the acquisition and dissemination of information is not usually treated explicitly in GE theory has much to do with the fact that the procurement of information is an indivisible activity which confers significant external benefits, so that the optimal provision of costly information cannot be guaranteed in a conventional GE framework.

Another source of externality is where one individual is concerned about the consumption pattern of another individual. This individual can then influence the welfare of the first by the way he acts. To rule this out, GE theory requires that each individual is concerned only with his own consumption pattern. He is purely selfish, in other words. A selfish individual who demands only tangible rather than intangible goods may be said to be materialistic. In this sense, selfish and materialistic preferences are hallmarks of conventional economic man as he appears in the GE model.

1.5 Uncertainty

The assumption about perfect information made in the GE model can be relaxed without causing too much damage to the efficiency results. Lack of information implies uncertainty and it was thought at one time that the presence of uncertainty would render optimization so fuzzy that the approach would become practically useless. But this is not, in fact, the case. The crucial requirement for optimization is that both objectives and constraints should be precisely specified. Perfect specification, rather than perfect knowledge, is what is required. Uncertainty can be handled very easily when it is assumed that the decision-maker is able to identify a set of mutually exclusive and collectively exhaustive possible states of the environment, and to associate a subjective probability with each of them. His preferences can then be defined, not over the set of all outcomes in a given state, but over the set of all possible combinations of different outcomes in different states. Moreover, preferences over the contingent outcomes may well satisfy the quasi-concavity condition, so that the decision problem remains sufficiently well defined for optimization to yield a unique choice.

When modified in this way the GE model shows that while the presence of uncertainty leads to suboptimization compared with full information, the allocation of resources will still be efficient conditional on the availability of information and its distribution between individuals. This qualification is nonetheless significant, because it means that some trade may occur which appears efficient *ex ante* but is not so *ex post*. In the context of speculative behaviour, for example, two people who attach different subjective probabilites to the outcome of some event can both gain *ex ante* from betting with each other, but one individual is bound to lose *ex post*. This individual is the one who attaches the lowest subjective probability to the outcome that actually occurs. The *ex ante* mutual welfare gain translates into an *ex post* redistribution of income between the winner and the loser. For the loser, optimization with imperfect foresight makes him worse off than he would have been had he adopted the suboptimizing strategy of not placing a bet at all.

The treatment of uncertainty in GE theory illustrates why conventional theory is criticized for being inherently static, for it is usually assumed that all the information that is ever likely to be available is available initially. In a typical multiperiod model, for example, the individual makes a single integrated lifetime plan at the outset which he has no reason to revise later because no new information emerges before the plan has expired. Even if such information does become available, it will normally be assumed that the possible forms this information might take can be anticipated in advance, and a contingent plan can be drawn up as to how it would lead to the modificaton of subsequent behaviour. This means that only information of a type that can be anticipated will appear. It also means that all learning activity is telescoped back into the preset, in the sense that, before taking the initial decision, the issue of what one would infer from certain information, were it to emerge, has already been considered.

It is rarely possible, however, to anticipate all the kinds of new information that might become available. Under these circumstances, plans need to be reconsidered every time unanticipated information becomes available. The question then arises whether such reconsideration should always be made. When present decisions have future consequences, a fully rational individual will have to take account of every one of these consequences and so, in the strongly interdependent economic system, a very complex analysis will be required (Hey, 1983).

If the individual has limited mental capabilities then it may be unreasonable for him to reconsider his plans in the light of every single new item of information that becomes available, because the expected benefit from such an exercise is less than the psychic cost involved. A detailed evaluation of whether these benefits exceed the cost in each particular case, however, is likely to be even more complex than the task it is designed to help avoid. It is therefore appropriate for the individual to adopt at the outset certain criteria which can be very simply applied. Individual rationality needs to be 'procedural' rather than substantive (Simon, 1983).

An important aspect of procedural rationality is the use of norms. A performance norm identifies a degree or success in decision-making which is considered satisfactory. A shortfall with respect to a performance norm indicates a problem, whose solution competes for attention with other matters. Another kind of norm is an expectation of what an observation, or similar item of information, will turn out to be. Discrepancy between expectation and realization causes surprise (Shackle, 1979). Surprising information points to the existence of a situation which previously seemed unlikely and suggests that a full reconsideration of plans may be worthwhile. Other things being equal, individuals with the poorest initial perception of the environment will encounter the most surprises. Individuals may differ in their response to surprise, however, with some passing the whole affair off as a kind of amusing novelty and others taking a more serious and deliberate approach.

People in the latter group may well reflect on why the new information seemed so surprising. In this way they may be able to detect certain biases in the way that they have drawn inferences from information previously available. An individual with limited mental capabilities may be able to improve his mental power by learning from his past mistakes. When new information is continually becoming available, this learning can itself become a continuous process. Changes in the environment, by providing new data, therefore provide a mechanism by which individuals, as they age, can accumulate experience which improves their decision-making capabilities (Tversky and Kahneman, 1974; see also Hogarth and Reder, 1986).

In practice, it seems, individuals often overlook not just a single possibility but an entire range of possibilities pertaining to events of a certain type. It is suggested below that this is particularly true of their failure to anticipate the way other people behave. The behaviour of other people is not important in an economy with a complete set of Walrasian markets, but it is in many other cases. A great deal of what people learn as they mature is concerned with how other people respond to their actions. The significance of this point is developed in section 1.9.

1.6 An Alternative Research Agenda

Preoccupation with the specific issue of the efficiency of the market system has led to a concept of economic man which has little relevance to wider issues. Crises in economic theory, it may be suggested, tend to occur when the need for urgent solutions to practical problems of policy pushes philosophical speculation about the market system into the background. It is the inability of conventional theory to tackle pressing practical problems outside the market arena that reveals the most serious limitations of economic man.

Recent concern over faltering productivity growth, for example, has focused attention on the discretionary nature of effort within teams and organizations. It is often difficult for supervisors to monitor effort and for owners of firms to monitor managers. Agency theory demonstrates that this gives selfish people an incentive to slack (see, for example, Arrow, 1985). Conventional economic man cannot be trusted: he is sure to take advantage of the situation. He must be given pecuniary rewards which, in the absence of direct measurements of effort, must be related through contingent contracts to a performance measure based upon output. Pecuniary incentives do not provide a complete solution to the problem, however, since when individual effort cannot be observed it is the output of the team or organization as a whole, and not the output of the specific individual, to which the payment is related.

Many of the most successful firms, it appears, tackle this problem not by pecuniary incentives but through moral suasion. They encourage individuals to supply effort unselfishly, by developing their commitment to various causes promoted – directly or indirectly – by corporate activity. In efficiency wage theory (Yellen, 1984), such commitments are reinforced by paying wages which workers perceive as fair and equitable. Individual preferences which are broad enough to encompass aspects of social welfare replace the narrowly self-centred interests of economic man (Akerlof, 1983).

The persistence of collusion between individuals is also difficult to explain in conventional terms. Trade union power relies heavily on the unwillingness of workers to compete for jobs by undercutting the wages of those already in employment (Akerlof, 1980) and on solidarity amongst strikers (Naylor, 1987). Informal collusion between producers through price leadership requires the leader to trust the followers not to undercut prices covertly. There are many other examples where collusion is sustained despite a short-term incentive for each individual party to cheat on the understanding or agreement. The prisoner's dilemma model shows that cheating may be individually rational independently of whether or not other individuals are expected to cheat (Schelling, 1960). Whilst in some cases cheating can be punished by collective action against the culprit, such collective action is itself liable to cheating, whereby not everyone participates in the punishment process. This is a special case of the more general free-rider problem, which inhibits economic man from successfully providing public goods to members of a group (Ng, 1979). The cohesiveness of social groups – whether collusive or not – is thus difficult to explain in terms of the behaviour of economic man.

In unemployment theory, the microfoundations of wage and price stickiness are also difficult to explain in conventional terms. Whilst nominal rigidities can be attributed to money illusion, it is difficult to explain why such illusion should persist if individuals are fully rational and basically well informed. Rigidities in real wages are difficult to account for too, except in terms of employee preferences which include the persistence of a customary minimum standard of living and the maintenance of traditional differentials between occupations.

Stickiness of retail prices is often explained in terms of goodwill, established through implicit contracts – or 'invisible handshakes' (Okun, 1981) – and sustained through reciprocity. Since the obligation to reciprocate cannot be legally enforced, however, it is once again difficult to rationalize such behaviour in terms of purely selfish motives.

There are certain areas of economics where conventional theory is notoriously weak. Scholarship in these areas is often dominated by economists who have defected from the mainstream of the profession and see the study of their field as providing an inductive basis for the creation of an alternative theory (Meier and Seers, 1984; Hill, 1986; Coleman, 1987). In the fields of economic history and economic development, for example, there is a long-standing difficulty in explaining international and interregional disparities in the standard of living and the rate of growth. Observed differences cannot be fully accounted for by differences in resource endowments and technological capabilities. Cultural factors, such as the Protestant work ethic, and the prevalence of entrepreneurial attitudes are said to be important, but proof is difficult because these factors are hard to quantify.

The preceding remarks suggest an alternative research agenda within economics, centred on the explanation of the historical evolution of economic institutions and the impact of such institutions on economic performance (Foster, 1987; Hodgson, 1988). This agenda embraces the establishment and growth of both formal institutions, such as governments and firms, and informal institutions, such as work groups, friendship circles and so on. The focus is on the comparison of institutional arrangements rather than on the more conventional comparison of market equilibria under different fiscal regimes.

A suitable theme for the new agenda is that individuals take a much wider view of their environment than does conventional economic man, and they care about things which may not directly affect them in a purely materialistic sense. This wider interest may seem, from a conventional standpoint, to lead to unwarranted interference in other people's affairs. From another standpoint, however, it highlights the ability of individuals to encompass their own immediate problems within a much wider view and to resolve conflict with others not merely through market forces but also through institutions which engineer the convergence of their preferences to reduce the scale of conflict between them.

1.7 Institutional Inflexibility

It is a feature of many of the problematic phenomena noted above that they involve the persistence of a particular pattern of behaviour, when conventional theory suggests that repeated short-term adaptations might be expected instead. When adjustment does occur, it is normally discrete, as when a new institutional form supplants an old one. The lumpiness of adjustment is most readily explained by fixed costs of evaluating and implementing adjustment.

When fixed costs of adjustment are large it is simply uneconomic to re-evaluate policy continually in the light of every minor change in the environment. Costless adjustment may well be a reasonable assumption when individuals are simply making buying and selling decisions in Walrasian markets. It may even be a reasonable approximation to the situation in real markets where there is intense competition and the costs of switching between alternative trading partners are negligible. But it does not apply in the context of organizational behaviour because organizations are created to deal with complex problems which conventional markets cannot easily solve. Short-term efficiency within an organization normally requires individuals to conform in their commitments to decision rules and working habits. The rules and habits to which members conform can normally be changed only by the leader, who may take some time to recognize the need for change. Such institutional inertia can significantly reduce the frequency, and increase the lumpiness, of adjustment.

Because of the time that must be invested in appraising change there is a tendency for leaders of different organizations to free-ride on one another's efforts (Conlisk, 1980). Each leader adopts a no-change strategy until he observes someone else make a change. He uses this as a cue to begin his own evaluation and then take the experience of the innovator as an input to his own calculations. This can lead to a delay in making the initial change and cause bunching as each leader subsequently makes up for lost time.

Another reason for the persistence of behaviour patterns is that it helps to build up both personal and corporate reputations, which enhance the efficiency of organizations and also facilitate trade by reducing transaction costs. To appreciate the significance of reputations it is necessary to present a critique of Walrasian market assumptions.

1.8 The Non-Walrasian Environment

Real markets operate in a manner that is substantially different from the Walrasian model. The main reason stems from the spatial dimension of transactions. This spatial dimension means that most transactions stem from bilateral encounters between individuals. These encounters are typically face to face. Sometimes the encounters are deliberately planned for purposes of trade – as when people go shopping – and sometimes they are a byproduct of other activities – leisure and recreation, for example.

Another consequence of the spatial dimension is that encounters themselves are spatially dispersed. This means that when negotiating a price in any encounter neither individual can be really sure of what price he would be able to obtain in an alternative trade.

Negotiation may be seen as a process in which each party attempts to influence the other party's perceptions of opportunity costs. A successful negotiation terminates when each party believes that the gain from further manipulating the other party's perceptions by protracting the negotiations is just outweighed by the advantages of concluding an agreement immediately. As a result, price setting is much more time consuming than in a Walrasian system. There will, moreover, be a spatial dispersion of prices across simultaneous transactions which will be greater, the greater are the geographical distances involved and the poorer is the quality of communications.

The execution of the resulting contract may also pose problems, for when exchanging bulky goods in a spatial economy it is often difficult to synchronize payment and receipt. The existence of leads and lags exacerbates the risk of default. Spatial dispersion also creates information asymmetry, where the seller knows the quality of the product better than the buyer – a factor which is difficult to correct for where quality is not reflected in the appearance of the good.

Transactions, it can be seen, involve a number of stages. Each stage typically involves an element of reciprocal externality: each party can take a decision which affects the other's welfare. At stages such as search and negotiation, which come before the contract has been concluded, there is no way of eliminating these externalities by incorporating incentives into the structure of the contract itself.

Transaction costs are typically fixed costs, independent of the volume and value of trade (Casson, 1982). This means that many markets in highly specialized rights cannot function because the potential gains from trade are insufficient to cover the fixed transaction costs. Trading in such goods will be diverted into markets for more versatile goods and services which can then be allocated to a specific use once the owner has gained possession of them.

Versatile goods are often traded between institutions (households, firms, government bodies) and within these institutions the markets that are too specialized to operate externally operate internally between the members of the institutions. Institutions are therefore a mechanism for internalizing the externalities that arise from the fact that conventional trade is costly to arrange. To economize on internal transaction costs it uses very different principles of trading from the external market. It places considerable emphasis on spontaneous cooperation underpinned by the trust that members of a stable institution learn to place in one another.

Individual members may develop a strong commitment to their institution. They form a social group whose organic structure becomes a vital concern of the members. This organic structure is the product of a division of labour within the group. Individuals may identify closely with their role within the group, particularly if they are assigned to it on a long-term basis.

Other social sciences – notably sociology – take the existence of the social group as in some ways more fundamental than that of the individual. Their analysis begins with the group as an organic entity, rather than with the individual as an isolated social atom. This organic view has much to recommend it, as it emphasizes the strength of the long-term non-market relations that exist between individuals in both their consumption and production activities. Conventional economics, with its emphasis on the individual isolated from others except through market transactions, is potentially misleading in this respect. The valid commitment to methodological individualism should not obscure the importance of social groups in economic coordination and the consequent restraint that this places on the speed with which the system adjusts to small environmental changes.

1.9 Reputation and Commitment within a Transaction Game

In the absence of Walrasian markets, almost any attempt at coordination must address a situation in which there are reciprocal externalities. The previous section showed that the typical transaction in fact involves a sequence of such reciprocal externalities.

Reciprocal externalities are the basis of non-cooperative games. When each stage of a transaction is considered separately, the pay-offs associated with the resultant games commonly share certain properties. The games belong to a small number of types, such as 'chicken' and prisoner's dilemma (Schelling, 1960). When these games are considered in the context of the entire sequence, however, the later games become subgames within an encompassing sequential game pertaining to the transaction as a whole (for biological analogies see Smith, 1982). At any one stage, the nature of the game that is entered at a subsequent stage depends upon the outcome at the current stage. The most obvious manifestations of this is that certain combinations of strategies at any stage can cause the transaction as a whole to fail, and the rest of the sequence to abort.

Given that individuals move on, within a spatial economy, from one encounter to another, each transaction has a potential successor. The outcome of one transaction can influence the nature of subsequent transactions through reputation effects. These occur when someone observes how a party behaves in a given transaction and uses it to infer how they are likely to behave in future transactions. Reputation mechanisms are most effective when bilateral transactions are readily observed by third parties; third parties constitute a reasonably impartial source of information on the transaction and act as a conduit for the dissemination of this information to people who are likely to deal in future with the partner concerned. Third party observation is most likely to occur amongst a relatively small number of transactors who are members of a stable group engaged in regular face-to-face contact within a compact territory.

Reputation effects mean that each transaction must itself be considered as an element within a sequence, with decisions made at any stage having the capacity to affect all future stages of the sequence. Given that each transaction is itself a sequence, the problem of deciding the optimal strategy at any given stage then becomes incredibly complex (on complexity see Loasby, 1977).

One way of coping with such complexity is to exploit the repetitive nature of the transaction experience and derive simple rules for transacting which can be applied without further analysis in each subsequent transaction (Axelrod, 1984). The fixed cost of developing the rule is then spread over a number of transactions. With sufficient repetition, these rules may be applied almost subconsciously because the individual has become habituated to them. The most widely studied rules involve trigger mechanisms that punish opponents who refuse to reciprocate cooperative behaviour.

A major cause of the complexity in sequential games is that each party is playing against an intelligent opponent. When both parties are equally intelligent, an attempt to find a winning solution that outwits the opponent may well be self-defeating. For every strategy one party investigates, the other will investigate the counter-strategies. As each attempts to uncover possible strategies that the other has overlooked, the dimensions of the game increase and the complexity accelerates further.

It is worth noting that conventional economic analysis typically handles such problems by restricting the vision of one or more of the players. In the Cournot model of oligopoly, for example, both players have restricted vision, in the sense that each takes the other's output as given when he could, in fact, influence it. The Cournot equilibrium is inherently myopic – which is confirmed by the fact that both parties could do better through collusion. In the Stackelberg model, the leader's vision of the game encompasses the follower's Cournot response, and so the follower's behaviour is endogenized in the leader's calculation of his optimal strategy. When both players have an encompassing vision, however, problems arise if they both persist in pursuing strategic self-interest. Neither can outwit the other through quantity adjustment, and any recourse to other instruments, such as advertising and research and development (R & D) strategies, can also be matched by the other party. They are therefore driven towards collusion, but the organization of collusion becomes itself just another game. Each is trying to outwit the other in extracting concessions over the distribution of profit and in organizing the marketing in order to maximize the chances of cheating by themselves and to minimize those for the other party.

Each party would find the game much easier to play if the other party were committed to a simple rule. But the other party would not make such a commitment because he would fear that he could be manipulated. If one party could make a commitment to non-manipulation, however, then the other party might well find it worthwhile, because of decision-making economies, to adopt a simple rule. Thus commitment by one party to a rule, and by the other to non-manipulation, may confer mutual benefit. Other forms of commitment, such as mutual commitment to complementary rules, might afford similar economies; but non-manipulation, being a principle, is potentially more flexible. There are two main problems with non-manipulation. The first is to define exactly what it means, and the second is to explain why a commitment to non-manipulation could ever be credible.

Non-manipulation is essentially a state of mind. It involves forbearing from pursuing one's own interests by exploiting a knowledge of other people's patterns of behaviour. It is impossible for observers to test for it directly, but there are certain symptoms by which it can be identified. One of these is a symmetric distribution of the benefits of a transaction. Benefit, of course, must be measured relative to opportunity cost, and is therefore a subjective concept itself. A group of independent observers may nonetheless be able to reach consensus over the degree of symmetry in the transaction – even if this consensus differs according to the cultural values of the group. A culturally specific concept of non-manipulation can then be defined.

Assume, therefore, that manipulation is detected through the distribution of benefits. Commitment to non-manipulation could, in principle, be encouraged through a system of rewards and penalties, but this leaves open the question of who is to have the power to enforce them. One solution is for people who are likely to transact with each other to enter into a preliminary contract in which they determine a mechanism for identifying manipulation according to agreed criteria and surrender to an enforcing power whatever instruments they have for evading or countering punishment. This only pushes the problem back one stage further, however, because whoever is given such power is clearly in a strong position to manipulate those who have surrendered it to them. How could the party concerned be trusted to exercise restraint?

Ultimately, it seems, the commitment to non-manipulation must be based on a credible personal commitment to exercise restraint in pursuit of self-interest. Such a commitment must have the property that the individual would punish himself were he to break it. He must be emotionally committed in the sense that default will cause feelings of guilt. To enter into such a commitment there must be some compensating advantages, however. Commitment to non-manipulation must have certain rewards of its own, which are anticipated at the time the commitment is made and are sufficiently real that the individual remains fearful of default. These rewards, it may be suggested, stem from the more intense psychic benefits obtained from outcomes which acquire special significance because they promote the objective to which the individual is committed.

Individuals may differ in their capacity for commitment of this kind. An individual with an established reputation for commitment to non-manipulation is likely to attract people to trade with him. He will benefit from this provided he is not himself the victim of manipulation. Since non-manipulation is a principle rather than a rule, an intelligent individual is not too vulnerable in this respect. He may also emerge into a leadership role in which people trust him with power and rely upon him as an independent third party to monitor their transactions. Part of the payment offered by the transactors may be their active support in punishing those who do attempt to manipulate the leader.

This leadership role is, in fact, rather akin to the role of the auctioneer in the GE system. The auctioneer is trusted by all transactors with the crucial role of price setting, acting as a clearing house for orders and consignments, and ensuring that contracts are enforced. Not only is he perfectly efficient, in the sense of operating costlessly, but he exercises remarkable self-restraint in not using his position as intermediator to set a monopolistic margin between buying price and selling price in each market. In practice, only an individual with impeccable credentials for non-manipulation would ever be entrusted with the responsibilities of the Walrasian auctioneer.

1.10 The Social Group

Commitment, it has been suggested, provides both direct emotional benefits and indirect benefits through the reduction of transaction costs.

The benefits from commitment are often most easily generated within the framework of a social group. A social group contains individuals who share the same commitment. Thus individuals who join the same group benefit both directly from the emotional support of the others and indirectly from the fact that transaction costs are lower when they trade with other members of the same group (Granovetter, 1985).

From an economic point of view, a particularly interesting type of group is the workgroup. Workgroups are found in firms both in shop-floor production and among managers making collective decisions. Within a workgroup individuals typically operate as a team, which means that failure by any one individual can seriously damage overall group performance. Within a team, the leader typically assigns each individual member to a role and sets a performance norm. In a well-run group the member will receive practical and emotional support in attaining these norms. If he is successful, he will experience satisfaction and receive the approval of the leader. If he fails, he will normally quit the group, finding another group – possibly committed to some other objective – within which he can perform better. The benefits of group membership can usually be assessed accurately only through experience. Individuals who are still seeking a worthwhile commitment and a workgroup to support it will tend to circulate between groups, whilst those who have found what they are looking for will stay with their group. The fact that breaking a commitment generates feelings of guilt discourages individuals from 'shopping around' once they have made their decision.

When membership of a group is voluntary, leaders can be regarded as effectively competing for the most able members in order to further their objectives. They may also compete on other fronts too, because their objectives conflict. Whilst competition between groups can often be useful in setting external norms against which each group can judge its performance, it can also degenerate into warfare unless all groups respect the rules of the competitive game. In this respect the morality of leaders themselves is crucially important. Integrity requires that they should be personally committed to the official objectives of their group, but not so committed that they abandon self-restraint by punishing weaker members severely for underperformance or by attacking rivals on the basis that victory is to be obtained at all costs. The requisite combination of dedication and restraint seems to be difficult to find in practice.

1.11 Ethical Man

This chapter began by inquiring whether there was a more relevant alternative to economic man. The preceding discussion suggests that an alternative may indeed exist. There may well, in fact, be several alternatives, but it is convenient to focus on just one. This alternative may be termed ethical man. It articulates a broader concept of human nature than the conventional economic man who is finely tuned to the requirements of GE theory. Ethical man has, in fact, a number of distinguished antecedents in the literature of economic philosophy (see in particular Hoyt, 1926; Knight, 1933; Macfie, 1936, 1943).

Ethical man, like economic man, is purposeful and intelligent (in this respect, but only in this respect, he is also similar to 'Austrian' man (Kirzner, 1986)). These restrictions mean that the concept is certainly not a vacuous one. Unlike economic man, however, his purposes are fixed only in the very general sense that he is seeking peace of mind. In any given situation this general purpose is translated into more proximate objectives. These proximate objectives are more precise and resemble more closely the preferences of conventional economic man. They are not autonomous, however. They can be influenced by the social group (or groups) to which the individual belongs. The individual searches across groups in pursuit of commitments that will give peace of mind. Within any group he conforms to the pursuit of the collective goal – willingly when membership is voluntary, but possibly as a result of coercion if it is not. Because the mechanism of preference change is well specified, the criticisms of endogenous preferences that are usually advanced do not apply.

Unlike economic man, ethical man, though intelligent, is not perfectly rational. He does not deal with perfectly specified hypothetical problems, but with complex real world problems where intuitive heuristic judgement is an essential adjunct to formal analysis. Ethical man relies heavily upon routine control procedures for recurrent types of decision. Routine procedures are reconsidered only when a problem emerges. A problem is identified when a performance norm fails to be satisfied. Some routine procedures may never be reconsidered – particularly where norms are low. In such cases individuals may reveal (to someone with higher norms) significant biases in their judgement. These biases will typically reflect the accumulated impact of past group influences, resulting in members of different groups making very different decisions under similar circumstances. In groups with low norms, therefore, considerable intergroup diversity may result. Where norms are higher, however, biases will tend to be eliminated through the learning process that is inherent in continued problem-solving. Intelligence ensures that the basic learning skills are present, so that groups with high norms will converge on best-practice decision procedures in the long run.

There is one sense in which ethical man is more rational – not less rational – than conventional man. Ethical man often takes a broader view of a problem than does economic man, encompassing aspects of the environment that economic man ignores. This is particularly true of the behaviour of other major players in the environment. Economic man often optimizes within the context of exactly specified models which fail to endogenize the responses of others to his own decisions. Ethical man endogenizes such responses, but recognizes that explicit analysis is often impossible because of the resulting complexity. Ethical man, for example, has sufficient vision to realize that when playing against an equally intelligent opponent cooperative strategies must be developed which involve reciprocal commitments. In some cases reputation effects may be sufficient to make commitments credible, whereas in other cases emotional commitment, secured by peace of mind on the one hand and guilt-feelings on the other, are necessary. Shared membership of a social group is instrumental in enhancing both reputation effects and emotional attachments, and so joining a group, even though it involves tampering with proximate preferences, can still be perceived as a reasonable step to undertake. Ethical man has sufficient intelligence to perceive this, but regrettably economic man, because of the narrow vision engendered by the Walrasian environment in which he operates, cannot. Ethical man is social, and indeed gregarious, whereas economic man is not (McIntosh, 1969; Roberts and Holdren, 1972; Hirschman, 1982).

Ethical man's capacity for commitment appears indirectly in game-theoretic analysis of reputation. Some models (e.g. Rosenthal, 1981) postulate a small probability of 'irrational' behaviour by potentially reputable people. The capacity for commitment may be interpreted as a 'rationalization' of such 'irrational' behaviour, as it is commitment to a particular pattern of behaviour that is crucial in such analysis.

The concept of ethical man demonstrates that people differ in many respects, and not just in their preferences for material goods and services. People differ in the objectives to which they are committed, in their personal norms, in their capacity to handle complex decisions, in the knowledge and in the biases they have inherited from previous experience and so on. The concept of economic man therefore makes it possible to recognize genuine personality differences between people and to address the crucial economic issue of how people with different personalities are to be matched to different roles within a social group. It is possible, in principle, to examine the requirements of each role in terms of the responsibilities that go with it and the qualities that are consequently needed to perform it effectively. This provides a much richer analytical structure than conventional economic theory with which to investigate the performance of groups, both large and small – from shop-floor workgroups to large firms and even to nation states themselves.

An important aspect of the division of labour within a group is the relation between leader and follower. Leaders have a valuable role in intermediating between followers and most particularly in building up trust between them. In one sense a leader resembles economic man more closely than his followers do, for his preferences tend to exhibit a higher degree of autonomy and his decision-making is often more calculating too.

A crucial issue is how far leaders also resemble economic man in being potentially devious and untrustworthy. It is important for the functioning of groups that leaders are committed both to the official objectives of the group and in particular to the non-manipulation of other people's commitments. The performance of the group hinges on the leader's being trusted, and indeed it is often the most trusted individual who emerges as the leader of a group. Because the concept of ethical man is so much broader than that of economic man, it provides plenty of opportunity to analyse the role of personality factors in leadership and to relate group performance to leadership style.

Ethical man is also better suited than economic man to dynamic analysis. Ethical man does not attempt to telescope the whole of the future into his present decisions, because he appreciates the complexity of decision-making that would result. Neither does he expect other individuals to enter into sophisticated contingent forward contracts for his benefit. The transactions costs involved are prohibitive. He recognizes that moral commitments to simple principles or rules are in many cases an adequate substitute. He copes with problems as and when they arise, relying for support upon the goodwill of other members of his social group. Taking this adaptive and evolutionary approach, he recognizes that economic success is not just an individual, but also a group phenomenon.

1.12 Conclusion

It is a hopeful sign that in the last 25 years or so the narrow concept of economic man has steadily been weakened – if not undermined – in the course of a number of imaginative applications of economic analysis to subjects of wider import (in addition to earlier references, see Margolis, 1982, and Sugden, 1986). This success has allowed economics to function, to some extent, as an imperial science, bringing the standpoint of methodological individualism to bear on social issues previously analysed chiefly from an organic standpoint (Hamlin, 1986). It has allowed economics to regain some of the ground that was lost to sociology and political science in the aftermath of the marginalist revolution (Hirshleifer, 1985).

It has been argued in this chapter that the concept of ethical man provides a more appropriate basis on which to continue this imperialistic movement. Ethical man harnesses the power of methodological individualism to analyse behaviour in a manner complementary to, rather than in conflict with, the insights that emerge from the organic perspective. Methodological individualism, through ethical man, can provide the 'bottom-up' perspective on the same sort of issues for which the organic perspective provides the 'top-down' view. This should permit a more sensible intellectual division of labour within the social sciences. The methods of economics can be used to develop the individualistic perspective across the whole range of sciences analysing the social system. Other social sciences can concentrate on the elaboration of the organic perspective. Because of the role of markets in decentralizing decisions, the individualistic perspective will tend to be of greatest relevance in analysing market behaviour. Conversely, within strictly hierarchical organizations, the organic view will reveal its greatest relative strength. Thus there will continue to be some association between market analysis and individualism on the one hand and hierarchical analysis and the organic approach on the other, but, where they interface, a better intellectual 'fit' should, in future, be obtained.

REFERENCES

Akerlof, G. A. (1980) 'A theory of social custom, of which unemployment may be one consequence', *Quarterly Journal of Economics* 94, 719–75.
Akerlof, G. A. (1983) 'Loyalty filters', *American Economic Review* 73, 54–63.
Arrow, K. J. (1985) 'The economics of agency', in *Principals and Agents: The Structure of Business*. Ed. J. W. Pratt and R. J. Zeckhauser, Boston, Mass.: Harvard Business School Press, pp. 37–51.
Arrow, K. J., and G. Debreu (1954) 'Existence of equilibrium for a competitive economy', *Econometrica* 22, 265–90.
Axelrod, R. (1984) *The Evolution of Cooperation*. New York: Basic Books.
Barrientos, A. (1988) 'Economic man, mathematics and the rise of neoclassical economics', Ealing Working Papers in Economics, No. 5.
Becker, G. S. (1976) *The Economic Approach to Human Behaviour*. Chicago, Ill.: University of Chicago Press.
Becker, G. S., and G. J. Stigler (1977) 'De gustibus non est disputandum', *American Economic Review* 67, 76–90.
Boland, L. A. (1982) *The Foundations of Economic Method*. London: Allen and Unwin.

Casson, M. C. (1982) *The Entrepreneur: An Economic Theory.* Oxford: Martin Robertson.

Coleman, D. C. (1987) *History and the Economic Past: An Account of the Rise and Decline of Economic History in Britain.* Oxford: Clarendon Press.

Conlisk, J. (1980) 'Costly optimisers versus cheap imitators', *Journal of Economic Behaviour and Organisation* 1, 275–93.

Foster, J. (1987) *Evolutionary Macroeconomics.* London: Allen and Unwin.

Friedman, M. (1953) 'The methodology of positive economics', in *Essays in Positive Economics.* Chicago, Ill.: University of Chicago Press, pp. 3–43.

Goldsmith, M. M. (1985) *Private Vices, Public Benefits: Bernard Mandeville's Social and Political Thought.* Cambridge: Cambridge University Press.

Granovetter, M. (1985) 'Economic action and social structure: the problem of embeddedness', *American Journal of Sociology* 91, 481–510.

Hamlin, A. P. (1986) *Ethics, Economics and the State.* Brighton: Wheatsheaf.

Hey, J. D. (1983) 'Towards double negative economics, in *Beyond Positive Economics?* Ed. J. Wiseman, London: Macmillan, pp. 160–75.

Hill, P. (1986) *Development Economics on Trial: the Anthropological Case for a Prosecution.* Cambridge: Cambridge University Press.

Hirschman, A. (1982) *Shifting Involvements: Private Interest and Public Action.* Oxford: Martin Robertson.

Hirshleifer, J. (1985) 'The expanding domain of economics', *American Economic Review* 85(b), 53–68.

Hodgson, G. (1988) *Economics and Institutions.* Oxford: Blackwell.

Hogarth, R. M., and M. W. Reder (eds) (1986) *Rational Choice: The Contrast between Economics and Psychology.* Chicago, Ill.: University of Chicago Press.

Hollis, M., and E. Nell (1975) *Rational Economic Man: A Philosophical Critique of Neo-classical Economics.* Cambridge: Cambridge University Press.

Hoyt, E. E. (1926) *Primitive Trade: Its Psychology and Economics.* London: Kegan Paul, Trench, Trubner.

Kirzner, I. M. (ed.) (1986) *Subjectivism, Intelligibility and Economic Understanding: Essays in Honour of Ludwig M. Lachmann on His Eightieth Birthday.* London: Macmillan.

Knight, F. H. (1933) *The Ethics of Competition: And Other Essays.* London: Allen and Unwin.

Leibenstein, H. (1976) *Beyond Economic Man: A New Foundation for Microeconomics.* Cambridge, Mass.: Harvard University Press.

Loasby, B. J. (1977) *Choice, Complexity and Ignorance.* Cambridge: Cambridge University Press.

Macfarlane, A. (1978) *The Origins of English Individualism: The Family, Property and Social Transition.* Oxford: Blackwell.

Macfie, A. L. (1936) *An Essay on Economy and Value: Being an Inquiry into the Real Nature of Economy.* London: Macmillan.

Macfie, A. L. (1943) *Economic Efficiency and Social Welfare.* London: Oxford University Press.

McIntosh, D. (1969) *The Foundations of Human Society.* Chicago, Ill.: University of Chicago Press.

Margolis, H. (1982) *Selfishness, Altruism and Rationality: A Theory of Social Choice.* Cambridge: Cambridge University Press.

Meier, G. M., and D. Seers (eds) (1984) *Pioneers in Development*. New York: Oxford University Press.

Myers, M. L. (1983) *The Soul of Economic Man: Ideas of Self-interest, Thomas Hobbes to Adam Smith*. Chicago, Ill.: University of Chicago Press.

Naylor, R. (1987) 'Strikes, free riders and social customs', Warwick Economic Research Papers, No. 275.

Ng, Y.-K. (1979) *Welfare Economics: Introduction and Development of Basic Concepts*. London: Macmillan.

Okun, A. M. (1981) *Prices and Quantities*. Oxford: Blackwell.

Roberts, B., and R. R. Holdren (1972) *Theory of Social Process: An Economic Analysis*. Ames, Iowa: The Iowa State University Press.

Rosenthal, R. W. (1981) 'Games of perfect information, predatory pricing and the chain-store paradox, *Journal of Economic Theory* 25, 92–100.

Schelling, T. C. (1960) *The Strategy of Conflict*. Cambridge, Mass.: Harvard University Press.

Sen, A. (1985) 'The moral standing of the market', in *Ethics and Economics*. Ed. E. F. Paul, F. D. Miller, Jr., and J. Paul, Oxford: Blackwell, pp. 1–19.

Shackle, G. L. S. (1979) *Imagination and the Nature of Choice*. Edinburgh: Edinburgh University Press.

Simon, H. A. (1983) *Reason in Human Affairs*. Oxford: Blackwell.

Smith, A. (1776) *An Inquiry into the Nature and Causes of the Wealth of Nations*. Ed. R. H. Campbell, A. S. Skinner and W. B. Todd, 1976, Oxford: Clarendon Press.

Smith, J. M. (1982) *Evolution and the Theory of Games*. Cambridge: Cambridge University Press.

Steintrager, J. (1977) *Bentham*. London: Allen and Unwin.

Stigler, G. J. (1982) *The Economist as Preacher*. Oxford: Blackwell.

Sugden, R. (1986) *The Economics of Rights, Co-operation and Welfare*. Oxford: Blackwell.

Tversky, A., and D. Kahneman (1974) 'Judgement under uncertainty: heuristics and biases', *Science* 185, 1124–31.

Wiles. P., and G. Routh (eds) (1984) *Economics in Disarray*. Oxford: Blackwell.

Yellen, J. L. (1984) 'Efficiency wage models of unemployment', *American Economic Review, Papers and Proceedings*, 94, 200–5.

2

The State and economic activity

D. A. Reisman

In 1949, riding high on the crest of a wave of interventionism which many felt would never break, Richard Henry Tawney wrote as follows about the capacity of wise and well-intentioned leaders to plan the collective future successfully:

> The increase in the freedom of ordinary men and women during the last two generations has taken place, not in spite of the action of the Governments, but because of it. It has been due to the fact that, once political democracy had found its feet popularly elected chambers began, under the pressure of their electors, to prescribe minimum standards of life and work, to extend public services, to pool surplus wealth and employ it for the common good. . . . The mother of liberty has, in fact, been law. (Tawney, 1966, p. 169)

Almost two centuries earlier, in 1755, Adam Smith, aware of what market capitalism required if it was to promote allocative efficiency and economic growth and convinced that State direction was normally ill informed and frequently counter-productive, had proposed a somewhat different mix for the mixed economy:

> Little else is required to carry a state to the highest degree of affluence from the lowest barbarism, but peace, easy taxes, and a tolerable administration of justice; all the rest being bought about by the natural course of things. (Quoted by Rae, 1895, p. 62)

Neither Tawney nor Smith denied the importance either of competitive markets or of State intervention – or of speculation on the State and economic activity such as constitutes the subject-matter of this essay. Where they differed was in the balance of their bias. Tawney's preferred principle was that of authority – the authority of good Governments, the super-authority of moral precepts. Smith's preferred principle was that of exchange – because the *quid pro quo* is natural to man and because the invisible hand of calculative self-interest is a potent source of progress. Each author, whichever was his preferred principle, had within his intellectual make-up distinctive elements of both. The same is likely to be true of the vast majority of his readers. The principle of authority and that of exchange are deep-seated social and psychological constructs. They are considered in the first section of this chapter. The second and third sections deal with the protective State and the productive State, respectively. (The terminology is taken from Buchanan, 1975.) The final section is concerned with public finance.

The tyranny of weasel words has led to the separation of economics from politics by means of an academic sleight of hand performed so skilfully that few students wishing to pass their examinations, and few lecturers wishing to publish their papers, pause to reflect upon the logic of an academic division of labour which by tradition and convention assigns authority to politics and exchange to economics. The division of labour is a wonderful thing, stimulating as it does intimacy of knowledge, the saving of time and the opportunity to make new discoveries; but it can also lead to stupidity, ignorance and mental mutilation, where the operative becomes stuck in his disciplinary rut and is unable to mould anew his instruments to suit the nature of his materials. Political economy is the interdisciplinary synthesis which seeks to put back the clock on the academic division of labour. This is entirely as it should be; for the fact is that the principle of authority and that of exchange are closely intertwined, complements rather than substitutes in the minds of most observers and in virtually every known social system. What is surprising is not that political economy now seeks to reunite the disparate but that two such interdependent principles were ever separated at all.

2.1 Authority and Exchange

The principle of authority and that of exchange are closely connected, both in the history of ideas and in the analysis of institutions. In the language of ideal types, however, they are separate.

The principle of authority is the principle of non-ego leadership and external guidance. It is in some ways the more easily assimilable of the two, since economic psychology begins with an infant socialization of which the central perception is that of benevolent despotism: the earliest order that most people hear is 'do as I say', the earliest justification given is 'because I say it', the earliest mode of legitimation is not the achieved status of election but the ascribed status of consanguinity, the earliest set of constitutional guidelines is rudimentary and sketchy – and all this is bound up with the warmth of love and affection, a sense of belonging and the sensation of loyalty. No less easy to understand than the instinctual tribalism that is first felt in the emotive bonding of the family environment and is subsequently experienced in situations evoking a similar collective commitment (situations involving, say, nationalism, imperialism, militarism, racialism, patriotism) is, however, the confidence in essences and absolutes which, alongside the urge-based non-rational, draws individuals to authority as the moth to the flame. Religious people, who will say that God exists and (much like any other father in that respect) propounds laws which are simply not open to creative modification and intellectual debate, will in this respect be able to make common cause with obsessive fact-gatherers and logic-choppers in asserting that reality is objective (not subjective) and independent of the contents of men's minds.

The emphasis of the investigators and the detectives on the uncovering of pre-existent truths, and their use of the powerful language of physics (the law of gravity, the position of equilibrium) and of the eternal verities of mathematics (including the maximization and the gradualism of the differential calculus), will appeal strongly to those attracted to the principle of authority because of a belief that it is more compatible with the perpetuation of the *status quo* than is the principle of exchange: these natural conservatives, attached as they are to habits, routines, conventions and customs, will derive satisfaction from the idea that there is momentum inhering in matter such as to promote stability and damp down revolutionary change that would be a threat to the identity. Others, less conservative, will be attracted to the principle of authority because, while in their eyes it does not repress innovative originality, at least it represses choice: the racialism of Gobineau and Sombart, the biological evolutionism of Darwin, the inexorability of Hegelian idealism, all breed fatalism, and none more so than Marxian historical materialism, with its account of an unstoppable march towards the expropriation of the expropriators as if guided by the invisible hand of self-transcending stages. Progress or cataclysm, after all, there is something intrinsically conforting about the sheer automaticity of that which must be. Gunnar Myrdal is only one among many to have pointed out that the road to a nervous breakdown is paved with extensive ranking of alternative scenarios, that Buridan's ass died of economizing and that a great number of people are genuinely afraid of freedom: 'Men, on the whole, do not want to be taught to think straight; they prefer to be told what they should believe' (Myrdal, 1955, p. 139). Whether told by the done thing or told by the wise and benevolent statesman, such natural followers will be attracted both to the principle of authority and to the scientistic conviction that there exists a non-ego constraint of circumstance to which individual freedom of choice must inevitably be subordinate.

Which is not to say that no persons who welcome choice will also be attracted to the principle of authority: on the contrary, since many persons who welcome choice-led change also want that change to be planned, not spontaneous, the result of conscious human deliberation and not the weakling's surrender to the automaticity of a natural order which invented horses, not cars, caves, not flats, cholera, not penicillin. Such natural improvers point to the amazing ingenuity and dedication shown by the scientists and engineers in putting satellites into space and men on the moon and.say that, in the light of such achievements, political economists ought at the very least to be capable of solving the problems of inflation and unemployment, poverty and slow growth: given better theories, better statistics and better computers, such improvers will say, what is needed is merely to press the right buttons, pull the right levers and employ the right tools (in the same manner as a skilled dentist selects the right drill) in such a way as optimally to suit the means available to the end desired. Without direction, such improvers will stress, scarce resources would be wasted in fruitless searching and false starts; whereas, because of direction, the coordination and steering problems are, in a knowledge-based society characterized by extensive division of labour, sensibly delegated to the experts and the intellectuals. Such specialists have overview as well as technique, and that in itself confers great benefits precisely because of the organic interdependence of the parts, the simultaneous determination of the magnitudes, that has been picked out by the macromodels of flows and networks that go back to Quesnay's *Tableau* of 1758: just as a physician would be ill advised indeed to operate on the spleen without taking into account the unintended effects on lungs, heart and liver of his action, so a businessman must not proceed atomistically lest the unexpected spin-offs include high wages, low prices, polluted rivers and congested roads. The principle of authority has the attraction of harnessing science in the service of the circular flow of phenomena in a situation where, as with the human body, the whole is something different from the mere sum of the parts.

Something different but perhaps also something better; and it was none other than Alfred Marshall who, much influenced by Kant on duty and T. H. Green on the unfolding of the true self in the united community, wrote in 1909 that 'morally everyone is a trustee to the public – to the All – for the use af all that he has' (Marshall, 1909, p. 464). Few would suggest that each soldier in an army be consulted on his individual preferences. Marshall's dictum seems to render society just such an army. Armies are led by experts. So too can the State be. Where a *national* purpose and a *national* interest are deemed to exist, there the German word *Volkswirtschaft* so much beloved of the romantics within the Historical School of economics comes – literally – into its own; and the way is then open for the collectivity to be governed, much as a father governs his family, by the firm but well-intentioned authority of specialist rulers such as the (physical and mental) elite that figures so prominently in Plato's ideal *Republic*. Plato's message – that individual citizens do not know best and that good rulers do know best, but only if they eschew property and renounce commerce – is not likely to win him many friends among adherents to the principle of exchange. Among those attracted by the principle of authority, however, the position is bound to be somewhat different: the section in book II of Aristotle's *Politics* where he defends slavery in terms of natural inequalities and concludes that some men are born to be slaves will, one suspects, be read with great appreciation not only by believers in the divine right of kings but also by a certain number of omniscient and beneficient leaders of mind and body in Whitehall, Westminster, Washington, D.C., and Harvey Road, Cambridge.

The principle of authority is the principle of leadership and planning. The principle of exchange, on the other hand, is the principle of individual self-determination and decentralized decision-making, of voluntary contracts and spontaneous cooperation. It is the principle of mutual benefits and the agreed-upon *quid pro quo* of revealed preferences and negotiated compensation. It is the principle of relativism and doubt, as opposed to the confidence and dogmatism of the logician and empiricist whose self-righteous conviction that he enjoys a hot-line direct to God has been castigated by James Buchanan as 'fundamentally illiberal and intolerant': '"Truth", in the final analysis, is tested by agreement. And if men disagree, there is no "truth"' (Buchanan, 1977, p. 113). It is the principle of *freedom from*, that the sentient individual being is alone in a position to know what is in his own best interest and that others have, as John Stuart Mill explains, only a very limited right to infringe the individual's sovereignty over self:

> The only purpose for which power can be rightfully exercised over any member of a civilized community, against his will, is to prevent harm to others. His own good, either physical or moral, is not a sufficient warrant. (Mill, 1859, p. 68)

It is the principle of self-interested maximization of utility and profit on the part of men and women who, fallen from grace and driven from the Garden of Eden to the state of nature, nonetheless manage to turn their energies from the violence and aggression of the Hobbesian *bellum omnium contra omnes* (a situation in which life is notoriously 'solitary, poor, nasty, brutish, and short': Hobbes, 1651, p. 82) to the peaceful industriousness of the Smithian market mechanism – a remarkable machine which is demonstrably capable of inputting 'Private Vices' and outputting 'Public Virtues' as if guided by an invisible hand:

> The natural effort of every individual to better his own condition, when suffered to exert itself with freedom and security, is so powerful a principle, that it is alone, and without any assistance, not only capable of carrying on the society to wealth and prosperity, but of surmounting a hundred impertinent obstructions with which the folly

of human laws too often incumbers its operations. (Smith, 1776, vol. II, pp. 49–50)

Powerful points all of them; and arguments which suggest that the principle of exchange is likely to have a particular appeal to persons who can believe, with Smith, that markets are allocatively efficient, with Mill, that liberty is good and coercion bad, and, with Buchanan, that the individual actor is alone in possession of the subjective data that is indispensable for the making of non-random economic choices. That appeal almost certainly owes a great deal, in the case of exchange as in that of authority, to the experience of early socialization: a child quickly learns to bargain swaps and trades with its parents ('I'll stop crying if you take me to the zoo'), it consciously or subconsciously absorbs the information that they regularly negotiate compromises with one another (exchanges ranging from the current arrangement to share household chores to the capital investment in a long-term relationship) and at school it comes into contact with the concepts of merit and achievement through grades proportioned to per-formance (to say nothing of competitive sports). Negative reactions to parents and teachers may well provoke an emotive revulsion towards figures of authority such as politicians and bureaucrats (just as good experiences may well provoke more positive attitudes); and the inevitable illustrations of political corruption, nepotism and patronage, and of bu-reaucratic inertia, delay and wastefulness, will naturally be taken as the rule rather than the exception by persons, whatever their socialization, who have developed an antipathy to other-directedness. The principle of exchange being that of the competitive market, they will reason, the multiplicity of buyers and sellers is in itself a check on the potential abuse of power. Where close substitutes exist, prices are less likely to be exploita-tive and quality is less likely to be substandard than where power is concentrated and reasonable alternativeness are non-existent.

Besides which, of course, the principle of exchange is more than a bulwark against the principle of authority: entrepreneurial alertness, im-aginative inventiveness, innovative risk-taking, all produce change in the institutional environment and rising standards of perceived economic welfare. The principle of exchange is thus more than merely a defensive mechanism, a means of protecting the person and property of the citizen against rulers who say that they are wise and show that they are strong. It is also a vote in favour of radical demand-led change: nicotine, cocaine, pornography, gambling, vitamin C tablets, puff pastry in outdoor cafes, violent gladiatoral sport, Sunday trading, clubs for homosexuals, brothels for prostitutes, the massive piece of meat that could nourish a starving family in the Third World for a week, the 20-foot car with long tail-fins, the all-Beethoven concert, the illustrated edition of Walras's *Elements* – these goods and many others the principle of exchange may be relied upon to supply or to supply in increased quantities should there be a swing of effective demand in their favour. The marketing of these goods and many others may be likened to the freedom of speech and their suppression may be regarded as analogous to the shouting down of a speaker whose social and political views one personally regards as profoundly immoral. As Milton Friedman puts it: 'Underlying most arguments against the free market is a lack of belief in freedom itself' (Friedman, 1962, p. 15).

The principle of authority is the principle of supra-individual guidance; the principle of exchange is the principle of independent units making choices and articulating desires. Conceptually, the two principles are as distinct from one another as the strict objectivity of the labour-cost theory of value (a dimension of non-ego authority) is distinct from the relativistic subjectivity of utility and scarcity or demand and supply (the essence of the catallactic orientation), as the Biblical injunction that 'Thou shalt not kill' is distinct from the enterprising initiator's maxim of 'Do your own thing'. In practice, too, the two principles retain their discrete uniqueness. Most consumers of ideas admittedly opt for a mixed portfolio which combines some authority (that of the community's conventional rules of the road, for example) with some exchange (the opportunity, let us say, to pay a non-fixed price for a non-prohibited glass of wine in a tavern which tailors its opening hours to the requirements of its clients). Not, however, for the same mix; and thus it is that real world consumers of ideas come to dwell, either alone or in clusters, at different points on the ideological spectrum that extends from one principle to the other. Real world participants in society are not so fortunate, compelled as they so often are to share their national dwelling-place with fellow citizens whose wants and actions emanate from different ideational perspectives and outlooks on life. Such citizens, in so far as they retain any desire at all to buttress belief systems with logic and evidence, will no doubt discuss and debate their respective ideological positions. However sincere their wish to maximize the scope for consensus and agreement, their recourse to reasoned persuasion will only partially succeed. Just as a man who suffers from agoraphobia will find it difficult to convince a man suffering from claustrophobia that his mental picture of external reality is a distortion and an aberration, so a man who fears the concentrated power of the State both because it is tyranical in itself and because it upsets the organic interdependence of social phenomena (society, Spencer warned the overconfident legislator, is *not* simply 'so much dough which the cook can mould as she pleases': Spencer, 1884, p. 116) will not find it easy to convert a man who fears the cutthroat aggressiveness of competition and the moral nihilism of revealed preference (a Tawney, for instance, whose first and last word on market capitalism was that it is 'not so much un-Christian as anti-Christian': Tawney,

1953, p. 170). Citizens who agree to disagree might, of course, opt for peaceful coexistence (for devolution to the local and regional levels, for example, and, through decentralization, maximal variety within the nation). Not everyone is prepared to accept, however, that pushpin is as good as poetry, red as good as blue, consumer sovereignty in the market-place for abstract ideas a fine thing, and intolerance of unpalatable opinions a great evil. Hayek, to take one instance, is not. Hayek insists that there are only two modes of social policy, collectivism and individualism – 'There is no third possibility' – and then blames the mixed economy interventionists for having paved the road to serfdom with their well-intentioned but ultimately misguided statism: 'By the time Hitler came to power, liberalism was to all intents and purposes dead in Germany. And it was socialism that had killed it' (Hayek, 1944, pp. 22–3). To tolerate Tawney is evidently to tolerate Hitler; and the inference is that there are certain limits even to tolerance.

2.2 The Protective State

Adam Smith was a believer in what he called the 'obvious and simple system of natural liberty' (Smith, 1776, vol. II, p. 208) but he would have had no wish to take issue with Friedman's evocative dictum that 'the consistent liberal is not an anarchist' (Friedman, 1962, p. 34). On the contrary, Smith believed that without the police and the courts, and the armies and the ambassadors, *homo homini lupus* would prowl the arteries of trade in search of booty and dominance, thereby rendering the smooth functioning of the decentralized market system all but unthinkable. For Smith, in other words, authority was not an alternative to exchange but, rather, a precondition for it in the two important areas of social life which constitute the protective State: law and order and national defence.

Law and Order

Smith assigned to the State 'the duty of establishing an exact administration of justice' (Smith, 1776, vol. II, p. 209) in a society characterized by conflicts and disturbances caused by the existence of the very property rights which needed to be protected: 'The preservation of property' is, Locke had written, 'the end of government, and that for which men enter into society' (Locke, 1690, p. 71). Locke's economic theory of the State puts one in mind of Adam Smith, but also of Karl Marx's famous declaration that 'the executive of the modern State is but a committee for managing the common affairs of the whole bourgeoisie' (Marx and Engels, 1848, p. 82), together, more generally, with Marx's fundamental methodological construct that it is the economic basis which determines the nature of the political superstructure:

> It is always the direct relationship of the owners of the conditions of production to the direct producers . . . which reveals the innermost secret, the hidden basis of the entire social structure, and with it the political form of the relation of sovereignty and dependence, in short, the corresponding specific form of the state. (Marx, 1891, p. 772)

It could have been either Smith or Marx (it was in fact the former) who penned the following piece of conjectural history concerning the origins and functions of political authority:

> Civil government, so far as it is instituted for the security of property, is in reality instituted for the defence of the rich against the poor, or of those who have some property against those who have none at all. (Smith, 1776, vol. II, p. 236)

In the absence of the class conflicts which private property calls into being, it would appear, the State might reasonably be expected to wither away. Private property does exist, however; so therefore, in the view of both Smith and Marx, do social tensions and divisions; and so therefore, in the analysis of both authors, must the law and order function of the protective State.

The conclusion is plausible but not, as it happens, entirely obvious. For one thing, self-interest is frequently complementary rather than zero-sum in a system of division of labour; and this organic interdependence, most notably where the interactions created through trade are iterated rather than one-shot, promotes a functional need to invest in a good reputation. Should the butcher, the brewer and the baker willingly pay their debts, of course, then the logic of exchange makes contracts self-enforcing and the *deus ex machina* of enforcing authority in effect redundant. Besides that, authority can take the form not of policemen and law courts but of internalized *ought-to-bes* which no sensitive social actor will wish to transgress lest he thereby expose himself to criticism from his peers and the spoiled self-image of a guilty conscience. Thus Alfred Marshall made much of the 'spirit of honesty and uprightness in commercial matters' (Marshall, 1920, p. 253) and indicated that truth-telling and promise-keeping were not only essential for the making of verbal agreements on the Stock and Cotton Exchanges (Marshall, 1920, p. 29) but also for the delegation by the shareholders of largely fiduciary powers to the executives of the modern joint stock company (Marshall, 1920, p. 253). A nation which has accumulated a healthy stock of moral capital is evidently in a strong position to ensure the maintenance of law and order even without reliance on specialist enforcers. Nor is there any particular reason why these specialist enforcers, always assuming neither economic exchange nor moral authority renders them obsolete, need be civil servants as well. Banks and office blocks obtain the services of security guards and night-watchmen not from the State but from the market; film stars hire private-sector bodyguards and pay directly for the protection of locks, bolts, safes and burglar alarms; insurance companies employ skilled investigators in cases of theft precisely because their financial incentive (not to pay compensation) so closely corresponds to the self-interest of their customers (to recover the stolen property); expert arbitrators have long been a less expensive, less time-consuming route to justice than the collectivized alternative; and the very success of these initiatives must inevitably provoke speculation about the viability of further departures along the same lines. Smith and Marx would regard the withering away of the State as contingent upon the antecedent withering away of enforceable rights in private property. Murray Rothbard's libertarian position is precisely the opposite, since for him the institution of the State-less community presupposes not the suppression of property rights but their extension, not the transcendence of self-love but its mobilization. Rothbard says: 'A private Central Park would be guarded efficiently in order to maximize park revenue' (Rothbard, 1973, p. 221). He applies the same logic to the privatization of the streets. It is a logic which anyone who currently includes in the service charge he pays for his flat an element for 24-hour porterage as well as an element for central heating and constant hot water will easily grasp: just as a landlord wishing to maximize his rents would be well advised to see to it that the roof of his building does not let in the rain, so would he be well advised to pay the company that supplies the streets a generous fee to ensure that those streets are swept clean of thieves as well as leaves. Criminals apprehended by the company and convicted by a private enterprise court freely selected by all parties concerned would be sent to an independent prison, self supporting and perhaps even profit-making because of the work of the inmates – work performed in the first instance, it must be stressed, in order to make restitution to the victim of the crime and restore the *status quo ante* with respect to the personal and property rights of the plaintiff. The net result is a state of protection but no protective State at all.

Adam Smith did not adopt so extreme a view with respect to law and order, but in most other areas of national life his personal bias was unambiguously in favour of free markets and competitive capitalism. One reason was the moral one; since Smith, very much the heir to the natural law school in this connection, tended to regard any movement away from *laissez-faire* as in itself a 'violation of natural liberty and justice' (Smith, 1776, vol. I, p. 157). Thus, when calling for freedom of trade in grain (as, for that matter, when attacking the Laws of Settlement and the Statutes of

Apprenticeship), Smith makes clear that his reasoning relates to ethics in economics as well as to allocative efficiency:

> To hinder . . . the farmer from sending his goods at all times to the best market, is evidently to sacrifice the ordinary laws of justice to an idea of public utility, to a sort of reasons of state. (Smith, 1776, vol. II, p. 48)

Not everyone would, of course, wish to ascribe *ougth-ness* to automaticity, or to identify the natural with the good; but there is undeniably a long tradition in economics of assigning normative significance to the outcomes generated by unguided processes. Thus even Aristotle regarded the just price as being the normal competitive price; while the late scholastic, Luis Molina, said that the just price was any price, normal or not, provided only that it was genuinely competitive and devoid of any monopolistic element such as collusive pricefixing. Molina also saw the functionality of short-run windfall gains caused by scarcity. And this from a Jesuit who would never have assigned such autonomy to the individual mind with respect to the moral authority of the Scriptures and of revealed religion! Molina's contribution is a reminder that there is a long tradition in economic science of treating competitive markets as just processes. Adam Smith's is one of the most sophisticated and interesting contributions in that tradition – so sophisticated and interesting, in fact, as to render all the more remarkable his reluctance to extend his theory of justice through markets to the administration of justice itself.

Smith had a personal bias in favour of justice through markets, but he was also prepared to make exceptions. These exceptions – two in particular – demonstrate the manner in which a socially – aware pragmatist might wish to maximize justice through authority and not through exchange.

The first case involves spillovers and externalities. No one who had learned of the 'greatest good of the greatest number' from the 'ne'er-to-be-forgotten' Francis Hutcheson himself was likely to end up so absolute an individualist that he was oblivious to the neighbourhood effects of human action. These, Smith argued, are inseparable from interdependence, and they must on occasion be allowed to take precedence over any natural rights which the individual may possess:

> Those exertions of the natural liberty of a few individuals, which might endanger the security of the whole society, are, and ought to be, restrained by the laws of all governments. . . .The obligation of building party walls, in order to prevent the communication of fire, is a violation of natural liberty, exactly of the same kind with the regulations of the banking trade which are here proposed. (Smith, 1776, vol. I, pp. 344–5)

Smith's instance is authority with respect to the regulation of banking. Other observers will suggest other occasions when wise laws avert unpleasant diswelfares – laws involving the specification of weights and measures, for example, or the date-stamping of food products, or the disposal of nuclear wastes, or the prohibition of untested medication, or the protection of the aesthetic environment that Galbraith has in mind when he invites the State to 'assert aesthetic priority against the industrial need' (Galbraith, 1967 p. 345): 'It is not imperative that the road which winds pleasantly along the lake or which accepts the contours of the valley should be widened and straightened today or even tomorrow. Those who use it can take a little more time in getting to their destination' (Galbraith, 1971, p. 132). The list of unpleasant diswelfares is potentially a long one; not every member of the community will have the same list ('To some of us rock music is noise pollution', Friedman observes; 'to others of us it is pleasure': Friedman and Friedman, 1980, p. 256); even where two members of the community happen to agree on the specification of a diswelfare, still there is no reason to suppose an identical *quantum* of subjective discomfort; and it is considerations of this kind which have led economists like Ronald Coase to argue that the principle of exchange be put before the principle of authority where neighbourhood effects are perceived to arise. *Ex post* Coase would recommend action through the courts: the damages awarded not only compensate the victim of an unwelcome externality for disutility suffered but also serve as a deterrent to the imposition of further diswelfares through malpractice, fraud, negligence, misrepresentation, unhygienic conditions, bad workmanship and similar modes of trespass on person and property. *Ex ante* Coase would propose direct negotiation between the affected parties: if a doctor has a right to tranquility in his waiting room, Coase says, then he must also have a right to alienate that right in favour of an exceptionally noisy confectioner in an adjacent building, always provided that he is given something in return (a large sum of money is a natural sweetener) which he personally ranks as superior (see Coase, 1960, especially pp. 2, 4). The benefits of such consensual agreement are not, of course, obtained without the transactions costs to which voluntary contracting always gives rise; and for that reason the sensitively tailored bargain between the doctor and the confectioner might prove uneconomic once some critical number of affected parties is reached. In such circumstances – where, say, the problem is the pollution of the air or the discharge of effluent into a river – there might simply not exist any *ex ante* bargaining solution that is not prohibitively expensive, and the alternative to action by authority might then realistically be no action at all. Even so, the economist sympathetic to the individualistic insights of Coase will point out, the principle of authority can never be more than a second-best substitute for the principle of exchange which remains the ideal.

The second case involves conflict of objectives. Smith, who had a personal bias in favour of justice through markets, was displeased to discover that natural liberty and economic growth were goals that, in at least one area of economic activity, were radically incompatible. That area was the market for loanable funds. Smith took the view that if the rate of interest were allowed to rise to its market-determined equilibrium level, the result would be to divert scarce resources away from growth-inducing outlets such as the accumulation of stock and the employment of productive labour and into the hands of 'prodigals and projectors' who would then 'waste and destroy' (Smith, 1776, vol. I, p. 379) that which ought to have become the wealth of their nation. Smith ignored the possibility of evasion and avoidance through black markets and hidden interest in his defence of the Usury Laws, and he neglected the concomitant disincentive effect on the supply of savings (perhaps because he, like Keynes, believed that the relevant interest elasticity was not high), but his point is clear enough – that there can exist a radical incompatibility of goals and that the State, via regulatory legislation duly enforced, migth on occasion have no choice but to rank one above the other. The retention of the interest ceiling in the work of Adam Smith is analogous in function to the taxation of industries experiencing diminishing returns, and the subsidization of industries experiencing increasing returns, that is proposed by Alfred Marshall (see on this Marshall, 1920, pp. 392, 416) – and to the imposition of a minimun wage that is recommended by Tawney not least because of the dynamic effects of higher pay on the long-run efficiency of a better-fed, better-housed labour force: 'That bad wages produce bad work is an experience as common as it is habitually disregarded' (Tawney, 1914, p. 113). A conflict of objectives can, of course, as easily be resolved in favour of the principle of exchange as an favour of that of authority. Protective tariffs, import quotas, export bounties, all could be dropped, despite the cost thereby imposed on infant industries promising higher average productivity in time. Union powers to restrict entry, to dispense with strike ballots, to enjoy legal immunity from prosecution for monopolistic practices, all could be eliminated, despite the consequent reduction in the standard of service they can then provide to unprotected groups in the labour force. Zoning regulations, urban planning, rent controls, all could be abolished, despite the impact on the poor, the old, the out of work and the ethnic minorities of replacing slum tenements with luxury flats inhabited by stockbrokers and speculators. Just as a conflict of objectives can be resolved by more direction, clearly, so it can be resolved by less. That it can arise, that it can present real problems for the socially responsible theorist of law and order within the protective State, is not, however, in question.

National Defence

Smith assigned to the State 'the duty of protecting the society from the violence and invasion of other independent societies' (Smith, 1776, vol. II, p. 208). He also said that 'defence . . . is of much more importance than opulence' (Smith, 1776, vol. I, p. 487). His views on the conflicts and disharmonies associated with the *bellum* abroad precisely parallel his observations on the need for law and order due to the threat of the *bellum* at home. His fear of aggression against person and property, whether on the part of imported barbarians of on the past of domestically produced louts, is a very real one; but it is surprising nonetheless to encounter a theorist with so powerful a belief in the principle of voluntary exchange who is able to articulate such great anxiety with respect to the imminence of involuntary authority. Rationally speaking, the butcher, the brewer and the baker may serve us not from benevolence but 'from their regard to their own interest' (Smith, 1776, vol. I, p. 18), but at least they do serve us. The butcher, the brewer, the baker, the philosopher and the common street porter are all interdependent and aware of their interdependence; so are the English and the Portuguese when they come to exchange cloth for wine according to the venerable criterion of comparative advantage; and the division of labour would thus appear to be a vote for *pax* rather than *bellum*, both at home and abroad, for the same reason that the heart simply cannot afford to separate from the lungs and the kidneys. One country might, of course, invade another because of a bullying propensity to prove itself the big fish that devours the small or, alternatively, because it wishes to impose its culture, its religion and its ideology on unenlightened foreigners. These non-commercial, non-rational motives for conquest might even be reinforced by that of direct economic imperialism, as where a large country dispatches a gunboat to a smaller one in order to protect not only the lives of its citizens but the property of its multinationals as well. The love of power, fanatical intolerance and the influence of investors over governments are no doubt causal variables that must be taken into account; but so too must the concern with a rising standard of economic welfare. Market-oriented economists tend to associate this ever-improving standard of living not with the redistribution towards self of that which others already enjoy (to say nothing of the punitive economic costs of conquering and occupying a nation that shows great antipathy to foreign rule) but rather with the on-going creation of new wealth by means of industry and trade. Adam Smith was such an economist. His politics of fear, with its overtones of Hobbesian pessimism and imminent bellicosity, comes in the circumstances as somewhat of a surprise.

Much of what he says, admittedly, is situated in the context of a debate with that which had gone before. The decline of feudalism and the rise of the nation state had given rise to the concept of a national interest. The idea must have appealed to the late medieval mind: feudalism itself had been a society of corporations (not of individuals), while Catholicism was hardly Calvinism in its emphasis on the integration of the isolated atom into the orderly whole. The mercantilists built upon that heritage – the very title of Mun's pamphlet has resonances of power politics and economic warfare: '*England's* Treasure by Forraign Trade'. The whole of the mercantilist intellectual system is geared to the might of the collectivity, not the utility of the consumer: interest ceilings and wage ceilings, monopolistic trading companies, import substitution, restrictions on emigration, the obsession with a favourable balance of trade and with the hoarding of stocks of specie – all this reflects a belief in the subordination of individual to national interests, a conviction that trade is a species of warfare and a fear of violence and invasion such as was spelled out with exceptional clarity by Josiah Child: 'Foreign trade produces riches, riches power, power preserves our trade and religion' (quoted by Schumpeter, 1954, p. 347n). Defence, it would be fair to say, was to Mun and Child (despite the close involvement of both in the profit-seeking enterprise of the East India Company) of much more importance than opulence; and so it was to Adam Smith.

Because of his concern with defence, Smith called upon the State to maintain a 'well-disciplined standing army' (Smith, 1776, vol. II, p. 307) and to cover the burden of this indivisible public good by means of general taxation: voluntary contribution provides too great a temptation to bad Samaritans to ride free, while a system of user-charges presents insuperable problems of assessment and administration. The taxation was to be compulsory but not the service itself: Smith did not propose conscription or say that each citizen had a moral duty to the national interest to translate defence into self-defence by paying his tax in time rather than in money. Nor did he propose privatization of the monopoly privilege: competitive tendering between alternative firms of mercenary soldiers for the opportunity to supply the well-disciplined standing army would, logically speaking, have had as beneficial an impact on the price and quality of standing armies supplied as it does in the market for apples and oranges, but this was not a logic about which Smith in the event chose to speak at all. His reluctance to relegate provision to the realm of exchange while retaining finance within the realm of authority is not one which will be shared by every market-oriented economist. Nor are the reasons for that reluctance ever spelled out in detail. Perhaps Smith harboured some fear of a State within the State that ultimately turned the power of the agent against the principal by enslaving, Leviathan-like, its employers – a fear inevitably magnified by his doubts as to whether the alienated labourers and the greedy capitalists of a mercantile commonwealth would be sufficiently patriotic to join a popular militia (let alone to indulge in guerrilla warfare). Perhaps, alternatively, he took the view that competing purveyors of force and violence would inevitably compete one another out of business (owing, say, to the exploitation of economies of scale such as breed and form the natural monopoly) – an argument for the nationalization of force and violence which Nozick uses in his defence of the minimal or night-watchman State against the assertion of extreme libertarians that even this function should be restored to exchange (see on this Nozick, 1974, especially Chs 2, 5 and 10). Perhaps, finally, Smith adopted the moralist's perspective that supplying and demanding is the natural training-ground for the traitor and the turncoat, and for the self-centred opportunist with a permanent incentive to renege on his promises, renegotiate his contracts and reshuffle his trading partners – a perspective well captured by Fred Hirsch when he reflects that a nation with market but no morals would simply not be safe from 'the first entrepreneur to be able to raise enough credit to buy the judge' (Hirsch, 1977, p. 143). The purpose of defence being security, these arguments point to insecurity. Individually or collectively (accompanied, naturally enough, by 'the tyranny of the *status quo*' and the fact that 'we start from here' which inevitably shape every intellectual's hidden assumptions by virtue of his personal socialization within the constraints of a given 'done thing'), they may well explain Smith's reluctance to recommend privatization of provision in the specific and unrepresentative instance of the standing army.

Smith goes beyond the provision of the standing army in his discussion of national defence and makes reference to defence-related economic policy as well. Thus he recommends (despite his general bias towards freedom of trade) that bounties be given for exports of British-made sailcloth and gunpowder in an attempt to stimulate artificially the expanded production of these strategic commodities at home (Smith, 1776, vol. II, p. 28), and he describes the Navigation Acts (which compelled British exporters to use British ships and British seamen even if the foreign competition were economically more attractive) as 'perhaps, the wisest of all the commercial regulations of England' (Smith, 1776, vol. I, p. 487). There are few if any areas of economic life, however, which cannot be said to be related in some way to national defence. This fact is unlikely to have entirely escaped the attention of special pleaders and vested interests. Industries specializing in military hardware are in a particularly strong position to press for additional public expenditure on weaponry and affiliated activities such as space exploration (and to oppose measures which they regard as retrograde such as restrictions on the sale abroad of state-of-the-art spy satellites or, for that matter, significant progress towards multilateral disarmament). These views are a specific instance of the more general proposition formulated by Anthony Downs that the producer-interest tends to enjoy disproportionate representation in the policy-making process:

> Men are more likely to exert political influence in their roles as income-receivers than in their roles as income-spenders, whether acting as private citizens or as members of a corporate entity. (Downs, 1957, p. 255)

One is moderately uncomfortable about the implications of this proposition when the result is high prices of food and wine, on the one hand, and large publicly purchased agricultural surpluses on the other. One is even less comfortable when the result is a limitation in the supply of licensed medical personnel, and therewith a rise in their fees. One is least comfortable of all when the result is massive and costly stockpiling of high-technology explosive devices throughout the world: given enough time, one of those devices might blow up the very nation which it was designed to defend. Such a scenario is difficult to reconcile with the *raison d'être* of the protective State.

2.3 The Productive State

Smith assigned to the State 'the duty of erecting and maintaining certain public works and certain public institutions, which it can never be for the interest of any individual, or small number of individuals, to erect and maintain' (Smith, 1776, vol. II, p. 209). Few things are less certain than 'certain'. That having been said, inclusion in this amorphous and open-ended category seems for Smith to have involved two criteria.

The first criterion is that of market failure – that, in certain cases, it can 'never' be in the pecuniary interests of the private sector to supply a particular good or service adequately, and that in such exceptional circumstances the 'natural order' and the 'invisible hand' demonstrably fail the community which they normally serve so well. One reason for this failure might be the accurate perception of discrete individuals in large groups, should they happen to be both self-interested and calculatively rational, that it is inherently logical to act the free-rider on the payment made by the suckered altruist: 'The larger the group, the farther it will fall short of providing an optimal amount of a collective good' states Mancur Olson (1965, p. 35) in language clearly relevant to the supply of unpriced public goods such as the services of policemen if funded on a strictly voluntary basis. Another reason for market failure might be the genuine ignorance of the social actor as to the personal and social benefits that would accrue to individual expenditure of effective demand: thus, calling for State subsidization of education, Adam Smith justifies his recommendation by observing that

> though the interest of the labourer is strictly connected with that of the society, he is incapable either of comprehending that interest, or of understanding its connection with his own. (Smith, 1776, vol. I, p. 277)

It would be fair to say that, even if the labourer did comprehend, being poor he might still not be able to pay; and that a community which wishes to enjoy the spillovers of his schooled skills and inculcated attitudes might have no real option, recognizing that low incomes can constitute a further reason for market failure, but to pay his contribution on his behalf. The alternative to State finance and even State provision is, after all, in the view of theorists of market failure such as John Kenneth Galbraith, no less dreadful than no provision whatsoever. Galbraith's proposals for 'social balance' embrace not only education but also Smith's infrastructure ('good roads, bridges, navigable canals, harbours': Smith, 1776, vol. II, p. 245) combined with Tawney's full welfare state (medical services, good housing, generous pensions, recreational facilities). Refuse and its disposal are a case in point:

> The more goods people procure, the more packages they discard and the more rubbish that must be carried away. If the appropriate sanitation services are not provided, the counterpart of increasing opulence will be deepening filth. The greater the wealth, the thicker will be the dirt. (Galbraith, 1958, pp. 210–11)

Galbraith writes as a man surrounded by rubbish. His appeal is to the authority of the State. His reason is the failure of market exchange.

The second criterion involves some notion of the 'public interest' as established by the leadership. Wise leaders, relying on advice gleaned from opinion polls and consultation with constituents, might indeed succeed in building up a picture of the nation's stock of revealed preferences. In a sense they must do so, since a ruling party in a democracy which propounds policies at variance with the national consensus runs the risk of losing votes, seats and elections. Not all citizens, however, are interested in or informed about political issues; and many, one suspects, will respond with a blank stare accompanied by stony silence if asked for their views on cost-plus pricing for public-sector contracts, on cross-subsidization of uneconomic by economic lines within the framework of nationalised industries, on the economies of large size allegedly enjoyed by a single State-run postal system – or, for that matter, on the potential for privatization of the collection of rubbish. What many citizens want, in an era of extensive specialization, is not so much to be involved in the formulation of policies as to be broadly satisfied with those aspects of those policies that affect them personally. The more optimistic among them will therefore vote on the basis of personalities, not of issues: the job of the leader is to lead, just as the job of the dentist is to drill, and in both cases it is the task of the rational consumer who is also reasonably optimistic about the exercise of fiduciary power first to select a professional he can trust and then to delegate to that employee the discretionary freedom to choose. The more pessimistic, meanwhile, aware of their own limitations of interest and information but unable nonetheless to put any faith in specialists in the art of leadership, will be driven by their anxieties to press for constitutional precommitment: distrusting discretion, they will say the range of choices should be preconstrained by multiperiod rules (a balanced budget rule, for example, or a money supply rule) lest the servants instead become the masters. No one can know, of course, whether politicians and bureaucrats genuinely wish to impose their own will on their fellow citizens or whether, alternatively, they see themselves merely as faceless automatons eager to please, and Schumpeter's warning is apposite, that 'it is unsafe to talk about individuals' motives. The only mind accessible to us is our own' (Schumpeter, 1954, p. 337n.). Unsafe or not, however, an informed guess must be made before any conclusion can be drawn as to whether the notion of the 'public interest' that forms the basis for the productive State in fact bubbles up from below or whether it is handed down from above, and Schumpeter leaves no doubt as to his own view on the direction of influence: 'The will of the people is the product and not the motive power of the political process' (Schumpeter, 1942, p. 263). No other outcome would, indeed, be conceivable if politicians were, in the real world, the self-interested maximizers which public choice theorists like Buchanan believe them to be:

> Within what he treats as his feasible set, the politician will choose that alternative or option which maximizes his own, not his constituents', utility. This opportunity offers one of the primary motivations to politicians. In a meaningful sense, this is 'political income', and it must be reckoned as a part of the total rewards of office. (Buchanan, 1975, p. 157)

The obsession of politicians with their personal utility in the work of Buchanan is matched by similar obsession on the part of bureaucrats in the work of Niskanen:

> Among the several variables that may enter the bureaucrat's utility function are the following: salary, perquisites of the office, public reputation, power, patronage, output of the bureau, ease of making changes, and ease of managing the bureau. All of these variables

except the last two, I contend, are a positive monotonic function of the total *budget* of the bureau during the bureaucrat's tenure in office. (Niskanen, 1971, p. 38)

Even where there is not actual corruption, nepotism and patronage, Buchanan and Niskanen would contend, politicians and bureaucrats still experience a strong temptation to slot in their own goals, to shape the 'public interest' in their own desired image. Marxists would go further still and assert that it is not the objectives of the class of rulers, narrowly defined, with which politicians and bureaucrats are primarily concerned so much as it is the objectives of the ruling class, broadly defined, of which they are but a part. Marxists would cite with approbation Smith's instance of educational subsidization, where Smith points out that the masses tend to suffer from 'mental mutilation' (Smith, 1776, vol. II, p. 308) caused by the division of labour and for that reason require paternalistic manipulation of revealed preferences such as to render them 'less liable . . . to the delusions of enthusiasm and superstition' and 'less apt to be misled into any wanton or unnecessary opposition to the measures of government' (Smith, 1776, vol. II, p. 309). Smith, one infers, sees the 'public interest' as something qualitatively different from the popular attitudes that might conceptually be communicated upwards, in a political democracy, from the individual voters to the expert professionals whom they employ. Whatever the precise specification of the 'public interest', however, what is clear is his conviction that it and it alone is the ultimate gatekeeper that determines which institutions and which works are to be permitted entry into the sheltered haven of the productive State.

Or, of course, denied admission, as is the case with one controversial but nowadays widespread form of collective intervention: income maintenance in states of dependence is conspicuous by its absence from Smith's account of the productive State. Smith scarcely mentions the Poor Laws. One reason is that he regarded man-made obstacles to mobility, both occupational (the Statutes of Apprenticeship) and geographical (the Laws of Settlement), as themselves causes of involuntary unemployment and the consequent distress precisely because 'the scarcity of hands in one parish . . . cannot always be relieved by their super-abundance in another' (Smith, 1776, vol. I, p. 157); the implication is that much distress can be alleviated, without the elaborate panoply of retraining schemes, youth employment subsidies, loan guarantees to labour-intensive enterprise and tax concessions in areas of high unemployment, merely through the abolition of restrictions on access to work, ranging from trades unions to the housing policies of local authorities. A second reason for Smith's lack of interest in absolute deprivation was his conviction that a growing economy such as his own was perfectly capable of creating enough jobs for all, and (in contrast with the Marxian prediction of technological displacement, the reserve army and low pay) at good wages: his reference to the manner in which, 'at the end of the late war, more than a hundred thousand soldiers and seamen, a number equal to what is employed in the greatest manufactures' (Smith, 1776, vol. I, p. 492) were thrown at once onto the labour market and easily absorbed by it is an eloquent illustration of the way in which private buoyancy might prove a viable alternative to public relief. A third reason for Smith's unwillingness to involve the State in income maintenance has to do with his confidence in the private sector emanating from moral sentiments such as those of benevolence, altruism and fellow feeling: 'The relief and consolation of human misery depend altogether upon our compassion for . . . the poor and the wretched' (Smith, 1759, p. 331). Our compassion but not, evidently, our duty – whereas to the English social democrats and theorists of welfare capitalism the kindly humanitarianism of the gift relationship was solidly underpinned by the citizenship rights of organic solidarity and the interdependent community. Thus the generous Titmuss, capable as he was of tracing the origins of an interventionist social policy to 'the expressed wish of all the people to assist the survival of some people' (Titmuss, 1963, p.39), also took the view that at least some of those in need of help had in effect pre-purchased their claim by virtue of the functional role they had played in the process of economic change: the obsolete skills of those made redundant by technological progress, to cite but one example, are the concomitant of rising living standards for those still in work, and for this reason it would be irresponsible and unjust to allow these social costs simply to 'lie where they fall' (Titmuss, 1974, p. 74). At least in the short run, authors such as Titmuss would say, there is a strong case to be made on grounds of equity as well as sympathy for assistance to the victims of collective advance (a case not dissimilar, it must be added, to the more familiar case commonly made in support of unearned incomes' being paid by the State to the war-wounded). The victims of national oversaving presumably merit unemployment benefits for the same reason. Should there be a genuine deficiency of aggregate demand, of course, then the State, preferring jobs to benefits, might wish to reflate; and it is in such circumstances that the expansionary fiscal policy of Keynesian economics comes to reinforce the welfareist aspirations of the social democrats, provided only that the desired pump-priming and fine-tuning take the form of an increase in public-sector spending and not a decrease in private-sector taxation. A ratchet effect then applies by virtue of the strong political incentive not to cut such spending in the subsequent upswing: even if the need to compensate the microeconomically displaced were to disappear, even if the macroeconomic deficiency in total demand were automatically to correct itself via across-the-board reductions in wages and prices, still there remain other potential outlets for State funding (social work and parks, the health service and the arts) to which a socially sensitive leadership (also known as a clique of vote-seeking elitists) would wish to turn its attention. Nor is there any clear evidence that the unemployed, the aged, the poor in work and the handicapped are about to wither away or that the voluntary sector (as typified by the Charity Organization Societies about which Marshall waxed so lyrical; see, for example, Marshall, 1893, p. 262, and Reisman, 1987, pp. 207–21) will prove able unaided to alleviate distress. No clear evidence at all; and that is why it may confidently be predicted that, just as the protective State will continue to be required if proper security against physical aggression is to be assured, so that dimension of the productive State which is concerned with the modulation of personal economic insecurities is likely to be a permanent part of the political landscape in a changing but also a caring community.

2.4 Public Finance

One of the principal objectives of economic investigation, in Adam Smith's view, was ultimately 'to supply the state or commonwealth with a revenue sufficient for the public services' (Smith, 1776, vol. I, p. 449). Almost 30 per cent of the text of *The Wealth of Nations* is directly devoted to that task – a fact as frequently neglected as the full title of Ricardo's great work: *Principles of Political Economy and Taxation*.

Taxation is one of the three modes of public finance. The second is borrowing at interest and the third is the creation of new money. Citizens always prefer the benefits of public expenditure to the costs of public finance, just as they consistently rank the consumption of the apple above the sacrifies of the shilling that is its price. They should be encouraged to think of the former category of costs and benefits in the same way as they would conceptualize the latter. No rational individual who is also law-abiding would expect to procure the apple without spending the shilling. Nor, therefore, should he expect the services of roads, schools and armies without the burden of taxes, bonds and paper which they entail. When he buys an orange he enters into market exchange. When he buys a policeman he enters into fiscal exchange. The principle of exchange is not that of authority; nor is the voluntary swap the visible hand of dominance. Citizens who repeatedly complain about the costs are perhaps not adequately appreciative of the benefits – or perhaps have not adequately been consulted as to their subjective trade-offs. Whatever the reason, a popular obsession with the burdens such as overshadows the services is *prima facie* evidence of a malfunctioning democracy in which the leaders and the people are not in touch. Public finance *per se* is not bad – only public finance widely perceived to be bad can be that. The shopper who genuinely wants the apple will freely sacrifice the shilling. The attitude of the citizen who genuinely wants the policeman ought to be no different with respect to the taxation, the borrowing and the money, the three modes of public finance which constitute the subject-matter of the three subsections which now follow.

Taxation

Smith adopted the Lockean perspective that a man's stake in his society is proportional to the property which he has and wishes to protect. From it he derived his recommendation that the taxation of personal revenues ought to proceed on the basis of a single fixed percentage:

> The subjects of every state ought to contribute towards the support of the government, as nearly as possible, in proportion to their respective abilities; that is, in proportion to the revenue which they respectively enjoy under the protection of the state. (Smith, 1776, vol. II, p. 350)

Proportionality is to be justified on the grounds of equality. It also fits in with his stress on certainty (since the assessment is impersonal and the magnitude far from arbitrary) and is fully compatible with his criterion of convenience (as is illustrated by the very name of the Pay-As-You-Earn system, which advertises the fact that the contribution is not required in advance of the taxable income out of which it is to be paid). With respect to Smith's final guideline of economy in collection, however, the position is more problematic: where each case must be individually assessed, the gap is greater between what the taxpayer spends and what the State receives than if there were to be a lump-sum poll tax of, say, £100 levied on each citizen irrespective of his actual earnings and expenses. A poll tax economizes on administrative costs (thereby conforming to Smith's fourth criterion), but it is regressive rather than proportional (£100 representing a greater percentage of a lower income of £1,000 than it does of a higher income of £5,000) and thereby offends against Smith's first principle, that of equality. This conflict of normative standards is a very real one, but it is also a conflict that can readily be resolved by recourse to a meta-principle that transcends both economy and equality, namely that of equity or justice. Such a meta-principle is notoriously difficult to apply. One possibility, however, is to link the requisite *ought-to-be* to a decision made *as if* situated behind a thick veil of ignorance such as is the case in John Rawls' 'original position': there,

> the parties have no basis for bargaining in the usual sense. No one knows his situation in society nor his natural assets, and therefore no

one is in a position to tailor principles to his advantage. We might imagine that one of the contractees threatens to hold out unless the others agree to principles favourable to him. But how does he know which principles are especially in his interests? (Rawls, 1972, pp. 139–40)

Justice as fairness given radical uncertainty, justice as good procedures not involving special pleading, is certainly a valuable tool for the precise formulation of specific *ought-to-bes*. Specific *ought-to-bes* but also relativistic ones; and it must be observed that not every student of society will be entirely satisfied with normative guidance that is at once so subjective and so kaleidoscopic.

The meta-principle of justice assists the community to reconcile conflicting criteria and in that way to establish precise rates of tax. It is unlikely that there would be unanimity of consensus (Wicksell's ideal benchmark) or even a 51 per cent majority (the normal second-best in the modern democratic referendum) in favour of the proposition that income tax be made a disproportionate burden on the less well paid: some will argue that the rich should be allowed to opt out of the costs of public services to the extent that they (by purchasing private medical insurance, eschewing local authority accommodation, educating their children in the private sector) demonstrably opt out of the benefits, but the representative citizen, reflecting perhaps how chagrined he himself would fell if the thick Rawlsian veil were to be drawn aside only to reveal him to be not a senior executive but a farm labourer, may reasonably be expected to regard the regressive income tax as imposing too harsh a penalty on those most at risk and in need. Support might, of course, be forthcoming for a flat-rate income tax such as was proposed by Smith: the principle of equality is even now legitimated by the meta-principle of equity in the case of corporation tax and capital gains tax, and it might well have a certain appeal to the self-interest of the rational citizen who regards his own future earnings as completely unpredictable. Income tax at rising (marginal) rates is a further possibility: the vast majority of countries having in fact opted for the progressive bias, one would like to think that their choice reflects something more than the envious wish of the also-rans to impose a penalty on the talented, the assiduous and the lucky, as indeed is the case with the reasoned arguments of both Marshall and Pigou. Marshall, a subjectivist with strong utilitarian leanings, personal sympathy towards the deprived and a missionary's zeal to do good, applied his marginal utility theory to income and found
; are not the same as perceptions: 'A shilling is the measure of
:, or satisfaction of any kind, to a rich man than to a poor one'
.920, p. 16). Equality of subjective sacrifice, Marshall concluded,
to inequality of objective aggregates. Marshall's logic, that the

market unaided fails to maximize utility, provides the foundation for Pigou's critique of consumer sovereignty, that

> *prima facie* all large inequalities of income entail social loss; for the ninth course of the plutocrat's dinner, despite the individual benefit that it may confer on his doctor, yields much less satisfaction on the whole than the milk which the cost of it might have secured for a poor man's child. (Pigou, 1935, p. 121)

Marshall and Pigou have been criticized for their propensity to make interpersonal comparisons of satisfaction and to derive policy inferences involving redistribution of income from perceptions the nature and intensity of which only an individual actor can ever know with any certainty. Whether or not these objections are justified, the fact is that Marshall and Pigou are hardly alone in ranking common sense above high theory in the way that they do – or in relying on imagination and empathy to convey subjective data about the wants and needs of others.

Some taxation is direct, in the sense that the taxes are imposed directly on incomes (personal and corporate). Some taxation is indirect, as is the case with the taxes (either lump-sum or *ad valorem*) that are levied on commodities. Such taxes are often regressive in their incidence (the poor man and the rich man, assuming that they both buy the same commodity, both support the same burden of tax despite the fact that their respective ability to pay is not the same) and frequently incorporate a social engineering function (as where, say, cigarettes are taxed at a discriminatory rate while milk is zero rated) – albeit a function operative only within limits by virtue of the fact that the power to tax is the power to destroy not merely the consumption of the commodity but also the public finance which that consumption would have occasioned: thus, Sir James Steuart advised the monarch, with respect to the taxation of 'spirituous liquors', that

> if you want to increase the revenue, from the propensity people have to poison themselves with spirits, your augmentations and alterations may be gentle and progressive. (Steuart, 1767, vol. I, p. 332)

Then, in addition to taxes on goods, there can be taxes on inputs such as land (Henry George's single tax – Walras actually recommended nationalization – had the advantage that the burden could not be passed on to the consumer and that the taxation of a non-functional surplus had no disincentive effect on supply) or, for that matter, labour (a selective employment tax, perhaps, which seeks to shake labour out of one mode of economic activity and into a different one). Some indirect taxes are transparent – the case of estate duty levied on the intergenerational transmission of wealth by inheritance. Others, however, are concealed:

there cannot be many consumers, for example, who know precisely what percentage of the price they pay for an imported car is the tariff. Tax consciousness (as typified by the pay-slip that sets out in detail all relevant deductions from income) is the *sine qua non* for a genuinely democractic system of fiscal exchange – as opposed to the deliberate fiscal illusion and the Machiavellian fiscal into which taxation without proper disclosure so easily degenerates.

Borrowing

Not all public spending is paid for out of current taxation. A part of public spending is financed through the sale of interest-bearing debt. Some authors, not least Ricardo, Pigou, Lerner and Barro, have denied that this means any intertemporal shifting of burdens: the present generation does, after all, have to forgo an equivalent amount of private consumption or private capital formation when it elects to buy the bonds issued. Future generations of taxpayers do, of course, have to pay interest on the debt; but the funds in question are only transferred to future generations of bond-holders, with the result that no net redistribution takes place between the generations. In Abba Lerner's words:

> The national debt is not a burden on posterity because if posterity pays the debt it will be paying it to the same posterity that will be alive at the time when the payment is made. (Lerner, 1944, p. 303)

Other authors, however, have been less than happy with this logic. James Buchanan, notably, has insisted that the objective transfer of resources from private sector to State is no proof that subjective sacrifice is being experienced: if the present generation voluntarily purchased the bonds, he says, it must have done so because it valued those assets above any other feasible alternative and must hence have gained (not lost) in utility. It is thus the future which is saddled with subjective sacrifice in the form of a burden handed on without consultation and consent – a burden rendered that much more unpleasant by the knowledge that (since, in Buchanan's estimation, long-lived capital expenditures constitute only 'a relatively small share of governmental outlays': Buchanan, 1986, p. 201) the future is being asked to shoulder the cost of benefits which others have already consumed. Buchanan finds such shifting unethical, as he does the concealment of expense which it embodies: the share of the government in the gross national product would be smaller, he argues, if the taxpayer–citizen were told the full facts about debt-finance and the true cost of public spending. It is not in the personal and collective interests of politicians and bureaucrats to make so expensive a disclosure, however; and that is why Buchanan proposes a multiperiod constitutional solution, legally as well as morally binding on generations to come and one which they cannot alter merely to suit their short-run convenience. That rule should institutionalize the balanced budget and therewith a return to the responsible practices which prevailed before the deficit-spenders arrived on the scene. The Victorian fiscal morality cannot itself be restored, but multiperiod law can nonetheless come to fulfil the same function. Can and must – on this point the theorist of the Fall who knows his Hobbes and fears his Keynes is absolutely clear:

> Having lived through the destruction of the fiscal morality by the Keynesian mind-set, we must make every effort to replace this morality with deliberately chosen constraints that will produce substantially the pre-Keynesian patterns of results. (Buchanan, 1986, p. 194)

What form such a multiperiod law would take in a country like Britain which has no written constitution and where no Parliament can bind its successor is somewhat less clear.

Money

The end of the Middle Ages which saw the rise of the nation state was also a period of political insecurity and an obsession with national power. It was a period of extravagant courts which needed funds and found feudal dues insufficient. It was a period of debasement of coinage followed by influx of specie and therewith by a price revolution the nature of which was not lost on contemporary observers. One of these was Jean Bodin who in his *Response* of 1568 was the first formally to present a quantity theory of money: the value of all commodities tends to fall, he reasoned, if demand remains unchanged when supply increases, and the value of a precious metal such as gold or silver is no exception. As with gold and silver, so with paper money, and it is therefore easy to see why the Suspension of Cash Payments in 1797 so greatly upset bullionists such as Thornton and Ricardo: in the absence of convertibility, they argued, banks acquire a license to print money and inflation is bound to be the result. The Gold Standard was ultimately abandoned in Britain in 1931; the Bank Charter Act of 1844 foresaw the concentration of the power of note-issue in the hands of the Bank of England; that central bank was nationalized in 1946 (it had long collaborated closely with the Treasury in any case); and present-day followers of Thornton and Ricardo will understandably be tempted to ask if any limits at all not exist on the power of governments to finance themselves by means of money creation. Not that new money is always and everywhere a bad thing. On the contrary, issuing paper is nothing less than Pareto efficient in an underemployed economy where the additional claims only set to work real resources that would otherwise have been idle. As full employment is reached, however, additional demand becomes less and less able to call forth additional supply; and the continuing injection of new money then causes a continuing rise in the price index. The public might attribute that rise to some well-publicized non-monetary force (foreign cartels, bad harvests, speculative hoarders and greedy unions are all conspicuous targets that have performed yeoman service as convenient enemies in the history of economic ideas and institutions). Where it does so, a money-issuing government makes a double gain. First, it buys popularity by means of paying for new undertakings without having to levy new taxes or contract new debts. Second, it reduces, through inflation, the real burden of interest on existing debt, at a real cost to every creditor caught in possession of non-indexed claims. Inflation redistributes income, acting in that way as a hidden tax imposed without Parliamentary approval. Inflation distorts markets, causing buyers and sellers to confuse specific signals with general signals. Inflation breeds expectations of further inflation, and these a money-issuing government will be only too happy to accommodate. Fearful of what happens to an honest man when confronted with temptation, some thinkers have gone so far as to recommend the introduction of a multiperiod law that would set a ceiling for the rate of growth of the money supply. More confident about the capacity of strong-willed Ulysses to shut out the Siren's song voluntarily, other thinkers have been entirely happy with discretion so long as it is accompanied by disclosure and democracy. The former group will read with pleasure Nassau Senior's statement that

> the government generally endeavours to extort from its subjects, not merely a fair compensation for its services, but all that force or terror can wring from them without injuring their powers of further production (Senior, 1836, p. 75)

and will neglect the fact that the same author, in more pragmatic mood, also declared that 'it is the duty of a government to do whatever is conducive to the welfare of the governed':

> It appears to me that the most fatal of all errors would be the general admission of the proposition that a government has no right to interfere for any purpose except for that of affording protection, for such an admission would be preventing our profiting from experience, and even from acquiring it. (Quoted by Robbins, 1952, p. 45)

The latter group will express its admiration for the far-sighted imaginativeness which led the American Economic Association to include in its original statutes of 1885 an Article III indicating that 'we regard the State as an agency whose positive assistance is one of the indispensable conditions of human progress' (quoted by Schumpeter, 1954, p. 756), and will be shocked to learn that this clause, looking backward to the programmatic zeal which had accompanied the establishment of the Verein für Sozialpolitik in 1872 and forward to the setting of the London School of Economics in 1895, was deleted only three years later, in 1888. The former group is likely to have a bias for the principle of exchange, and the latter a bias for the principle of authority. The arguments presented by the adherents of both principles must be examined with respectful tolerance as much as with scientific detachment by every member of society with a genuine interest in a topic at once as complex, as multidisciplinary, as ideology ridden – and as important – as is the State and economic activity.

REFERENCES

Buchanan, J. (1975) *The Limits of Liberty*. Chicago, Ill.: University of Chicago Press.
Buchanan, J. (1977) *Freedom in Constitutional Contract*. College Station, Tex.: Texas A & M University Press.
Buchanan, J. (1986) *Liberty, Market and State*. Brighton: Wheatsheaf.
Coase, R. (1960) 'The problem of social cost', *The Journal of Law and Economics* 3, 1–44.
Downs, A. (1957) *An Economic Theory of Democracy*. New York: Harper and Row.
Friedman, M. (1962) *Capitalism and Freedom*. Chicago, Ill.: University of Chicago Press.
Friedman, M., and R. Friedman (1980) *Free to Choose*. Harmondsworth: Penguin.
Galbraith, J. K. (1958) *The Affluent Society*. Reprinted 1968, Harmondsworth: Penguin.
Galbraith, J. K. (1967) *The New Industrial State*. Reprinted 1974, Harmondsworth: Penguin.
Galbraith, J. K. (1971) *Economics, Peace and Laughter*. Reprinted 1975, Harmondsworth: Penguin.
Hayek, F. A. (1944) *The Road to Serfdom*. Reprinted 1976, London: Routledge & Kegan Paul.
Hirsch, F. (1977) *Social Limits to Growth*. London: Routledge & Kegan Paul.
Hobbes, T. (1651) *Leviathan*. Reprinted 1957, Oxford: Blackwell.
Lerner, A. (1944) *The Economics of Control*. Reprinted 1970, New York: Augustus M. Kelley.
Locke, J. (1690) *The Second Treatise of Government*. Reprinted 1946, Oxford: Blackwell.
Marshall, A. (1893) 'Preliminary statement and evidence before the Royal Commission on the Aged Poor', in *Official Papers by Alfred Marshall*. Ed. J. M. Keynes, reprinted 1926, London: Macmillan, pp. 197–262.
Marshall, A. (1909) 'Letter to Lord Reay dated 12 November 1909', in *Memories of Alfred Marshall*. Ed. A. C. Pigou, reprinted 1925, London: Macmillan, pp. 461–5.

Marshall, A. (1920) *Principles of Economics*. Reprinted 1949, London: Macmillan.

Marx, K. (1891) *Capital*, vol. III. Reprinted 1962, Moscow: Foreign Languages Publishing House.

Marx, K., and F. Engels (1848) *The Communist Manifesto*. Reprinted 1967, Harmondsworth: Penguin.

Mill, J. S. (1859) *On Liberty*. Reprinted 1974, Harmondsworth: Penguin.

Myrdal, G. (1955) *The Political Element in the Development of Economic Theory*. Cambridge, Mass.: Harvard University Press.

Niskanen, W. (1971) *Bureaucracy and Representative Government*. Chicago, Ill.: Aldine-Atherton.

Nozick, R. (1974) *Anarchy, State, and Utopia*. New York: Basic Books.

Olson, M. (1965) *The Logic of Collective Action*. Cambridge, Mass.: Harvard University Press.

Pigou, A. C. (1935) *Economics in Practice*. London: Macmillan.

Rae, J. (1895) *Life of Adam Smith*. Reprinted 1965, New York: Augustus M. Kelley.

Rawls, J. (1972) *A Theory of Justice*. Oxford: Oxford University Press.

Reisman, D. (1987) *Alfred Marshall: Progress and Politics*. London: Macmillan.

Robbins, L. (1952) *The Theory of Economic Policy in English Classical Political Economy*. London: Macmillan.

Rothbard, M. (1973) *For a New Liberty*. New York: Macmillan.

Schumpeter, J. (1942) *Capitalism, Socialism and Democracy*. Reprinted 1976, London: George Allen & Unwin.

Schumpeter, J. (1954) *History of Economic Analysis*. London: George Allen & Unwin.

Senior, N. (1836) *An Outline of the Science of Political Economy*. Reprinted 1965, New York: Augustus M. Kelley.

Smith, A. (1759) *The Theory of Moral Sentiments*. Reprinted 1966, New York: Augustus M. Kelley.

Smith, A. (1776) *The Wealth of Nations*. Reprinted 1961, London: Methuen.

Spencer, H. (1884) *The Man Versus the State*. Reprinted 1940, Caldwell: Caxton.

Steuart, J. (1767) *An Inquiry into the Principles of Political Œconomy*. Reprinted 1966, Chicago, Ill.: University of Chicago Press.

Tawney, R. H. (1914) *The Establishment of Minimum Rates in the Chain-making Industry Under the Trade Boards Act of 1909*. London: G. Bell.

Tawney, R. H. (1953) *The Attack and Other Papers*. London: George Allen & Unwin.

Tawney, R. H. (1966) *The Radical Tradition*. Harmondsworth: Penguin.

Titmuss, R. M. (1963) *Essays on "The Welfare State"*. London: George Allen & Unwin.

Titmuss, R. M. (1974) *Social Policy*. London: George Allen & Unwin.

3

Competition

Roger E. Backhouse

Competition is fundamental to most economic theory. According to John Stuart Mill, 'only through the principle of competition has political economy any pretension to the character of a science' (Mill, 1848, p. 147). When discussing the theory of value and price he explained that he was considering those cases 'in which values and prices are determined by competition alone', the reason being that 'In so far only as they are thus determined, can they be reduced to any assignable law' (Mill, 1848, p. 267). Furthermore, much economic theory assumes not simply competition, but perfect competition. In much contemporary writing the term 'competitive equilibrium' is used to refer to equilibrium with perfect competition. The importance of the assumption of perfect competition was clearly pointed out by John Hicks when he wrote that

> a general abandonment of the assumption of perfect competition . . . must have very destructive consequences for economic theory. . . . It is, I believe, only possible to save anything from this wreck – and it must be remembered that the threatened wreckage is the greater part of general equilibrium theory – if we can assume that the markets confronting most of the firms with which we shall be dealing do not differ very greatly from perfectly competitive markets. (Hicks, 1939, pp. 83–4)

Whilst they find that they are forced to make this assumption in their economic theories, however, many economists consider it to be unrealistic.

In addition to its being thought unrealistic, perfect competition deals with a situation where competition, as the term is commonly understood, is absent. There are two aspects to this. The first is that competition is often

I wish to thank John Creedy and participants in seminars at Birmingham University and University College Cardiff who provided useful comments on an early draft of this chapter. I am particularly indebted to John Beath, Ken George, Lynn Mainwaring, Denis O'Brien and Prasanta Pattanaik for directing my attention to material that I would otherwise have overlooked. Needless to say, none of these can be held responsible for the use I have made of their ideas.

thought of in terms of a dynamic process in which new products are developed and new markets are created and where firms seek new ways of making profits. The theory of perfect competition, however, is concerned with situations in which firms merely break even, a market's competitiveness being defined simply in terms of the ability of individual firms to influence the price of their own product. The second is that perfect competition describes markets where 'strategic competition', in which firms take account of how their competitors will respond to their actions, is absent. To quote Edward Chamberlin,

> One never hears of 'competition' in connection with the great markets [e.g. commodity markets], and the phrases 'price cutting,' 'under-selling,' 'unfair competition,' 'meeting competition,' 'securing a market,' etc. are unknown. (Chamberlin, 1933, p. 10)

Strategic competition is associated with oligopolistic and monopolistic markets, not with perfectly competitive markets. There are thus many aspects to the concept of competition.[1]

There are several ways in which the material covered in this chapter could be arranged. The arrangement followed here is to start with competition as a dynamic process, the interpretation of competition with the longest history, and then to move on to consider the static concept of competition. It is here that the concept of perfect competition comes in. The role of numbers in competition, because of its importance, is considered separately in section 3.3. Conclusions are drawn in the final section.

3.1 Competition as a Dynamic Process

The Classical View of Competition

Adam Smith, the economist who is perhaps most closely associated with the notion of competition, used the term in a way very different from that found in most contemporary economics. This is illustrated by the fact that he almost invariably used a definite or indefinite article when referring to competition, the following quotations from *The Wealth of Nations* being typical: 'A competition will immediately begin among them . . .'; 'Their mutual competition will . . .'; 'a competition between capitals'; 'the competition of the East India Companies with private traders' (1776, vol. I, pp. 64, 69, 375, 271). Competition was thus an activity in which people engaged, the economic world being the scene of many competitions between traders, all trying to buy or sell at the expense of their rivals.

The nearest Smith comes to the modern usage of the term is in the following passage:

that free and universal competition which forces everyone to have recourse to it for the sake of self-defence. (Smith 1776, vol. I, p. 165)

In many instances where we would use the term competition, Smith uses the term 'liberty'. For example, Smith argues that the price of something will be forced down to its normal level, not where the market is competitive, but where there is 'perfect liberty' and 'everyone may change his trade as often as he pleases' (Smith, 1776, vol. I, p. 63; cf. pp. 70 and 111). The emphasis is thus purely on what Joan Robinson has called 'the long-period aspect' of competition (Robinson, 1956, pp. 181–2). Smith thus defines liberty in terms of the absence of restraints:

> All systems either of preference or of restraint, therefore, being thus completely taken away, the obvious and simple system of natural liberty establishes itself of its own accord. Every man, as long as he does not violate the laws of justice, is left perfectly free to pursue his own interests his own way, and to bring both his industry and his capital into competition with those of any other man, or order of men. (Smith, 1776, vol. II, p. 208)

Smith's usage of the term, emphasizing competition as a process, or activity, was characteristic of English classical economics. This notion of competition explains the way the classical economists wrote about markets. Ricardo, for example, wrote that

> commodities are not only at a monopoly price, when by no possible device their quantity can be augmented; and when, therefore, the competition is wholly on one side – amongst the buyers. (Ricardo, 1817, p. 217)

He draws a contrast with the situation for agricultural produce where 'there is competition among the sellers as well as amongst the buyers' (Ricardo, 1817, p. 258). Ricardo did, however, distinguish the effects of monopoly from those of differential productivity. Rents, he argued, do not imply a monopoly price for the produce, for it is scarcity of land, not monopolistic restrictions on output and an absence of competition amongst sellers, that imposes a limit on the capital that can be employed.

A different approach was adopted by Samuel Bailey, one of Ricardo's most influential critics. Fundamental to Bailey's treatment of the problem was a threefold division of markets into (a) monopolies, or markets protected from competition, (b) markets where some producers have special advantages and (c) markets where competition operates without restraint (Bailey, 1825, p. 185). The characteristic of monopoly was not the existence of a single seller, but restictions on entry. A monopoly might therefore be dominated by either one seller or many sellers. It was only in the former case (i.e. no entry and a single seller) that price would be raised to the maximum consistent with demand. Bailey's second type of market covered, amongst other things, markets for agricultural produce. In such markets there are increasing costs, but new entrants lack some of the advantages (e.g. the most fertile land) possessed by existing producers. This means that the existing, lower-cost, producers have a limited degree of monopoly power: the extent that they can raise prices is

> limited by the watchful competition, which is ever ready to act upon it the moment it has exceeded a particular point. (Bailey, 1825, pp. 193–4)

Bailey recognized that monopoly was a special case of this. Finally, we have competition without restraint: 'free competition'.

To modern economists, Bailey's definition of monopoly seems un-natural, yet it was a natural one given the classical characterization of competition in terms of factor mobility rather than in terms of the demand conditions faced by individual producers. Other economists followed the same approach. Nassau Senior, for example, adopted essentially the same classification of markets, introducing the term 'equal competition' to describe Bailey's third category of market, 'where all persons can become producers, and that with equal advantages' (Senior, 1836, p. 102).

To appreciate the extent to which the classical economists thought of competition as a dynamic process involving the movement of resources from one activity to another, we have only to look at the work of Cairnes and Bagehot, writing at the very end of the classical period. Bagehot, in examining the postulates underlying 'English' political economy, picked out mobility of capital and labour between occupations. Defending the assumption of competition, he defended the notion that there was (albeit subject to certain limitations, which it was vital to recognize) considerable factor mobility. Furthermore, in analysing this he used competition in exactly the same sense as Smith:

> A free circulation of labour . . . involves an incessant competition between man and man. (Bagehot, 1876, p. 42)

Cairnes's approach is revealing because he is concerned with the absence of competition, arguing that within a country there are a number of 'non-competing groups' of producers. Within each group 'the existence of an effective competition [note the indefinite article] amongst those engaged in industrial pursuits' (Cairnes, 1874. p. 63) results in a situation where cost of production regulates normal values. When we go outside any group, however, values are determined by reciprocal demand. Reciprocal de-mand, Cairnes argued, not only was relevant to international trade, but was 'applicable to all cases in which groups of producers, excluded from reciprocal industrial competition, exchange their products' (Cairnes, 1874, p. 99).

The Competitive Process

The classical analysis of the competitive process was laid down by Adam Smith and was based on the concept of natural price which was 'what it really costs the person who brings [a commodity] to market', comprising not only 'prime cost' but also profit at 'the ordinary rate' (Smith, 1776, vol. I, pp. 62–3).

> Natural price is . . . the central price, to which the prices of all commodities are continually gravitating. (Smith, 1776, vol. I p. 65)

If the market price of a commodity rises above its natural price, the profits obtained in the industry concerned will be higher than those available elsewhere. Capital will then move into the industry and output will expand.[2] The working of this mechanism is clearly shown by Ricardo.

> Let us suppose that all commodities are at their natural price, and consequently that the profits of capital in all employments are exactly at the same rate. . . . Suppose now that a change of fashion should increase the demand for silks, and lessen that for woollens; their natural price, the quantity of labour necessary to their production, would continue unaltered, but the market price of silks would rise, and that of woollens would fall; and consequently the profits of the silk manufacturer would be above, whilst those of the woollen manufacturer would be below, the general and adjusted rate of profits. . . . This increased demand for silks would however soon be supplied, by the transference of capital and labour from the woollen to the silk manufacture; when the market prices of silks and woollens would again approach their natural prices, and then the usual profits would be obtained by the respective manufacturers of those commodities. (Ricardo, 1817, pp. 113–14)

This competitive process is also found in Walras's general equilibrium model in which equilibrium requires not only that effective supply and demand are equal in all markets, but also that the selling price of every commodity must equal its cost of production. If we define market price as the price at which supply and demand are equal, this is equivalent to the classical condition that market prices equal natural prices. Where Walras departed from the classics was in analysing the process in terms of his *tâtonnement*, or groping, in which prices were raised whenever demand exceeded supply and were lowered whenever supply exceeded demand. This was not an account of any dynamic competitive process, for it was rendered timeless by the assumption (needed in order to make the problem manageable) that neither production nor exchange took place until an equilibrium set of prices had been established.

Despite providing a static analysis of competition, however, Walras, like the classical economists, saw competition as a dynamic process. He saw his static equilibrium as an ideal, not as describing any real state:

> Equilibrium in production, like equilibrium in exchange, is an ideal and not a real state. It never happens in the real world that the selling price of any given product is absolutely equal to the cost of the productive services that enter into that product, or that the effective demand and supply of services or products are absolutely equal. Yet equilibrium is the normal state, in the sense that it is the state towards which things spontaneously tend under a regime of free competition in exchange and production. (Walras, 1874, p. 224)

The reason why equilibrium is never attained is that the world is constantly changing.[3]

> Such is the continuous market, which is perpetually tending towards equilibrium without ever actually attaining it, because the market has no other way of approaching equilibrium except by groping, and, before the goal is reached, it has to renew its efforts and start all over again, all the basic data of the problem [stocks of goods, technology and tastes] having changed in the meantime. (Walras, 1874, p. 380)

The economist analysing equilibrium prices was like someone explaining the level of a lake the surface of which is disturbed by storms, an analogy also used by Walras's contemporary, John Bates Clark (Clark, 1899, pp. 401ff.).

Evolutionary Theories of Competition

A different, but nonetheless dynamic, perspective is contained in theories which view competition as an evolutionary process. The most important such theory is that of J. A Schumpeter (1911). Schumpeter was concerned with the problem of economic development, which he defined as 'such changes in economic life as are not forced upon it from without but arise by its own initiative, from within' (Schumpeter, 1911, p. 63), this concern leading him to a view of competition in which innovation was central. The impulse to capitalist development comes, he argued, 'from the new consumers' goods, the new methods of production or transportation, the new markets, the new forms of industrial organization that capitalist enterprise creates' (Schumpeter, 1934, p. 83), these innovations arising as entrepreneurs seek new ways of making profits. The process of competition is thus one of 'creative destruction' where one firm makes an innovation (perhaps a new consumers' good) and as a result is able to obtain higher than normal profits. Over time, however, the innovation is imitated by other firms and the innovator's profits are eroded. As this happens old production techniques and old commodities are displaced by new ones. He compared this perspective with the traditional conception of competition in the following way:

> But in capitalist reality as distinguished from its textbook picture, it is not that kind of competition which counts but the competition from the new commodity, the new technology, the new source of supply, the new type of organization (the largest-scale unit of control for instance) – competition which commands a decisive cost or quality advantage and which strikes not at the margins of the profits and the outputs of the existing firms but at their foundations and their very lives. This kind of competition is as much more effective than the other as a bombardment is in comparison with forcing a door. . . . (Schumpeter, 1934, p. 84)

Evolutionary theories such as Schumpeter's are inevitably very complicated. Not only is technology constantly changing, but firms in competition with each other differ as regards both size and the technology to which they have access. Thus although many economists have found Schumpeter's vision of the competitive process attractive, far fewer have managed to work with it.

Schumpeter's work has, nonetheless, inspired some important work on what has come to be known as 'technological competition'. Dasgupta and Stiglitz (1980), for example, have investigated the relationship, suggested by Schumpeter, between industrial concentration, the level of research and development (R & D) expenditure and innovative activity.[4] They have developed models in which the level of R & D expenditure in an industry will be positively correlated with the level of concentration, as Schumpeter had suggested. However, the causation was not one way. Firms with a large market share have a greater incentive to engage in R & D, but at the same time high R & D expenditure serves to lower costs and create entry barriers.

The Schumpeterian perspective is one of competition as an evolutionary process in which firms struggle for survival. Armen Alchian (1950) drew from this the conclusion (very important if it is true) that competition would eliminate firms which did not maximize profits. Thus even if firms wish to pursue other objectives (see, for example, Simon, 1955; Baumol, 1959) only profit-maximizing firms will survive. This argument has been widely discussed (notably by Friedman, 1953, pp. 19–23; Koopmans, 1957, pp. 139–42) but the first economist to provide a formal model of the competitive process capable of analysing the problem was Winter (1964; see also Nelson and Winter 1982, especially part V).[5]

Winter's argument was that the assumptions of profit maximization and equilibrium had to be abandoned, the reasons being that the essence of the Schumpeterian perspective is that choice sets are not given and that when novel situations arise there may be no choice that is clearly best *ex ante*. Firms that face the same market circumstances may thus respond differently. In this context competition performs two functions: it permits a variety of responses to be explored; and it rewards those choices that prove good and penalizes those that prove bad, eventually eliminating firms that consistently make mistakes, or forcing them to reform (see Nelson and Winter, 1982, pp. 276–7). The model used was one in which successful innovation is rewarded by temporary monopoly power, but where the R & D expenditure required to be an innovator is more costly than that needed to imitate competitors' innovations. Winter showed that provided, amongst other assumptions, that some firms try a profit-maximizing strategy and that profitable firms expand, it will be true that 'the responses of surviving firms to situations that occur persistently will be profit maximizing responses' (Winter, 1964, p. 268). This conclusion, however, applies only where there is no novelty, in the sense that 'every conceivable state of the world occurs not once, but repeatedly' (p. 268). Where there is novelty, or where information is costly, it it not true that competition will eliminate firms that do not maximize profits.

3.2 The Static Concept of Competition

The Law of One Price

All the above remarks concern long-period competition. As regards short-period competition, Schumpeter's remark that 'the competitive case was the obvious thing, familiar to all, that they did not bother to analyze its logical content' (Schumpeter, 1954, p. 545) is well justified. It was agreed that the existence of competition implied that there could never be more than one price in a market. As J. S. Mill put it,

> There is no proposition which meets us in the field of political economy oftener than this – that there cannot be two prices in the same market. (Mill, 1848, p. 149)

It was recognized that a precondition for this was that individuals on both sides of the market must be actively pursuing their own interests, or, in J. S. Mill's words, 'The buyers must be supposed to be as studious to buy cheap as the sellers to sell dear' (Mill, 1848, p. 267). It is the latter aspect of competition that Mill had in mind when he argued that 'competition, in fact, has only become in any considerable degree the governing principle of contracts, at a comparatively modern period' (Mill, 1848, p. 148). He distinguished two determinants of prices, competition and custom, arguing that over time the influence of competition had increased. It is Mill's use of these two factors influencing price that allows him to refer, in a way that his predecessors did not, to the amount of competition. Economists, he argued, 'must consider not only what will happen supposing the maximum of competition, but how far the result will be affected if competition falls short of the maximum' (Mill, 1848, p. 151). Though it may be tempting to see falling short of maximum competition in terms of imperfect competition, this would be a mistake: Mill has in mind the possibility of non-maximizing behaviour, not the problems which arise when there are few competitors.

Jevons and Exchange

Jevons's theory of competition is unusual in that it is based on the concept of a 'trading body', this being 'any body either of buyers or sellers' (Jevons, 1871, p. 135). It may comprise 'any number of people whose aggregate influence in the market . . . we have to consider' (Jevons, 1871, p. 135). Though he argued that a trading body might comprise either a single individual or 'the whole inhabitants of a continent', the case Jevons analysed was that where trading bodies were each made up of a large number of individuals. Given that he assumed that individuals had no influence over prices, his theory makes sense only if his dealers are two typical individuals taken from a larger number. That Jevons may have been thinking along these lines is suggested by correspondence in which he analysed trade between 'Jones and Brown', clearly intended as two representative individuals (see Creedy, 1986, p. 74).

Jevons's analysis of competition centred on his 'law of indifference'.

> When a commodity is perfectly uniform or homogeneous in quality, any portion may be indifferently used in place of an equal portion: hence, in the same market, and at the same moment, all portions must be exchanged at the same ratio. . . . in the same open market, at any one moment, there cannot be two prices for the same kind of article. Such differences as may practically occur arise from extraneous circumstances, such as the defective credit of the purchasers, their imperfect knowledge of the market, and so on. (Jevons, 1871, p. 137)

Individuals have a monopoly as regards their own produce, but provided that 'different persons own property of exactly the same kind' (Jevons, 1871, p. 69) such monopoly will be limited by competition, no owner being able to obtain more for his goods than what owners of exactly similar goods are prepared to accept. Though Jevons's terminology was different, there was nothing new in this.

Jevons, however, went on to use his law of indifference in a novel way. Exchange, he recognized, took place over time, which meant that, as successive units of a commodity are exchanged, the price will change, the reason being that once the first portion has been exchanged the conditions of demand and supply will change. It follows that the ratio in which small increments of the commodity are exchanged (dy/dx, where x and y are the quantities of the two goods being exchanged) need not equal the ratio in which the total quantities traded are exchanged (y/x). This, Jevons argued, was a dynamic problem, and on the grounds that it was sensible to consider the statics first, he assumed that 'the last increments in an act of exchange must be exchanged in the same ratio as the whole quantities exchanged' (Jevons, 1871, p. 139). All transactions between two trading bodies, therefore, would occur at rate y/x. From here he went on to show that exchange would continue to the point where, for each trading body, the ratio of marginal utilities equalled the ratio of exchange.

There is thus an ambiguity in Jevons's theory of competitive equilibrium. He is clearly concerned with competitive exchange (where there is a large number of both buyers and sellers), and yet, because he wants to argue in terms of the ratio of a quantity of goods traded, rather than in terms of prices, he has to consider exchange between two traders (his trading bodies).

Walras and Price Taking

In contrast with Jevons and Edgeworth, Walras was prepared to define 'free competition' (*libre concurrence*) in terms of price-taking behaviour.

> Value in exchange, when left to itself, arises spontaneously in the market as the result of competition. As buyers, traders make their demands by outbidding each other. As sellers, traders make their offers by underbidding each other. . . . The more perfectly competition functions, the more rigorous is the manner of arriving at value in exchange. The markets which are best organized from the competitive standpoint are those in which purchases and sales are made by auction, through the instrumentality of stockbrokers, commercial brokers or criers acting as agents who centralize transactions in such a way that the terms of every exchange are openly announced and an opportunity is given to sellers to lower their prices and to buyers to raise their bids. (1874, p. 83–4)

For Walras, therefore, competition is judged in terms of how closely the market concerned works like an auction market, where an outsider sets prices and individual traders simply decide the quantities they wish to buy and sell at those prices. The best organized markets are thus financial markets and the like. After these come markets for fish, poultry and vegetables: partly organized, but effective. Competition works adequately, however, even in unorganized retail markets.

When he came to analysing the *tâtonnement*, the process whereby markets actually reach equilibrium, Walras used two models. In the first, used to analyse equilibrium in exchange, the auctioneer cries out prices expressed in terms of a *numéraire*. In the second, the prices cried out are the relative prices of every pair of goods in the economy. In this second model, therefore, arbitrage is needed if a full general equilibrium is to be achieved. Furthermore, the equations of general equilibrium have to be written differently to take account of there being many more prices in the system. Walras came close, therefore, to a notion of competition based on arbitrage, but he never managed to free himself from the auction model of competition.

To put Walras's achievement in perspective it is important to point out that although he did not make much progress in analysing the nature of competition itself, he posed, and made substantial steps towards answering, many of the technical questions concerning general competitive equilibrium. He tackled the problems of existence and stability in a way which his predecessors had failed to do. In addition he formulated many of the concepts which have become standard in general equilibrium theory: for example, the *numéraire*, the *tâtonnement* (involving not only the adjustment of prices according to excess supply and demand, but also the assumption that no trading is allowed to take place until the economy is out of equilibrium) and the distinction between stocks of factors and flows of factor services.

Walras's theory of free competition was developed by his successor at Lausanne, Pareto. Pareto distinguished between two types of behaviour: behaviour which takes 'the state or condition of the market' as given (Pareto's type I) and behaviour which seeks to modify the conditions of the market to achieve desired ends (type II). Type I is found 'where there is competition among those who act according to it'. In a dynamic context type I behaviour occurs where agents assume that their current actions will have no influence on future prices; in a static context it amounts to assuming that individuals are price-takers. Type II behaviour, in contrast, is much more straightforward. It is the behaviour of monopolists.

Pareto uses a number of adjectives to describe competition.

1 He refers to competition being 'incomplete' when production stops at a point where producers are at an internal profit maximum and 'complete'

when prices are such that producers increase output 'up to the terminal point which the other conditions of the problem impose on him' (Pareto, 1906, p. 134; cf. p. 152).

2 A second attribute of competition is introduced where Pareto argues that type I behaviour 'is the more pure as competition is the more widespread and the more perfect' (Pareto, 1906, p. 116). Pareto has moved away from Walras's auctioneer, for he argues that sellers 'clearly modify the prices'. Such price changes, however, are 'without previous design; it is not the purpose, but the effect of their actions' (Pareto, 1906, p. 116). Nonetheless, there is nothing to suggest that Pareto is not using the term perfection in the same sense as Walras: denoting the degree to which competition is like that involved in an auction market, in which there is free communication between many buyers and sellers and in which there is no collusion between traders.

Pareto recognized the possibility that, as an individual traded goods, the price at which he could buy or sell successive portions could change. He dismissed this, however, claiming that 'this hypothesis yields strange and highly unrealistic consequences' and that 'the hypothesis which conforms best to reality is the one of equal prices for successive portions' (Pareto, 1906, p. 157). The purchase of successive portions at different prices was a characteristic of speculative markets, but speculation, he argued, was a secondary phenomenon, modifying the 'principal' phenomenon which adjusts consumption to production. This dismissal of price variation seems akin to Jevons's dismissal of non-uniform prices as a dynamic phenomenon, too complex for analysis.

Jevons and Walras both analysed markets in which the law of one price prevailed. This characterization of competition was criticized by Bertrand (1883) who argued that sellers compete on price and that it is misleading to assume that firms necessarily charge the same price. However, if buyers always purchase from the cheapest available seller and if firms take their competitors' prices as given, then every firm will face a perfectly elastic demand curve and will behave as though it were a price-taker. Prices will be set at the same level as in a Walrasian model.

Perfect and Imperfect Competition by 1920

By 1920, because of the work of Jevons, Walras and their successors, the static theory of competition had been much more fully worked out than it ever was in the classical period. One of the most complete accounts of competition in the first two decades of the twentieth century was that contained in Wicksell's *Lectures on Political Economy* (Wicksell, 1901, revised in 1911). He viewed competition in terms of price-taking behaviour, explaining the more or less fixed prices which occur on an open market in terms of Jevons's 'law of indifference'. This, Wicksell argued, was 'nothing else than the old "free competition"' (Wicksell, 1901, p. 52). What sustained the equilibrium price was the risk that if some sellers raised their price (perhaps hoping to sell a part of their output at a high price, disposing of the remainder more cheaply later on) they would run the risk that they might not be able to sell their output at all, or that the price might fall far below what they would have got had the equilibrium price prevailed from the start.

Perfect competition was seen to depend on a number of conditions. There must be a uniform product, firms must be small in size and there must be constant returns to scale. These last two conditions were related, for constant returns might prevail either because there were constant returns at all levels of output or because 'all productive enterprises have already reached the limit beyond which a further increase in the scale of production will no longer yield any advantage' (Wicksell, 1901, p. 126). There are two aspects to this: firms must operate at their 'optimum' scale (the point of constant returns) if they are not to be undercut by other firms, and new firms must be established until entrepreneurial profit is zero (Wicksell, 1901, pp. 129–30). The elimination of entrepreneurial profit, Wicksell argued, might come about either through the price of output falling, or through the bidding up of wages and rents. Perfect competition will be sustained only if the optimum scale of an enterprise is sufficiently small for the market to contain a large number of firms operating at optimum scale (Wicksell, 1901, pp. 130–1).

In addition to discussing monopoly (in a conventional manner, though he did point out, citing as an example the Standard Oil Company of America, that fear of intervention might cause a monopoly to charge the competitive price – 1901, p. 89) and bilateral exchange (following Edgeworth), Wicksell considered imperfect competition. His main example here was retail trade, which departed from perfect competition in three ways. First there was the problem of large overhead costs and joint supply. Second there was a general desire for stability of prices. Finally, retailers possessed a local monopoly caused by their location. In such a situation, Wicksell argued, new entry might raise prices, not lower them. The reason was that if a new shop was established between two existing ones, the existing shops would lose customers. With three shops, overhead costs per unit sold would be higher, and prices would have to rise.

Wicksell, therefore, had an excellent understanding of perfect competition and perceived some aspects of what Chamberlin was later to call monopolistic competition.[6] His analysis of the latter, however, was incomplete for he failed to see that free entry could result in a zero-profit equilibrium even when firms had a local monopoly. Wicksell stated explicitly that 'the tendency of entrepreneurial profits to zero . . . holds only under perfect competition' (Wicksell, 1901, p. 229).

Similar remarks can be made concerning Marshall's successor, Pigou. Pigou distinguished between simple competition, monopolistic competition and monopoly. The term simple competition was used to denote what Pareto called perfect competition: a situation 'where the supply of each seller is so small a part of the aggregate supply that his advantage is best consulted if he accepts market prices without trying, or set purpose, to modify them' (Pigou, 1912, p. 180; quoting Pareto, 1896, vol. I, p. 20). Monopolistic competition occurred 'when each of two or more sellers supplies a considerable part of the market with which they are connected' (Pigou, 1912, p. 192). He argued, in line with what had by then become the generally accepted view, that output under monopolistic competition would, within certain limits, be indeterminate. His main argument ran in terms of what has since been labelled conjectural variation:

> The output, which at any moment will be most profitable to A, depends on the output which B is undertaking, and vice versa. The output undertaken by each, therefore, depends on his judgement of the policy which the other will pursue, and this judgement is indeterminate. (Pigou, 1912, p. 193)

It is worth noting, in view of the emphasis that Chamberlin was later to place on selling costs, that these are taken into account by Pigou. In discussing the factors which lead to the monopolization of an industry he listed not only structural conditions (an optimal plant size that is large relative to the market, and economies of scale in business organization) but also 'advertisement economies' (Pigou, 1912, p. 189). If two businesses could be combined, they would not have to persuade people to buy one of their products rather than the other.

Many of the ideas discussed by Wicksell and Pigou are to be found in the work of earlier economists, notably Marshall. Their writings show, however, that by about 1920 the static theory of competition had progressed significantly beyond what was available to the classical economists in that the concept of perfect competition was fairly well understood and economists were beginning to move towards having a worked out theory of imperfect competition.

Chamberlin and Market Structure

Chamberlin's *The Theory of Monopolistic Competition*, published in 1933 though written between 1925 and 1927, was perhaps the most important contribution to the theory of competition since Cournot. Chamberlin's concern was with situations where both monopolistic and competitive forces combine in determining prices, and as a result he provided a much clearer classification of markets than had previously been attempted.

Defining monopoly as a situation where a supplier has 'control over the supply and therefore over the price' (Chamberlin, 1933, p. 7), Chamberlin defined pure competition in terms of the absence of monopoly. This requires that the number of suppliers be sufficiently large that no one finds it worthwhile to attempt to influence price (it does not have to be infinite). Despite his criticisms of Pareto (Chamberlin, 1933, p. 10), Chamberlin would appear to be adopting the same distinction as him. In addition, if control over price is to be completely absent, it is necessary that the product be homogeneous and that consumers have no reason to prefer one seller to another. This concept of pure competition was distinguished from perfect competition in that the latter required not only pure competition, but also perfect knowledge and an absence of friction.

Chamberlin then pointed out that there were two distinct ways of blending competition and monopoly: numbers might be small, or there might be product differentiation. As regards the former problem, though he invented the term oligopoly, he had little to add to previous contributions, arguing that the reason for their different results was that 'Duopoly is not one problem, but several' (1933, p. 53). Under different circumstances different results will obtain. The result of moving in the other direction, assuming a large number of firms producing differentiated products, led to what he termed monopolistic competition. In such a situation each firm has a monopoly of its own product, but its control over price is limited by the availability of substitutes. Monopolistic competition, Chamberlin claimed, was what most people usually meant by competition.

Chamberlin went on to analyse monopolistic competition in terms of the now familiar diagram, with marginal cost equal to marginal revenue and with the demand curve tangential to the average cost curve when competition forces profits to zero. Despite the familiarity of this model, however, it is necessary to point out some features of Chamberlin's treatment.

1 Because each firm produced a unique product, it was no longer possible to define an industry as comprising all firms producing a particular product. Instead, Chamberlin referred to 'groups' of firms producing products which are close substitutes for each other (Chamberlin, 1933, p. 81).

2 Product differentiation in an otherwise competitive market creates a role for advertising and other means of changing the firm's 'product'.[7] Though such selling costs had been recognized previously (e.g. by Pigou, discussed above), Chamberlin was the first economist to analyse them so formally.

Marshall and Robinson

Despite the similarities in their theories, Robinson's work on competition was undertaken against a very different background, and with very different goals, from Chamberlin's. *The Economics of Imperfect Competition* (1933) has to be seen as part of the movement away from Marshall towards a more formal theory of economic equilibrium. To understand this we have to examine Marshall's theory of competition.

Although in certain respects Marshall is closer to Jevons, Walras and their successors, in his treatment of competition he is closer to the English classical economists. At the beginning of his *Principles* he wrote

> The strict meaning of competition seems to be the racing of one person against another, with special reference to bidding for the sale or purchase of something. (Marshall, 1890, p. 4)

For Marshall, the opposite of competition is not monopoly, but cooperation. Marshall did not characterize individual behaviour in terms of profit maximization, but in terms of

> a certain independence and habit of choosing one's own course for oneself, a self-reliance; a deliberation and yet a promptness of choice and judgement, and a habit of forecasting the future and of shaping one's course with reference to distant aims. (Marshall, 1890, p. 4)

He saw these characteristics as resulting not simply in competition, but also in cooperation. He thus disagreed with Mill in that he did not see history in terms of a movement from custom to competition. Marshall was thus concerned to analyse not a competitive economy, but one where individuals were motivated in this more complicated way. Like Adam Smith, though for different reasons, Marshall spoke of 'economic freedom', rather than competition.

Marshall's work contains a problem as regards his attitude towards competition. His concern was, like Smith's, with the determinants of normal value, which he analysed in terms of supply and demand. Natural values were the values 'which economic forces tend to bring about in the long run' (Marshall, 1890, p. 289). As Cournot and Edgeworth (see below) had clearly shown, the use of supply curves presupposes perfect competition, but Marshall was not willing to assume this: 'Of course,' he wrote, 'Normal does not mean Competitive' (Marshall, 1890, p. 289). Marshall's algebraic analysis of competition was substantially the same as that of contemporaries such as Wicksell, but in Marshall's text we find a much looser analysis: more realistic, but not as rigorous.

The origins of Robinson's work lie in the 'cost controversy' of the 1920s. Sraffa (1926) argued that increasing returns to scale were incompatible with competition and suggested that the way out was through a theory of monopoly. There followed an intense debate involving, amongst others, Harrod, Pigou, Robbins and Robinson on Marshallian value theory and the role of the firm. In this debate a number of developments occurred: (a) the derivation of the marginal revenue curve, and the recognition that the supply curve disappeared when competition was not perfect (Harrod, 1930); (b) the abandonment of Marshall's 'representative firm' (Pigou, 1928; Robbins, 1928), which led in due course to the replacement of Marshall's notion of an industry made up of a number of different firms, with the simpler notion of an industry made up of identical firms.

In Robinson's book the main characteristic of competition is free entry. She starts with equilibrium for a monopoly and then shows that if there is competition profits will be reduced to zero, with the demand curve tangential to the average cost curve. It is only if there is perfect competition that the demand curve will be horizontal, and price will equal marginal cost. Although the basic framework is thus the same as Chamberlin's, she is doing no more than providing what she describes as 'a box of tools'. Where Chamberlin was attempting to bring Marshall's analysis up to date and to make it more realistic, Robinson was simplifying Marshall's theory to the point where a formal equilibrium model could be constructed.

3.3 The Role of Numbers in Competition

Cournot

In the first half of the nineteenth century only one researcher examined the concept of competition in a modern way: Augustin Cournot, Professor of Mathematics at Lyons, author of the remarkable *Researches into the Mathematical Principles of the Theory of Wealth* (1838). Cournot defined his subject-matter, wealth, in terms of the market value of goods, and then he proceeded systematically to investigate what determined market values, in particular the effects of competition:

> Every one has a vague idea of the effects of competition. Theory should have attempted to render this idea more precise; and yet, for lack of regarding the question from the proper point of view, and for want of recourse to symbols (of which the use in this connection becomes indispensable), economic writers have not in the least improved on popular notions in this respect. These notions have remained as ill-defined and ill-applied in their works, as in popular language. (Cournot, 1838, p. 79)

As did the classical economists, Cournot used the term competition in the sense of a contest between one or more parties. He thus separated 'the competition of customers' from 'the competition of producers'. The former was assumed throughout his analysis, but 'the competition of producers' was analysed in three stages, starting with the simplest case where it was absent: monopoly.

Cournot implicitly recognized that the term monopoly was understood in a wider sense, for he had to explain that he was discussing monopoly 'in its most absolute meaning', namely the case of a single producer (Cournot, 1838, p. 56). A single producer will maximize profits subject to the demand function, from which Cournot deduced the condition that marginal cost equals marginal revenue: $D + (dD/dp)[p - c'(D)] = 0$, where D is produce demanded, p is price and $c(D)$ the cost function. The derivative dD/dp is given by the demand function.

He then introduced the theory for which he is now best known, introducing another producer so as to analyse competition between two producers. As is well known, he analysed this problem by assuming that each producer maximizes profit on the assumption that the other producer will keep its output unchanged. Cournot introduces this assumption without any suggestion that he realizes how vital it is:

> Proprietor (1) can have no direct influence on the determination of $D2$: all that he can do, when $D2$ has been determined by proprietor (2), is to choose for $D1$ the value which is best for him. (Cournot, 1838, p. 80)

The phrase 'all that he can do' suggests that Cournot regards this as a natural assumption. It is clear that by 'the value which is best for him' Cournot means the best given the other firm's current output, for he goes on to say that the proprietor will 'be able to accomplish this by properly setting his price, except as proprietor (2) . . . may adopt a new value for $D2$' (Cournot, 1838, p. 80). As his subsequent use of the diagram showing reaction curves makes clear, Cournot is here describing the dynamic process which operates when the two producers both behave according to this rule.

This theory was, for Cournot, the first step in an analysis of competition between producers. He assumed that, when the number of producers increased, competition amongst the producers increased, and so he went on to consider the case of n producers, analysing it in the same way. The limiting case, unlimited competition, occurred when any individual producer was insignificant relative to the market as a whole.

> The effects of competition have reached their limit, when each of the partial productions Dk is inappreciable, not only with reference to the total production $D = F(p)$ [the demand function], but also with

reference to the derivative $F'(p)$, so that the partial production Dk could be subtracted from D without any appreciable variation resulting in the price of the commodity. (Cournot, 1838, p. 90)

If any 'partial production', taken alone, is negligible, price will equal marginal cost for all producers:

$$p - ck'(Dk) = 0.$$

Each of these equations can be solved for Dk as a function of p, and they can then be summed to give D (total production) as a function of p. It follows that

$$S(p) = D(p)$$

where $S(p)$ is the function derived from the price–marginal-cost equations. Cournot then plotted these supply and demand functions, observing that marginal costs, and hence the supply function, had to be increasing (otherwise revenue would be less than cost, and there would be no limit on production). He went on to use these curves to analyse taxation, deriving the familiar textbook results.

Cournot's achievement, writing in 1838, was remarkable. He started from the same concept of competition as Smith and his followers and showed how price and output would depend on the number of producers competing with each other. His demonstration that 'unlimited competition' required that competitors be infinitesimally small was unequalled until Edgeworth's work over 40 years later. Not only this, but he showed how under unlimited competition price would equal marginal cost, and how such a market could be analysed in terms of supply and demand. He clearly recognized that it was inappropriate to use supply and demand curves when the number of competitors was finite, a point recognized by Edgeworth but, largely owing to Marshall's influence, forgotten by many economists until it was 'rediscovered' by Harrod and Robinson around 1930. In his analysis of imperfect competition Cournot did not name the concepts of marginal cost and marginal revenue but this is simply because he managed perfectly adequately using mathematical notation. Marginal cost, for example, is not named but $C'(D)$ is discussed in detail.[8]

Edgeworth

Unlike Jevons, Edgeworth was unwilling to assume price-taking behaviour, approaching the problem of competition through examining the bargains that individuals, each pursuing their own self-interest, might strike with each other. His approach to the problem of competition was to argue that at any moment there will be a series of contracts which have been made between individuals concerning exchanges of goods, but that individuals will recontract (enter a new contract with different individuals) if it is in their interests to do so. He was thus led to focus on 'final settlements': contracts which can be varied neither with the consent of all the parties involved nor by individuals choosing to recontract.[9]

Competition enters naturally into this framework, Edgeworth defining 'the field of competition' as 'all the individuals who are willing and able to recontract about the articles in question' (Edgeworth, 1881, p. 17). A normal competitive field is characterized by free communication between all the individuals involved (they are either all at the same place, or connected by telephones). In addition to this, a perfect field of competition has four further properties (Edgeworth, 1881, p. 18):

I. Any individual is free to recontract with any out of an indefinite number.
II. Any individual is free to contract (at the same time) with an indefinite number.
III. Any individual is free to recontract with another independently of, without the consent being required of, any third party.
IV. Any individual is free to contract with another independently of any third party.

Using these definitions he was able to show that

(a) Contract without competition is indeterminate, (b) Contract with perfect competition is perfectly determinate, (c) Contract with more or less perfect competition is less or more indeterminate. (Edgeworth, 1881, p. 20)

To prove this he started, like Cournot, with two traders, showing that every point on the contract curve consistent with both traders being at least as well off as if they opted out of trade was potentially a final settlement. He then introduced further traders to show, using diagrams that are copied almost exactly in modern textbooks (e.g. Weintraub, 1974; Hildenbrand and Kirman, 1976, ch. 1), how the line containing potential final settlements shrank as the number of traders increased. In the limit, where anyone could contract and recontract with an indefinite number of traders, there was a unique final settlement.

Edgeworth was thus able to show that the familiar equilibrium conditions for a perfectly competitive market could be derived 'from the first principle: Equilibrium is attained when the existing contracts can neither be varied without recontract with the consent of the existing parties, nor by recontract within the field of production' (1881, p. 31). He commented, quite correctly, that his method of deriving what were, from the work of Jevons, Walras and Marshall, familiar equilibrium conditions had the advantage that it was applicable to the case of imperfect competition, where the conceptions of demand and supply at a price were no longer appropriate.

It is worth noting that in Edgeworth's work we have a very different usage of the term competition from that found in earlier literature. When, at the start of his exposition, he discusses whether 'economic competition' is peace or war, he uses the term in its traditional sense. Later, however, he refers, in a more modern manner, to a state of perfect competition and to imperfect competition (Edgeworth, 1881, e.g. pp. 30–1, 44). It is also significant that market imperfection was defined in terms of small numbers, not in terms of non-maximizing behaviour (cf. J. S. Mill).

Modern Work

In the past 40 years economists have examined further the role of numbers in competition, rediscovering and generalizing the concepts first developed by Cournot and Edgeworth. The basis for this work, as for much of the work examined in the following section, has been the theory of games, developed by von Neumann and Morgenstern (1944), for this has provided a general perspective from which problems of market organization can be viewed. Of particular importance has been the distinction between cooperative and non-cooperative games.

One approach to the theory of competition has been to analyze it in terms of bargaining, the crucial step here being the rediscovery of the 'core', Edgeworth's line of final settlements. It was shown more rigorously and more generally than Edgeworth had been able to do how the core of an economy shrank as the number of agents increased, the limit, in which all agents are infinitesimally small, being a single point: the Walrasian, perfectly competitive, equilibrium (Shubik, 1959; Scarf, 1962; Debreu and Scarf, 1963; Aumann, 1964).[10]

The other main approach has been to follow Cournot in examining competition as a non-cooperative game. In a non-cooperative game agents are assumed to have well-defined strategies, with the outcome of the game depending, in some precisely specified manner, on these strategies. An equilibrium in such a game is

> a combination of strategies with the property that no agent has an incentive to modify them given the conjectures he has on the reaction of other agents. (Mas-Colell, 1980b, p. 2)

This is clearly a generalization of Cournot's equilibrium in which each firm's strategy was to set output to maximize profits given its competitors' output. Cournot's result has been established more rigorously and attempts have been made to generalize it by extending it from partial equilibrium analysis of a single market to general equilibrium analysis.[11]

An interesting extension of this approach has been to investigate the circumstances under which agents will wish to pursue a non-cooperative strategy rather than cooperating, for if this is not the case a non-cooperative equilibrium is unlikely to be viable. Radner (1980), for example, has shown that, if the market game is repeated a finite number of times, the larger the number of traders, the more likely it is that the outcome will be close to the Cournot equilibrium. In other words, that non-cooperative behaviour is more likely if there is a large number of traders. Given that with a large number of firms the Cournot equilibrium will be close to the competitive Walrasian equilibrium, this means that a competitive equilibrium is more likely if the number of traders is large.

In the Cournot model the crucial factor determining the degree of competition is the number of firms in the market. However, this result has been challenged by economists who have argued that it is the size of the firm relative to the economy as a whole, not a particular market, that is important. One of the most important contributions has been made by Hart (1979). Consider an economy in which there are two commodities A and B where a single agent owns the entire stock of A, but where ownership of B is divided between n identical agents. The owner of good A is thus a monopolist and can benefit from her or his monopoly power. The interesting result to emerge is that as n, together with the total stock of good B, increases the gains that A can obtain from acting as a monopolist diminish. As n approaches infinity the relative price of A and B approaches the competitive price ratio and the gains from acting as a monopolist approach zero.[12]

This result is related to the work of Ostroy (1980) and Makowski (1980) who use what they call a 'no-surplus' condition to characterize a perfectly competitive equilibrium. A no-surplus economy is one where every individual is obtaining the maximum utility possible, subject to the constraint that all other individuals in the economy are no worse off than they would be if the individual concerned were absent and they were to reallocate resources amongst themselves (Ostroy, 1980, p. 65). In such an economy each individual is receiving his or her marginal product: the amount he or she could expect to obtain from joining the economy. This characterization of perfect competition is interesting for a number of reasons. Firstly, it is a description of perfect competition that is not logically tied to the assumption of a large number of agents: the conditions for perfectly competitive equilibrium are essentially the same in an economy with a small number of agents as in one with many agents. The difference is simply that perfect competition is more likely if there are many agents. Secondly, the 'no-surplus' approach to competitive equilibrium 'almost always' (for clarification see Ostroy, 1980) yields the same conclusions as the seemingly very different approach, discussed above, using the 'core'. The difference is summarized by Ostroy in the following way.

> With the core criterion, perfectly competitive equilibrium is obtained as the residual outcome after all groups of agents cooperate in the interests of improving upon any given allocation but no group is able to hold together to use its potential monopoly power to extract a more favourable outcome. With NS [no-surplus], just the opposite occurs. Only small groups (individuals) are able to form but they are relied upon to bargain as monopolists for the maximum they can possibly extract. . . . Which interpretation – the core or NS condition – is the preferred description of what will frequently be equivalent mathematical conditions characterizing perfectly competitive equilibrium should be judged on its eventual connections to the theory of imperfect competition. (Ostroy, 1980, p. 88)

Contestability

For many years perfect competition has been taken as the benchmark against which to appraise market structures. This has recently been questioned by Baumol and his associates (Baumol, 1982; Baumol, Panzar and Willig, 1982) who have proposed the alternative of what they term a 'perfectly contestable market'. This is defined as a market in which 'entry is absolutely free, *and exit is absolutely costless*' (Baumol, 1982, p. 3). Free entry requires that potential entrants must be able to produce goods that are perceived as being of equal quality to those of the existing producers and that they can produce goods just as cheaply. Costless exit means that there are no 'sunk' costs: costs that cannot be recovered (e.g. by selling assets) should the firm decide to cease production. These conditions imply that a perfectly contestable market is vulnerable to 'hit and run' entry, for should prices rise above cost a new entrant could enter the market, make a profit and leave the market (without incurring any cost) should the incumbent firms respond by lowering their prices. It follows that in a perfectly contestable market no firm will be able to make more than normal profits, even if the number of firms is very small. In addition, Baumol argued, price will always equal marginal cost in a perfectly contestable market, provided that there are at least two firms in the industry.[13]

A perfectly contestable market will therefore exhibit important features of a perfectly competitive market, even though there may be very few firms in the market. What keeps price equal to marginal cost is *potential* competition and the fact that firms already in the market take account of potential competition in setting their prices. Contestability theory, therefore, turns attention away from demand conditions facing firms already in an industry towards conditions of entry and exit. Although Baumol and his associates are providing a rival to the static theory of perfect competition, therefore, their theory is in some respects closer to that of the classical economists, discussed in section 3.1 above.

The major problem with this theory is that it assumes that new entrants into a market will be able to enter more quickly than incumbent firms will be able to lower their prices in retaliation. If this condition is not satisfied new entrants will be unable to make any profit, which means that they will not wish to enter: there will be no threat to incumbent firms. Given that prices in most markets, can be changed far more quickly than newcomers can enter, it seems unlikely that many, if any, markets are perfectly contestable. The concept of a perfectly contestable market is nonetheless useful as an ideal type against which other markets can be assessed. Baumol and his associates may not have managed to displace the concept of perfect competition as they intended, but they have nonetheless succeeded in forcing economists to pay attention to the important issue of entry barriers and potential competition, something of which economists have long since been aware but without, perhaps, paying it sufficient attention.[14]

3.4 Conclusions

For Adam Smith and most of the classical economists the concept of competition was so familiar that its logical content was, as Schumpeter pointed out, to a great extent unanalysed. As a result, the term competition, when used by economists, retained much of its everyday meaning. When economists became more interested in the individual producer and as the more formal mathematics came to be used, the content of the term was examined more closely. As this happened, however, there was a shift of emphasis away from the dynamic view we find in classical writings towards a more static concept of competition. Dynamic issues, involving entry into and exit from markets, were still relevant, but they were pushed into the background, with much of the analysis being of situations where dynamic forces had worked themselves out and brought markets into equilibrium.

Since the World War II there have been two major developments, both stimulated by game theory. The first is that our understanding of perfect competition has been increased as economists have shown that it can be characterized in many ways. In virtually all recent work, whether competition is viewed (following Edgeworth) in terms of a cooperative game or (following Cournot) in terms of a non-cooperative game, perfect competition arises as a limiting case when the number of competitors increases towards infinity (though in some such sequences the limiting case is still imperfectly competitive). It is quite likely that the relative fruitfulness of these different interpretations will depend on what they can teach us about imperfect, not perfect, competition.

The second major development has been that economic theorists have begun to take account of the fact that competition involves much more than simply price competition. According to Stiglitz,

> It is now widely recognised that the nature of competition in market economies is far more complex (and more interesting) than the simple representation of price competition embodied in, say, the Arrow–Debreu model. Not only are there alternative *objects* of competition: firms compete not only about price but also about products and R & D. But also, the *structure* of competition, the 'rules' which relate the pay-offs to each of the participants to the actions they undertake, may differ markedly from those in the standard model. (Stiglitz and Matthewson, 1986, p. 399)

He elaborates on this last point in the following way:

> Most of us are familiar with sports competitions. There are a variety of rules of the game under which these competitions are conducted. Only a single prize may be awarded, or alternatively, the difference between the winning prize and the losing prizes . . . may be relatively small. There may be handicaps, and almost any contest imposes a variety of restrictions on the set of 'feasible' actions which the participants can undertake . . . . (Stiglitz and Matthewson, 1986, p. 442)

The literature on technological competition, for example, discusses patent 'races' and 'tournaments'. There has thus been a 'rediscovery' of the everyday meaning of the term competition.

NOTES

1 Because of the scope of the subject there is much that cannot be covered in this chapter. General discussions of the history of the concept of competition are given by Moore (1905), Stigler (1957) and Clark (1961). Some important aspects of the theory of imperfect competition that are not covered here are examined by O'Brien (1983). For useful survey of some recent work on strategic competition and oligopoly see Dixit (1982), Geroski, Phlips and Ulph (1985) and Morris et al. (1986).

2 It is worth noting that it is not inevitable that entry into an industry will reduce profits. This issue has recently been explored, albeit in a model very different from Ricardo's, by Novshek and Sonnenschein (1986).

3 This, according to some economists (Roncaglia, 1978; Dumenil and Levy, 1987), is the classical view of competition.

4 For a simpler more general discussion, see Dasgupta (1986).
5 Mention should also be made of Downie (1958) who also analysed a Schumpeterian model, though his concern was with its implications for firm size rather than with maximizing behaviour.
6 Cf. Moss (1984), who argues that the concept of perfect competition was not fully developed until it emerged as a byproduct of the theory of imperfect competition in the 1930s.
7 Since Chamberlin there has been extensive discussion of whether perfect competition is compatible with product differentiation. Robinson (1934) and Kaldor (1935) argued that Chamberlin was wrong to claim that perfect competition required a homogeneous product. Examples from the recent literature include Hart (1985a, b), Perloff and Salop (1985) and Dixit and Stiglitz (1977). Beath and Katsoulacos (forthcoming, ch. 7) give a useful discussion of this.
8 Compare the different assessments of Samuelson (1967) and Shackle (1967).
9 For a useful exposition of Edgeworth's theory see Creedy (1986).
10 For more comprehensive discussion of recent work on this area see Hildenbrand (1974).
11 For further references on this see the symposium introduced by Mas-Colell (1980a). Mas-Colell's introduction covers the issues discussed in this and the following paragraph.
12 A simple exposition of Hart's model is provided by Beath and Katsoulacos (forthcoming).
13 For details of why two firms are required, see Baumol (1982).
14 See, for example, Clark (1907), pp. 380–1. Entry barriers and potential competition are most frequently discussed in the context of oligopoly.

REFERENCES

Alchian, A. A. (1950) 'Uncertainty, evolution and economic theory', *Journal of Political Economy* 58, 211–22.
Aumann, R. J. (1964) 'Markets with a continuum of traders', *Econometrica* 32, 39–50.
Bagehot, W. (1876) *The Postulates of English Political Economy*. Reprinted 1885, London: Longman Green.
Bailey, S. (1825) *A Critical Dissertation on the Nature, Measure and Causes of Value*. LSE Series of Reprints, no. 7. London: London School of Economics.
Baumol, W. J. (1959) *Business Behaviour, Value and Growth*. New York: Macmillan.
Baumol, W. J. (1982) 'Contestable markets: an uprising in the theory of industrial structure', *American Economic Review* 72, 1–15.
Baumol, W. J., J. C. Panzar and R. D. Willig (1982) *Contestable Markets and the Theory of Industry Structure*. San Diego, Calif.: Harcourt Brace Jovanovich.
Beath, J. A., and Y. S. Katsoulacos (forthcoming) *The Economic Theory of Product Differentiation*. Cambridge: Cambridge University Press.
Bertrand, J. (1883) 'Théorie mathématique de la richesse sociale', *Journal des Savants* , 499–508.

Cairnes, J. E. (1874) *Some Leading Principles of Political Economy*. London: Macmillan.

Chamberlin, E. H. (1933) *The Theory of Monopolistic Competition*. Cambridge, Mass.: Harvard University Press.

Clark, J. B. (1899) *The Distribution of Wealth*. 2nd edn, 1902, New York.

Clark, J. M. (1907) *Essentials of Economic Theory*. New York: Macmillan.

Clark, J. M. (1961) *Competition as a Dynamic Process*. Washington, D.C.: Brookings Institution.

Cournot, A. A. (1838) *Researches into the Mathematical Principles of the Theory of Wealth*. Trans. N. T. Bacon, 1927, New York.

Creedy, J. (1986) *Edgeworth and the Development of Neoclassical Economics*. Oxford: Blackwell.

Dasgupta, P. (1986) 'The theory of technological competition', in *New Developments in the Analysis of Market Structure*. Ed. E. Stiglitz and G. F. Matthewson, London: Macmillan, pp. 319–47.

Dasgupta, P., and J. E. Stiglitz (1980) 'Industrial structure and the nature of innovative activity', *Economic Journal* 90, 266–93.

Debreu, G., and H. Scarf (1963) 'A limit theorem on the core of an economy', *International Economic Review* 4, 235–46.

Dixit, A. K. (1982) 'Recent developments in oligopoly theory', *American Economic Review, Papers and Proceedings* 72, 12–17.

Downie, J. (1958) *The Competitive Process*. London: Duckworth.

Dumenil, G., and D. Levy (1987) 'The dynamics of competition: a restoration of the classical analysis', *Cambridge Journal of Economics* 11, 133–64.

Edgeworth, F. Y. (1881) *Mathematical Psychics*. London: Kegan Paul.

Friedman, M. (1953) 'The methodology of positive economics', in *Essays in Positive Economics*. Chicago, Ill.: Chicago University Press, pp. 3–43.

Geroski, P. A., L. Phlips and A. Ulph (1985) 'Oligopoly, competition and welfare: some recent developments', in *Oligopoly, Competition and Welfare*. Ed. P. A. Geroski, L. Phlips and A. Ulph, Oxford: Blackwell, pp. 1–18.

Harrod, R. F. (1930) 'Notes on supply', *Economic Journal* 40, 232ff.

Hart, O. (1979) 'Monopolistic competition in a large economy with differentiated commodities', *Review of Economic Studies* 46, 1–30.

Hart, O. (1985a) 'Monopolistic competition in the spirit of Chamberlin: a general model', *Review of Economic Studies*.

Hart, O. (1985b) 'Monopolistic competition in the spirit of Chamberlin: special results', *Economic Journal* 95.

Hicks, J. R. (1939) *Value and Capital*. 2nd ed, 1946, Oxford: Oxford University Press.

Hildenbrand, W. (1974) *Core and Equilibria of a Large Economy*. Princeton, N.J.: Princeton University Press.

Hildenbrand, W., and A. P. Kirman (1976) *Introduction to Equilibrium Analysis*. Amsterdam: North-Holland.

Jevons, W. S. (1871) *The Theory of Political Economy*. Ed. R. D. C. Black, 1971, Harmondsworth: Penguin.

Kaldor, N. (1935) 'Market imperfection and excess capacity', *Economica*, 33–80.

Koopmans, T. C. (1957) *Three Essays on the State of Economic Science*. New York: McGraw-Hill.

Makowski, L. (1980) ' A characterization of perfectly competitive economies with production', *Journal of Economic Theory* 22, 208–21. Reprinted in *Noncooperative Approaches to the Theory of Perfect Competition*. Ed. A. Mas-Colell, New York: Academic Press.

Marshall, A. (1890) *Principles of Economics*. 8th edn, 19, London: Macmillan.

Mas-Colell, A. (1980a) 'Noncooperative approaches to the theory of perfect competition: presentation', *Journal of Economic Theory* 22, 121–35. Reprinted in *Noncooperative Approaches to the Theory of Perfect Competition*. Ed. A. Mas-Colell, New York: Academic Press.

Mas-Colell, A. (ed.) (1980b) *Noncooperative Approaches to the Theory of Perfect Competition*. New York: Academic Press.

Mill, J. S. (1848) *Principles of Political Economy*. 6th edn, reprinted 1873, London: Longman Green.

Moore, H. L. (1905) 'Paradoxes of competition', *Quarterly Journal of Economics* 20, 211–30.

Morris, D. J., P. J. N. Sinclair, M. D. E. Slater and J. S. Vickers (1986) 'Strategic behaviour and industrial competition: an introduction', *Oxford Economic Papers* 38 (supplement), 1–8.

Nelson, R. R., and S. G. Winter (1982) *An Evolutionary Theory of Economic Change*. Cambridge, Mass.: Harvard University Press.

von Neumann, J., and O. Morgenstern (1944) *The Theory of Games and Economic Behaviour*. New York.

Novshek, W., and H. Sonnenschein (1986) 'Non-cooperative Marshallian-like foundations for general equilibrium theory', in *Contributions to Mathematical Economics in Honor of Gerard Debreu*. Ed. W. Hildenbrand and A. Mas-Collel, Amsterdam: North-Holland.

O'Brien, D. P. (1983) 'Research programmes in competitive structure', *Journal of Economic Studies* 10, 29–51.

Ostroy, J. M. (1980) 'The no-surplus condition as a characterization of perfectly competitive equilibrium', *Journal of Economic Theory* 22, 183–207. Reprinted in *Noncooperative Approaches to the Theory of Perfect Competition*. Ed. A. Mas-Colell, New York: Academic Press.

Pareto, V. (1896) *Cours d'Economie Politique*. Reprinted in *Oeuvres Completes*, vol. 1, 1964, Geneva: Librarie Droz.

Pareto, V. (1906) *Manual of Political Economy*. Trans. A. S. Schwier, 1972, London: Macmillan.

Perloff, J., and S. Salop (1985) 'Equilibrium with product differentiation', *Review of Economic Studies*.

Pigou, A. C. (1912) *Wealth and Welfare*. London: Macmillan.

Pigou, A. C. (1928) 'An analysis of supply', *Economic Journal* 38, 238–57.

Radner, R. (1980) 'Collusive behaviour in noncooperative epsilon-equilibria of oligopolies with long but finite lives', *Journal of Economic Theory* 22, 136–54. Reprinted in *Noncooperative Approaches to the Theory of Perfect Competition*. Ed. A. Mas-Colell, New York: Academic Press.

Ricardo, D. (1817) *Principles of Political Economy and Taxation*, 3rd edn, 1821. Ed. R. M. Hartwell, 1971, Harmondsworth: Penguin.

Robbins, L. (1928) 'The representative firm', *Economic Journal* 38, 387–404.

Robinson, J. (1933) *The Economics of Imperfect Competition*. London: Macmillan.

Robinson, J. (1934) 'What is perfect competition', *Quarterly Journal of Economics* 49, 104–20.

Robinson, J. (1956) *The Accumulation of Capital*. London: Macmillan.

Roncaglia, A. (1978) *Sraffa and the Theory of Prices*. New York: Wiley.

Samuelson, P. A. (1967) 'The monopolistic competition revolution', in *Monopolistic Competition Theory: Studies in Impact*. Ed. R. E. Kuenne, New York, pp. 105–38.

Scarf, H. (1962) 'An analysis of markets with a large number of participants', in *Recent Advances in Game Theory*. Ed. H. Scarf, Princeton, N.J.: Princeton University Press.

Schumpeter, J. A. (1911) *The Theory of Economic Development*. Trans. R. Opie, 1934, Cambridge, Mass.: Harvard University Press.

Schumpeter, J. A. (1934) *Capitalism, Socialism and Democracy*. 5th ed, 1976, London: George Allen & Unwin.

Schumpeter, J. A. (1954) *History of Economic Analysis*. New York: Oxford University Press.

Senior, N. (1836) *Outline of Political Economy*. Reprinted 1938, London: George Allen & Unwin.

Shackle, G. L. S. (1967) *The Years of High Theory*. Cambridge: Cambridge University Press.

Shubik, M. (1959) 'Edgeworth market games', in *Contributions to the Theory of Games, IV*. Ed. A. W. Tucker and R. D. Luce, Princeton, N.J.: Princeton University Press, pp. 267–78.

Simon, H. A. (1955) 'A behavioural model of rational choice', *Quarterly Journal of Economics* 69, 99–118.

Smith, A. (1776) *An Inquiry into the Nature and Causes of the Wealth of Nations*. Ed. E. Cannan, 1976, Chicago, Ill: Chicago University Press.

Sraffa, P. (1926) 'The laws of returns under competitive conditions', *Economic Journal* 36, 535–50.

Stigler, G. J. (1957) 'Perfect competition historically contemplated', *Journal of Political Economy*. Reprinted in *Essays on the History of Economics*. Ed. G. J. Stigler, Chicago, Ill.: Chicago University Press, pp. 234–67.

Stiglitz J. E., and G. F. Matthewson (eds) (1986) *New Developments in the Analysis of Market Structure*. London: Macmillan.

Walras, L. (1874) *Elements of Pure Economics*. Trans. W. Jaffé, 1954, London: George Allen & Unwin.

Weintraub, E. R. (1974) *General Equilibrium Theory*. London: Macmillan.

Wicksell, K. (1901) *Lectures on Political Economy*. Trans. E. Classen, ed. L. Robbins, 1938, London: Routledge.

Winter, S. G. (1964) 'Economic "natural selection" and the theory of the firm', *Yale Economic Essays* 4, 224–72.

4

Marginalism and the margin

Lynn Mainwaring

The margin is an analytical technique associated with the school of economics which came into being in the 1870s through the innovations of Jevons, Menger and Walras and which 20 years later was regarded (at least in Britain) as representing economic orthodoxy. The marginal 'revolution', if that is what it was, succeeded in these two decades in ousting from its position of dominance the system of thought of the classical school initiated by Smith, refined by Ricardo and polished by Mill. But the margin itself is nothing more than a tool and its historical associations need not bind its practitioners to a particular viewpoint. It is, says Hicks (1976, p. 212), 'no more than an expression of the mathematical rule for a maximum (or minimum)'. In that case it matters little whether the maximizing is done by individual agents operating in a totally decentralized economy, the problem that preoccupied Jevons and Walras, or whether it is done by policy-makers and planners with some degree of central control. The use of optimization in decision-making is referred to by Lange (1963) (following the Austrians) as 'praxiology' and is promoted by him as a basic tool in the 'economics of control'. But whereas for Lange there is a sharp distinction between the praxiological uses of the margin and that branch of economics which adopted its name, for Hicks 'any sort of economics is marginalist that is concerned with maximising'. Hick's definition thus appears to deny the school any other identifying characteristics.

Lange's view is implicitly supported by Dasgupta (1985, pp. 79–80) according to whom Marginalism (distinguished henceforth by a capital M when referring to the paradigm rather than the technique) has three defining characteristics:[1] first is the stress on prices as allocators of resources; second is that distribution is an endogenous outcome of the determination of prices; and third is that consumption rather than accumulation is the 'mainspring' of economic behaviour. It is true that these characteristics emerged historically through the medium of marginal

I should like to thank John Creedy and Ken George for helpful comments on the first draft of this chapter. The final version is, of course, entirely my responsibility.

theorizing, yet it will be argued, in consonance with Lange, that the margin is no longer essential to any of them.

Section 4.1 sketches the historical background to the Marginal revolution and, in particular, presents a somewhat schematized picture of classical theory as a counterpoint to the ensuing discussion. In sections 4.2 and 4.3 the marginal theories of utility and productivity, successive building blocks in the construction of the 'alternative cost' theory of value, are briefly discussed. The debate on the 'adding-up' properties of marginal productivity theory leads naturally to a discussion of the role of the entrepreneur (section 4.4). Section 4.5 contrasts classical and Marginalist justifications for the payment of interest and relates this debate to the preceding discussion of the entrepreneur. In sections 4.6 and 4.7 some technical issues relating to the identification of the marginal products of labour and capital are examined and it is conceded that the difficulties involved may be bypassed without sacrificing the core of Marginalist philosophy by abandoning the traditional marginalist formulation in favour of one in terms of general equilibrium theory. Section 4.8 attempts to summarize this philosophy and identifies its principal limitation as arising out of an essentially static methodology. Section 4.9 considers both the descriptive relevance of Marginalism to the capitalist market and its prescriptive relevance to the economics of control under socialism. The somewhat agnostic conclusions are supplemented by a suggestion that 'satisficing' rather than 'optimizing' procedures might be more fully exploited in both these spheres.

4.1 Historical Overview

Precursors of Marginalism

It was the application of marginal techniques to individual consumer behaviour that initiated the Marginal revolution and gave Marginalism its special character, for the maximand in this case was utility, and in utility, rather than the 'real cost' of production, was located the source of value. Only subsequently were the marginal techniques applied widely to production and, by implication, to distribution, but even then utility maintained a theoretical dominance in the Marginalist system. It is this subjective element – the focus on individual choice – that gives Marginalism its special character and makes it something more than a collection of marginal applications. And it is one reason why the near simultaneous writings of Jevons, Menger and Walras may be said to constitute a revolution. None of these writers can be credited with the discovery of the principle of (diminishing) marginal utility.[2] Lloyd (1834), Longfield (1834) and Senior (1836) had all stated the principle unambiguously 40 years before Jevons's *Theory*. But none of these writers properly integrated it into the general body of his work and used it as an essential component of an alternative theory of value (see Blaug, 1978, p. 339). Their expositions seem to have been motivated mainly by a desire to resolve the 'paradox of value'.[3]

Sophisticated statements of the principle of diminishing marginal utility also appeared in the later work of Dupuit (1844), Jennings (1855) and, most notably, Gossen (1854) and, unlike their predecessors, these writers made full application of the principle. Their failure to initiate a revolution by gaining wide acceptance for their ideas has been ascribed by Stigler (1972) to a lack of professionalism in the discipline at the time. The occurrence of such multiple discoveries over a 40-year period is enough for Blaug to be sceptical of the idea of a 'revolution' in the 1870s but the continuing speculations of historians will not be pursued here.[4]

Just as Jevons, Menger and Walras were innovators rather than discoverers of marginal utility, so it is generally argued that the principle of marginal productivity long-predates its universal application in Marginalism in the 1890s. According to Blaug (1978, p. 322), 'there is as much marginalism in Ricardo as in Jevons or Walras but it is applied to different things'. What Blaug has in mind is the theory of differential rent which made four independent appearances in 1815, the others being due to West, Torrens and Malthus.[5] It will be argued later that this theory is not an application of the marginal technique and therefore not a forerunner of the marginal productivity theory of factor rewards (and, consequently, not a contribution to Marginalism). There were forerunners, however, notably Turgot's theory of intensive rent and Longfield's theory of the marginal productivity of capital.

The Ricardian System

The purpose of this section is partly to outline the theory of differential rent so that its relationship to marginal productivity theory can be evaluated later (section 4.3) but, more importantly, to provide a brief sketch of the classical system (mainly as expounded by Ricardo) as a counterpoint to the ideas of Marginalism.

For the classical economists the central questions were the causes, the growth in and the social distribution of the wealth of nations, where wealth was conceived as a surplus of output over the necessaries of production. The core of these classical concerns can be seen most clearly in the so-called corn-ratio model of Ricardo's *Essay* (1815).[6]

In the corn-ratio model, corn is the only means of consumption and the only means of production. Consumption is determined directly by the size of population (the growth of which follows Malthusian principles), implying zero elasticity of demand. Corn can be produced on various grades of land which can be ranked in descending order of natural fertility: 1, 2, 3 . . . etc. If, with a given technology, the availability of grade 1 land is insufficient to satisfy demand, resort has to be made to inferior grades. (Variation of technology with a given grade, implying intensive rent, is ruled out for the present.) On any particular grade i the process of production can be described as follows:

$$c + wl \rightarrow C_i$$

where c is the amount of corn per acre sown at the beginning of the year, l is the number of worker-hours per acre, w is the hourly wage rate reckoned as a quantity of corn advanced, and C_i is output per acre on grade i at the end of the year. An hour of labour is assumed to be equally irksome whichever grade of land it is applied to, and competition between labourers thus ensures that w is uniform. The level of w is determined by the presence of surplus labour (again ensured by Malthusian mechanisms) at a historically defined subsistence level.

The quantity $c + wl$ may be thought of as Mill's (1848) 'dose' of capital plus labour, though strictly, since wl is in the form of an advance, it is entirely capital. In extending production these equal doses are applied to successive acres, proceeding down the ranking of goods. The 'margin of cultivation',[7] i.e. the last grade n brought into use, is determined by the size of population (with allowance for intermediate requirements c per acre). The physical surplus S_i from grade i is net output less wages:

$$S_i = (C_i - c) - wl \tag{4.1}$$

and the fertility ranking implies that $S_1 > S_2 > \ldots > S_n$. The surplus itself is divided between the rents of the landlords and the profits of the capitalists. (Capitalists may also be landlords but it is perhaps easier to think of them as tenant farmers.) Because the capital (a quantity of corn) is mobile it will be shifted from one location to another in search of the highest return, which will therefore tend to uniformity. This is not possible with land and so rent, the payment for 'the original and indestructible powers of the soil' (Ricardo, 1817, p. 67) will vary from grade to grade. If R_i is rent per acre on grade i and r the uniform rate of profit (return to capital), then

$$r = \frac{S_i - R_i}{c + wl} \tag{4.2}$$

from which it follows that

$$R_i = S_i - r(c + wl) \qquad (i = 1, \ldots, n) \tag{4.3}$$

That is (since $r(c + wl)$ is uniform from grade to grade), the ranking of rents corresponds to the ranking of fertilities. In searching for the highest profits, capitalists will bid most (pay most rent) for the best land. One loose end remains to be tied up; the n equations (4.3) have $n + 1$ unknowns: n rents R_i and the rate of profit r. The system is made determinate by the requirement that

$$R_n = 0 \tag{4.4}$$

i.e. that the marginal land is no-rent land. Equation (4.4) is justified on the grounds that as long as there is no excess demand for grade n it is a free good. As soon as excess demand becomes positive the margin shifts to grade $n + 1$.

The corn-ratio model is one of diminishing returns at the extensive margin of cultivation. Diminishing returns at the intensive margin, in which additional doses are applied to land of a given quality, have been ruled out by assumption. Although the concept of intensive variable returns was enunciated by Turgot as long ago as 1768 (see Cannan, 1924, pp. 147–8), it formed no significant part of the classical story. Despite the use of the word 'margin' in discussions of extensive diminishing returns it will be argued subsequently (following Wicksteed) that the theory does not constitute a proper application of marginal analysis.

The one-good assumption of the corn-ratio model severely limits its generality. The introduction of reproducible luxury goods presents no problems but the inclusion of necessities (goods which enter workers' consumption or which are direct means of production) means that the rate of profits can no longer be calculated as the ratio of homogeneous physical quantities. It was this difficulty that drove Ricardo's search for a theory of value and, in particular, for an invariable standard of value. His failure to find an invariable standard led to the compromise solution of using the labour embodied in a commodity as a measure of its value. Since labour was irksome this could be taken as an indication of its 'real' cost. What this account suggests is that the theory of value was not a focal point of classical political economy. It was a secondary consideration deriving from the need to shore up the foundations of the dynamic structure.

Three features of the classical approach may now be noted. First, it has just been seen that the role of prices was primarily as indexes of aggregation to allow the evaluation of heterogeneous commodities. There was, of course, an allocative role because capitalists shifted resources according to profitability but there was virtually no stress on the allocative function of prices in the face of scarcity. Second, one key distributive element, the wage rate, was exogenous to the theory. The rate of profit was determined by the productivity of marginal land and rent followed as a residual. It was simply not possible within the structure of the model to determine all three distributive elements endogenously. Third, while workers had no scope to use wages for anything other than immediate consumption and landlords were also assumed to consume their rents, the capitalists were assumed to be strongly motivated by a desire for accumulation. Accumulation and consumption both had claims on the disposition of profits. In a letter to Malthus, Ricardo once wrote: 'Consumption adds to our enjoyments, accumulation to our power, and they both equally promote demand' (quoted by Sweezy, 1942, p. 82).

The corn-ratio model also illustrates clearly the classical preoccupations with social class and with dynamic analysis, even if in the latter case certain important interactions (between investment, wages and population) have been glossed over here. The model gave backing to Ricardo's attempt to gain repeal of the Corn Laws: lower duties on corn would have reduced the real cost of feeding labour and so postponed the stationary state. In this pursuit he was championing the interests of capitalists against those of landlords whose incomes would be eroded by freer competition.

From Ricardianism to Marginalism

If Ricardo was the capitalists' advocate, others were quick to draw from his theory a critique of capitalism. There was no problem in identifying labour's contribution to national wealth: the toil of work. What was less clear was what the capitalist contributed. If Adam Smith could say of the landlords that they 'love to reap where they never sowed' (Smith, 1776, p. 56), could not the same be said of the capitalists? And if the Malthusian mechanism were rejected and the long-run wage allowed to rise, it could only do so at the expense of profits. Thus, in the writings of the early Ricardian Socialists, and later and more comprehensively in those of Marx, Ricardo's theory came to be seen as representing capitalism as a system of antagonism and discord.

Whereas the Ricardian Socialists argued the workers' claim to the whole produce of their labour, others, notably Senior and Longfield, attempted to justify the capitalists' share in ways which though different were later to be united by the Marginalists. Senior's defence was the more direct: the capitalist contribution was 'the deferring of enjoyment' or 'abstinence' which 'stands in the same relation to Profit as Labour does to Wages' (1836, pp. 58–9). This formulation was taken on board by Mill and other 'orthodox' Ricardians who reduced them both to 'sacrifices', the 'real' costs of production. But this created a difficulty. Postponement of enjoyment and labour may both be sacrifices but they are of a different nature and cannot be added together. A value theory based on real cost is therefore only operational when commodities are produced with equal proportions of labour and abstinence. This is effectively the same limitation of the labour theory of value as in the work of Ricardo and Marx (where the requirement would be referred to as 'equal organic compositions of capital'). It is also, with some irony, the limitation of the Marginalists' aggregate production function (see section 4.7). For Senior himself abstinence was simply a moral argument and not a component of a theory of value (see Bharadwaj, 1978, p. 25). As one of the discoverers of the law of diminishing marginal utility he had the building blocks of the Marginalist theory of interest but he failed to put them together.

Longfield's defence was not directly a moral defence, but a defence based on appeal to laws 'framed by the Great Author of our being' and consisted in his substitution of Ricardo's theory of profits by a remarkably complete anticipation of marginal productivity theory. According to Longfield, competition reduces profit to a lesser limit 'determined by the efficiency of that capital which without imprudence is employed in the least efficient manner' (1834, p. 188). In his view natural laws placed both wages and profits beyond the ability of both labour combinations and legislatures to influence, a conclusion which he hoped would not 'be unpleasing to the benevolent mind'.

Whether Senior and Longfield saw themselves as merely extending and patching up the classical system or whether, as Dobb would have it (1973, p. 111), they were 'consciously in retreat' from these doctrines, there is little doubt that important elements of the classical story were weakened as a result. Capitalists were no longer accumulating for its own sake but simply to defer enjoyment, while Longfield's natural laws, effectively the laws of supply and demand, suggested the endogenization of the real wage. Even if Jevons, consciously in the revolt against the Ricardian system, believed himself to be propounding essentially new doctrines, one can easily see in these earlier contributions an embryonic Marginalism.

4.2 Utility

The Marginal revolution was initially a marginal utility revolution. The behaviour of the individual in the act of choosing became the foundation of a new theory of value. A commodity would no longer be valuable because it was costly to produce but because its services yielded utility. Its relative price would now be determined by its 'alternative' cost: the utility sacrificed in order to produce or acquire a small increment in its supply. This fundamental reorientation of value theory is easily overlooked in favour of the technical developments of demand theory as such. These have been extensively documented in the literature[8] and only the briefest of sketches will be presented here.

The central axiom in the earliest expositions of utility theory was the 'law' of diminishing marginal utility to which appeal was largely made on the basis of introspection.[9] The three founders of the revolution all postulated an additive utility function using which it is easy to establish the well-known rule that utility is maximized when the individual distributes expenditure such that the last (very small) unit of money spent on each good yields the same satisfaction. This principle, sometimes known as Gossen's third law, was propounded by that hapless economist 17 years before Jevons's *Theory* but almost totally ignored. It was restated by Jevons (1871) and Menger (1871) but only Walras succeeded in going beyond it to the construction of individual and market demand curves and thence to a theory of the determination of prices in a competitive economy.

Walras did not investigate the properties of the demand curves, however. It was left to Pareto (1892) to show that with an additive utility function they would be downward sloping, but this comfortable finding did not survive Edgeworth's (1881) generalization of the utility function. A thorough understanding of the generalized function and the rigorous derivation of demand curves had to await the explorations of Slutsky (1915) and Hicks and Allen (1934).

In the opinion of Stigler progress in the utility-based theory of demand was painfully slow, the efforts yielding scant reward. Jevons popularized the utility function in 1871, Edgeworth generalized it in 1881 and Slutsky finally derived its full implications in 1915. The resulting 'law' of demand

> was the chief product – so far as hypotheses on economic behaviour go
> – of the long labours of a very large number of able economists. These
> very able economists, and their predecessors, however, had known all
> along that demand curves have negative slopes, quite independently
> of their utility theorising. (Stigler, 1950, pp. 395–6)

So was marginal utility theory much ado about very little?

Whatever its contribution to demand theory as such, and there are surely strong grounds for scepticism, the marginal utility theorists, and especially Walras, did succeed in putting demand, as the aggregation of individual choice, at the centre of the theory of price determination. Relative prices became the mechanism for allocating scarce resources and the ends to which these were directed were the satisfactions obtained from consuming goods. If there was a revolution then it surely consisted in the replacement of an objective real-cost theory of value with a subjective alternative-cost theory.[10] Perhaps the most important consequence of this was the explanation of savings (and hence accumulation) in terms of the optimal allocation of consumption over time.

The following sections concentrate on marginal productivity theory but it should be borne in mind that the demand for factors is a derived demand and the pre-eminence of utility should not be overlooked.

4.3 Productivity

The main novelty in the works of Jevons, Menger and Walras was the theory of utility. Extension to production of the underlying marginal principles was either absent (in the case of Walras who initially used fixed coefficients in production) or rudimentary.[11] The germ of the idea is found in Menger's work. Jevons gives his approval to Ricardian rent theory (ironically, of the differential variety) and uses a marginal theory to determine the rate of interest but he fails to bring these applications together in a unified theory of distribution. The origins of a complete theory must be located in Wicksteed's remarkable essay on *The Co-ordination of the Laws of Distribution* (1894) and an essay by J. B. Clark (1889). The theory may be considered as a generalization of the theory of *intensive* rent which the classical economists understood well enough but made little use of.

Consider an individual (or firm) producing output Q by the employment of factors $a_1, \ldots, a_n$, such that

$$Q = Q(a_1, \ldots, a_n)$$

and

$$Q_i > 0 \qquad Q_{ii} < 0 \qquad\qquad (i = 1, \ldots, n) \qquad (4.5)$$

If p is product price and w_i the cost of factor i, then profit is

$$\pi = pQ(a_1, \ldots, a_n) - \sum_{i=1}^{n} w_i a_i$$

which is maximized when

$$pQ_i = w_i \qquad\qquad\qquad (4.6)$$

or

$$p = \frac{w_i}{Q_i} = \text{marginal costs} \qquad\qquad (4.7)$$

Under competition, supplies of the factors and demand for output are perfectly-elastic and so (4.6) implies that the firm takes on each factor up to the point where its marginal revenue product pQ_i has fallen to the price of the factor. The relationship of this reasoning to that of intensive rent is easy to see. Suppose that there are only two factors and that labour is available in any quantity a_1 at a given wage w_1. Land of *uniform* quality is in fixed supply $\bar{a}_2$ and its rent w_2 is to be determined. (The problem is simplified here by the absence of profit.) Labour will be applied more and more intensively until its marginal revenue product has fallen to w_1. This determines labour input, commodity output and rent as a residual:

$$w_2 \bar{a}_2 = pQ(a_1, \bar{a}_2) - a_1 \, pQ_1(a_1, \bar{a}_2)$$ (4.8)

Wicksteed's approval of this classical reasoning was matched by his disapproval of its confinement to the determination of intensive rent. By a symmetrical argument, the application of varying areas of homogeneous land to a fixed labour force would allow the determination of the 'rent' of labour:

$$w_1 \bar{a}_1 = pQ(\bar{a}_1, a_2) - a_2 pQ_2(\bar{a}_1, a_2)$$ (4.9)

There is no reason, however, why the analysis should be confined to two or even three factors. In fact, Wicksteed explicitly rejected the threefold classification into land, labour and capital which are, of course, aggregates with many heterogeneous components:

> We must regard every kind and quality of labour that can be distinguished from other kinds and qualities as a separate factor and in the same way every kind of land will be taken as a separate factor. Still more important is it to insist that instead of speaking of so many £-worth of capital we shall speak of so many ploughs, so many tons of manure and so many horses, or foot-pounds of power. (1894, p. 33)

By this means, and in conjunction with the essential principle of substitutability, Wicksteed was able to deny any peculiarity of land due to its fixity. Like any type of labour or piece of equipment a particular type of land could be switched from one use to another so as to equate its price with its marginal revenue product.[12] Although he admitted that there may be limits to the degree of substitutability, he claimed that, in general, there would be sufficient substitutability at the margin for the process to be effective (1933, pp. 360–2). In another, subsequent, terminology, the elasticity of substitution between any two factors would generally be non-zero.

To determine equilibrium factor prices, individual firms' demands, implicit in equation (4.6), have to be aggregated and equated to the fixed supplies. But these demands are themselves derived from those of final commodities. The simultaneous determination of factors and commodity prices must be pursued in the Walrasian manner. This Wicksteed failed to do, though the general idea is implicit in his notion of alternative cost. Factors which produce one thing cannot produce another; cost of production is thus 'simply and solely "the marginal significance of something else"' (1933, p. 382). In this he was at one with the Austrians and with Walras.

Wicksteed's disaggregated approach to the classification of factors leads, as will be seen in section 4.4, to some problems in relation to the laws of returns. Clark (1899), however, was content to aggregate factors into labour and capital. (He was even more emphatic than Wicksteed in denying land a role as a separate factor.) In this respect, Clark was clearly the more influential on the succeeding generation of Marginalists but the difficulties of measuring capital at a macro-level, which he glossed over, left a serious weakness in this particular version of Marginalism (see section 4.7).

Wicksteed on Extensive Rent

If Wicksteed regarded his theory of distribution as a generalization of the classical theory of intensive rent a special word should be reserved for his view of the theory of differential rent. The critical difference between the two is that in the intensive case there is a functional relationship between output and the variable factor as applied to *homogeneous* land. In the extensive case the relationship between output and labour inputs is not a functional one. The lands in this case are not homogeneous and the 'doses' of capital plus labour are intentionally ordered so that they apply to lands of declining fertility.

When land and labour are both homogeneous it is not possible to say which unit (of either) is the marginal unit: any and every unit is marginal. It matters not which is removed; output will decline by some small amount. The margin can only be identified by adding or subtracting one unit. It requires, in other words, a potential change in the level of output (see Bharadwaj, 1978, pp. 44–6). The extensive margin, however, is immediately identifiable as a particular (not necessarily small) plot of land which happens to occupy the right-hand position in a diagram because that is where it has been put. No potential change is necessary to identify this plot. Wicksteed sums up his critique as follows:

> Ricardo's celebrated law of rent really asserts nothing except that the superior article fetches the superior price, in proportion to its superiority. (1933, p. 790)

Strictly, Wicksteed is perfectly correct in his judgement, but in his eagerness to dismiss any claims of Ricardian rent theory to be a contribution to Marginalist thought he surely undervalues the ingenuity of the construction as a component of the classical dynamic story.

A more sophisticated version of Ricardian rent theory has been developed by Sraffa (1960, ch. 11) who, ironically, calls on Wicksteed to pre-empt any charge of Marginalisms being levelled against his revision (1960, pp. v–vi). It may be noted that his version is also immune to the alternative charge that the better land fetches the better price, because it does not attempt to rank land according to fertility while the ranking according to profitability is not independent of distribution (see Mainwaring, 1984, ch. 12).

4.4 Euler's Theorem and the Entrepreneur

For both Wicksteed and Clark confirmation of the logic of the marginal productivity theory required the overriding demonstration that payments to factors according to their marginal productivities exhausted the product. The ensuing debate on this issue, rather like that on demand theory, absorbed a disproportionate amount of the energies of the early Marginalists.[13]

Consider, for simplicity, the two-factor model represented by (4.8) and (4.9). Whatever its use of land, the firm varies its labour input until the wage equals the marginal revenue product of labour. Equation (4.8) then *defines* the rent payment as a residual. Similarly, whatever its labour use, land is hired until its marginal revenue product equals rent per acre. Equation (4.9) then defines the wage bill as residual. The question is: are these equations consistent? Is the residual $w_i\bar{a}_i$ in one equation equal to the payment according to marginal productivity in the other? In short, do a_1pQ_1 and a_2pQ_2 'add up' to pQ? Wicksteed first posed the problem in *Co-ordination* (1894). His affirmative demonstration, based on the assumption of universal constant returns, involved a long and tortuous argument which was considerably simplified by Flux (1894) who related the problem to Euler's theorem on homogeneous functions. The Wicksteed–Flux solution however, was, soon criticized for its assumption of constant returns.

Wicksteed contended that, given his classification of factors, constant returns would necessarily prevail. It is true that factors so defined are not all perfectly divisible and that if a divisible factor is applied in increasing amounts to an indivisible one it is likely that returns will vary. But constant returns require that a doubling of *all* factors leads to a doubling of output and, in Wicksteed's view, the replication of factor 'bundles' (a 'plant') leads, tautologically, to the replication of output (1894, p. 33). It was the universality of this implication that appeared to create difficulties in relation to the competitive assumptions of the analysis. Faced with constant prices of outputs and inputs, a firm which is operating with constant physical returns has no limits on the extent to which it may expand. If so, might not a single firm come to dominate the market and competition consequently break down? Barone and Walras, and Wicksell (1901), thought so and proposed a way out of the difficulty.[14]

Universal constant returns imply a horizontal long-run average cost curve. What Walras and Wicksell showed was that the 'adding-up' theorem could be sustained provided that constant returns prevailed at the point of competitive equilibrium. This would be consistent with a U-shaped long-run average cost curve, in which increasing returns (falling average costs) were succeeded by decreasing returns, because competitive equilibrium coexists with instantaneous constant returns at the bottom of the 'U'. This solution itself raises a problem in relation to the laws of returns, for the natural question, especially given Wicksteed's classification of factors, is: why should returns increase or decrease?

So far as increasing returns go, one might begin by questioning Wicksteed's 'truism' that doubling factors necessarily doubles output, no more and no less. This is precisely what Wicksell does (see Stigler, 1941, p. 378n.) when he refers to the enhanced possibilities of exploiting division of labour. In other words, two workers operating two *adjacent* machines may be able to get more than twice the product of one worker from one machine because of specialization in operation functions. But what of decreasing returns? Wicksell's references to the increased costs of marketing or raw materials (1901, p. 129) are not relevant to the characteristics of production (especially under competitive conditions). If there are increasing costs it must be because of the presence of an indivisibility, and the most obvious candidate for this is entrepreneurship. The coordination of a high level of activity is more difficult than the coordination of a low level. But if entrepreneurship is more or less indivisible, what determines its rewards and does exhaustion of the product still follow?

Joan Robinson (1934) suggests three ways of treating entrepreneurship: (a) following Wicksell, that there is no role for the entrepreneur; (2) that entrepreneurship is merely a form of labour and can be supplied on a divisible basis at a fixed price per unit; and (c) that each firm has a single indivisible unit of entrepreneurship. In the first case the question of entrepreneurial rewards is irrelevant; in the second the rewards are determined like those of any other factor by the principle of marginal productivity. Note, however, that neither of these cases provides reasons why the cost curve should rise. In the third case increasing costs are possible but the principle of marginal productivity is inapplicable. The problem of distribution, however, can be solved by use of the generalized Euler theorem, as applied to the remaining divisible factors. (see Wicksell, 1901, p. 128). With variable returns

$$\sum_{i=1}^{n} a_i Q_i \gtreqless Q$$

as

$$\lambda Q \gtreqless Q(\lambda a_1, \ldots, \lambda a_n)$$

Thus if diminishing returns prevail the product exceeds the payments to the divisible factors on the basis of their marginal contributions and there is a positive residual for profits, the reward of the entrepreneur. With increasing returns profits are negative. This solution, as Robinson points out, is perfectly consistent with the economic logic of cost curves.

Although it is not possible to define the marginal product of entrepreneurship with respect to the output of the firm, it may be possible to do so with respect to the industry. The decrement of the industry's output following the withdrawal of one entrepreneur is 'the output of one firm *minus* the output which the factors employed by that firm would produce if they were dispersed among the remaining firms' (Robinson, 1934). Then, if there are constant returns *to the industry* and if entrepreneurship can be regarded as divisible with respect to the industry, it follows from Euler's theorem that the reward to the entrepreneur is indeed its marginal product with respect to the industry. If entrepreneurship does not come in such small packages, however, the adding-up theorem will fail to apply even at the industry level.

The concept of the entrepreneur does create something of a dilemma for Marginalism in relation to the choice of maximand. The Marginalists adopted uncritically the classical assumption that firms maximize profits. Yet the Marginalist revolution has its essence in the notion that individuals maximize utility. An entrepreneur who maximizes both (supernormal) profit and utility has, in Scitovsky's view (1943), a very particular psychology. Scitovsky considers the case in which profits are a continuous function of entrepreneurial effort. (This obviously implies some continuity of supply of entrepreneurship but it is not inconsistent with a minimum effort necessary to bring the firm into existence and is thus a compromise between Joan Robinson's cases (b) and (c) above.) For profits to reach a maximum with respect to entrepreneurial effort, then maximizing both profits and utility implies that the marginal utility of effort is zero. According to Scitovsky, the most plausible interpretation of such behaviour is that the entrepreneur is 'so keen on making money that his ambition cannot be damped by a rising income'. The wider implications of this conclusion will be considered in section 4.5.

4.5 Accounting for Interest

The Three Grounds

The Marginalist determination of the rate of interest is via the supply of and demand for loanable funds by households and firms. Until Fisher's (1907, 1930) synthesis, analysis of these two sources of excess demand were generally conducted separately.

The approach to individual or household savings has been hinted at in the use of the word 'abstinence' which was adopted by some of the Marginalists (though Marshall preferred 'waiting'). Stripped of its moral overtones, what it implies is that individuals place a premium on present consumption. A positive rate of interest is thus needed to induce people to delay part of consumption to a future period. But why should this particular time preference be assumed? One reason, following directly from the principle of diminishing marginal utility, is that if incomes in general are growing (or expected to grow) then less utility is lost in giving up a unit tomorrow than is gained in adding a unit today. In a stationary economy, however, individual borrowings (for lumpy purchases like houses) should be just cancelled by individual lendings without the need of a positive interest rate *unless* there is any reason why individuals in general should place a greater weight on present consumption.

These considerations form the basis of von Böhm-Bawerk's (1889) first two 'grounds' for the existence of a positive rate of interest. The first is expected growth of per capita income. The second is the existence of *pure* time preference: the total utility of a volume of consumption today is greater than the total utility of the same volume tomorrow. More 'impatient' consumers will borrow from less impatient ones but the latter will still need to be compensated for postponing their enjoyments. Thus, even in a stationary state, there is a function for interest.

These two grounds are not sufficient to determine the equilibrium rate of interest, however, for it is necessary that borrowers be in a position to pay back lenders at interest. In the aggregate this requires that the economy be productive. In a subsistence economy consumption can be brought forward (by running down capital) but that would leave nothing in future periods to pay interest. (In fact, the economy would collapse.) The extent of interest payments is thus bounded by the future availability of resources, i.e. by the productivity of the economy. This gives rise to von Böhm-Bawerk's third ground: the technical superiority of more 'roundabout' (capital-intensive) processes.

As early as 1871, Jevons had proffered a marginal productivity explanation of the rate of interest. Both he and von Böhm-Bawerk used the notion of the 'period of production' as a measurement of capital intensity, though in neither case is the concept satisfactory except on highly simplifying assumptions.[15] Jevons's explanation, divested of the period of production, was given a clearer statement by Wicksteed (1889). Let K be the 'quantity of capital' used up (through wear) per period and let $v = v(K)$ be the 'net periodical productiveness' of the capital (gross output less wear and raw materials). If the capital is applied to a fixed quantity of labour, it is assumed that $v' > 0$ and $v'' < 0$ and the marginal net periodical productiveness $v'(K)$ is equated to what Wicksteed calls 'the rate of *hire* of capital' or the rate of interest. It may be worth entering a note of caution at this point. The rate of interest is a pure number, so it is necessary that v' (K) also be a pure number. In the case of labour, say, the marginal (value) product is a ratio of a value term to a term representing physical labour and so has the dimension of value per hour (say) of work, which is also the dimension of the wage rate. The corresponding payment for the use of a bundle of capital goods would be the net rental rp_K where p_K is the value of a unit bundle. The rental and the interest rate are identical only if $p_K = 1$. For Wicksteed's argument to hold wherever it is applied it is therefore necessary *either* that output and capital are the same single (or composite) good *or* that capital and output are measured in terms of a common set of prices. In either case, the marginal product will then be a ratio of elements with like dimensions and consequently dimensionless. Wicksteed, in fact, is referring to a price-taking producer and is thus valuing both input and output at the prevailing prices.[16]

To proceed from the price-taking firm to the economy in general, the individual excess demand curves for capital funds implicit in the preceding argument must be aggregated and added to those of the household sector. Neither von Böhm-Bawerk (who believed his three grounds to be independent reasons for the existence of interest) nor Wicksteed endeavoured to make this integration. It was Fisher who first achieved the synthesis by confronting intertemporal preferences with an intertemporal transformation curve (with a diminishing marginal rate of transformation). The equilibrium rate of interest is immediately determined as the price which yields zero excess demand for consumption and production loans. This way of posing the problem is now standard in modern texts.

Classical and Marginalist Conceptions of Interest

Consider an economy with zero aggregate growth so that von Böhm-Bawerk's first ground plays no part in the general determination of the rate of interest. Moreover, with zero pure time preference there is no reason why individuals should supply savings at any positive rate of interest. If such a rate is demanded it must be because of pure time preference. Some writers, including Marginalists like von Böhm-Bawerk and Wicksteed, have stressed the 'imprudence' of such myopic behaviour. Nevertheless, as long as there is a perceived utility gain in bringing forward a unit of consumption, those who are asked to forgo present enjoyments will require a return for their 'sacrifice'. For Marginalists like Jevons and Clark (and many others) this was sufficient moral justification for the payment of interest.

In the classical conception of society, workers have little income to spare after acquiring the immediate necessaries of life. Saving is thus largely a function of the capitalist class. (Landlords were generally assumed to be profligate, but that is of no immediate importance.) Because growth depends on saving, capitalists have a central role in the creation of wealth. For Ricardo this was enough to justify the promotion of capitalist interests. It did not occur to him to ask whether capitalists 'deserved' their reward, but it did occur to the Ricardian Socialists and to Marx, in whose view the payment of interest (or 'profit' in the classical sense[17]) to capitalists is due to their monopoly of capital and arises, therefore, out of the exploitation of labour.

The concept of abstinence, employed by Senior in his defence of profits, has been refined into the Marginalist concept of time preference. Whether or not myopic behaviour is reprehensible, these substitutable concepts have their basis in the Marginalist notion that the ultimate purpose of economic activity is consumption for, apart from leisure, it is consumption, and consumption only, which yields utility. Wicksteed is very clear about the futility of increasing wealth for its own sake: 'Aristotle said long ago that only the man who has no defined ends desires the strictly indefinite accumulation of means' (1933, p. 156). For Wicksteed, ends are clearly equated with satisfaction from consumption and accumulation for its own sake is a pointless irrational activity. Both Ricardo and Marx, on the contrary, saw accumulated wealth as representing power and power as an end in itself. Thus accumulation for accumulation's sake was not pointless.[18]

It is at this point that Scitovsky's analysis of the motives of the entrepreneur once again becomes relevant. Scitovsky showed that the entrepreneur who simultaneously maximizes profit and utility desires money (wealth) for its own sake 'because it is an index and token of his success in life. . . . [T]he desire for success is more insatiable than the demand for material goods'. Thus, in assuming a profit-maximizing capitalist, the classical economists 'were concerned with a type of businessman whose psychology happened to be such that for him maximising profits was identical with maximising satisfaction'. But the same assumption in Marginalism has precisely the same implication.

The classical and the abstinence views could hardly be more different in their ethical implications. As Dasgupta says,

> Once you take accumulation as the motive force behind economic activity, as the classical economists do, you at once recognise the existence of a capitalist class who, by virtue of their ownership of capital, enjoy the privilege of employing labour. (1985, pp. 79–80)

In contrast, the abstinence view implies not a privilege but a sacrifice. But Marginalism cannot have a profit-maximizing abstaining entrepreneur. It can have a profit-maximizing or an abstaining entrepreneur, but it cannot have both. Since the entrepreneur is likely to be a major source of savings, even in the class-free Marginalist world, acceptance of the profit-maximizing assumption seriously undermines the justification for the receipt of interest on the basis of abstinence or time preference.[19]

4.6 A Wage Grumble

In the traditional formulation of marginal productivity theory, the production function (4.5) is differentiable. Defining the marginal product of factor i as its partial derivative Q_i means that a_i is being subjected to an infinitesimal change while all other factors are being held constant. If output is capable of a marginal response to a marginal change in just one of the factors then, in Samuelson's words (1947, p. 35), 'all factors are perfectly indifferent substitutes' at the margin.[20] Perfect substitutability at the margin and differentiability of the production function are one and the same thing and in this case there is no problem in defining the marginal product. But the confinement to differentiable production functions is a severe one and it gave rise to one (perhaps the most important one) of Dennis Robertson's famous 'Wage grumbles' (1931) in which he assessed various criticisms of the marginal productivity theory in relation to wages.

Following hints from Taussig and Cassel, Robertson considered an example in which nine men equipped with nine spades were set to dig a pit. Adding a tenth man would increase output only if a tenth spade were also added. The other factor, therefore, does not remain constant (at any rate on Wicksteed's 'physical' definition), so how does one find the marginal product of labour? Robertson notes two possible solutions to the problem, one suggested by Clark and one by Marshall. Clark, it has been noted, preferred not to think in terms of individual pieces of capital equipment but to measure capital in value terms. If the value is held constant then that effectively means that the capital is malleable:

> Any increase or diminution in the amount of labour that is employed in connection with a given amount of capital causes that capital to change its forms. (1899, p. 159)

Or, as Robertson puts it, more concretely, the ten men 'will be furnished with ten cheaper spades instead of nine more expensive ones'. Marshall's solution is to define the marginal product of labour as the increase in the value of the output *less* the additional expenditure on the other factors. In other words, the cost of an extra spade is deducted from the value of the tenth man's addition to output. The increment so defined is referred to as a 'net' product (1890, p. 517). Whereas Marshall's solution violates the traditional definition of the margin as a partial derivative, Clark's keeps faith provided that the constancy of other factors is interpreted in value terms. The relationship between the two and also the traditional (Wicksteed) approach are explored by Bliss (1975, ch. 5) whose thoughts are worth pursuing not only because they show how marginal concepts can be adapted to deal with non-differentiability but also because they are relevant to the problems of defining the marginal product of aggregate capital (see section 4.7).

Consider the production function

$$Q = Q(\mathbf{S}, L)$$

where $\mathbf{S}$ is a vector of types of capital equipment (types of spade, say) and L is labour; Q, $\mathbf{S}$ and L have corresponding prices p, σ and w. The firm's problem is to maximize profit:

$$\text{Max } \pi = pQ - \sigma\mathbf{S} - wL \qquad \text{subject to } Q = Q(\mathbf{S}, L)$$

Bliss suggests a two-stage solution. First, fix L arbitrarily at $\bar{L} \geqslant 0$, maximize

$$Z = pQ - \sigma\mathbf{S} \qquad \text{subject to } Q = Q(\mathbf{S}, L)$$

and denote the solution by $Z(\bar{L})$. This is equal to profit plus labour cost $w\bar{L}$. Next choose L so as to find

$$\max[Z(L) - wL]$$

The resulting value of $Z(L)$ is Marshall's net value product of labour, i.e. the value of output less the cost of equipment when both equipment and labour are optimally chosen to maximize profits. If $Z(L)$ is differentiable, then the solution to the second stage implies

$$\frac{dZ}{dL} = pQ_L - \sigma\mathbf{S}_L = w \tag{4.10}$$

or the marginal net value product equals the wage. This may be compared with the traditional formulation in which the wage is equal to the marginal value product – equation (4.6), reproduced here as

$$pQ_L = w \tag{4.11}$$

Equation (4.11) may be regarded as a special case of (4.10) in which the optimal adjustment of other factors is zero (i.e. $\mathbf{S}_L = 0$) because, at the margin, labour and equipment are perfect substitutes.

The discussion is illustrated in figure 4.1 in which max Z is plotted as functions of L. The lower function refers to variation in L when $\mathbf{S}$ is held constant, the upper function to variation in L when $\mathbf{S}$ is optimally adjusted. The upper function is the envelope of lower functions and the distinction relates in an obvious way to that between the Marshallian long and short runs. Figure 4.1(a) refers to the differentiable case. At point E, the tangent to the lower curve measures the traditional marginal value product while the tangent to the upper curve measures the marginal net value product.

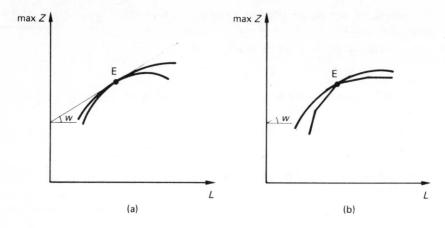

Figure 4.1 Net value product functions (a) where the traditional
marginal product is defined and (b) where it is not.

The two are clearly the same in this case. Robertson's example is illustrated in figure 4.1(b). Here the traditional margin is not defined because
of the kink at E. In this case the wage will lie between the right and left
margins:

$$(pQ_L)_{dL>0} < w < (pQ_L)_{dL<0} \tag{4.12}$$

The net margin will be defined, however, if the upper function is differentiable. (If not, the wage will also lie between the left and right net
margins.)

The assumption that $S_L = 0$ effectively avoids the wage grumble by
assuming it away, i.e. by supposing that there is no problem of input
complementarity. There is a second way in which (4.11) may be reached
from (4.10), however: by the much weaker assumption that $\sigma S_L = 0$. This
is Clark's approach in which nine high-quality spades are replaced by ten
poorer ones of equal cost. This second assumption yields a concept of the
marginal product that is free from any 'deductions', unlike Marshall's, yet
which is more capable of dealing with complementarity than the traditional
approach and thus more likely to yield a wage–marginal-product equality
(4.11) than the inequalities (4.12). (Since it implies a constraint on the
firm's actions which is weaker than freezing equipment in a physical sense
but stronger than allowing optimal adjustment, it implies, in figure 4.1, a
third $Z(L)$ function which lies between the two illustrated.)

Both the Clarkian and the Marshallian definitions of marginal product
have the peculiarity of depending on the prices of cooperating factors. In
Bliss's opinion this is precisely as it should be: ordinarily the demand for

labour can be expected to depend on the prices of capital goods. But if Bliss dismisses this as of no consequence for equilibrium theory, it is because he is thinking always in terms of *general* equilibrium theory, in which relations like (4.11) and (4.12) hold (depending on the presence or absence of the requisite differentiability) but do not imply anything about the behaviour of input demands with respect to their own prices. This is true, but it must be acknowledged that there is a vast body of modern partial equilibrium theorizing to which both long- and short-run input demand curves are taken to be downward sloping.

On the assumption of diminishing marginal productivity the labour demand curve follows from (4.11) when all prices other than labour are kept constant.[21] As applied to the long run (where transmission of effects to other sectors will have time to work themselves out), this procedure is particularly suspect. As Steedman explains, in comparing long-period positions, it is not possible 'to change one input price (wage, etc.) relative to other input prices without also changing the relativities among the latter' (1985, p. 169). Clark's Q_L requires for its definition sufficient lapse of time to allow the firm to restructure its capital stock. Within such time it is unreasonable to suppose that σ will remain unchanged. But since Q_L depends on σ it is no longer certain that the demand curve is non-positively sloped. In particular, if some components of **S** are complements to labour, the demand curve may be upward sloping (see 'example 3' of Steedman, 1985).

4.7 Capital Grumbles

The modern critique of Marginalism initiated by Sraffa (1960) had as its central objective the restoration of the classical modes of analysis. Its earliest and most successful target was the naive capital theory deriving from the work of Clark. Clark, as noted earlier, applied the theory to a single entity called 'capital'. It has been seen how this procedure could imply the mutability of capital goods in such a way as to allow a *definition* of the marginal product of some other factor (section 6.6). But in order to obtain the marginal product of capital by differentiating the production function in which capital is an argument *and* for that marginal product to be equal to the rate of interest at any point along the function, it is necessary (exceptional cases apart) that capital and output are the self-same commodity (rather as in Ricardo's corn-ratio theory). With a diminishing marginal product there follows a downward-sloping demand curve. More accurately, in Clark's two-factor macromodel, the capital-to-labour ratio is an inverse monotonic function of the ratio of the interest rate to the real wage (r/w). The difficulties of obtaining a capital aggregate with the requisite properties, skated over by Clark but clearly understood by Wicksell, did not hinder many neoclassicals from believing that the basic insights of Clark's approach continue to hold good in a world of many capital goods. The Sraffian critics showed conclusively that this implicit generalization was invalid. (see Harcourt, 1972).

The demonstration does not require the strict format of Sraffa's model. In virtually any theory of capital it is possible to identify, for a given technique of production, a negative relation between the equilibrium real wage and the rate of interest or profit:

$$w = w(r) \qquad\qquad w' < 0 \qquad\qquad (4.13)$$

It is also possible to identify for each technique a relation between the value c, of consumption per worker and the rate g of growth of capital:

$$c = c(g) \qquad\qquad c' < 0 \qquad\qquad (4.14)$$

Under certain widely assumed conditions (which necessarily hold in a one-commodity world; see Mainwaring, 1984, ch. 5) these two relations are dual when referring to the same technique, i. e. $c(r) = w(r)$. National accounts, in per worker terms, may be written as

$$y = w + rk = c + gk \qquad\qquad (4.15)$$

(where y is the value of net output and k is the value of capital), from which it follows that

$$k = \frac{c - w}{r - g} \qquad\qquad (4.16)$$

These relationships are illustrated in figures 4.2(a) and 4.2(b) for two particular cases.

Consider, first, figure 4.2(a). Each straight line represents the dual $w(r)$ and $c(g)$ relations for a particular technique. It follows from (4.16) that for $r \neq g$ (specifically, suppose $g < r$) the slope of each measures k. Suppose that there is an infinite number of such techniques such that the upper envelope of the relations contains a single point from each. Given r, the profit-maximizing technique is that which yields the greatest w which may, therefore, be read off the envelope curve. Suppose also that as k changes continuously along the envelope one technique gives way to the next also in a continuous fashion. It can then be seen that, as k rises from its minimum to its maximum, net output per worker rises from y_{min} to y_{max} in a continuous manner. This construction thus implies the Clark-type production function in which k is inversely related to r/w. The marginal properties of the latter may be confirmed by totally differentiating (4.15):

$$dy = dw + rdk + kdr \qquad\qquad (4.17)$$

$$= dc + gdk + kdg \qquad\qquad (4.18)$$

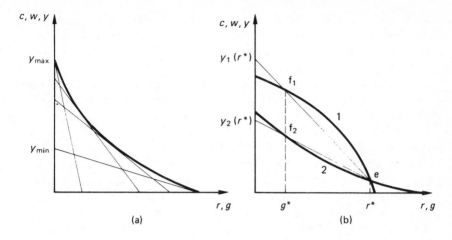

Figure 4.2 Dual *w–r* and *c–g* frontiers for (a) Clark-type technologies and (b) more general technologies.

From (4.17), $dy/dk = r$ provided that $k = dw/dr$, which must be true for any point on the envelope because at each point the slope of (4.13) is equal to k.

Figure 4.2(a) is drawn on the basis of some severely limiting assumptions. It refers to either a single-commodity model or one in which capital-to-labour ratios are uniform across sectors. It assumes an infinite number of ways of combining capital and labour and it requires important continuity properties. Figure 4.2(b), although itself a special case, is more representative in so far as it does not imply these assumptions. In this case, (4.16) implies that, for (say) $g = g^*$ and $r = r^*$, the value of capital per worker for technique i ($i = 1, 2$) is equal to the slope of the line ef_i and that $y_i = y_i(r^*)$. Given the concavity of the $w(r)$ relation for technique 1 it is immediately apparent that there is no longer an inverse relation between k and r/w. Marginal products are clearly still defined using (4.17) and (4.18), but they are no longer *necessarily* equal to the rate of interest. Two cases may easily be considered.[22]

The first is the 'real' Wicksell effect arising out of a switch of techniques as at point e. Since the techniques are equiprofitable at e then, by definition, there is no change in w and r and so $dy/dk = r^*$ follows directly from (4.17). Note that the coexistence of techniques at a switchpoint implies that prices are the same for each technique. There is thus no price change involved in taking the derivative dy/dk, which explains why it is equal to a pure number. The second is the 'price' Wicksell effect which refers to a move between adjacent points on the $w(r)$ relation for a single technique. Here dw and dr are non-zero. However, if, by assumption, dg = dc = 0 then, from (4.18), dy/dk = g. (If g = 0, dy/dk = 0; if g (>0) and r are related – as by the Cambridge equation g = sr – then dy/dk is equal to neither r nor g.)

Although dy/dk may be defined for a price Wicksell effect, it is less clear that it can be dignified with the description 'marginal product', as traditionally understood. Unless the $w(r)$ relation is a straight line adjacent points will be associated with marginally different prices and, by definition, with marginally different values of w and r. This means that both inputs and outputs are measured at varying prices, a procedure which is not typically applied to other factors. If, on the contrary, the marginal product is measured in terms of the constant prices of a single state then the traditional (weak inequality) relations between the margins and the interest rate are restored (Bliss, 1975, ch. 5). Consider two states (1 and 2) with a common growth rate. Letting y = pq, w = pm and k = ph, the first equation of (4.15) may be written for each state as

$$p_1 q_1 = p_1 m_1 + r_1 p_1 h_1$$

$$p_2 q_2 = p_2 m_2 + r_2 p_2 h_2$$

In terms of the prices and interest rate obtaining in state 1, that state is the more profitable in which net output minus interest payments are greater (i.e. in which the real wage is greater). This is state 1 if

$$p_1 \Delta q - r_1 p_1 \Delta h \leqslant 0$$

(where $\Delta q = q_2 - q_1$ etc.), from which it follows that

$$\left(\frac{p_1 \Delta q}{p_1 \Delta h} \right)_{\Delta h > 0} \leqslant r_1 \leqslant \left(\frac{p_1 \Delta q}{p_1 \Delta h} \right)_{\Delta h < 0} \tag{4.19}$$

Equalities in (4.19) will occur where the two states are equiprofitable and the change implies a real Wicksell effect. Otherwise strict inequalities will hold. This places the marginal product of capital on the same footing as that of other factors (compare relations (4.19) and (4.12)). Whether this strengthens the appeal of the concept as applied to capital depends on one's view of its usefulness as applied to primary factors of production. That in turn depends on whether one prefers to operate in a partial equilibrium framework and is prepared to overlook the inherent limitations of that method.

Margins in General Equilibrium

The critique of naive capital theory has generally been conceded. The counter-critique of 'neo-Ricardianism' has been conducted on a more sophisticated level, that of a fully general equilibrium theory in which capital is approached in the manner of Wicksteed (individual items of capital equipment) rather than Clark (a value aggregate). Given the requisite differentiability, it is possible to show that the marginal product of each factor, so defined, is equal to its reward in equilibrium (either a real wage rate or a real rental) (see Hahn, 1982). Indeed, all the standard marginal conditions hold with the appropriate interpretation. Thus the intertemporal version contains a straightforward generalization of the Fisherian analysis in which the marginal rates of substitution between commodities (identified by physical properties and dates of delivery) are equal to the corresponding marginal rates of transformation (see Nuti, 1974). Yet, despite the fact that marginal concepts may be there to be found, they are in no way essential to general equilibrium theorizing.[23] This point is made quite explicitly by Bliss:

> the equation between the payment for the service of a factor and the value of the marginal product of that factor plays no part in the discussion and derivation of equilibrium for the atemporal economy. The same is necessarily true for the equilibrium of the intertemporal economy. . . . However, there is no implication that marginal ideas are in any way in conflict with the theory that has made no appeal to them. . . . (1975, ch. 5)

In relation to the capital theory debates this leaves general equilibrium theory essentially unscathed. The theory has no need of monotonic relationships between quantities demanded or supplied and marginal utilities or marginal products; nor does it imply such relationships. The limitations of naive theory identified by Sraffa and his followers could just as easily have been detected from the general equilibrium perspective. (That they were not is another matter.) What is true of capital is true of other factors. Monotonic input demand curves are creations of partial equilibrium theorizing that is difficult to defend (Steedman, 1985). General equilibrium theorists make no attempt to offer a defence. Some, like Hahn (1982), are content with the claim that Sraffa's economics is merely a special case of general equilibrium theory.

4.8 Marginalist Science and Marginalist Ethics

As a consequence of the Marginalist revolution the dynamic preoccupations of the classical economists gave way entirely to static preoccupations. The utility theorists were concerned with how individuals obtain maximum satisfaction from allocating a fixed budget. Extension to production involved no real novelties: the marginal principle of choice was applied to the entrepreneur whose aim was to maximize profits which, with perfect competition, implied making the most efficient use of given resources. The hierarchical division of economic functions – acquiring utility from the services of consumption goods, producing consumption goods, producing production goods, etc. – is most explicit in the work of Menger and the Austrian school, but the essential idea of derived demand is common to all Marginalists. The consequence was that both value and cost have been given a new interpretation. The irksomeness of production is no longer the cause of value. A commodity has value jointly because of its utility and its scarcity and it has a cost because its acquisition means giving up something else of value. In equilibrium relative prices are equal to relative costs and, in turn, everybody's relative marginal evaluations (rates of substitution). Relative prices thus constitute a feedback mechanism: they inform individual maximizing decisions and are themselves the outcome of the aggregate of those decisions. Their primary function is not valuation but allocation.

Through continuous refinement and generalization these ideas have evolved into the modern theory of general equilibrium. But can a theory which has no need of the margin be considered as Marginalist? At the purely technical level, marginal analysis is simply a particular method of obtaining a maximum. It is a method that is limited by its assumptions. Modern general equilibrium theory has succeeded in removing many of these limitations but it is 'necessarily in harmony with marginal concepts where these are applicable' (Bliss, 1975, p. 94). At the more conceptual level it may be that many of the predictions of simple, traditional Marginalism are overturned when interdependences are fully accounted for. But the essential characteristics of Marginalism, as identified for example by Dasgupta, all survive the generalization; the allocative role of prices, the endogenous treatment of distribution and the emphasis on consumption are all retained. General equilibrium theory is thoroughly Marginalist in spirit but, because it has no need of margins, 'it can', says Bliss, 'suffer no crisis on their account' (1975, p. 94).

It is clear from this brief account that Marginalism did succeed in creating a radically different vision of capitalism. It may not be quite so clear from the foregoing that any claim to greater generality than its predecessor cannot be sustained. It could be argued that the greater emphasis on demand gave greater generality in the determination of prices, especially in so far as it encompassed those cases which classical theory was forced to ignore, such as non-reproducible goods and joint products and short-run price determination where constant costs cannot be assumed to prevail. But gain in generality in some respects was paid for dearly by loss in others (an ironic example of opportunity cost!). The most grievous loss was the confinement to static analysis. According to Shackle the static method is a necessary consequence of the assumption of rational choice which is the hallmark of Marginalism:

> *All individuals simultaneously* must, if they are each to act rationally, have a knowledge, at the moment when each makes his choice, of what each other individual is choosing. . . . If all such actions are simultaneous, it follows that the world we study must be deemed a timeless or momentary world. Rationality and time are alien to each other. This is the severe limitation imposed upon the analyst by his chosen method, that method to which marginalism must be taken to belong if it is to have its full meaning and effect. (1972, pp. 593–4; italics in original)

It follows from what has already been said that Shackle's indictment applies with equal force to general equilibrium theory. If there is a critical weakness in the Marginalist conception then surely this is it.[24]

There were, of course, other losses and other gains. Lost were 'class' and class discord; gained were 'individuals', 'factors' and 'social harmony'. It is not entirely surprising, therefore, that some historians have interpreted Marginalism as fundamentally an apologetic for the existing order. It is an interpretation that gained credance from the explicit views of some of the major innovators of Marginalism but it is difficult to sustain the charge that Marginalism was in any way a conspiracy to overthrow Ricardian offsprings on purely ideological grounds.[25] Jevons's well-advertised distaste for Ricardian doctrine and his belief in the harmony and legitimacy of capitalism (1871, ch. 8) were related rather more to the notion of abstinence and the 'natural laws' of competition than to an appeal to Marginalist principles. (see Steedman, 1972). Nevertheless, there were aspects of Marginalism which, as Longfield might have put it, were 'not unpleasing' to the defenders of capitalism and it was probably J. B. Clark, that 'made-to-order foil for the diatribes of a Veblen' (Stigler, 1941, p. 297), who was the least subtle in promoting them.[26] In asserting that a factor's marginal product is its just reward, he too invoked natural laws:

> As real as gravitation is the force that draws the actual pay of men *toward* a standard that is set by the final productivity law. This law is universal and permanent. . . . We are to get what we produce. (1899, p. 180)

Clark was well aware that in competitive equilibrium a factor's marginal product is determined by its natural scarcity and talents and by the availability of cooperating factors, but he failed to make it clear why justice should be a function of chance (see Blaug, 1978, pp. 450–1).

4.9   Principles of Economic Rationality

Optimization and the Economics of Control

Out of the synthesis of Walrasian equilibrium theory and Paretian welfare economics have come Arrow's (1951) fundamental welfare theorems concerning the competitive economy: (a) every competitive equilibrium is Pareto optimal; and (b) every Pareto optimum can be attained as a competitive equilibrium by an appropriate redistribution of initial endowments. Given the requisite differentiability of utility and production functions, the conditions of Pareto optimality can, of course, be stated in terms of well-known marginal equalities. Those theorems, while they do not rule out the possibility of Pareto-efficient monopolistic equilibrium, nevertheless establish a strong presumption in favour of perfect competition and, therefore, of policies to attain or to mimic perfect competition. In economies where there is no central coordination of the allocative mechanism the marginal principles of welfare economics have been translated into partial equilibrium policy rules, subject to modification by second-best considerations, increasing returns etc. A familiar example is the use of marginal-cost pricing in public-sector industries but a dozen other examples could be quoted from tax and tariff policies alone.

What may prove, historically (and perhaps a little ironically), to be of greater significance is the increasing acceptance of praxiological methods within centrally planned economies (see Meek, 1972). Proposals for the centralized mimicking of the Walrasian *tâtonnement* or some other iterative market-clearing procedure have been common in the West since the work of Lange (1936–7). Their absorption into the mainstream of Soviet planning culture, however, has been hampered by the ideological associations of the margin and of Marginalism, the former connected to the latter, and the latter understood as an apology for capitalism. The theory of marginal productivity, in particular, was regarded as opposing Marx's theory of exploitation. The erosion of these traditional and deep-seated prejudices has been a slow and relatively recent process. That it began at all may be because the leading proponents of 'optimal planning' have evolved their ideas not from traditional marginal principles but from linear programming methods from which it is much easier to establish connections with orthodox Marxian categories.[27]

Such connections may have been politically necessary but they are largely superficial (cf. Nove and Nuti, 1972, p. 349). Marx's economics was an outgrowth of Ricardo's and, whether or not it is compatible with some aspects of Marginalism,[28] its optimizing features are limited to the capitalists' maximization of the rate of profit. Marx's analytical concepts, which relate to the dynamics of capitalist economies, have limited relevance to the rational organization of a socialist economy. But might it not be wondered whether the same is true of the margin and, *a fortiori*, of Marginalism?

It should be clear by now that the margin and its sophisticated relatives are ideologically neutral and not necessarily tied to any particular paradigm. So far as Marginalism goes one might begin by questioning its relevance to capitalism. It is a paradigm about utility maximization in the presence of scarcity in which equilibrium and optimality are attained by a pseudodynamic process called *tâtonnement*. Doubt has already been cast on the implied consumption-optimizing motives of the capitalist-entrepreneur. And doubt can just as quickly be cast on the axiom that scarcity is *the* economic problem of capitalism, as of any other form of organization. Baran and Sweezy describe how the ordinary citizen is bemused by the wisdom of conventional textbooks:

> If he is a worker, the ubiquitous fact of unemployment teaches him that the supply of labour is always greater than the demand. If he is a farmer, he struggles to stay afloat in a sea of surpluses. If he is a businessman, his sales persistently fall short of what he could profitably produce. Always too much, never too little. (1966, p. 114)

They go on to note, pertinently: 'This condition of affairs is peculiar to monopoly capitalism'. But if modern capitalism *is* monopoly capitalism, how relevant is the Marginalist vision of free price-taking entrepreneurs? The last and, perhaps, most important question concerns the actual mechanism of allocation. How realistic is the Walrasian *tâtonnement* even as a description of market clearing under competition? Who or what is the auctioneer and how can it ensure that transactions are only undertaken at equilibrium prices?

If these arguments suggest scepticism about the descriptive relevance of Marginalism to capitalism, what is its prescriptive relevance to socialism? Consider the purely normative proposition that the role of the socialist planner is to maximize an intertemporal social welfare function, implying the choice of a particular Pareto optimum. Can the principles of economic rationality be so applied by a central authority?

The first thing to note is that the auctioneer can be given real form in this context, in the shape of the central planning agency. A *tâtonnement* or other iterative procedure for the forthcoming plan can be prosecuted (in real time) while the previous plan is being executed. The major problems here are the resource requirements of information and computation and the limited availability of time. Second, firms, no matter how large, could be instructed to act in a particular way at centrally given prices; in particular, they could be told to act as competitive profit-maximizers. Important problems in this respect are the incentives firms have to disregard instructions and the existence of non-convexities in production. Third, if approximately efficient plans were attainable, the second welfare theorem would imply the possibility of reconciling them with more general social objectives. But there is a difficulty here also. If, in capitalism, the application of the second welfare theorem is hindered by the vested interests of the dominant class, it may be similarly fettered under socialism by the self-interests of politicians and bureaucrats.

These brief remarks suggest that adapting Marginalist principles to the economics of control is not a straightforward matter. Consider, for example, the problem of non-convexity in production. The root of the difficulty is that increasing returns to scale are inconsistent with competitive equilibrium. In particular, input demand curves may be discontinuous so that a supply–demand equilibrium may fail to exist. Not surprisingly, planning procedures such as Lange's, which attempt to mimic the Walrasian market (for which convexity is a requirement) are also incapable of dealing with increasing returns. Alternative procedures using quantity rather than price signals can handle non-convexities but only by adding to informational requirements.

'Satisficing'

Of the earlier utility theorists, Wicksteed explored most thoroughly the boundaries of the theory's applicability. In the *Common Sense* (1933) there are thoughtful passages on irrational behaviour, altruism, 'alienation' (though he does not use that word) and the importance of habitual and instinctive choice. This last is particularly notable, for Wicksteed here completes the groundwork for a 'satisficing' theory of rational choice without quite appreciating the potential, both constructive and destructive, of his efforts. He begins by noting that time and mental energy, which are both inputs into real decision-taking processes, are themselves scarce commodities:

> A vast amount of the work of the world is probably done, to the great advantage of all concerned, and to the saving of much fretting upon the higher strings of motive and efforts of will, by the mere drift and momentum of acquired habit. (1933, p. 119)

He is determined to retain this territory within the domain of marginal calculation, however, for the extent of 'fretting on the higher strings' is itself the result of an optimizing calculation, albeit one under uncertainty: 'The alert mind is always willing to open a question, but only on an estimate, instinctive or deliberate, of the probable advantages to be gained by doing so' (pp. 199–20). The time and energy devoted to thinking about one question has, in other words, an opportunity cost in being diverted from some other question, and the probable returns from allocating these precious resources to alternative speculations are equalized at the margin. And thus the wise (i.e. rational) man 'will not only think wisely, but will know how much to think and when not to think at all, (p. 121). This extension of the marginal principle is suspiciously tautological. A 'deliberate' calculation of the optimal degree of optimization would, in many cases, require nearly as much knowledge as the calculation of the global optimum anyway. Any compromise on deliberation implies a willingness to 'satisfice'. In his references to 'instincts' and 'impulse', Wicksteed effectively gives the game away.

Simon (1955), in taking these arguments to their logical conclusion, has developed what is probably the most important critique of the description of economic behaviour or of the prescription of economic policies in terms of standard optimization procedures. The main applications of his theory of 'bounded rationality' have been to the firm, but Simon also notes its relevance to normative decision theory[29] and, by implication therefore, to the economics of control. In real decision-taking where the computational requirements for reaching a global optimum are too large the rational agent will accept a 'satisficing' solution of some sort. This could be through the choice of a 'satisfactory' simplified model in which a (simplified) optimum is sought or by forgoing optimization altogether and selecting directly a 'satisficing' solution. Simon's insights remain underexploited both in positive and in normative economics.

4.10 Conclusion

The Marginalist revolution consisted of a marriage of marginalist technique and a vision of the capitalist market economy which involved the reconstruction of value theory around the idea of choice under scarcity. This vision found its complete expression in a system of general equilibrium. Yet, because the modern theory of general equilibrium does not rely on differentiable functions, in this sphere the margin has largely been relegated to a heuristic role. However, in partial equilibrium its relative simplicity and intuitive appeal have sustained the margin as a basis for policy formulation while, in applied economics, it remains a favourite vehicle for Marginalist ideas. It is at the partial level, however, that its application is most problematic, the 'good behaviour' of supply and demand functions resting heavily on the heroic assumption of *ceteris paribus*. With whatever method Marginalism is practised, its major limitation is its essentially static character.

The growing sophistication of Marginalism as a paradigm accompanied the growing sophistication of optimizing techniques and thus a broadening of the praxiological application of the marginal 'spirit'. Despite the reservations of the behaviourists, rationality is still synonymous for most economists with optimization and, for many, with the equating of margins.

NOTES

1 On the validity of the Kuhnian concept of 'paradigm' to Marginalism, see Deane (1978). Among others who regard Marginalism as a distinctive philosophy are Meek (1972), Dobb (1973) and Bharadwaj (1978). For a view more in keeping with Hicks, see Blaug (1978).

2 According to Howey (1972) the word 'marginal' in this context did not appear in English until Wicksteed's (1888) *Alphabet*. It seems to have been a translation of the German *grenze* employed by Weiser. In his *Theory*, Jevons (1871) talked of 'final degree of utility', while Walras (1874) used the term *rareté* in the *Elements*.

3 See Smith (1776, pp. 32–3). The major classical writers treated this problem (unsatisfactorily) by distinguishing between utility and value and declaring that utility was necessary to value but did not determine it. For a modern discussion see Bowley (1972).

4 See Blaug (1978) and contributions to Black, Coats and Goodwin (1973). It may be noted in passing that the mathematician Bernoulli (1738) in his investigation into the 'St Petersburg paradox' also formulated a utility function with the property of diminishing marginal utility. Blaug concedes Bernoulli as an 'outlier'.

5 In fact the theory of extensive diminishing returns to agriculture also has its less successful precursors in Stuart and Anderson. For an account of classical rent theory see O'Brien (1975).

6 The reconstruction is Sraffa's (1951, vol. I, Introduction). See also Pasinetti (1959).

7 The first known use of the word 'margin' in this context (cf. note 2) was by Chalmers (1832). It was subsequently adopted by J. S. Mill. See Howey (1972).

8 See especially the excellent survey by Stigler (1950).

9 Though Jevons also invoked physiological laws concerning stimulus and response.

10 The early Marginalists were all clear on this. Walras, for example, entitled lesson ten of the *Elements*, '*Rareté*, The Cause of Value in Exchange'.

11 See Stigler (1941) for a comparative survey of ten leading Marginalist theorists.

12 Wicksteed also denied the practical possibility of distinguishing land from capital because virtually all land had benefited from improvements (1933, p. 365).

13 For a detailed account of the major contributions, see Stigler (1941, ch. 12).

14 Barone's reservations were communicated to Walras and noted by him in the third (1896) edition of the *Elements*. Samuelson (1947, pp. 78–9) has since argued (convincingly) that even if a single firms has 99.9 per cent of the market it must, under these conditions, remain a price-taker. If it tries to raise its price other firms would simply undercut it.

15 See Samuelson (1966) and Steedman (1972) on the Austrian and Jevonian theories, respectively.
16 This in no way contradicts his assumption in *Co-ordination* of separate types of capital.
17 For Marginalists 'pure' profit is 'gross' profit less interest. In classical long-period equilibrium pure profit is zero and interest equals 'gross' profit.
18 Marx's views on this are well known and do not need repeating. On Ricardo, see section 4.2.
19 On the implications for the theory of interest of including wealth in the utility function, see Steedman (1981).
20 This proposition originates with Viner's (1937, pp. 515–6) observation that the incremental cost of production in terms of each factor is the same at the margin, as indicated by equation (4.7). It does not, of course, imply that the elasticity of substitution at the margin is infinite.
21 In fact, neither differentiability nor convexity is necessary to establish the slightly weaker result that $\Delta L/\Delta w \leq 0$. See, for example, Steedman (1985).
22 Craven (1977) identifies four cases. The other two, arising out of the dual properties of the model, are not explained here.
23 The classic statement of modern equilibrium theory, by Debreu (1959), contains not a single reference in its index to the words 'margin' or 'marginal'.
24 In the continuing debate between Marginalists and the modern classical school a critique along these lines has been formulated by Dumenil and Lévy (1985).
25 On this, see Meek (1972). An alternative thesis, offered by Mirowski (1984), was that the Marginalist revolution was impelled by the desire of its leading participants to repeat in economics the success of the energetics revolution in physics by a metaphorical extension of its leading principles.
26 Caution on the part of others should not be taken too hastily as a sign of disapproval; cf. Stigler (1982, p. 19): 'the appeal of productivity ethics for income distribution commands wide support not only from the public but also from the economists when they are watching their sentiments rather than their words'.
27 The most important figure is probably Kantorovich; see Kantorovich (1960). On other contributors, see Nove and Nuti (1972, part 5), and Ellman (1973) who also discusses early Soviet attitudes to marginalism, in his Introduction.
28 Cf. Johansen (1963). Johansen, in fact, demonstrates only the compatibility of Marxian economics with marginal utility (deprived of its intertemporal interpretation) and only then for single-product industries.
29 See Simon (1979) for a discussion of applications and a defence against his marginalist critics.

REFERENCES

Arrow, K. J. (1951) 'An extension of the basic theorems of classical welfare economics', in *Proceedings of the Second Berkeley Symposium on Mathematical Statistics and Probability*. Ed. J. Neyman, Berkeley, Calif.: University of California Press, pp. 507–32.

Baran, P. A., and P. M. Sweezy (1966) *Monopoly Capital*. New York: Monthly Review Press. References to 1968 edition, Harmondsworth: Penguin.

Bernoulli, D. (1738) 'Exposition of a new theory on the measurement of risk', English translation, 1954, *Econometrica* 22, 23–36.

Bharadwaj, K. (1978) *Classical Political Economy and the Rise to Dominance of Supply and Demand Theories*. New Delhi: Orient Longman.

Black, R., A. Coats and C. Goodwin (eds) (1973) *The Marginal Revolution in Economics*. Durham, N. C.: Duke University Press.

Blaug, M. (1978) *Economic Theory in Retrospect*, 3rd. edn. Cambridge: Cambridge University Press.

Bliss, C. (1975) *Capital Theory and the Distribution of Income*. Amsterdam: North-Holland.

von Böhm-Bawerk, E. (1889) *The Positive Theory of Capital*. English translation, 1891, London: Macmillan.

Bowley, M. (1972) 'The predecessors of Jevons – the revolution that wasn't', *Manchester School* 40, 9–29.

Cannan, E. (1924) *A History of the Theories of Production and Distribution*, 3rd edn. London: P. S. King.

Chalmers, T. (1832) *On Political Economy in Connection with the Moral State and the Moral Prospects of Society*. Glasgow.

Clark, J. B. (1889) 'Possibility of a scientific law of wages', *Publications of the American Economic Association* 4, 37–69.

Clark, J. B. (1899) *The Distribution of Wealth*. London: Macmillan.

Craven, J. (1977) 'On the marginal product of capital', *Oxford Economic Papers* 29, 472–7.

Dasgupta, A. K. (1985) *Epochs of Economic Theory*. Oxford: Blackwell.

Deane, P. (1978) *The Evolution of Economic Ideas*. Cambridge: Cambridge University Press.

Debreu, G. (1959) *Theory of Value*. New Haven, Conn.: Yale University Press.

Dobb, M. (1973) *Theories of Value and Distribution since Adam Smith*. Cambridge: Cambridge University Press.

Dumenil, G. and D. Lévy (1985) 'The classics and the neoclassics: a rejoinder to Frank Hahn', *Cambridge Journal of Economics* 9, 327–46.

Dupuit, J. (1844) 'On the measurement of the utility of public works'. English translation, 1952, *International Economic Papers* 2, 83–110.

Edgeworth, F. Y. (1881) *Mathematical Physics*. London: Kegan Paul. LSE Series of reprints, 1932.

Fisher, I. (1907) *The Rate of Interest*. New York: Macmillan.

Fisher, I. (1930) *The Theory of Interest*. New York: Macmillan.

Flux, A. W. (1894) Review of Wicksteed (1894), *Economic Journal* 4, 305–13.

Gossen, H. H. (1854) *Entwickelung der Gesetze des manschilchen Verkehrs*, 3rd edn. 1927, Berlin: Prager.

Hahn, F. (1982) 'The neo-Ricardians', *Cambridge Journal of Economics* 6, 353–74.

Harcourt, G. C. (1972) *Some Cambridge Controversies in the Theory of Capital*. Cambridge: Cambridge University Press.

Hicks, J. R. (1976) '"Revolutions" in economics', in *Methods and Appraisal in*

Economics. Ed. S. J. Latsis, Cambridge: Cambridge University Press, pp. 207–18.

Hicks, J. R. and R. G. D. Allen (1934) 'A reconsideration of the theory of value', *Economica, New Series* 1, 52–76 and 196–219.

Howey, R. S. (1972) 'Origins of Marginalism', *History of Political Economy*, 4, 281–302. Reprinted in *The Marginal Revolution in Economics*. Ed. R. Black, A. Coats and C. Goodwin, 1973, Durham, N. C.: Duke University Press.

Jennings, R. (1855) *Natural Elements of Political Economy*. London: Longman.

Jevons, W. S. (1871) *Theory of Political Economy*. London: Macmillan.

Kantorovich, L. V. (1960) *The Best Use of Economic Resources*. English translation, 1965, Oxford: Pergamon.

Lange, O. (1936–7) 'On the economic theory of socialism', *Review of Economic Studies* 4, 53–71 and 123–42.

Lange, O. (1963) *Political Economy*, vol. I. New York: Pergamon.

Lloyd, W. F. (1834) *A Lecture on the Notion of Value*. London.

Longfield, M. (1834) *Lectures on Political Economy*. Dublin. Reprinted 1931, LSE Series of reprints, London: London School of Economics.

Mainwaring, L. (1984) *Value and Distribution in Capitalist Economies*. Cambridge: Cambridge University Press.

Marshall, A. (1890) *Principles of Economics*. London: Macmillan.

Meek, R. L. (1972) 'Marginalism and Marxism', *History of Political Economy* 4, 499–511. Reprinted in *The Marginal Revolution in Economics*. Ed. R. Black, A. Coats and C. Goodwin, 1973, Durham, N.C.: Duke University Press.

Menger, C. (1871) *Principles of Economics*. English translation, 1950, Glencoe, Ill.: The Free Press.

Mill, J. S. (1848) *Principles of Political Economy*. Ed. D. Winch, 1979, Harmondsworth: Penguin.

Mirowski, P. (1984) 'Physics and the Marginalist revolution', *Cambridge Journal of Economics* 8, 361–79.

Nove, A., and D. M. Nuti (eds) (1972) *Socialist Economics*. Harmondsworth: Penguin.

Nuti, D. M. (1974) 'On the rates of return on investment', *Kyklos* 27, 345–69.

O'Brien, D. P. (1975) *The Classical Economists*. Oxford: Oxford University Press.

Pareto, V. (1982) 'Considerazioni sui Principii Fondomentali dell'Economia Politica Pura', *Giornale degli Economisti, Series 2* V.

Pasinetti, L. L. (1959) 'A mathematical reformulation of the Ricardian system', *Review of Economic Studies* 27, 78–98.

Ricardo, D. (1815) *An Essay on the Influence of a Low Price of Corn on the Profits of Stock*. Reprinted in *The Works and Correspondence of David Ricardo*, vol. IV. Ed. P. Sraffa. 1951, Cambridge: Cambridge University Press.

Ricardo, D. (1817) *Principles of Political Economy and Taxation*. References to *The Works and Correspondence of David Ricardo*, vol. I. Ed. P. Sraffa, 1951, Cambridge: Cambridge University Press.

Robertson, D. H. (1931) 'Wage grumbles', in *Economic Fragments*. London: P. S. King. Reprinted in *Readings in the Theory of Income Distribution*. Ed. W. Fellner and B. F. Haley, 1946, Philadelphia, Pa.: Blakiston, pp. 221–36.

Robinson, J. (1934) 'Euler's theorem and the problem of distribution', *Economic Journal* 44, 398–414.

Samuelson, P. A. (1947) *Foundations of Economic Analysis*. Cambridge, Mass.: Harvard University Press.

Scitovsky, T. (1943) 'A note on profit maximisation and its implications', *Review of Economic Studies* 11, 57–60.

Senior, N. (1836) *An Outline of the Science of Political Economy*. London.

Shackle, G. L. S. (1972) 'Marginalism: the harvest', *History of Political Economy* 4, 587–602. Reprinted in *The Marginal Revolution in Economics*. Ed. R. Black, A. Coats and C. Goodwin, 1973, Durham, N.C.: Duke University Press.

Simon, H. A. (1955) 'A behavioural model of rational choice', *Quarterly Journal of Economics* 79, 99–118.

Simon, H. A. (1979) 'Rational decision making in business organisations', *American Economic Review* 69, 493–513.

Slutsky, E. E. (1915) 'On the theory of the budget of the consumer'. English translation in *Readings in Price Theory*. Ed. K. E. Boulding and G. Stigler, 1953, London: George Allen & Unwin, pp. 27–56.

Smith, A. (1776) *The Wealth of Nations*. References to 6th Cannan edition, 1961, London: Methuen University Paperbacks.

Sraffa, P. (ed.) (1951) *The Works and Correspondence of David Ricardo*. Cambridge: Cambridge University Press.

Sraffa, P. (1960) *Production of Commodities by Means of Commodities*. Cambridge: Cambridge University Press.

Steedman, I. (1972) 'Jevon's theory of capital and interest', *Manchester School* 40, 31–52.

Steedman, I. (1981) 'Time preference, the rate of interest and abstinence from accumulation', *Australian Economic Papers* 20, 219–34.

Steedman, I. (1985) 'On input demand curves', *Cambridge Journal of Economics* 9, 165–72.

Stigler, G. (1941) *Production and Distribution Theories*. New York: Macmillan.

Stigler, G. (1950) 'The development of utility theory', *Quarterly Journal of Economics* 68, 307–27 and 373–96.

Stigler, G. (1972) 'The adoption of the marginal utility theory', *History of Political Economy* 4, 573–86. Reprinted in *The Marginal Revolution in Economics*. Ed. R. Black, A. Coats and C. Goodwin, 1973, Durham, N.C.: Duke University Press.

Stigler, G. (1982) *The Economist as Preacher*. Oxford: Blackwell.

Viner, J. (1937) *Studies in the Theory of International Trade*. New York: Harper.

Walras, L. (1874) *Elements of Pure Economics*. English edition, trans. W. Jaffe, 1954, London: George Allen & Unwin.

Wicksell, K. (1901) *Lectures on Political Economy*, vol. 1. English translation, 1934, London: Routledge & Kegan Paul.

Wicksteed, P. H. (1888) *Alphabet of Economic Science*. London: Macmillan.

Wicksteed, P. H. (1889) 'On certain passages in Jevons's *Theory of Political Economy*', *Quarterly Journal of Economics* 3, 293–314. Reprinted in P. H. Wicksteed, *The Common Sense of Political Economy*. Ed. L. Robbins, 1933, London: Routledge.

Wicksteed, P. H. (1894) *The Co-ordination of the Laws of Distribution*. London: Macmillan. LSE Series of reprints, no. 12, 1932.

Wicksteed, P. H. (1933) *The Common Sense of Political Economy*. Ed. L. Robbins, London: Routledge.

5

Value

Peter C. Dooley

Value theory is often called price theory, because it explains the empirical phenomenon of market prices, but it began with controversies that were substantially religious, ethical or political in character such as the notion of the just price, the philosophy of property rights and the doctrine of *laissez-faire*. The Scholastic Doctors, moral philosophers and political economists who first wrote on value theory were not primarily interested in empirical analysis. They struggled with fundamentally different issues: what is sinful, what is just, what is politic. These are normative questions, which ask what ought to be. No unifying principle can resolve them, but an analysis of market prices is essential to them. The early economists needed to understand reality, so they introduced concepts, like scarcity and utility, that still exist today.

The concepts have become more refined and the analysis more rigorous. The questions have become narrower and more tractable, but the changes have been slow and irregular. Moral and political controversy did not vanish at the dawn of science; they continued to be mixed with empirical analysis well into this century, even to this day. While the questions have changed, the method has not. Value theory has been deductive, axiomatic or mathematical in method from the start; and its convention of credibility has been logical consistency: what is valid. The quest for logical consistency has driven the evolution of value theory since the eighteenth century, when Adam Smith set the course for modern economics.

Smith is taken as the starting point, not because his theory of value was the first of any importance, but because it was sufficiently persuasive and authoritative to command the attention of his immediate followers. Classical economics may be considered a 'school' of economics because its members – Malthus, Ricardo, Marx and others – shared the common task of criticizing and improving the theory of value that began with Smith. As a first approximation, the classical economists explained the value of a commodity by the labour embodied in it; but no logical variation on this theme could account for the value of something that cost no human effort or sacrifice to produce. The neoclassical economists gave a logical solution to this problem in the 1870s, when they developed the marginal utility theory. They traced the value of a thing to its scarcity relative to its usefulness. This explanation applied not only to commodities produced by man, but also to free gifts of nature. The neoclassical economists – Menger, Jevons, Walras and their followers – belong to a 'school' of economics in the sense that they all attributed the phenomenon of value to utility.

To say that value theory since the time of Adam Smith has evolved through a series of logical refinements does not imply that the history of value theory has been ahistorical. While Smith intended his theory to apply at all times and places, he based his analysis on the social and economic conditions of eighteenth-century Britain: the legal institutions of private property and free contract; an extensive division of labour, money and credit; and three social classes corresponding to three factors of production – land, labour and capital. After Smith constructed the classical framework for value theory, however, new economic conditions did not influence the development of the subject much. Classical economists applied their theory to new facts, but no new facts can explain the change from classical to neoclassical economics. The old theory failed to explain old facts.

Smith addressed three distinct concepts of value, which his classical and neoclassical critics accepted and followed: (a) the origin of value, or why things have value in principle and in the abstract; (b) the measure of value, or the quantity by which values are reckoned; and (c) the regulation of value, or what determines the relative value or price of commodities. The brief survey in this chapter is organized around these three concepts, because they are the key to understanding the classical labour theory of value and, therefore, to distinguishing between classical and neoclassical economics (see Whitaker, 1968, p. 12). The classical economists needed to keep these concepts separate and distinct, because they sometimes explained each of them with a special theory. The early neoclassical economists employed the same concepts, but they did not always clearly separate them. They believed that utility provided a unified and consistent theory of them.

5.1 Origin of Value

The controversy over the origin of value is difficult for modern economists to understand, since it disappeared from the literature around the turn of the century. Modern theory treats only the measure and regulation of value. The origin of value has been called the 'ultimate nature' or 'essence' of value by Whitaker (1968, p. 13), the 'original source' or 'real foundation' of value by Ricardo (1951–73, vol. I, pp. 13, 25) and the 'substance' of value by Marx (1961, vol. I, p. 38). Why things have value may be considered a prescientific or philosophical question about the nature or cause of value. It does not ask what determines prices; it does not ask how values are measured; it asks why a thing should have the characteristic, quality or essence of value. The classical economists approached this question by asking what produces value over time; and they answered that labour produces value. The neoclassical economists asked why things have value at a point in time; and they answered that things have value if they are scarce in comparison with their usefulness. Both these theories existed before the time of Smith, though sometimes they were embedded in philosophical speculations.

John Locke (1960, p. 315), for example, who clearly influenced Smith, maintained that *'labour makes the far greatest part of the value* of things'; and he went on to assert that labour is the moral justification for private property and that title to property originates in the labour devoted to its production.

> Though the Earth, and all the inferior Creatures be common to all Men, yet every Man has a *Property* in his own *Person*. This no Body has any Right to but himself. The *Labour* of his Body, and the *Work* of his Hands, we may say, are properly his. Whatsoever then he removes out of the State that Nature hath provided, he hath mixed his *Labour* with, and joyned to it something that is his own, and thereby makes it his Property. (1960, pp. 305–6)

While this is an ethical theory, strictly speaking, and not an economic theory, it is an ethical theory about economic values, for economics is concerned with the exchange of property rights. Locke's ethical theory requires an economic theory, however, where labour and capital jointly produce commodities. If a man works for a master who pays him in cash or in kind, how much should his wages be? Where each man works in isolation on his own account, no ethical problem can arise about the distribution of income. But in civil society, where the labourer must share with the landlord and the master, both the ethical and economic questions about income distribution are present; and many economists have tried to answer both questions, sometimes unconsciously, as if they were one.

Two centuries later, J. B. Clark (1956) presented a neoclassical variation on Locke's ethical principle. Instead of restricting the moral justification of private property to labour alone, Clark extended it to all the factors of production, to capital as well as labour – land being treated as a species of capital. Any agent that does not receive the value of what it creates is a victim of institutional robbery, a victim of an institutional arrangement that threatens the moral foundation of society. Under a regime of perfect competition, Clark argues that every factor of production will receive its marginal product, the extra output produced by an extra unit of either labour or capital. Labour is not deprived of its product; it receives the value of what it creates. Capital is also productive, and it receives the value of what it creates. Thus, the law of nature is in harmony with the rule of capitalism.

Before the time of Adam Smith, the value of things was also commonly attributed to utility. Despite his labour theory of property rights, Locke (1960, p. 312) maintained that 'the intrinsick value of things . . . depends only on their usefulness to the Life of Man'. Hutcheson, Smith's professor of moral philosophy, argued that 'the prices of goods depend on these two jointly, the *demand* on account of some use or other which many desire, and the *difficulty* of acquiring, or cultivating for human use' (1973, p. 31). And Galiani, perhaps the most modern of Smith's contemporaries, thought that value depended on utility and scarcity, which he explained as follows: 'By utility I mean a thing's capacity to bring happiness. . . . By scarcity I mean the proportion between the quantity of a thing and the use made of it' (1924, pp. 284, 289). While this sounds like neoclassical economics, Galiani went on to state that 'labour . . . is the sole source of value' (1924, p. 290). This was the tradition in economics that Smith inherited; and, while many of his ideas can be found in the works of his predecessors, none of them presented a systematic theory of value. They often explained the origin of value with incompatible cost and utility theories.

Smith avoided this dilemma by abandoning utility as an explanation of value. He observed (1976, pp. 44–5) in his famous paradox of value that the word value has two different meanings: value in use and value in exchange. Value in use is an individual, introspective and subjective concept, which lies behind exchange; value in exchange is an objective and social phenomenon, which is observed in the market. This ancient distinction can be traced back to Aristotle, and Smith merely recited it to define the word value. After defining the word, he scarcely referred to value in use again, because it had no formal place in his theory. His main interest was value in exchange, which he attributed to labour, not utility. Jevons, however, took value in use to mean total utility, the foundation on which neoclassical value theory rests; and he related value in exchange to the 'final degree of utility' or the marginal utility that an individual expects to derive from a particular commodity.

Labour as the Origin of Value

Smith's theory of the origin of value is somewhat obscure and confusing, because it contains elements of Locke's earlier ethical theory and Marx's later labour theory of value. His main position comes in the first sentence of *The Wealth of Nations*.

The annual labour of every nation is the fund which originally supplies it with all the necessaries and conveniences of life which it annually consumes, and which consist always, either in the immediate produce of that labour, or in what is purchased with that produce from other nations. (1976, p. 10)

Labour is therefore both the original and the immediate source of all production in every nation; and the value created by labour provides the funds needed to purchase the produce of other nations. The omission of capital and land is striking. On occasion, however, Smith alludes to the 'spontaneous produce of uncultivated land' (1976, p. 334); and he often refers to the annual produce of society as the annual produce of land and labour (1976, p. 12 and elsewhere). Whether Smith conceived of land as a value-creating substance is doubtful; he apparently believed that in primeval times, before the accumulation of capital, land and labour were the only extant factors of production and that land was a free gift of nature. This follows Locke (1960, p. 312).

The value of all goods comes from labour: 'Labour was the first price, the original purchase-money that was paid for all things' (Smith, 1976, p. 48). And, as Smith taught in the first chapter of his book, the division of labour directly increases the wealth of nations. Capital indirectly extends the division of labour; but capital itself is simply so much crystallized or congealed labour-time, as Smith makes clear in his much disputed chapter on productive and unproductive labour (compare, for example, Blaug, 1978, Meek, 1956, and Myint, 1965). The analytic significance of productive labour in *The Wealth of Nations* arises from the fact that the stock of capital is a collection of physical things. The title of the chapter reveals his purpose: 'Of the Accumulation of Capital, or of Productive and Unproductive Labour'. Productive labour adds value to physical things that survive the period of production, whereas unproductive labour does not. Capital goods are a subset of the output of productive labour, which 'is, as it were, a certain quantity of labour stocked and stored up to be employed, if necessary, upon some other occasion' (Smith, 1976, p. 330). Capital is not an original factor of production; it is accumulated labour, following Locke (1960, p. 316).

Rent and profit are deductions from the whole produce of labour. In primitive society, before the accumulation of capital and the appropriation of land, neither profit nor rent can exist, so that 'the whole produce of labour belongs to the labourer' (Smith, 1976, p. 65). But, 'as soon as land becomes private property, the landlord demands a share of almost all the produce which the labourer can either raise, or collect from it. His rent makes the first deduction from the produce of the labour which is employed upon land' (Smith, 1976, p. 83). In agriculture, 'profit makes a second deduction from the produce of the labour which is employed upon land' (Smith, 1976, p. 83). Similarly, the master manufacturer who employs a crew of workmen 'shares in the produce of their labour, or in the value which it adds to the materials upon which it is bestowed' (Smith, 1976, p. 83). While in civil society 'the whole produce of labour does not always belong to the labourer' (Smith, 1976, p. 67), labour still produces all commodities; and labour is the sole value-creating substance, which is the fundamental proposition of Marxian economics.

In his theory of the incidence of taxation, Smith contended that a tax on rent or on profit would not affect production, provided that the tax on rent applied to all the alternative uses of land and that the tax on profit applied to only the interest on capital, excluding any premium that may be necessary to induce the capitalist to enter risky or disagreeable occupations (1976, p. 848). This is consistent with his theory of the origin of value, but not his theory of capital accumulation. Rent could be taxed away, because such a tax has no tendency to reduce the produce of land or 'to raise the price of that produce' (1976, p. 828). It falls wholly on the landlord. Similarly, profits on the stock of capital could be taxed away, but Smith recommended against such a tax on practical grounds. As a practical matter, capital is commonly concealed, so that a tax on capital would be difficult to assess. Furthermore, unlike land, capital can be removed from the country if taxes are too high (1976, pp. 847–9). If rent and pure profit were taxed away, labour would receive the value of what it creates in civil society just as it would in a Lockean state of nature.

Smith also has a pure labour-embodied theory of the *regulation* of value, i.e. a theory of relative prices, but it only applies to primitive societies. Where capital is accumulated and land is appropriated, Smith abandons labour as his explanation of the regulation of value, though he keeps it as his explanation of the origin of value. In civil society, the whole price of any commodity resolves itself into some one or another of three component parts of price: wages, profit and rent. This is commonly called a cost of production theory of value, and it will be discussed at greater length later.

Ricardo's theory of value is particularly difficult to follow, because he often failed to recognize that the origin, measure and regulation of value are separate concepts. After quoting Smith's example of the beaver and the deer, Ricardo offered this criticism:

> Adam Smith, who so accurately defined the original source of exchangeable value, and who was bound in consistency to maintain, that all things became more or less valuable in proportion as more or less labour was bestowed on their production, has himself erected another standard measure of value, and speaks of things being more or less

valuable, in proportion as they will exchange for more or less of this standard commodity. (1951–73, vol. I, pp. 13–14)

The 'original source of exchangeable value' refers to the origin of value; 'all things became more or less valuable in proportion as more or less labour was bestowed on their production' explains the regulation of value; and the 'standard measure' is a measure of value. Here, in a single sentence, Ricardo undeniably treats Smith's theories of the origin, measure and regulation of value as if they were a single concept. He misinterpreted Smith, because he frequently confused Smith's three concepts of value.

Even though Ricardo borrowed Smith's language, he did not present a metaphysical rationale for the origin of value. Ricardo wanted to explain the empirical phenomenon of value in exchange with a logically consistent theory that was based on the doctrine that labour 'is really the foundation of the exchangeable value of all things' (1951–73, vol. I, p. 13). His theory of the regulation of value is, therefore, an attempt to extend Smith's theory of the origin of value to a theory of price determination; but Ricardo did not treat labour as the only source of value. He attributed the whole value of any commodity to wages plus profits; yet, he asserted that the quantity of labour embodied in different commodities regulates or determines the relative value of them. Later he modified this thesis. In addition, he noted that, where commodities are naturally scarce or artificially monopolized, their values are unrelated to the labour embodied in them, so he treated them as exceptions to his labour theory of value and explained their value by scarcity, a theory which had never disappeared from the literature. Both his theories require a thing to be useful before it can be valuable: 'Utility then is not the measure of exchangeable value, though it is absolutely essential to it' (1951–73, vol. I, p. 11). The means of measurement of a phenomenon is, of course, distinct from its essential nature, just as a thermometer is distinct from heat. He meant that useful things have value if they are scarce or if they contain labour. 'Possessing utility, commodities derive their exchangeable value from two sources: from their scarcity, and from the quantity of labour required to obtain them' (1951–73, vol. I, p. 12). Ricardo realized that Smith failed to explain the value of naturally or artificially scarce commodities.

Marx followed Smith when he argued that labour is the sole value-creating substance; and he followed Ricardo when he attempted to explain the regulation of value by labour-time: 'The basis, the starting point for the physiology of the bourgeois system – for the understanding of its internal organic coherence and life process – is the determination of *value by labour-time*' (Marx, 1963–71, vol. II, p. 166). While commodities must be useful or possess utility before they can have value, their value is simply so much crystallized or congealed labour-time. For Marx, commodities are capital goods, which he divided into the means of production and the means of subsistence. The means of production are called *constant capital*, because they cannot create any new value. They merely transfer the labour-time that is already embodied in them to a new commodity as they are used up in production. Consumer goods provide the means of subsistence for the labourer; and he called them *variable capital*, because only labour can create new value (Marx, 1961, vol. I, pp. 208–9). Labour is the origin of value; or, in Marx's terminology, labour is the 'substance' of value (Marx, 1961, vol. I, pp. 35–83).

The classical economists approached the origin of value from the perspective of a Lockean state of nature, which Smith called the early and rude state of society. From this perspective, nature provides its bounty to man free of charge; it has no value. But the labour-time spent gathering or collecting the fruits of nature adds value to them; and the labour-time spent fashioning them into commodities creates more value. The value of anything is simply the labour-time spent producing it. The value of a capital good, therefore, consists of an accumulation of labour-time; and that value is transferred to new commodities as the capital good is used up in production. If, for example, a family gathers saplings and constructs a ladder to pick wild berries, those berries are worth the current labour-time spent harvesting them plus that part of the past labour-time which is embodied in the ladder and is used up while picking them. Since the value of the berries includes part of the labour-time previously spent constructing the ladder, the theory is backward looking: classical values have a history. The value of any commodity is its cost price, which consists of labour-values alone, so that supply rather than demand regulates values in a Lockean state of nature. However, the theory does not provide a satisfying account of things that are naturally scarce or artificially monopolized, which is why Ricardo treated them as exceptions to his theory; and the inclusion of rent and profit in prices complicates the analysis still further. The labour theory of the origin of value permitted Marx to turn classical economics into a powerful political indictment of capitalism, because it led him to the conclusion that capitalists acquire profits by exploiting labour.

Utility as the Origin of Value

The neoclassical concept of the origin of value has been clearly treated by Menger (1950, pp. 114–21). For Menger, value originates in the relation between man's need for various things and the quantities of them that are available. Men economize in the use of things that are scarce in relation to their usefulness, where usefulness is correlative with utility. The theory is forward looking. Economic goods are scarce compared with their prospective usefulness; non-economic goods are not. This defines the scope of econ-omics. As a man acquires additional units of an economic good, the usefulness of the last unit declines. This is the basic principle of marginal utility theory. Menger's definition of economics and his entire research programme are based on the idea of economizing in the use of things that are expected to be scarce relative to their usefulness.

Menger's theory was stated even more forcefully by von Wieser, who began his book *Natural Value* with a chapter on the origin of value, in which he asked: 'Whence do things get their value?' (1956, p. 3). Like his classical predecessors and his neoclassical contemporaries, von Wieser believed that the origin of value is the foundation of economic analysis. He criticized Smith for presenting two contradictory explanations of value, a 'philosophical' account based on labour and an 'empirical' account based on the cost of production. von Wieser (1956, p. xxx) advertised that he would 'explain reality by reality'; but he based his own account of the origin of value on utility, which is a theoretical construction, not an empirical phenomenon. Where goods are scarce, von Wieser (1956, p. xxxii) said, 'utility creates value'.

Walras and Jevons discussed the origin of value in much the same terms as Menger and von Wieser. In his lesson on the exposition and refutation of Adam Smith's and J. B. Say's doctrines of the origin of value in exchange, Walras credited the 'correct solution' to the problem of the origin of value to Burlamaqui and to A. A. Walras, his father, who traced the origin of value to *rareté*, the Walrasian term for marginal utility (1954, p. 201). In his section 'On the Origin of Value', Jevons belittled Ricardo's labour theory of value: but he began his own theory by declaring:

> Repeated reflection and inquiry have led me to the somewhat novel opinion, that *value depends entirely upon utility*. Prevailing opinions make labour rather than utility the origin of value; and there are even those who distinctly assert, that labour is the *cause* of value. (1871, p. 2)

Jevons also proclaimed that his value theory was derived from Bentham's utilitarianism, so that, at least for Jevons, the neoclassical theory of the origin of value has a philosophical basis.

Marshall defended Ricardo against the criticisms of Jevons, Walras, Menger and von Wieser by showing that their theory of the origin of value suffers from the same fault as the labour theory (but see von Böhm-Bawerk, 1962). Marshall (1961, vol. I, p. 816) wrote that Ricardo did not always 'state clearly, and in some cases he perhaps did not fully and clearly perceive how, in the problem of normal value, the various elements govern one another *mutually*, and not *successively* in a long chain of causation'. For Marshall, the value of anything is determined over a period of time by the interaction of a complex of forces; however, Ricardo's neoclassical critics attempted to disprove his doctrines by referring to 'the ultimate tendencies, the causes of causes, the *causæcausantes*, of the relations between cost of production and value, by means of arguments based on causes of temporary changes, and short-period fluctuations of value' (1961, vol. I, p. 821). For Marshall there was no such thing as a single cause of value, which Ricardo had recognized. Both utility and labour may be considered 'philosophical' explanations of the origin of value. Both theories are intended to explain the real foundation, ultimate nature, substance or essence of value; but value cannot be explained by a single cause.

The neoclassical economists approached the origin of value from the perspective of a Robinson Crusoe economy. the neoclassical equivalent of a Lockean state of nature. Crusoe knows his own wants; and he can look about his island and see what are available to satisfy them. The theory is individual, introspective and subjective. Given his technical knowledge, he can choose what to produce and how to allocate his resources to maximize his satisfaction. Crusoe is looking forward into the future and deciding what he needs, so that future demands rather than past costs regulate values in his economy: bygones are forever bygones. In a more complex society, however, no individual can know the wants, resources and technical possibilities of everyone else. Market prices tell each individual what is scarce relative to its usefulness; and market prices are determined by the interaction of many individuals: value in exchange is a social phenomenon.

5.2 Measure of Value

A measure of value is some commodity or bundle of commodities that serves as a standard for calculating the values of other commodities. One unit of the standard commodity is implicitly assigned a value of unity, and other commodities are said to be worth so many units of the standard commodity. A measure of value is necessary to compare and to aggregate heterogeneous and otherwise incommensurable things, such as Smith's beaver and deer. A measure of value can ignore metaphysical speculations about the origin of value, and it can be independent of any theory of the regulation of value. A measurement without theory, however, may be a meaningless tool, so that both the classical and neoclassical economists developed measures of value that are consistent with their theories of economic welfare.

Measuring value has several dimensions: static, interspacial, intertemporal, interpersonal. A static measure compares the values of commodities at a point in time. This occurs spontaneously in the simple act of exchanging one thing for another: the value of one thing is equal to the quantity of another thing that is given for it. An interspacial measure compares values between two points in space; and, like all measures of value, it requires at least one common denominator. An intertemporal measure compares the value of commodities at two different points in time. With exceptions such as loan contracts and futures markets, exchange between points in time is generally impossible; yet growth theory requires an intertemporal measure of value. Finally, if welfare economics is to measure the aggregate well-being of different individuals, it must make interpersonal comparisons. The classical and neoclassical schools considered all these measures of value.

Classical Measures of Value

Smith needed a *universal* measure of value to compare the wealth of nations at all times and places. While Ricardo and most economists after him denied that such a measure is possible, it was logically necessary for the task that Smith addressed in *The Wealth of Nations*. As the individuals in society and as the collection of goods and services differ from nation to nation and from age to age, it is necessary to make heroic assumptions to determine whether one nation is richer than another or whether one nation has grown over time.

Smith used three measures of value: money, corn and labour. Money is an exact measure of value in the instant that a transaction occurs, because equal values are given in exchange: the money itself and the money's worth in goods. Money is also a relatively stable measure of value over short periods of time, since new gold and silver mines, the source of the metallic money in Smith's day, are only discovered occasionally. Over long periods of time, corn is a more stable measure of value than money because of the limited capacity of the division of labour to increase the productivity of agriculture and to reduce the relative value of corn. Over short periods of time, however, good and bad harvests make the value of corn much less stable than money. Since neither money nor corn is a perfectly stable measure of value, Smith adopted labour as 'the only universal, as well as the only accurate measure of value, or the only standard by which we can compare the values of different commodities at all times and at all places' (1976, p. 54). Smith's theory of the measurement of value is therefore consistent with his theory of the origin of value; both are labour theories of value.

A standardized unit of labour sacrifice is Smith's universal measure of value. He assumed that a given sacrifice is equal in value to every labourer. Labour is assumed to be homogeneous, and the 'toil and trouble' of labour is assumed to be an absolute value that does not vary over time and space. Smith used this *universal measure of value* to compare the income per capita of different nations; but, to the great confusion of his readers, he ' constructed two different labour measures of value: the real price of labour and the real price of commodities.

First, the *real price of labour* is the subsistence of the labourer, which is intrinsically variable. Since the real wage of labour depends on the advancing, stationary or declining state of society, it is an approximate measure of economic welfare.

> In this popular sense, therefore, labour, like commodities, may be said to have a real and a nominal price. Its real price may be said to consist in the quantity of the necessaries and conveniencies of life which are given for it; its nominal price, in the quantity of money. (Smith, 1976, p. 51)

However, the subsistence of the labourer cannot measure the wealth of nations, because that wealth includes all the commodities produced in a nation; and those commodities are distributed to the landlord and the capitalist as well as the labourer. Second, the *real price of commodities* is the value of commodities measured by a standardized unit of labour-time. It measures the value of all commodities, along with wages, profit and rent (1976, pp. 51, 67–8).

Smith's theory of the real price of commodities is his labour-command theory of value, which is based on his theory of the origin of value, for it supposes that labour and labour alone produces all value. An individual who exchanges one commodity for another commodity is, according to Smith, exchanging one quantity of labour for another.

> The value of any commodity, therefore, to the person who possesses it, and who means not to use or consume it himself, but to exchange it for other commodities, is equal to the quantity of labour which it enables him to purchase or command. Labour, therefore, is the real measure of the exchangeable value of all commodities. (1976, p. 47)

Similarly, the wealth of any individual can be measured by the quantity of labour that he can command, which is the same thing as the total output that he can command. The quantity of labour and the produce of labour are the same thing, because labour is the sole value-creating substance (see Gladen, 1975, p. 511). The real price of commodities, Smith's labour-command measure of value, is output per unit of labour sacrifice.

Since one hour of work may involve unequal degrees of hardship and ingenuity, one hour of work may require a greater sacrifice than another and produce a greater value. What, then, is a unit of labour sacrifice? Smith (1976, pp. 48–9) maintained that hardship and ingenuity are compensated in the market, so that wages measure the sacrifice of labour. And later he wrote that labourers tend to avoid occupations which are under-compensated and to seek those which are overcompensated, so that 'the whole of the advantages and disadvantages of the different employments of labour and stock must, in the same neighbourhood, be either perfectly equal or continually tending to equality' (1976, p. 116). For the net advantages of different employments to be equal, labour must be perfectly homogeneous. Before labourers choose their occupations, they must possess the same preferences as well as the same innate abilities for different occupations; otherwise, the whole of the advantages and disadvantages of different occupations will not tend to equalize. The wealth of nations can therefore be measured and compared by the amount of output that a given type of labour – say, unskilled labour – can produce. Under these conditions, labour-time would be an objective measure of value.

Ricardo's criticism of Smith's measure of value arises from a misreading of *The Wealth of Nations*. He interpreted Smith's measure of value in the light of his own theory of the regulation of value, the central proposition of which is that the value of commodities is 'governed by the relative quantities of labour bestowed on their production' (1951–73, vol. I, p. 47). However, Ricardo divided price into two component parts: wages and profits. If the ratio of wages to profits is the same in every industry, the relative value of any two commodities will be the same as their relative wages. It will also be the same as their relative profits. Profits will only be on the same level, however, if the capital structure, i.e. the labour-to-capital ratio, is the same in every industry. If one industry is more capital intensive than the average, its profits will account for a greater than average proportion of its price, because competition assures that the rate of profit will be the same in all industries.

The lack of uniformity in the capital structure in different trades required Ricardo to introduce 'a considerable modification to the rule, which is of universal application when labour is almost exclusively employed in production; namely, that commodities never vary in value, unless a greater or less quantity of labour be bestowed on their production' (1951–73, vol. I, p. 38). If profits fall, the relative value of commodities produced in capital-intensive industries will fall, even though the quantity of labour embodied in their production remains constant. Ricardo, like Smith, ended up with a cost of production theory of the regulation of value.

Ricardo rejected Smith's theory of the measurement of value on the grounds that there is no commodity 'which is not subject to require more or less labour for its production' (1951–73, vol. I, p. 44). For Ricardo, a perfect measure of value would always have the same quantity of labour embodied in it; but, even if there were such a commodity, say corn, its value would change compared with the value of all other commodities that did not have the same capital structure whenever the ratio of wages to profits changed. But Smith did not say that the labour embodied in the production of any commodity is perfectly constant. Neither gold nor corn is a perfect measure of value; labour sacrifice, the 'toil and trouble' of labour, is Smith's universal measure. He rendered the sacrifice of labour constant by assumption.

Ricardo clearly saw the difficulty of measuring values in a changing economy, even though he misinterpreted Smith. After struggling with the problem for several years, he confessed that 'there is no such thing in nature as a perfect measure of value' (1951–73, vol. IV, p. 404). For the sake of exposition, Ricardo used gold as his measure of value on the supposition that it is produced with an average capital structure. For simplicity, Marx (1961, vol. I, p. 94) used gold, too. All this was the focus of Sraffa (1960).

Neoclassical Measures of Value

In the neoclassical literature, the measure of value has been most clearly treated by Walras in his *Elements of Pure Economics* (1954). Walras called his measure of value a *numéraire*. A *numéraire* is that commodity by which the values of other commodities are reckoned. In a state of general equilibrium, where the relative values of all commodities are already established, any commodity can be selected to serve as the *numéraire*. The price of any other commodity is measured by the number of units of the *numéraire* that must be given in exchange for it. The price of the *numéraire* itself is unity.

Walras introduced the concept of the *numéraire* to simplify his exposition. Prices are simply relative values; and the exchange rate between any two commodities can be expressed by two prices: the price of A in terms of B or the price of B in terms of A, for example. Instead of treating the relative value of each commodity in terms of every other, it is sufficient to express the price of each commodity in terms of the *numéraire*. Since all prices are expressed in terms of the *numéraire*, values can be aggregated to measure the wealth of a nation at a given point in time.

Utility measures the welfare of each individual considered separately, but utility cannot directly measure the welfare of society, because in the neoclassical theory the utilities that individuals derive from their activities are considered to be incommensurable (on utility measurement see Majumdar, 1966). In a state of general equilibrium, however, all consumers buy and sell at the same prices; and , when they maximize their total utility, the ratio of the marginal utilities of any two commodities will be equal to the ratio of their prices for all consumers, where the prices of all commodities are expressed in terms of the *numéraire*. The *numéraire* is an indirect measure of utility.

The *numéraire* is an unambiguous measure of economic welfare in a given state of general equilibrium for a single economy, but it cannot compare two different states of equilibrium. It cannot compare two different societies, because the preferences of consumers, the quantities consumed and the prices differ from society to society; and it cannot compare two different states of equilibrium for a single economy, because relative prices differ from one equilibrium to another. If prices change, every consumer may change the quantity of every commodity purchased or sold, so that the welfare of everyone may be altered; and, when relative prices change, it is not possible to determine whether the value of the *numéraire* or the value of other commodities has changed. The Walrasian measure of value is only valid at a static point of equilibrium. It cannot compare the wealth of nations.

Pareto, who succeeded Walras to the chair in economics at the University of Lausanne, developed a measure of value that could compare two different states of equilibrium for one society. It employs the concept of the *Pareto optimum*, a state of equilibrium in which no one can improve his position without reducing the well-being of someone else. Pareto's optimal points are not comparable. But, if it were possible to improve the position of some consumers without decreasing the economic welfare of anyone else, then, wrote Pareto (1971, p. 451), 'it is obvious that the new position is more advantageous'. The new position is said to be Pareto superior to the old. Modern welfare economics employs this concept to compare social alternatives.

Marshall used money as his measuring rod of economic activity, but in a restricted way. He analysed how a change in the price of one commodity, considered in isolation from other commodities, would affect supply and demand; and he explained how such a change in price would affect the economic welfare of buyers and sellers. This is a partial equilibrium analysis, as opposed to the general equilibrium analysis of Walras, because it treats only a single market; and it is an exercise in comparative statics, because it compares one static point with another.

Marshall intended his theory of consumer demand to approximate observed reality; and he maintained that it would be a good approximation where a consumer's 'expenditure on any one thing, as, for instance, tea, is only a small part of his whole expenditure' (1961, vol. I, p. 842). Where this condition obtains, it would be legitimate to 'neglect possible changes in the general purchasing power of money' (1961, vol. I, p. 62). 'If a change in the price of one commodity does not affect real income, then the marginal utility of income may be considered constant. This constancy assumption simplified Marshall's derivation of the individual demand curve and his measure of consumer's surplus.

The marginal utility of each commodity considered separately diminishes, and the individual maximizes total utility where the last penny spent on each line of expenditure produces the same benefit. In other words, if a consumer gained more utility from the last penny spent on ale than on lager, he would buy more ale and less lager until he could no longer improve his position. Since marginal utility of the last penny spent is assumed to be constant, utilities can be converted into prices by the constant marginal utility of money. The individual's demand curve for a commodity is therefore simply a transformation of his marginal utility curve; and it is downward sloping because of the principle of diminishing marginal utility.

Consumer's surplus is Marshall's measure of economic welfare. An individual demand curve shows the highest price that a person would be willing to pay for each quantity of a commodity; and the price that is actually paid measures the cost of alternative commodities forgone. The consumer's surplus is 'the excess of the price which he would be willing to pay rather than go without a thing, over that which he actually does pay' (1961, vol. I, p. 124). If the price of a commodity increases, owing to a tax, for example, the consumer suffers a loss in economic welfare that can be measured in terms of money (see Hicks, 1939).

The economic welfare of society is not so easily measured, however, because it requires comparing the well-being of heterogeneous individuals. To begin with, Marshall proposed treating every individual the same; for 'it would naturally be assumed that a shilling's worth of gratification to one Englishman might be taken as equivalent with a shilling's worth to another' (1961, vol. I, p. 130). But Marshall knew that this was not generally true. Some people may be more sensitive and some may be richer than others, so that money would not be a uniform measuring rod of economic welfare. Yet, if consumers as a group could gain more by a reduction in price than producers would lose and 'if a general agreement could be obtained among consumers, terms might be arranged which would make such an action amply remunerative to the producers, at the same time that they left a large balance of advantage to the consumers' (1961, vol. I, p. 472). This is the compensation principle; and it employs the equivalent of Pareto's criterion for an improvement in social welfare, which Marshall stated, but did not pursue, before Pareto began to write on economics.

Marshall's measure of consumer's surplus and Pareto's optimum are not ethically neutral. They suppose that the free and independent individual is the best judge of his own economic welfare; and they measure welfare by the economic values or wealth possessed by the individual, who is assumed to be entirely self-interested without any regard for the well-being of other individuals. An unambiguous gain in welfare is said to occur if some individuals become wealthier while no one else becomes poorer. Since the analysis of Pareto, in particular, precludes interpersonal comparisons of utility, it cannot evaluate policies that redistribute income and wealth; it is a conservative guide to the status quo. Where Marshall and Pigou consider treating individuals as if they were comparable and homogeneous, they can analyse the effect of policies that redistribute income; they have a criterion to determine what is just, but the analysis is still based on the possessions of rational, free, independent and selfish individuals.

5.3 Regulation of Value

The regulation of value is usually called price theory or microeconomics; it explains what determines the relative value of different commodities – why water is ordinarily cheap and diamonds dear, for example. The classical economists began their theory with the notion that labour is the cause of value; but their logic sooner or later led them to the conclusion that, where competition prevails, the value of different commodities depends on their cost of production. The neoclassical economists arrived at much the same conclusion when they discussed the cost of production; but they began their theory with an explanation of how individuals economize in the use of scarce resources, which also allowed them to explain the value of commodities that cost nothing to produce. The mainstream of both classical and neoclassical economics viewed the market as being governed by competition, monopoly being treated as a special topic. This section presents how a few of the most influential economists explained competitive prices.

Classical Cost of Production Theories

The classical theory of the regulation of value has a common starting point: Smith's statement that in primitive society 'the proportion between the quantities of labour necessary for acquiring different objects seems to be the only circumstance which can afford any rule for exchanging them for one another' (1976, p. 65). In civil society, however, where capital has been accumulated and land appropriated, profit and rent are component parts of price; and the price of each commodity tends to equal its cost of production. This raises two interrelated questions, which Smith treated separately: (a) what determines the natural price of commodities, and (b) what determines the natural rates of wages, profit and rent.

First, Smith began his explanation of what determines the natural price of a commodity on the supposition that the ordinary or average rates of wages, profit and rent that prevail at any time or place are their natural rates. He then defined the following terms: (a) the *natural price* of a commodity is its cost of production at the natural rates of wages, profit and rent; (b) the *effectual demand* for a commodity is the quantity demanded at its natural price; and (c) the *market price* is the price at which the commodity actually sells. He then went on to explain how competition tends to equate the market price with the natural price. On the one hand, 'when the quantity of any commodity which is brought to market falls short of the effectual demand, . . . the market price will rise more or less above the natural price' (1976, pp. 73–4) as buyers bid up the price. Since a deficient supply raises the price, the demand curve must be downward sloping. As the price rises, some of the resource owners will be paid above their natural rates, so that it will be in their interest to increase the quantity produced, which will tend to depress the market price. On the other hand, 'when the quantity brought to market exceeds the effectual demand, . . . the market price will sink more or less below the natural price' (1976, p. 74) as sellers compete against each other. As the price falls, some of the factors of production will earn less than their natural rates; and they will tend to reduce the quantity supplied, which will raise the market price toward the natural price. 'The natural price, therefore, is, as it were, the central price, to which the prices of all commodities are continually gravitating' (1976, p. 75). It is what Marshall called the long-run equilibrium price.

Second, the proportions of land, labour and capital that are employed in a country ultimately determine the natural rates of wages, profit and rent. As a country progresses, capital accumulates and population grows, while land is immutable, so that factor proportions change. Therefore the natural rates of wages, profit and rent also tend to change, which causes the relative value of commodities that are produced with different proportions of land, labour and capital to vary.

The natural rate of wages depends on the demand for labour and the size of the population. The demand for labour consists of a wages fund, which is previously accumulated from past production and is annually renewed from current production. Smith defined the wages fund as the excess of funds that is over and above the personal needs of the employers of labour. The wages fund is a portion of the capital stock of the nation, and it grows as capital accumulates: 'The demand for those who live by wages, therefore, naturally increases with the increase of national wealth, and cannot possibly increase without it' (1976, p. 87). The accumulation of capital per capita bids up the wage of labour, which encourages the growth of the population: 'The liberal reward of labour, therefore, as it is the effect of increasing wealth, so it is the cause of increasing population' (1976, p. 99). In the progressive state of society, wages are sufficiently high to increase the size of the population and the supply of labour. If capital accumulates more rapidly than population grows, the natural rate of wages tends to rise; but, if the accumulation of capital should cease, population would continue to expand until wages fell to subsistence, at which point population growth would stop and society would be in the stationary state. Society would fall into a declining state, if anything should destroy a part of the capital stock and push wages below subsistence, causing population to decline. The natural rate of wages varies with the growth of the wages fund in comparison with the population. This is Smith's statement of the population principle, which Malthus (1986) refined.

The natural rate of profit declines as the stock of capital in any nation accumulates, in part because wages rise and depress profits and in part because markets become more competitive as capital accumulates. Where capital is accumulating more rapidly than population is growing, wages tend to rise and profits fall, as each labourer is more abundantly equipped with capital. The rate of profit will continue to fall as capital accumulates until the stationary state arrives, when profits will be 'so low as to render it impossible for any but the very wealthiest people to live upon the interest of their money' (Smith, 1976, p. 113). In the stationary state, capital accumulation stops because profits are not sufficiently high to increase the supply of capital. In the declining state, as wages fall below subsistence, the rate of profit rises.

Labour and capital are homogeneous before they are committed to particular trades, and they are virtually unlimited in quantity as society progresses. All labourers are assumed by Smith to have the same preferences as well as the same innate abilities before they choose their occupations, as has already been discussed, so that the real or imaginary circumstances that may differentiate particular trades tend to be compensated in the market. Labourers tend to enter the more advantageous and avoid the less advantageous occupations until all occupations possess the same net advantages. Similarly, before a capitalist invests his funds in one project or another, he will weigh the net advantages of various alternatives and choose the most advantageous. In equilibrium, competition tends to establish a uniform rate of profit in all industries subject to such adjustments as may be necessary to reflect their riskiness or disagreeableness. Since labour and capital are assumed to be homogeneous at all times and places, Smith (1976, pp. 158–9) concluded that relative wages and relative profits in different trades are not much affected by the progress of society.

The rent of land is paid for the use of the free gifts of nature, and those free gifts are inherently heterogeneous and limited in quantity. Rent, therefore, is partly determined by the fertility or locality of a tract of land and partly determined by the advancing, stationary or declining state of society. As society progresses, the natural rent of land is price determined, not price determining (1976, p. 162). As population grows and the demand for food increases, land becomes increasingly scarce, and the rent of land naturally tends to rise.

In a civilized country, land devoted to the production of food always affords a rent, though other land may not. Forest land, for example, will only yield a rent when wood becomes scarce: 'The scarcity of wood then raises its price' (Smith, 1976, p. 183). As society progresses and the demand for food increases, corn land must compete with pasture land and pasture land with forest land. A man will not plant a forest unless his harvest of trees promises him as large a rent as the cattle and corn he must forgo. The alternative uses of land make rent a cost of production in each alternative use, not only to the farmer, but also to the society (see Knight, 1965, p. 150). If the market price of any ordinary crop should fall below its natural price and depress the rent of the land below its natural rate, 'the interest of the landlords will immediately prompt them to withdraw a part of their land' (Smith, 1976, p. 75). A tax on the rent of a particular type of land, such as a tax on barley land (Smith, 1976, pp. 892–3), will tend to reallocate resources, whereas a general tax on the rent of land in every alternative use will not affect production. Smith did not, perhaps, fully and distinctly formulate his theory of rent, for Ricardo and others apparently did not understand it.

Smith's theory of the regulation of value is incompatible with his theories of the origin and measure of value. If the wood in a virgin forest has value, that value cannot logically be attributed to labour. Labour cannot be the origin of its value, and its real price cannot be measured by the labour embodied in it. Ricardo, Marx and many others reproached Smith for his logical inconsistencies.

Ricardo began his theory of value on the classical theme that labour is the 'foundation' of value, but he immediately introduced a series of modifications that led him to a cost of production theory. He stated that the labour embodied in a commodity does not create the whole value of it. Prices are proportional to, but less than, the wages bill. This formulation obliged him to clarify the following points: (a) how wages measure the quantity of labour; (b) whether the capital stock is simply canned labour; (c) how profits affect prices; and (d) whether rent affects prices (for further discussion of Ricardo's theory of value see Knight, 1956; Meek, 1956; Stigler, 1965; Blaug, 1978; and Hollander, 1979).

Ricardo accepted Smith's conclusion that relative wages are not much affected by the progress of society; but he did not mention Smith's assumption that, before labourers enter various occupations, they may be treated as if they were homogeneous. Unless labour is homogeneous, no correspondence need exist between the quantities of labour employed in dissimilar occupations and the wages that are paid. Competition will not tend to equalize the net advantages of occupations that require special natural talents – the occupations of a baritone and a ballerina, for example. Since Ricardo (1951–73, vol. I, p. 22) quoted Smith's conclusion, it may seem reasonable to infer that he accepted his assumption, but Ricardo presented another argument. Where relative wages are constant, any *change* in the quantity of labour bestowed on the production of a commodity will cause a *change* in its value; however, such a change in values need not be proportionate to the change in the employment of any particular type of labour, unless different types of labour are employed in fixed proportions.

The value of capital goods is determined in precisely the same manner as the value of all other commodities; and the cost of production of any commodity includes the value of the capital goods that are used up in its production. In commenting on Smith's example of the beaver and the deer, Ricardo observed:

> Without some weapon, neither the beaver nor the deer could be destroyed, and therefore the value of these animals would be regulated, not solely by the time and labour necessary to their destruction, but also by the time and labour necessary for providing the hunter's capital, the weapon, by the aid of which their destruction was effected. (1951–73, vol. I, p. 23)

While Ricardo's language may suggest that capital goods are simply so much crystallized or congealed labour-time, he included both wages and profits in the cost of production of commodities.

Ricardo contended that profits were 'only a just compensation for the time' (1951–73, vol. I, p. 37) during which capital is employed, so that profits on capital accrue like compound interest on a principal sum of money; and he explained that profits motivate men to allocate their capital among its alternative uses (1951–73, vol. I, pp. 88–9).

If the rate of profit tends to equality in all the alternative uses of capital, values will only be proportionate to the wages bill if every industry has the same capital structure, as has already been discussed. One commodity would cost more to produce than another, even though the same quantities of labour were directly and indirectly expended on their production, if one required a more durable plant or a longer time to produce than the other. Their absolute values would differ, as, for example, the value of wine is typically greater when it is well aged than when it is young. But Ricardo did not assign much importance to the absolute values of particular commodities; he gave more emphasis to *changes* in relative values as society progresses. For Ricardo, as for Smith, relative values change as society progresses, because factor proportions and therefore factor prices change. If profits fall relative to the wages as society progresses, commodities produced in capital-intensive industries will fall in value relative to commodities produced in labour-intensive industries.

For Ricardo, rent is not a cost of production. In the strictest sense of the term, he defined rent to be 'that portion of the produce of the earth, which is paid to the landlord for the use of the original and indestructible powers of the soil' (1951–73, vol. I, p. 67). Ricardo's theory of rent rests on two criteria: the heterogeneity and the scarcity of land. The heterogeneity of land generates a *differential rent*. If land were of three qualities – qualities no. 1, no. 2 and no. 3, to use Ricardo's example – and if the produce of the land decreased as successive qualities of land were brought into production, land no. 1 would earn a rent as soon as land no. 2 was brought into production. Unless people were willing to pay the wages and profits that must be paid to bring land no. 2 into production, corn would not be grown on that land. Since no. 1 produces a surplus above the expenses incurred on no. 2, the landlord can claim that surplus as a rent for the use of his higher quality land. But land no. 2 would never be brought into production unless no. 1 were scarce. If land of the first quality were scarce, it would afford a rent as soon as the demand for it exceeded the available quantity, even though other lands were too poor to farm. This is called a *scarcity rent*. Ricardo recognized this possibility when he wrote that 'in such a case, capital will be preferably employed on the old land, and will equally create a rent; for rent is always the difference between the produce obtained by the employment of two equal quantities of capital and labour' (1951–73, vol. I, p. 71). The rent of land arises from the law of diminishing returns: as successive doses of labour plus capital are applied to a fixed quantity of land, output increases at a diminishing rate. The cost of production rises on the margin of cultivation as society progresses, which raises the price of corn. Land on the margin of cultivation is called *no-rent land*, because wages and profits exhaust the whole value of the product. On the extensive margin of new land and on the intensive margin of old land, rent is not a cost of production; and Ricardo did not include it as a component part of price.

Wages plus profits determine Ricardian values; and the Malthusian population principle determines wages, so that profits are a residual. As capital accumulates, the market rate of wages tends to rise above subsistence and to increase the population; but, for Malthus and Ricardo, the response of population to an increase in wages is sufficiently rapid that wages tend to subsistence, where the level of subsistence depends on the customary or habitual standard of living that exists in any society. If wages are at subsistence, profits must fall as society progresses, because the extra output that an extra dose of labour plus capital can produce from a given amount of land diminishes. As capital accumulates, population grows and the price of corn rises on the margin of cultivation. Ricardo advocated repealing the Corn Laws that restricted the importation of corn, the subsistence of labour, because they artificially inflated the price of corn and raised the subsistence wage of labour in terms of Ricardo's invariable measure of value. This reduced the rate of profit, discouraged the accumulation of capital and retarded the progress of society.

Marx (1963–71, vol. II, p. 165) accused Smith of moving 'with great naïveté in a perpetual contradiction'. On the one hand, Smith explained the 'esoteric' nature of bourgeois society – labour as the origin of value. On the other hand, he explained the 'exoteric' nature of capitalism as seen by the unscientific observer – cost as the regulator of value.

> One of these conceptions fathoms the inner connection, the physiology, so to speak, of the bourgeois system, whereas the other takes the external phenomena of life, as they seem and appear and merely describes, catalogues, recounts and arranges them under formal definitions. (1963–71, vol. II, p. 165)

Marx accepted as self-evident the proposition that labour is the substance of value, that only labour produces value; and he sought to explain how the exploitation of labour leads to capital accumulation and economic growth – the process of capitalist development. He praised Ricardo for his contribution to the science; but, like Ricardo, logical consistency required him to introduce a considerable modification to his theory.

Marx presented a pure labour-embodied theory of value in volume I of *Capital*. The whole value of every commodity, including labour itself, is produced by labour. The wages of different types of labour are determined by the labour power that is necessary to raise and train them. The food, the clothing and the housing – in short, the subsistence of the labourer – all count as so much labour. Skilled labour, therefore, can be counted as so many units of unskilled labour; and labour may be considered a homogeneous aggregate. Values are determined by the quantity of labour that is socially necessary to produce different commodities, where what is socially necessary is simply the average labour-time that is used up in the production of a commodity in a particular industry in a given society.

Marx divided the whole value of any commodity into three parts: (a) the *variable capital* expended on the subsistence of the labourer; (b) the labour value of the *constant capital*, the means of production, used up in production; and (c) the *surplus value* expropriated by the capitalist. Surplus value arises because the capitalist buys labour power at its value in exchange, at the value of the labour embodied in it; but he acquires the right to use labour for the whole working day, which Marx called the value in use of labour. If a labourer takes six hours in a ten-hour day to reproduce the value of his subsistence, the capitalist acquires a surplus value that is worth four hours of production. Since only active living labour can create new value, surplus value arises entirely from the employment of variable capital; and the rate of surplus value, the ratio of surplus value to variable capital, is an exact expression for the degree of exploitation of labour, which is governed by the class struggle between labour and capital.

The capitalist considers surplus value to be his profit; and he allocates his total capital, variable plus constant capital, to maximize his profits. Competition tends to produce a uniform rate of profit in all industries as capital moves from low- to high-profit industries. If the capital structure, which Marx called the organic composition of capital, is everywhere the same and if the rate of surplus value is also the same in every industry, then market prices are proportional to the labour embodied in production, as in Ricardo's theory. They are proportional to the variable capital plus the constant capital used up in production. But, if the capital structure is not the same in every industry, market prices will exceed labour values in those industries which are relatively intensive in the use of constant capital. This theoretical possibility, which is the empirical reality, required Marx to introduce his own considerable modification to his labour theory of value in volume III of *Capital* when he discussed the so-called transformation problem. He argued that competition apportions the mass of surplus value created in all the different spheres of production to establish a uniform rate of profit (1961, vol. III, pp. 155–8). After values are transformed, market prices no longer equal Marxian values; they are roughly equivalent to Ricardo's cost of production prices (on the transformation problem, see Meek 1977; Pasinetti, 1977; and Steedman, 1981).

Not only does the classical theory of the regulation of value explain what determines relative prices at a point in time, but it also explains the forces of motion that cause relative values and factor incomes to change over time. For Smith, 'the desire of bettering our condition' (1976, p. 341) drives the engine of economic progress. As capital accumulates and population grows, factor proportions change, which changes factor incomes and relative prices. Ricardo took his theory from Smith; Marx from Ricardo. Marx explained how capital accumulation leads to a falling rate of profit and the immiseration of labour; but his discussion of the historical tendencies of capitalism goes well beyond his theory of value. The classical economists needed a theory of value to explain the historical development of society.

Neoclassical Price Theories

Neoclassical price theory started with the marginal revolution of the 1870s, when Jevons, Menger and Walras independently formulated the marginal utility theory. All three of the founders of neoclassical price theory approached the subject from different perspectives: Jevons developed the calculus of pleasure and pain as a mathematical science; Menger treated the allocation for scarce resources among alternative uses as the logic of choice; and Walras presented the general equilibrium for an economy as a system of simultaneous equations. In England, Jevons's *Theory of Political Economy* soon gave way to Marshall's *Principles*, which dominated economics, at least in the English-speaking world, for nearly half a century; on the continent, Menger founded the Austrian School, which included von Böhm-Bawerk, von Wieser and many others, while Walras established the School of Lausanne, which included Pareto, Barone and others. Since a short review cannot cover the whole of neoclassical price theory, two of the most important contributions will be contrasted: the partial equilibrium theory of Marshall and the general equilibrium theory of Walras.

Walras addressed the purely theoretical question of what conditions are logically necessary for the determination of equilibrium simultaneously in all markets at a point in time, whereas Marshall investigated the more practical question of how a single market adjusts to equilibrium over time. Like the classical economists, Marshall wanted to explain the forces of motion that cause change vided time. He divided time into three periods: the temporary period, when the stock of goods on hand in a single market limits supply; the short period, when the existing productive capacity in an industry limits supply; and the long period, when only the consumer preferences, the resources and the technology of a given economy limit the supply for any one industry. He assumed that consumer demand is given over all three periods.

In the temporary period, buyers come to market with a sum of money and with expectations about the future course of prices. They expect to acquire a commodity at a price that will give them more utility than the alternatives on which they could spend their money. Sellers come to market with a given stock of a commodity, which they expect to sell at a price that will increase their utility. If the commodity is durable, like corn, sellers can withdraw from the market until another day; but, if it is perishable, like fish, consuming it is the only rational alternative to selling it. In the temporary period, cost is not relevant; utility theory explains the regulation of prices.

Buyers and sellers are in disequilibrium at the start of the market day, because they expect to gain from trade. Both buyers and sellers can alter the market price by 'waiting'. If the price is too high, buyers will wait; and 'by waiting they help to bring the price down' (Marshall, 1961, vol. I, p. 333). If the price is too low, sellers will wait and 'by waiting help to bring the price up' (Marshall, 1961, vol. I, p. 333). Prices adjust to the available quantity in the temporary period: however, transactions take place at various prices during the day, so that buyers and sellers may experience windfall gains or losses as the price changes, which could cause them to revise their plans and alter the true equilibrium price. Marshall tried to avoid this logical problem by supposing that the marginal utility of money income is constant, i.e. by supposing that windfall gains and losses do not affect the real income of traders. At the end of the day, both buyers and sellers are in equilibrium in the sense that neither can gain from further transactions. However realistic it may be to allow trading at disequilibrium prices, it renders the whole analysis logically imprecise, because Marshall cannot explain the prices at which transactions actually occur.

In the short run, the productive capacity of the firm and the industry restrict production; and price determines the most profitable rate of capacity utilization. The 'prime' cost of a unit of business consists of the labour and materials that are used in production, and it necessarily increases as production increases because of the law of diminishing returns, whereas the 'supplementary' cost of the buildings, machinery and permanent staff are invariable over a short period of time. The businessman maximizes profits by setting production at the point where the prime cost of the last unit of production, i.e. the marginal cost of production, equals the price that he expects to receive: quantity adjusts to price. As the price rises, production increases, so that the short-run supply curve is upward sloping for the firm and in the market. The intersection of the market supply and demand curves determines the price.

The utility-maximizing behaviour of labourers gives the supply of labour, while decisions that were made in the past fix the structures, equipment and other resources which are available for production. The profit-maximizing behaviour of the businessman leads the firm to employ labour up to the point where it receives the value of its marginal product, but the owners of the business obtain a quasi-rent that, except by coincidence, is unrelated to the original cost of their investment, so that the stock of capital is in disequilibrium. In the short run, prices are partly governed by labour cost and partly by consumer demand.

The Marshallian long run is a planning period during which all inputs are variable. Traders are looking forward into a logical future where consumer demand, factor supply and production technology are hypothetically held constant. Firms adjust their productive capacity to the prices that they expect to prevail in the long run. The production technology stipulates that each firm experiences increasing returns to scale, so that average cost falls as the firm grows. Since the largest firm will have the lowest cost, it will tend to become a monopoly unless something retards its growth. Marshall argued that cost rises as the entrepreneur grows old, which checks the growth of the firm (for criticism, see Sraffa, 1926 and Robbins, 1928).

In the long run, the owners of capital tend to receive the market rate of interest. If profits in any market exceed the rate of interest, new businesses will enter, which tends to depress the price: and, if profits fall below the rate of interest, firms withdraw and prices rise. In the long run, the price of the product must cover the real sacrifice of labour and the 'waiting' of savers; otherwise, neither labour nor capital will be forthcoming. Therefore the price tends to equal the cost of production, as the classical economists maintained; but, before the long run arrives, unforeseen events disturb the market, so that, for Marshall, the capital stock is always in disequilibrium.

Marshall was a strong defender of the received tradition in economics, especially the work of J. S. Mill; and he intended his theory of value to reconcile the classical cost of production theory with the neoclassical utility theory and to show how utility and cost play different roles in the regulation of value. Utility receives top billing in the temporary period; real cost in the long run. Each period begins in a state of disequilibrium, and Marshall tells how market forces tend to establish equilibrium over time. His theory has frequently been criticized, however, on grounds of logical consistency.

The general equilibrium theory of Walras required him to stress conceptual clarity and logical rigour more than any previous economist, because he wanted to show what could and what could not be proven mathematically. His method occasionally required him to invent artificial conditions and institutions, such as equilibrium at a point in time and auction markets for all commodities, to make his theory mathematically tractable. While Walras frequently asserted theorems that he could not prove, his system of simultaneous equations laid the foundation for much of modern value theory, as in the work of Debreu (1959).

A Walrasian economy comprises (a) consumers with heterogeneous preferences, (b) initial endowments of commodities that are arbitrarily distributed among consumers and (c) a production technology that specifies how various inputs can produce various outputs. The economy is coordinated by a hypothetical auctioneer, who establishes equilibrium prices where the quantity demanded equals the quantity offered for every commodity. Walras viewed equilibrium as the solution to a system of simultaneous equations at a point in time, which he examined under three different sets of initial conditions: general equilibrium in exchange without production, general equilibrium in exchange with production, and general equilibrium in exchange with production and capital accumulation.

His theory of general equilibrium in exchange without production corresponds to Marshall's temporary period, where costs are irrelevant and where relative prices are governed by the utility-maximizing decisions of the traders; and, like Smith's analysis of market prices, it proceeds in terms of excess supplies and excess demands. Prices clear the market for the existing quantities of commodities. The distinction between the Marshallian and Walrasian stability conditions rests, at least in part, on the element of time. Marshall (1961, vol. I, pp. 345–6) stated his stability conditions in the context where time permits the 'scale of production' to adjust to expected prices. Walras's (1954, pp. 108–13) conditions apply to general equilibrium in exchange without production, so that prices adjust to clear the market for predetermined quantities. Like Smith and Marshall, Walras did not give a logically rigorous explanation of how market forces establish equilibrium prices in a pure exchange economy; he let arbitrage transactions determine prices without the aid of an auctioneer, which he introduced somewhat later. Arbitrage entails 'false trading', trading at disequilibrium prices.

In his theory of production, the consumer begins with an arbitrary and unexplained endowment of commodities consisting of both consumer goods and producer goods. The marginal utility of each commodity considered separately diminishes as the consumer acquires a greater quantity of it. Since the preferences of consumers are subjective, individual and heterogeneous, each consumer has distinctive marginal utility functions or curves. Once prices have been set, the consumer can exchange some of his initial endowments for other commodities that yield a greater degree of utility. Some labour-time may be traded for apples, for example, and some land may be rented for oranges. All exchanges are by barter, for the economy has no money in the sense of a medium of exchange. In equilibrium, the consumer maximizes total utility, or buys those commodities which he most prefers, subject to the constraint of his initial endowment. The total purchases of each consumer are equal in value to his total sales or market income.

The initial endowments of the economy are heterogeneous; they include many kinds of land, labour and capital goods. Consumers can either sell the services of their factors of production or use them as consumer goods. A farmer, for example, implicitly sells part of his land, labour and capital to himself as an entrepreneur to grow his crops and reserves part of his labour-time for leisure, part of his land for his homestead and part of his capital goods for his household. In a static economy, markets exist for only the services of the factors of production, not the factors of production themselves. Neither consumers nor producers need to buy land or capital goods, since they can procure as much of the services of the factors of production as they can afford.

Entrepreneurs rent land, hire labour and lease capital goods from consumers to make new goods and services, which they then sell to consumers. The production technology gives the blueprints for producing new commodities. Walras first represented the production function for each commodity by an equation of fixed coefficients, which specified how much of each factor service is needed to produce one unit of output. Later he incorporated the marginal productivity theory into his system of equations to allow for diminishing returns, factor substitution and cost minimization. Entrepreneurs maximize profits by adjusting output to the auctioneer's prices, but entrepreneurial profits only exist in a state of disequilibrium. In equilibrium, competition eliminates these profits, so that entrepreneurs receive income from their initial endowments like other consumers.

Walras's theory of production does not really correspond to Marshall's short run or long run. It does not correspond to his short run, because the entrepreneur can vary all the inputs that he employs; and it does not correspond to the long run, because the predetermined collection of heterogeneous capital goods may not be optimal in view of the state of technical knowledge, consumer preferences and other resources. In his theory of capital accumulation, new capital goods are produced; but the production of new capital goods belongs to his theory of economic growth. It explains the determination of the rate of interest in the progressive state of society and corresponds to the growth theories of Smith and Ricardo. Unlike Smith and Ricardo, however, Walras stops his theory of accumulation at the point where the new capital goods are produced, but before they enter production, so his theory remains static.

In his theory of production, Walras did not work from the analogy of the Robinson Crusoe economy where competition would be impossible. Unlike Crusoe's values, Walrasian prices cannot be forecast by any agent, because no agent can know the preferences and initial endowments of every consumer and the cost of production of every commodity; but prices provide each consumer and entrepreneur with the information that they need to make their utility-maximizing and profit-maximizing calculations. Walras invoked his hypothetical auctioneer to establish equilibrium prices. The auctioneer begins by crying an initial set of prices at random. Consumers and entrepreneurs submit provisional tickets to the auctioneer showing how much of each commodity they are willing to buy or sell at those prices. The auctioneer then computes the total quantity offered and demanded for each commodity; and, if the quantities offered and demanded are not equal, he cries a new set of prices. He raises the prices of commodities where the quantity demanded exceeds the quantity offered and lowers them where the offers exceed the demands. This is the process of groping toward equilibrium. The auctioneer reaches equilibrium when the quantity demanded equals the quantity offered for every commodity; and the provisional tickets become binding contracts, so that production can proceed and transactions occur.

If trading occurred at disequilibrium prices, however, two forces would disrupt the economy: resources might go into the production and consumption of commodities that would not be demanded at equilibrium prices, which would waste scarce resources and make it impossible to reach the true equilibrium; and income might be redistributed by windfall gains and losses as prices changed, which would alter the quantities of commodities offered and demanded by consumers and change the true equilibrium. Both equilibrium and the path to equilibrium would be indeterminate. The auctioneer, or a similar hypothesis, is logically necessary for a consistent theory of competitive prices. Any disturbance to the economy requires the auctioneer to establish a new equilibrium. If consumer preferences, the initial endowments or production technology change, the auctioneer must repeat the process of groping until he discovers the new set of equilibrium prices, which cannot be known beforehand. Since, for example, farmers and country gentlemen may put their land to different uses, even a redistribution of the existing endowments among the same consumers may cause a change in commodity prices and factor payments.

In equilibrium, prices are set where the quantity demanded equals the quantity offered for every commodity, including the services of the factors of production. Each consumer maximizes total utility where the ratio of the marginal utility of one commodity to another equals the ratio of their prices. Prices signal what commodities and how much of each commodity will be produced and what factor services and how much of each factor service will be used. Households purchase consumer goods with the income they receive from selling their factor services. Each entrepreneur maximizes profits where the price of each factor service equals the value of its marginal product and where the price of each commodity equals its marginal cost. Since competition reduces excess profits to zero, the price of each commodity equals its average cost of production. Production is efficient in the sense that the value of total output is the maximum that is possible with the given wants, resources and technology of the economy. If any factor service could produce a greater value in an alternative use or if any commodity could be produced at a lower cost, profits would not be maximized and production would not be efficient.

Walras was fully aware that his system of equations did not explain disturbances to competitive equilibrium; but he thought that his static analysis was an important step forward, because it proved for the first time 'the superior general rule' of *laissez-faire* (1954, p. 256). He criticized early economists, such as Smith, for failing to demonstrate their results rigorously; and he chastised others for extending the doctrine of *laissez-faire* to cases where it does not apply, such as the questions of public goods, monopoly and justice. Walras's advocacy of *laissez-faire*, however, is a statement of what ought to be; it belongs to what Walras (1954, p. 63) himself called '*moral science* or *ethics*'.

Smith and Walras conceived of the economy as being governed by a hypothetical regime of competition, which they knew did not exist in reality; but they approached value theory from fundamentally different perspectives and often asked different questions. Smith began his analysis in a Lockean state of nature, where labour alone regulates values; then he switched to a cost of production theory for civil society, where land is appropriated and capital is accumulated. In equilibrium, price equals the cost of production: wages, profits and rents. The emphasis is on supply: wages are not only the incentive to work, but also to population growth; and profits are the incentive not only to allocate capital, but also to accumulate capital. The growth of population and accumulation of capital cause factor incomes and therefore commodity prices to change over time. Smith had a theory of economic history. Walras began with unexplained initial endowments of land, labour and capital, which are distributed to consumers like manna from heaven; and he sought to explain how competition establishes equilibrium at a point in time. The Walrasian theory does not explain what determines the available resources; and it does not explain change; it is entirely static. In equilibrium with production, Walrasian prices equal costs, but the cost of production consists of the wages, profits and rents that must be paid to induce consumers to sell their factor services on the market rather than consume them at home. For Walras, cost is simply an alternative benefit forgone, so that, given the initial endowments and the state of technical knowledge, relative values are determined by the demand. Walras treats all the factors of production in the same way that Smith treats land: he treats them as if they were free gifts of nature.

5.4 Conclusions

Adam Smith set an ambitious agenda for economics when he inquired into the nature and causes of the wealth of nations. His immediate concern was economic growth, economic welfare and economic policy; but, to compare different nations and policies, he needed to measure the value of output and income and to explain the determination of relative values and factor incomes as society progressed. His whole analysis rested on value theory, which was still in its infancy. He inherited an incoherent mixture of labour and utility theories, which he found wanting; but he confused his successors by leaving them with a bewildering account of the origin, measure and regulation of value.

The origin of value refers to the question of why things have value in principle and in the abstract, which Smith approached from the perspective of a Lockean state of nature, where land is free and labour creates value. This conception gave rise to the classical labour theory of value, which Ricardo, Marx and others applied to civil society, where land is appropriated and capital accumulated. Menger, Jevons and Walras – the early neoclassical economists – rejected the labour theory of value, because it could not explain why the free gifts of nature have value; but they accepted the concepts of the origin, measure and regulation of value. Their theory of the origin of value proceeded from the perspective of a Robinson Crusoe economy where things have value if they are scarce relative to their usefulness, which is an introspective and subjective concept. They maintained that utility was the origin of value even when, as in the case of Walras, such a proposition was inconsistent with their own theory of the regulation of value. Both the labour and the utility theories of the origin of value are 'philosophical' as opposed to 'empirical' explanations of value. They suppose that value has a cause of causes, which is neither logically necessary nor empirically true. In a market economy, individuals cannot know whether things are physically scarce in relation to their aggregate usefulness. They can only know whether things have market prices, and prices are simultaneously determined by the activities of all individuals.

Smith needed a universal measure of value to compare the wealth of nations over time and space, but Ricardo demonstrated that there is no such thing as a perfect measure of value. As society progresses, relative values change; and it is impossible to observe whether one value has remained constant. Smith assumed that labour is homogeneous across time and space, so that he could measure the wealth of nations by the output that a standardized unit of labour produces, which, by assumption, is an objective concept. Ricardo restricted his analysis to a single country and examined how economic growth affects relative values and factor incomes, which only requires a measure of value over time. Ricardo used gold as his measure of value on the assumption that gold is produced under average conditions, but he knew that his measure was not perfect. Utility cannot be used as an empirical measure of value, because utility is not observable and individuals are not comparable. However, Marshall and Pareto developed measures of economic welfare that could compare two states of equilibrium, but their measures restrict economic analysis to comparative statics. Under some conditions, their measures can compare the effects of alternative economic policies.

Price theory explains the determination of relative values in a market economy. The classical economists needed value theory to explain how market forces cause the economy to change over time. Smith presented two theories of the regulation of value: a labour theory for primitive societies and a cost of production theory for advanced societies. Ricardo and Marx adopted Smith's labour-embodied theory; but they soon discovered that they could not account for the value of commodities that are produced with different capital structures, so they ended up with a cost of production theory of market prices like Smith. The neoclassical marginal utility theory swept away the classical cost of production theory, however, because the classical economists had no theory of consumer demand and could not explain the value of naturally or artificially scarce commodities.

Marshall's theory of value is a synthesis of the classical and neoclassical theories, because he attributes the cost of production to real sacrifices and he explains consumer demand with marginal utility. Marshall's analysis begins at a point in time when traders are in a state of disequilibrium and are looking forward into the future, which he divides into three time periods: the temporary period, the short run and the long run. He used different time periods because it takes different amounts of time to make a transaction, to produce a commodity or to expand the productive capacity of a firm. Like the classical economists, he wanted to explain the forces of motion that cause prices to change over time. However, his disequilibrium analysis was criticized by many economists, because it was not always logically consistent. Neoclassical theory found its most logical expression in the general equilibrium theory of Walras; but Walras restricted his analysis to decisions made at a point in time, because his system of simultaneous equations is intractable under changing conditions.

The historical controversy over value theory has been fought on grounds of logical consistency; and it has produced an accumulation of negative results, which has forced economists to modify their research agenda. While the concept of the origin of value was not needed and disappeared from the literature, analytical and empirical work requires a measure of value, though values are not easily measured. Without a robust measure of value, many important economic questions such as whether one nation is richer than another or whether one nation has grown over time have no answers. Policy analysis also requires a measure of value; but economic policy frequently involves the question of justice, which is a matter of what ought to be. Marshall and Pigou, among others, were prepared to treat all individuals as if they were the same, which permitted them to discuss policies that redistribute income and wealth; but making interpersonal comparisons is generally disputable, so policy analysis has been restricted to Pareto improvements, which takes social reform off the agenda of economics. And, as Marshall (1961, vol. I, p. vii) observed, the element of time is 'the chief difficulty of almost every economic problem', because the economy is constantly changing, but little can be said about disturbing factors and changing conditions: disequilibrium analysis has proven intractable. General equilibrium theory is the most advanced form of value theory; it provides an elegant and logically valid explanation of relative values under a hypothetical regime of perfect competition at a point in time.

REFERENCES

Bladen, V. (1975) 'Command over labour: a study in misinterpretation', *Canadian Journal of Economics* 8, 504–19.
Blaug, M. (1978) *Economic Theory in Retrospect*, 3rd edn. Cambridge: Cambridge University Press.

von Böhm-Bawerk, E. (1962) 'The ultimate standard of value', in *Shorter Classics of Eugen von Böhm-Bawerk*. Trans. C. W. Macfarlane, South Holland, Ill.: Libertarian Press, pp. 303–70.

Clark, J. B. (1956) *The Distribution of Wealth*. New York: Kelley and Millman.

Debreu, G. (1959) *Theory of Value*. New York: Wiley.

Galiani, F. (1924) *Della Moneta*. Reprinted in *Early Economic Thought*. Ed. A. E. Monroe, Cambridge, Mass.: Harvard University Press, pp. 279–307.

Hicks, J. R. (1939) *Value and Capital*. Oxford: Clarendon Press.

Hollander, S. (1979) *The Economics of David Ricardo*. Toronto: University of Toronto Press.

Hutcheson, F. (1973) *A System of Moral Philosophy*. Reprinted in *Precursors of Adam Smith*. Ed. R. L. Meek, London: Dent, pp. 23–41.

Knight, F. H. (1956) *On the History and Method of Economics*. Chicago, Ill.: University of Chicago Press.

Knight, F. H. (1965) *The Economic Organisation*. New York: Harper & Row.

Locke, J. (1960) *Two Treatises of Government*. Ed. P. Laslett, Cambridge: Cambridge University Press.

Majumdar, T. (1966) *The Measurement of Utility*. London: Macmillan.

Malthus, T. R. (1986) *An Essay on the Principle of Population*. Reprinted in *The Works of Thomas Robert Malthus*, vol. 1. Ed. E. A. Wrigley and D. Souden, London: William Pickering.

Marshall, A. (1961) *Principles of Economics*, 2 vols. Ed. C. W. Guillebaud, London: Macmillan.

Marx, K. (1961) *Capital*, 3 vols. Moscow: Foreign Languages Publishing House.

Marx, K. (1963–71) *Theories of Surplus Value*, 3 parts. Moscow: Progress Publishers.

Meek, R. L. (1956) *Studies in the Labour Theory of Value*. London: Lawrence & Wishart.

Meek, R. L. (1977) *Smith, Marx and After*. London: Chapman and Hall.

Menger, C. (1950) *Principles of Economics*. Trans. and ed. J. Dingwall and B. F. Hoselitz, Glencoe, Ill.: Free Press.

Myint, H. (1965) *Theories of Welfare Economics*. New York: Kelley.

Pareto, V. (1971) *Manual of Political Economy*. Trans. A. S. Schwier, ed. A. S. Schwier and A. N. Page, New York: Kelley.

Pasinetti, L. (1977) *Lectures on the Theory of Production*. London: Macmillan.

Ricardo, D. (1951–73) *The Works and Correspondence of David Ricardo*. Ed. P. Sraffa with the collaboration of M. H. Dobb, 11 vols. Cambridge: Cambridge University Press.

Robbins, L. (1928) 'The representative firm', *Economic Journal* 38, 387–404.

Smith, Adam (1976) *An Inquiry into the Nature and Causes of the Wealth of Nations*, 2 vols. Ed. R. H. Campbell and A. S. Skinner, Oxford: Clarendon Press.

Sraffa, P. (1926) 'The laws of returns under competitive equilibrium', *Economic Journal* 36, 535–50.

Sraffa, P. (1960) *Production of Commodities by Means of Commodities*. Cambridge: Cambridge University Press.

Steedman, I. (1981) *Marx after Sraffa*. London: Verso.

Stigler, G. J. (1965) *Essays in the History of Economics*. Chicago, Ill.: University of Chicago Press.

Walras, L. (1954) *Elements of Pure Economics*. Trans. W. Jaffé, Homewood, Ill.: Richard D. Irwin.

Whitaker, A. C. (1968) *History and Criticism of the Labor Theory of Value in English Political Economy*. New York: Kelley.

von Wieser, F. (1956) *Natural Value*. Trans. C. A. Malloch, ed. W. Smart, New York: Kelley and Millman.

6

Social welfare

Randall G. Holcombe

The conclusions of economic analysis can be divided into two categories: positive and normative. Positive analysis draws conclusions about the facts of the world, while normative analysis draws conclusions about the way that the world should be. Normative conclusions cannot be drawn without making some value judgements about what constitutes a desirable state of affairs. Social welfare is a concept that attempts to provide a foundation for normative analysis by drawing conclusions regarding the public interest. Presumably, a change would be desirable if it would cause an increase in social welfare. The purpose of this chapter is to explain several criteria for evaluating the social welfare.

Before analysing specific criteria, however, it is important to realize that the concept of social welfare is a normative concept and rests on value judgements rather than facts. Because of this, some economists do not even recognize this type of normative analysis as a part of economics. For example, Alchian and Allen (1972, pp. 6–7) state:

> Economic theory is 'positive' or 'non-normative.' It gives no generally accepted criteria for determining which consequence or type of behavior or economic policy is good. . . . Economics can only tell the consequences of certain conditions, policies, or choices. It is no more proper for the economist than for any other person to sit on Mt. Olympus and decree what is desirable, though everyone may in fact make such pronouncements.

There is much truth in what Alchian and Allen say. The value judgements of economists are no better than the value judgements of anyone else. However, as they also note, everyone makes such judgements, and the likelihood that individuals will make sound and consistent judgements will increase if they understand and can articulate the reasons for believing that something is in the public interest. Theories of social welfare provide such reasons.

Since they are normative theories, it cannot be concluded that theories of social welfare are true or false in the same way as can be done with theories of interest rates, inflation or unemployment. But the assumptions and underlying logic of theories of social welfare can be examined to see whether a theory seems to capture reasonably the spirit of the public interest. There is a final reason for taking theories of social welfare seriously despite their normative foundations. Societies make collective decisions continuously, mostly through government, and presumably they try to pursue policies that are in the public interest. How is one to know whether a policy is in the public interest? Theories of social welfare attempt to answer this question.

6.1 Individual Welfare and Social Welfare

Throughout most of recorded history, individual citizens have been viewed as having the duty of serving the interests of the state. This holistic view of social welfare sees the strength and survival of the state as the proper criterion for evaluating the desirability of a policy. Only within the past several centuries have social philosophers accepted individualistic theories of social welfare. Individualistic theories of social welfare envisage that the role of the state is to serve its citizens rather than the other way around. Today, all prominent theories are individualistic rather than holistic. In all the theories discussed in this chapter, social welfare can be improved only by improving the welfare of the individuals in the society.

While this individualistic postulate provides a common ground for theories of social welfare, the theories start to diverge when individuals within a society are affected differently by some proposed change. If a policy is proposed which improves the welfare of every individual in a society, all individualistic theories agree that the group is better off when all individuals in the group are better off. The problem arises when some individuals are made better off while others are made worse off – which is the case with almost any policy in the real world. This is the point at which theories of social welfare diverge.

Before departing on these divergent paths, one more point of commonality should be noted. All theories in this chapter agree that the individual is the appropriate judge of when the individual's well-being is improved. Thus, theories of social welfare are in general agreement that social welfare is a function of the welfare of the individuals in the society, and they are further in agreement that the individual is the proper judge of his or her own welfare. The question now arises how to aggregate the welfare of a group of individuals into a single concept of social welfare.

Two major questions arise in attempting this aggregation. The first is how to deal with potential changes that would improve the well-being of some people but harm others, as will be the case with almost any policy in the real world. Saying that the group is better off implies that the gain to the gainers more than offsets the loss to the losers. In sections 6.2–6.5, on utilitarianism, the Pareto criteria, potential compensation and the social welfare function, ways in which economists have approached this issue are discussed. The second major question involves the distinction between procedures and outcomes in evaluating social welfare. Many criteria for social welfare look only at the state of the world to judge social welfare – they evaluate the outcome – while others are based on the argument that the outcome cannot be judged independently of the procedures that generate the outcome. The distinction between procedures and outcomes plays an important part in sections 6.6–6.9, on contractarian models, fair outcomes and fair processes, procedural and non-procedural theories of welfare, and revealed preference and social choice. The concluding section of the chapter attempts to summarize the relationships between the various concepts of social welfare.[1]

6.2 Utilitarianism

Over two centuries ago, Jeremy Bentham suggested that policies improved the social welfare if they produced the greatest good for the greatest number. Bentham's concept is intuitively appealing but, unfortunately, is not very precise. Presumably, a policy that provided great benefit to most people and caused only a few people a minor inconvenience would produce the greatest good for the greatest number, but what about a policy that benefited many people a little while harming a few people a great deal? A more precise definition of exactly what constitutes the greatest good for the greatest number is needed if Bentham's criterion is to be useful for evaluating the social welfare in the real world.

Bentham's approach to social welfare is called utilitarianism because he attempts to take account of the relative well-being, or utility, of everyone in the society by weighing the utility gained by some people against the utility lost by others. But if such a weighing is actually to take place, there must be some way to measure the utility gain to the gainers and the utility loss to the losers in order to know whether a policy actually does create the greatest good for the greatest number.

By the latter half of the nineteenth century, utilitarians such as John Stuart Mill considered utility to be something that was cardinally measurable, at least in theory. According to these utilitarians, utility could be denominated in utils just as income can be denominated in pounds, francs or dollars. A person's utility could thus be added up and compared with another person's utility in the same way that one person's income could be compared with another's.[2] If utils can be compared among individuals in this way, only one more step need be taken to arrive at the utilitarian concept of social welfare. Utilitarians measure the social welfare by adding up the utilities of everyone in the society. The higher the total, the greater is social welfare.

Some of the earliest applications of utilitarianism were to problems of income distribution. Utilitarians reasoned that income provided diminishing marginal utility so that a franc of additional income provided less utility to a rich person than to a poor person. Therefore, if a franc were taxed away from a rich person and given to a poor person, total utility would be increased and the social welfare would be improved.

This type of utilitarianism is subject to criticism on a number of grounds. First, contemporary economists do not believe that utility is cardinally measurable. In the above example, there would be no way to compare the utility loss of a franc to a rich person with the utility gain of a franc to a poor person. As a practical matter, it might be that the rich person works harder to earn more money because she derives more utility from income than the poor person does, who does not work as hard. But more fundamentally, utility just cannot be compared across people in the same way that people's heights can be compared to see who is taller.[3]

Assume, for example, that a woman wins a talent contest and then 20 years later her daughter enters the same contest and is placed second. Does this mean that the woman has more talent than her daughter? Clearly it does not, because there is not a common standard of measurement between the years. There is also not a common standard of measurement of utility among different persons, so interpersonal utility comparisons are questionable for the same reasons.

Even if interpersonal utility comparisons were possible, utilitarianism has also been objected to on ethical grounds. Utilitarianism implies that a policy enhances the social welfare as long as the utility gained from the gainers is greater than the utility loss to the losers. Taken to its logical conclusion, this means forcing one person to do something for another person if the second person gains more than the first person loses. For example, if one person would gain more utility from having a slave than another person would lose from being a slave, then slavery would represent a gain in social welfare following the tenets of utilitarianism.[4]

Despite these criticisms of utilitarianism, contemporary utilitarians argue that, in the real world, virtually any proposed policy is going to benefit some people and harm others. As a result, there is really no way to make policy recommendations other than to try to weigh fairly the benefits to some against the losses of others. Policy-makers and social philosophers can attempt to cover their value judgements with as much scientific-sounding jargon as they want, but ultimately any policy recommendation must come down to an evaluation of the costs to the losers versus the gains to the winners. Contemporary utilitarians would like to see these value judgements openly admitted rather than to have policy proposals clouded in scientific-sounding terms that really amount to no more than arguing that the proposer believes that the gains to the gainers outweigh the losses to the lossers.[5]

6.3 The Pareto Criteria

The Pareto criteria, named after economist and sociologist Vilfredo Pareto (1848–1923), provide a means for evaluating social welfare without making the interpersonal utility comparisons inherent in utilitarianism. Pareto reasoned that, because there is no sound basis for making interpersonal utility comparisons, the only way that one can be sure that the social welfare has actually been enhanced by a change is if at least one person is made better off but nobody is made worse off. Such a change is called a Pareto improvement.

If a situation arises in which nobody can be made better off without making someone else worse off, then no Pareto improvement can be made. If no Pareto improvement can be made, then the situation is called a Pareto optimum. There are two Pareto criteria, then. The criterion for a Pareto improvement requires that at least one person's welfare is improved while nobody else is harmed, and constitutes an improvement in social welfare. A Pareto optimum is a situation where one person's welfare cannot be increased without decreasing the welfare of someone else.

The Pareto criteria can be illustrated with the assistance of the Edgeworth box diagram shown in figure 6.1. The diagram illustrates the utility functions for two individuals, called X and Y, and some of their indifference curves for the two goods, numbered good 1 and good 2. X's origin is at the lower left corner of the diagram and his indifference curves are convex to his origin, while Y's origin is located at the upper right corner of the diagram. Points further to the right of the diagram indicate more of good 1 for Y and less for X, while points closer to the bottom of the diagram indicate more of good 2 for Y and less for X.

Consider first a point like point A in the diagram, at which the indifference curves of the two people intersect. At this point, both can be made better off by moving to point B, where each is on a higher indifference curve. Therefore, a movement from A to B is a Pareto improvement. Similarly, a movement from point B to point C is a Pareto improvement. Since the indifference curves of the individuals are tangent at point C, further Pareto improvements are not possible, so point C is a Pareto optimum.

From any point that is not a Pareto optimum, it is possible to make a

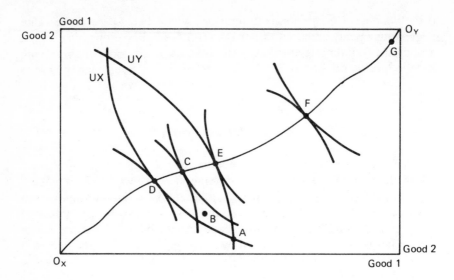

Figure 6.1 The Pareto criteria.

Pareto improvement but, as illustrated in the move from A to B, a Pareto improvement does not necessarily produce a Pareto optimum. Also note that, from a non-Pareto-optimal point, it is possible to make Pareto improvements to many different Pareto-optimal points. For example, from point A, movements to points C, D and E are all Pareto improvements, and all result in Pareto optima.

The curve drawn through D, C, E and F is the contract curve, which is the locus of all Pareto-optimal points. From the diagram, it is easy to see that it is possible to make a move that is not a Pareto improvement from a non-Pareto-optimal point to a Pareto-optimal point. A move from A to F is an example.

Using figure 6.1 as a point of reference, it is possible to consider the Pareto criteria as measures of the social welfare. A movement from A to C is a Pareto improvement and so enhances the social welfare. The same is true of a movement from A to D or from A to E. Which movement enhances social welfare the most? Unfortunately, the Pareto criteria provide no guidance. As the diagram shows, a movement from A to E places individual X on a higher indifference curve but leaves Y on the same indifference curve, so person X is made better off while person Y's welfare is unchanged. Similarly, a move from A to D improves Y's well-being while leaving X's welfare unchanged. Both people benefit from a move from A to C. The Pareto criteria identify all these moves as improvements in social welfare, but provide no method for choosing which of the points is most preferred.

The criterion of Pareto optimality indicates that, from points C, D and E, no change can take place that can be identified as an improvement in social welfare. A movement from D to E, for example, will make person X better off but will make person Y worse off. Such a change cannot be evaluated using the Pareto criteria because the Pareto criteria do not make interpersonal utility comparisons. This example illustrates that the Pareto criteria cannot rank all points, since there is no way to determine whether C, D or E provides more social welfare.

Consider next the case of moving from A to F. Point F is a Pareto optimum, but the movement from A to F is not a Pareto improvement. Therefore, at point F, the Pareto criteria cannot identify any points that improve the social welfare, but the Pareto criteria also cannot judge the movement from A to F. Since individual X is made better off but individual Y is made worse off, the Pareto criteria have no way of determining whether the improvement in X's welfare compensates for the losses imposed in Y. Likewise, the Pareto criteria cannot judge a move from F to A. Even though F is a Pareto-optimal point and A is not, one cannot say that F provides more social welfare than A. Since one person is made better off but one person is made worse off, the move cannot be evaluated.

The big advantage of the Pareto criteria is that they do not require interpersonal utility comparisons. Therefore, only a small value judgement is required to say that they reflect the social welfare. As long as one is willing to agree that an improvement in one person's welfare that does not harm anyone else improves the social welfare, the Pareto criteria can be accepted as a way of determining whether a change is in the public interest.

The Pareto criteria have some drawbacks as indicators of social welfare as well. First, as noted above, the Pareto criteria do not rank all possible outcomes so that, for many changes, the Pareto criteria will offer no guidance as to whether the change improves the social welfare. In figure 6.1, the Pareto criteria were unable to tell whether C was better than D or whether A was better than F. In the real world, almost any possible change will make someone worse off so, strictly interpreted, the Pareto criteria will not be very useful for evaluating policies in the real world.

A frequently heard defence of this criticism is that often policy changes will make almost everyone better off but, unless absolutely nobody objects to a change, it will not be a Pareto improvement; this defence moves toward utilitarianism. If the change is 'almost' a Pareto improvement, then some people are being made worse off, and the defence amounts to saying that the utility gain of the vast majority should count more than the utility loss of the small minority. The Pareto criteria must be taken literally if they are not to dissolve into utilitarianism but, if taken literally, they will not be able to pass judgement on most changes that occur in the real world.

Another problem with the Pareto criteria is that they tend to legitimize the status quo. While everyone may not view this as a problem, consider the situation where, for some reason, persons X and Y begin at point G in figure 6.1. At point G, X has almost all of both goods, leaving individual Y with very little. But following the Pareto criteria, only changes that do not make X worse off can be judged to be improvements in the social welfare. This would be a problem if one judged that the initial starting point of G was unfair to begin with, although the Pareto criteria would never make such a judgement.

Examples of that type of situation might be slavery in the pre-civil war United States or apartheid in South Africa. One might judge that the elimination of slavery would enhance the social welfare even though the former slave owners would be worse off, but the Pareto criteria would not judge the abolishment of slavery to be an improvement in the social welfare unless the former slave owners were compensated for their losses. The examples show how one might view the legitimization of the status quo as a drawback in using the Pareto criteria to judge the social welfare. The Pareto criteria are widely accepted but, like all criteria for judging social welfare, they are basically value judgements.

6.4 Potential Compensation

One method of overcoming some of the criticisms of the Pareto criteria is to substitute the weaker criterion that the social welfare would be improved if it were possible for the gainers from any change to use their gains to compensate the losers for their losses such that everyone would be made better off. Under this criterion of potential compensation, the compensation would not actually have to be paid. It would only have to be possible to compensate the losses of the losers with the gains from the gainers.

The compensation in this case would be paid in the *numéraire* good – money. The test of potential compensation therefore compares the money value of the gains to the gainers from a change with the money value of the loss to the losers. If the gain is worth more money to the gainers than the loss costs the losers, then the potential compensation criterion says that the social welfare is improved by the change. If the gainers actually pay the compensation to the losers, then a Pareto improvement will take place but, while at first glance the potential compensation criterion looks similar to the Pareto criteria, there are important differences.

One important difference is that the test of potential compensation requires interpersonal utility comparisons. It is utilitarian in that it measures the money value of the utility gains and losses and is willing to declare that the social welfare is improved if the money value of the utility gain to the gainers outweighs the money value of the utility loss to the losers. On the negative side, one might be reluctant to accept a criterion that will automatically justify any losses to the losers by saying that the gainers gain more than the losers lose. Would the social welfare be enhanced if Mr Smith's house were knocked down and replaced by a highway? This criterion would argue that it should if the money value of the gain to drivers on the highway outweighed the money value of the loss to Mr Smith. Mr Smith need not be compensated. The criterion would only argue that Mr Smith could potentially be compensated from the gains of the gainers.

A partial defence of this criticism is that the government makes many decisions every day in which there are gainers and losers. It would be impractical to compensate the losers each time, but over a large number of issues one would expect to be a gainer on average as often as anyone else. If the value of the gains to the gainers consistently outweighed the value of the loss to the losers, then each person would expect to be a net gainer over a large number of issues. While one might want to protect individual rights more carefully on certain issues (like Mr Smith's house), for most issues potential compensation would be sufficient to ensure that the typical individual would, on net, gain from the government's policies.

One advantage of the potential compensation criterion is that it is able to rank more points than the Pareto criteria. With the Pareto criteria, one could not judge the effect on the social welfare if a change made some people better off but some worse off. With the criterion of potential compensation, such changes could be evaluated by comparing the money value of the gains and losses.

The potential compensation criterion has Paretian characteristics and utilitarian characteristics. If compensation were actually paid, it would be Paretian but, without compensation being paid, it is a kind of utilitarianism that denominates utility in money. This subjects potential compensation to the critique of interpersonal utility comparisons that was made of utilitarianism, but also subjects it to the critique of the Pareto criteria that it justifies the status quo. Under the potential compensation criterion, the utilities of individuals are weighted by their wealth, since people could compensate at most their entire wealth, and probably would be willing to compensate less for a particular change.

However, one might object to weighting utility by wealth even if one were a utilitarian. In defence of the potential compensation criterion, if all changes were made in which the value of the gains to the gainers outweighed the losses to the losers, the total value of a society's wealth would be maximized. If maximization of social wealth is synonymous with social welfare, then the potential compensation criterion looks appealing.

6.5 The Social Welfare Function

The social welfare function is basically a mathematical concept. It can be explained without the use of mathematics, but it owes its existence to the development of mathematical theories and the fact that, in mathematical models, economists can use the tools of mathematics to maximize functions. Analytically, the social welfare function appears to be very similar to the utility function for an individual. The social welfare function contains social indifference curves which pass through all points of the choice set and are assumed to have the same properties as individual indifference curves. A typical depiction of a social welfare function is given in figure 6.2.

In figure 6.2 the horizontal axis registers the utility of individual X and the vertical axis registers the utility of individual Y. The curve CC represents the contract curve, and has the same significance as the contract curve in the Edgeworth box diagram. At any point on the contract curve, one person's welfare can be improved only if the other person's welfare is reduced. At a point such as point A, below the contract curve, a movement toward the upper right of the figure would improve the welfare of both individuals and so would be a Pareto improvement. However, the social welfare function uses different criteria for evaluating social welfare.

As with individual utility functions, the social welfare function judges welfare to be improved if a change results in a movement to a higher indifference curve, meaning one farther from the origin. Therefore, a Pareto improvement, which implies a movement toward the upper right corner of the figure, would also be an unambiguous improvement in social welfare according to the social welfare function. Since the Pareto criteria seem so reasonable as indicators of social welfare, it is satisfying to find that a Pareto improvement will always improve the social welfare according to the social welfare function.

The social welfare function is able to indicate considerably more than the Pareto criteria, though. Since social indifference curves pass through every point in the issue space, any possible point can be compared with any other. With the Pareto criteria, a change that improved one person's welfare but harmed another could not be evaluated, but the social welfare function provides a definite ranking of all possible outcomes.

Like utilitarianism, the social welfare function is able to weigh the welfare gain of one individual against the welfare loss to someone else to

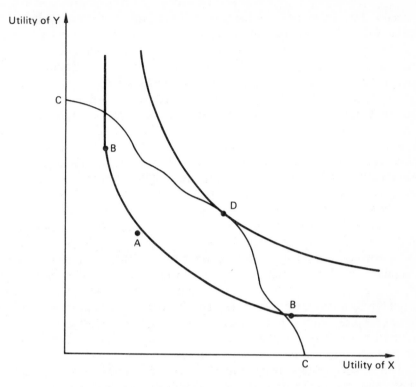

Figure 6.2 The social welfare function.

determine whether the social welfare has, on net, been improved. But unlike the simpler variants of utilitarianism, the social welfare function does not simply add the utility of all persons to arrive at a total social utility. More complex relationships are possible so that, for example, if the social indifference curves were to become vertical or horizontal after some point, the social welfare function would show that, if one individual's utility were very low relative to another's, no utility gain to the higher-utility individual could offset any utility loss for the lower-utility individual. This is illustrated on the social indifference curve labelled BB in figure 6.2. The points beyond B at either end of the indifference curves are the points for which there would be no trade-off in utility. This illustrates the considerable flexibility embodied in the concept of the social welfare function.

Finding the point of maximum social welfare is analytically the same as the problem of individual utility maximization. The contract curve, or utility possibilities frontier as it is sometimes called, provides a constraint and the social welfare function is maximized subject to that constraint. The social indifference curve that is tangent to the utility possibilities frontier defines the point of maximum social welfare. This is point D in figure 6.2.

The mathematical properties of the social welfare function were mentioned earlier, and they should now be apparent to the mathematically inclined reader. Maximization subject to a constraint is a standard calculus exercise, so the social welfare function has pleasant mathematical properties that make it easy in theory to derive mathematically the properties of the real world which lead to maximum social welfare. All that is required is the social welfare function and the constraints. The social welfare function was used most frequently in international trade models in the 1940s, but beginning in the 1950s and up through the 1970s it found its most prominent uses in models of income redistribution.[6]

The social welfare function is analytically very tractable in theory, but in practice some difficult questions arise about how a real world social welfare function could ever be derived. As already noted, interpersonal utility comparisons must be made and, although the concept of the social welfare function sounds very scientific, there is in reality no scientific method by which one person's utility can be compared with another's to determine whether a gain to one person outweighs the loss to another. Therefore, the social welfare function leaves itself open to many of the same criticisms as utilitarianism. It is simply a method of disguising one's value judgements behind a mask of pseudo-scientific jargon.

The defence to this criticism is that in the real world such value judgements must be made all the time. Policy-makers must continually decide whether particular policies that benefit some but harm others are in the public interest. The Pareto criteria are unable to pass judgement on such questions, but in the real world such questions are the rule rather than the exception. The social welfare function, seen in this light, is not a guide to policy-makers but rather a representation of the preferences of policy-makers which allows some rigorous economic analysis to take place with regard to public policy decisions. In other words, the social welfare function depicts policy choices within a framework similar to that in which the choices are actually made. The economist does not choose the social welfare function for the policy-maker, but simply recognizes that there is some function that represents a ranking of public policy alternatives. The mathematically tractable social welfare function is an economist's tool that makes it easy to analyse the setting in which public policy decisions are made.

This defence is not entirely satisfactory for a number of reasons. First, it sidesteps the issue of what really constitutes an improvement in social welfare by making the concept into a concept embodying some individual's (or group's) preferences. Second, such a defence fails to analyse the motivations behind the policy-makers when they make their decisions.

Might it be possible, for example, for a policy-maker to make a decision specifically to benefit some special interest group – or even the decision-maker himself – rather than to further social welfare more generally conceived?[7] But if the concept is accepted as a true measure of social welfare, other problems arise. As already noted, the social welfare function makes interpersonal utility comparisons, and there is no way that such comparisons can be made without individual value judgements in the real world, regardless of how scientific the concept appears in theory. The social welfare function may be especially misleading since it clouds in scientific jargon the fact that someone will have to make a personal value judgement regarding how much one person's well-being is worth compared with another's.

While this criticism of the social welfare function sounds devastating, it must be considered in the context of the discussion of social welfare. Since any concept of social welfare is normative, one should not be surprised to find that the social welfare function is based ultimately on a value judgement. The problem is that the social welfare function leaves the questions of whose value judgement is used and how any aggregation of values takes place quite unspecified.

6.6 Contractarian Models

Another prominent line of analysis of social welfare is undertaken by contractarian models of the State. The concept of social welfare is important because it is desirable for public policy decisions to improve the social welfare but, as the discussion thus far has illustrated, attempting to define what it meant by social welfare is a difficult proposition. If the purpose of public policy is to improve the social welfare, and if – as all the policies evaluated in this chapter agree – social welfare is no more than the aggregate of the welfare of all the individuals in a society, then this provides a starting point for analysis of public policies and the role of government.

As viewed by contractarian models, the government provides a mechanism whereby individuals can undertake collective projects that would not be feasible in the private sector. There is an analogy between a government and a club, then, in that both types of organization are composed of groups of people who undertake collective activities for the benefit of the group. Social welfare is improved when the club or government undertakes these activities for the collective benefit.

This leaves open the question of what types of activity the government should pursue in order to enhance social welfare. In the contractarian view, the government's activities are described by the social contract, which is an agreement that binds individuals and the State. There is no actual social contract to which everyone has agreed. Most people are simply born in a country and live under that government without having agreed to anything. But the contractarians argue that there may be a conceptual agreement under which individuals are bound to follow the government's policies.

The social contract theory is not new,[8] but the theory is still developing. Contemporary contractarians have been concerned with the question of under what conditions individuals could be said to be in agreement with the social contract. The question is important to the concept of social welfare because in the contractarian view the social welfare is enhanced when the government does those things which are agreed to under the social contract.

The most prominent twentieth-century contractarian is John Rawls, who in his book *A Theory of Justice* (1971) argues that individuals would be in conceptual agreement with the social contract if they agreed to its provisions behind a veil of ignorance. Rawls's analysis proceeds in the following manner in trying to determine what the government should do to improve the social welfare. First, he imagines that everyone in a society is behind a veil of ignorance where they do not know who they will be when they take their roles in the real world. Individuals do not know their race or their gender. They do not know whether they will be born rich or poor, intelligent, athletic, musically inclined or with any other personal characteristic. Behind this veil of ignorance where individuals do not know who they will eventually be in society, all individuals must agree upon the rules under which they will live. Do they want the government heavily involved in welfare? Do they want highly progressive taxation? Should the government produce health care or should it be left to the private sector?

Since individuals do not know their individual characteristics from behind the veil of ignorance, Rawls reasoned that they would choose to have the government pursue those activities that are in the collective best interest. The social welfare is improved when the government pursues those activities agreed to from behind the veil of ignorance.[9] What Rawls is saying is that the government should pursue those activities that people would generally agree would further the social welfare if the people agreeing had no knowledge about how the government's actions would specifically benefit or harm them. This concept has some common sense appeal. For example, people might agree that the government should collect taxes in order to provide some type of welfare to the neediest people in a society if, when asked, they did not know whether they would be one of the needy ones.

The contractarian model differs in some important ways from the concepts of social welfare discussed earlier. It does not look at the welfare of individuals *per se*, but rather considers what they would agree would benefit the group. This avoids any interpersonal utility comparisons. One might imagine the social contract specifying that if an able-bodied person chose not to work when the opportunity arose, that person would not be entitled to receive any income from the State. This would be so regardless of whether a utilitarian argued that the utility gain to the poor person would be greater than the loss to a rich person if a transfer of income were to be made, or regardless of whether it was claimed that the transfer would move the society to a higher social indifference curve. The contractarian response would be that such interpersonal utility comparisons are not valid in the first place and, in the second place, that the policy that furthers the social welfare is that which is agreed upon in the social contract.

The key to the contractarian model is agreement. Individuals, without considering their own narrow self-interests, agree that certain social policies further the social welfare. If social welfare is nothing more than the aggregate welfare of the individuals in a society, and if the individuals themselves are the best judges of their own welfare, then the social policies agreed upon by those individuals will be the policies that enhance social welfare.

The contractarian model can be criticized on several grounds. First, the whole concept is based on a fiction that individuals agree to a social contract. In fact, there is no contract and individuals are simply born into a country and are subject to the laws of that government. The agreement referred to in the contractarian model is a conceptual agreement. While this may provide some guidelines to public policy by suggesting that policies enhance the social welfare if individuals, not considering their own narrow interests, agree that they are in the public interest, it also glosses over the fact that even the most benevolent government forces its citizens to obey its rules. Critics of the contractarians charge that government is ultimately based on force, not agreement as implied by the contractarians.

Another problem with the contractarian model is that it does not actually say what policies would enhance the social welfare. Policies that individuals would agree to if they considered the public interest rather than their own narrow self-interests would improve social welfare, but what policies are these? Rawls (1971) has suggested policies that he thinks people would agree to, but others, while accepting his contractarian framework, have disagreed with the policies Rawls believes would be agreed to within the contract and have even suggested that there is no conclusive way to know that policies would be approved under such hypothetical circumstances.[10] Ultimately, then, the contractarian model provides a framework for considering when policies enhance the social welfare, but it does not identify the specific policies. This criticism sounds harsh, but it applies to all the other concepts of social welfare as well.

6.7 Fair Outcomes and Fair Processes

A relatively recent development in concepts discussing the social welfare is the development of what has been called fairness theory. Fairness theory attempts to judge whether certain states of the world are fair, using a relatively specific set of criteria. The original inspiration for this line of inquiry was the work of Duncan Foley (1967), and good overviews are presented by Baumol (1982, 1986).

At first glance, it may seem that there is a substantial difference between fairness and social welfare. One might imagine, for example, a situation in which the outcome is fair, but lowers social welfare. However, when one remembers that the social welfare is nothing more than the aggregate of the individual welfare of everyone in a society, and when one considers the conceptual difficulty in making interpersonal utility comparisons, it is really not possible just to add up everyone's individual welfare to arrive at the social welfare. The social contract theory provides one way around that problem by arguing that the social welfare is improved whenever the people in a society agree that it is improved. Agreement of this sort seems to be a just or fair method of determining social policy. Rawls (1971) titles his book *A Theory of Justice* and argues that justice and fairness are the same thing. It makes sense that policies that are just and fair will be the policies that will enhance the social welfare, especially if it is recognized that it is not possible to add up individual utilities in order to obtain a measure of social welfare.

The fairness theory that has recently appeared in the economics literature rests on a specific definition of the term envy. In fairness theory, one person envies another if the person would rather have what the other person has.[11] A situation is defined as fair only if there is no envy. Starting from Foley's (1967) original definition, if one person would be willing to trade places with another, including taking the job of the other person, living in that person's home and so forth, then there is envy and the situation is not fair.

This concept of fairness has intuitive appeal. One can imagine, for example, a victim of racial discrimination who would like to have the job of another person, along with that person's income and lifestyle, but is barred from it because of discrimination. There is envy and, according to Foley, the situation is not fair. The definition runs into some problems when some people have unusual talents, or are more productive than other people. One might wish to trade places with a great professional athlete or a talented professional musician but, without those special talents, a typical individual could not produce output of the same value as the professional athlete or musician under any circumstances. Is it fair for those professionals to receive the income they receive as a result of using their talents?

Foley suggests an exception for these types of people, but the problem arises in considering production in general. If one person works harder than another and ends up with more goods at the end of the day, then at the end of the day the individual who did not work as hard will envy the goods belonging to the harder worker. Is it fair for the more productive individual to have more goods? Because of difficult questions such as this, rigorous analyses of fairness tend to look at exchange models rather than models that contain production and exchange.[12]

Baumol (1982) applies a model of this type to rationing policy to show that rationing is fair because without it individuals with less income will envy individuals with more income who can then buy more of the good that is to be rationed. This model of fairness produces clear answers to the questions asked in the preceding two paragraphs. It is not fair for the professional athlete or musician to receive the income they receive from their professions if another person would like to trade places with them. It is not fair for an individual who works harder to have more at the end of the day, for it produces envy among people who have less.

How should these types of answer be evaluated? First, note that these answers are consistent with much real world social policy, such as rationing, as noted above, and progressive income taxation that redistributes from higher-income individuals to lower-income individuals without considering whether the higher-income individuals worked harder or applied any special talents to earn those incomes. Following the definition of fairness in this section, these policies are fair, and they are also fair according to the perceptions of many individuals in the real world.

This idea of fairness contrasts sharply with Rawls's idea of justice as fairness, however, because Rawls's idea (and the contractarian idea in general) examines the process whereas contemporary fairness theory examines the outcome. This difference is important enough to warrant further exploration.

6.8 Procedural and Non-procedural Theories of Welfare

Assume that one finds that the final score of a basketball game was 75 to 48. Was this a fair game? Following the fairness theory outlined in the previous section, it was not, because the losing team would rather have had the points of the winning team. The fairness theory described here looks only at the outcome to decide whether there is envy and, if there is, the outcome is not fair. A procedural theory such as the contractarian theory would look at the rules of the game to decide if they were fair. Did both teams agree to the rules ahead of time? Were the referees unbiased in their judgement? If the rules and the environment were agreed to beforehand, then the procedure that produced the outcome is fair, and therefore the outcome is fair.

Note this important distinction between judging the outcome and judging the process to determine whether the outcome is fair. A procedural theory argues that the outcome cannot be judged independently of the process that produced the outcome, and that fair outcomes are the results of fair processes. Many theories are not procedural and judge the outcome without looking at the process that produced it.[13]

The reader might at this point consider whether it seems reasonable that the process that produced an outcome must be judged in order to decide whether the outcome enhances the social welfare. Most of the theories of social welfare discussed in this essay have not been procedural theories, but some have. The fairness theory described in the previous section is not a procedural theory. Neither is utilitarianism or the concept of the social welfare function. Both of these ideas measure an outcome against some yardstick of social welfare. The social welfare function uses a potentially complex relationship among individuals, but still judges how an outcome ranks on the social welfare function. Utilitarianism simply adds up individual utilities. In both cases, one can easily imagine one individual working hard and producing valuable output, and some of that output being transferred to individuals who do almost no work, because the gain in utility to the lazy people outweighs the utility loss to the hard workers. Does this enhance the social welfare? According to some measures, it could. Only the outcome is judged in many measures of the social welfare, so the process by which the wealth was produced in the above example is not relevant.

The contractarian theory is a procedural theory because it examines whether the procedure that produced the outcome was agreed to by the participants. If it was, then the process is fair, and therefore the outcome is fair. Utility is not compared directly. Rather, contractarianism looks to see whether the process that produced the outcome was agreed to, and if it was, then the outcome improves the social welfare.

The concept of Pareto improvement is a procedural concept, but Pareto optimality is not. With Pareto optimality, one looks at the outcome to see whether any individual's welfare can be improved without harming someone else. If not, then the situation is Pareto optimal, and there is no examination of how the Pareto-optimal situation arose. A Pareto improvement, however, examines whether a change makes at least one person better off without harming anyone. Therefore, it examines the process by which the new outcome is produced, and judges the outcome to be a Pareto improvement only if someone benefits and nobody is harmed in the process. Therefore, the Pareto improvement is a procedural theory of social welfare. The outcome cannot be judged independently of the procedure that produced the outcome.

Recall the basketball game outcome of 75 to 48. Sometimes this outcome might be fair and sometimes it might not. Referring back to figure 6.1, would point E be a Pareto improvement? It would if the movement was from A to E, but it would not if the movement was from B to E. With a procedural theory, the outcome cannot be judged independently of the process that produced the outcome.

This concept is so important that it cannot be overemphasized. There is often the tendency to try to judge whether some social condition is good or bad, or whether some social policy should be instituted to improve the social welfare, and often the judgement is attempted without considering the process that led up to the condition in question. Procedural theories will tend to emphasize equality of opportunity rather than equality of result. One should be aware that many criteria of social welfare are not procedural criteria and so do not consider the process that produced the result in judging the result. If one chooses to use such a concept of social welfare, one should at the minimum be aware of what one is choosing to ignore by using that criterion.

6.9 Revealed Preference and Social Choice

All the concepts of social welfare considered up to this point have been so abstract that, even if one agreed with the concept in principle, there would still not be a clear-cut way to formulate public policy from the concepts. The concepts have relied on measuring and comparing utilities, or on trying to determine what people might agree to under hypothetical circumstances. These ideas might provide some general guidance to policymakers in the real world, but they do not provide specific policy guidance.

The concepts of social welfare examined thus far have significant differences, but they also have the common elements that all of them consider the individuals themselves to be the best judges of their own welfare, and they consider that social welfare will be enhanced when the individuals within the society are made better off. Why worry about these abstract concepts then? Why not just ask people directly whether a change will improve their welfare?

There are two potential problems with trying to maximize social welfare based on individuals' statements about their own welfare. First, individuals may not have an incentive to reveal their true preferences. The free-rider problem is a good example of this. If individuals will have to pay for the goods they demand, they might understate their demands for goods that they can benefit from if others pay for them. National defence is a standard example. But if individuals do not directly pay for the goods they demand, they have an incentive to demand goods that are not cost effective, because others will pay for them. Individuals in a neighbourhood might not be willing to pay for the costs of a neighbourhood park, but would gladly vote for a park in their neighbourhood if the government were to provide it and ask all taxpayers in the nation to share the cost.

The second problem is that even if everyone's individual preferences were known, there is not a good way to aggregate the revealed preferences to produce the optimum allocation of resources. Kenneth Arrow, in *Social Choice and Individual Values* (1951), demonstrated that, under seemingly reasonable circumstances, it would not be possible to aggregate individual preferences into a rational social preference ordering. Consider, for example, the preference ordering given in table 6.1, where individuals 1, 2 and 3 have the preference rankings shown for outcomes A, B and C, and thus individual 1 would most prefer outcome A, would prefer B next, and would find C to be the least desirable outcome.

If simple majority rule is used to determine which option is to be chosen, A defeats B, but C defeats A and B defeats C. Therefore, the outcome of the election will depend upon which options are voted on first. For example, if A and B run against each other and the winner faces C in another election, A will beat B, but then C will beat A to win the election. If the winner from A and C faces B, then B will win, but A will win if B and C face each other first. The winner of the election depends upon the order in which the alternatives are considered. This problem is called the cyclical majority because the winner in a pairwise competition always loses against the third alternative, which sets up an endless cycle of majority rule winners.[14]

The type of election just described is not uncommon. Political parties may hold primary elections to decide which candidate will face the opposing party in a general election, and the winner could be an artefact of the order in which the options are voted on rather than the outcome that truly maximizes social welfare. The problem is not unique with this election procedure. The reader can examine the preference orderings in table 6.1 to see that, even with all the information in the table, there is no basis for choosing any of the options as the one that most enhances social welfare.

The notion of trying to derive a measure of social welfare from the revealed preferences of the members of a society is intuitively appealing,[15] but the cyclical majority example shows that more than a simple rank ordering of preferences is needed in order to guarantee that one outcome can be selected as the most preferred outcome. Consider, for example, the preferences shown in table 6.2, which has the same rank ordering of outcomes as in table 6.1 but this time includes the monetary value that each individual attaches to the particular outcome.

Table 6.1   A cyclical majority

	Individuals	
1	*2*	*3*
A	B	C
B	C	A
C	A	B

Table 6.2   Cyclical preferences with an
efficient outcome: monetary value of
outcome to individual

	Individuals		
	1	*2*	*3*
A	$1000	$1	$2
B	$2	$3	$1
C	$1	$2	$3

If a simple majority rule election is to take place with the preferences listed in table 6.2, the reader can confirm that the same cyclical majority problem arises here as with the preferences in table 6.1. There is no clear majority rule winner. In this case, however, the additional information about the value of the outcomes to the three individuals reveals that outcome A is far more valuable to individual 1 than any of the other outcomes are to any of the other individuals. But while the optimal outcome clearly is A, there is no guarantee that a simple majority rule election will select A.

If there actually were only three voters, all of whom knew each other, there would be a possibility of vote trading that could produce the optimal outcome. Individual A could offer to pay the other two for their votes, or could agree to vote for something they wanted in the future in exchange for their votes now. In elections where there are a small number of people in the voting group, this type of vote exchange occurs frequently and can facilitate producing the outcome that is most valuable to the individuals who are voting. Small groups of voters exist in parliaments and congresses, for example. Unfortunately, it is not always the case that the outcome most valuable to the people in the parliament who are voting will also be the outcome most valuable to the population at large.[16]

The difference between the examples in tables 6.1 and 6.2 is that in table 6.1 only a preference ordering is given, whereas in table 6.2 the relative values of those preferences are also provided. If the relative values of the outcomes can be ascertained in addition to a rank ordering of preferences, then it will be possible to overcome the problems that Arrow identified and select a Pareto-optimal outcome.[17] The problem then is to devise a voting system that asks voters how much they value various options and at the same time gives them an incentive to provide a true answer. This is not an easy task. If voters are asked to pay the amount that they value the option, they have an incentive to understate their preferences to minimize the cost (and free-ride off the votes of others) but, if they do not have to pay the amount that they say they value the option, they have an incentive to overstate their preferences for goods and services that will be provided to them at the expense of others.[18]

There is a voting system that can accomplish these goals, though, which was explained by Clarke (1971) and with more clarity by Tideman and Tullock (1976). Under this voting system, the voter places a monetary value on all the options under consideration. Summing the monetary values of the options provides a monetary value of the benefits of each option which can then be weighed against the cost. In order to provide the incentive to each voter, the voter is required to pay a tax equal to the marginal social cost that the voter imposes on all other voters by casting the vote rather than abstaining.[19]

The fundamental point is that, if each voter is responsible for paying the marginal social cost that his vote imposes on others (by altering the outcome of the election), then voters have the proper incentives to reveal their true preferences. An election system of this type would be complex – probably too complex to be used in place of most existing majority rule elections – but this election system does demonstrate the possibility in theory of designing an election process that can lead voters to reveal their true preferences and produce a Pareto-optimal outcome.

It makes a great deal of sense to link the notion of social welfare with the analysis of the results of social choice through voting. All theories of social welfare that are based on the aggregation of individual welfares (as all the concepts discussed here are) are merely empty theoretical concepts until they are filled out with the actual preferences of individuals. Therefore, there must be a way to discover the individual preferences that form the foundation for the concept of social welfare, and voting is a method of doing so. Even if the true preferences of individuals are revealed, though, there will still be normative disagreements about which Pareto optimum will be the one that maximizes social welfare. But if there is an accurate method for preference revelation, at least the first step is taken in trying to decide which public policies will maximize social welfare.

6.10 Conclusions

The concept of social welfare is a normative one, so ultimately there are no absolutely right answers and there is no way to identify one criterion that is the ultimate true measure of social welfare. Despite the normative foundations that make the concept of social welfare a difficult one to analyse, there are important reasons for studying concepts of social welfare and trying to understand the various competing notions. Public policy decisions must be based on some criteria, either explicit or implicit. At a minimum, the basis for public policy decisions can be better understood if one has a good grasp of the concepts of social welfare, and it is possible that better public policy decisions could be made if the criteria for evaluating the social welfare are laid out explicitly ahead of time.

While all these concepts of social welfare are normative, the Pareto criteria enjoy a greater general acceptance than any of the others. In particular, every concept of social welfare discussed in this essay would agree that social welfare is not maximized unless the society is at a Pareto optimum. The problem is that there are an infinite number of Pareto-optimal outcomes and the criterion of Pareto optimality does not identify which of the Pareto optima is the one that maximizes social welfare. This means that some other criteria must be used to choose among Pareto optima.

The concept of Pareto superiority also enjoys widespread agreement, at least to the extent that every concept discussed here would agree that a Pareto-superior move would enhance the social welfare. But again, there are many possible Pareto-superior moves and, in addition, many of the concepts discussed would argue that social welfare can only be maximized if changes are made that are not Pareto-superior moves. The concept of Pareto superiority gives special status to the status quo since a move cannot be Pareto superior unless nobody is made worse off. If, however, some criterion judges that a person's well-being is higher than the person deserves, then, according to that criterion, a non-Pareto-superior move must be made to maximize social welfare. There is general agreement that a Pareto-superior move will enhance social welfare, but there is not general agreement that social welfare can be maximized by making only Pareto-superior moves.

Since the Pareto criteria do not rank all possible outcomes, one can either accept these limits or look for other methods of evaluating the social welfare. Utilitarians are willing to make explicit trade-offs of one person's utility for another's in search of social-welfare-maximizing public policies. The same types of interpersonal utility trade-offs are implied in the social welfare function. Contractarians, in contrast, look for policies that would be agreed upon under certain circumstances and use this agreement as the basis of the search for policies that enhance the social welfare. Each of these lines of reasoning has its strengths and weaknesses, but all have the common problem that they do not explicitly identify the policies that enhance the social welfare. Rather, they are theoretical frameworks within which public policy choices can be analysed.

One significant feature of the contractarian framework is that it considers the process by which an outcome was generated to evaluate the outcome, rather than looking at the outcome alone. There is a tendency to look at an outcome, such as an income distribution, and judge it as desirable or undesirable without considering the process that produced the outcome. Perhaps some people work harder or invest more in income-producing skills so that they deserve the higher income that they receive, which is what produces an unequal income distribution. As a normative statement, this is open to debate, but it does seem to be important to consider the process that produces an outcome in addition to the outcome itself when examining issues of social welfare.

Because of the problems involved in tying these theoretical constructs of social welfare to the real world, it is desirable to try to link concepts of social welfare to the political systems that make social choices. Social choices, after all, are not made by an omniscient decision-maker who is able to examine social indifference curves, measure and compare the utilities of individuals or step behind a Rawlsian veil of ignorance. Rather, social choices are made through political processes that economists have only begun to analyse in recent decades.[20] Since the examination of social choices is the ultimate goal of social welfare analysis, future progress in the understanding of the concept of social welfare will be linked closely to developments in social choice theory.

NOTES

1 Recent related works of interest are by Elster and Hylland (1986) and Pattanaik and Salles (1983).
2 In order for one person's utility to be compared with another's, utility must be cardinally measurable. For an excellent discussion of cardinality, see Alchian (1971).
3 Problems of utility measurement were well recognized even as the utilitarian paradigm was being rigorously defined in the nineteenth century. F. Y. Edgeworth (1881, pp. 58–60), for example, noted that individuals might differ in the amount of utility they would get from identical consumption bundles (which Edgeworth called the capacity for happiness) and in the disutility they received from work (which Edgeworth called the capacity for work). Nevertheless, Edgeworth felt that adjustments could be made for these differences and took as axiomatic that utility could be measured and compared among individuals.
4 This argument is made by Ricketts (1981).
5 See Yeager (1985) for an elaboration of this theme.

6 See Samuelson (1956) for a discussion of some of these points as well as a defence of the concept of a social welfare function.
7 There is a considerable literature in economics on this point. See Buchanan (1975b) for a discussion about economic analysis of the motivations of politicians.
8 The idea of the social contract can be traced back at least to Locke and Rousseau, and Barker (1960) traces the concept as far back as Plato.
9 Scott Gordon (1976) gives a good summary of the ideas of Rawls and of Buchanan (1975b) and Nozick (1974), whom Gordon calls the new contractarians.
10 See, for example, Buchanan (1975b).
11 Note that this definition is not exactly the dictionary definition of envy. One person might like to have the possessions of another, but might feel that the other person has worked hard and deserves those possessions, and so does not envy the other person according to the dictionary. But there would be envy according to this economic definition. Holcombe (1983) argues that economists should not redefine words like this for their own purposes, but the word will be used as it has been redefined in the literature.
12 Varian (1974) discusses the problems involved in this definition of fairness when production is involved and decides that models with production do not lead to the same clear results as pure exchange models.
13 Holcombe (1983) examines this distinction with regard to the fairness theory described by Baumol (1982).
14 Note that even if there were a unique majority rule winner, there is still no guarantee that the outcome chosen by a majority would maximize social welfare. With a majority imposing its preferences on a minority, some people are made better off while those in the minority are made worse off. Without an interpersonal utility comparison there is no way to conclude that the benefits to the majority outweigh the costs imposed on the minority. See Buchanan (1962) for an elaboration of this theme.
15 See Coleman (1966) for an argument that a social welfare function can be derived in this way. Comments by Park (1967) and Mueller (1967) suggest difficulties with the approach.
16 An important seminal work in this area is by Buchanan and Tullock (1962). A more recent discussion of these issues is given by Holcombe (1985).
17 Recall, however, that there are many possible Pareto-optimal outcomes, so selecting one of them would not ensure that social welfare is maximized according to some of the other social welfare criteria.
18 In his seminal articles on public goods, Samuelson (1954, 1955) stressed the problem of getting people to reveal their true preferences for these goods, and made the argument that without a way for accurate preference revelation the market could not provide the goods efficiently. Public goods, therefore, would be best supplied by government. Samuelson did not analyse how the government could calculate the optimal amount of the good to be produced.
19 The mechanics of the system are too complex to discuss in the space allotted for this essay, but the reader can look to Tideman and Tullock (1976) for a relatively straightforward explanation of how the system works.

184 R. G. Holcombe

20 Buchanan (1975a) discusses the economic analysis of political processes that has been making much progress recently, but was only begun as a serious area of modern inquiry after World War II.

REFERENCES

Alchian, A. A. (1971) 'The meaning of utility measurement', in *Readings in Microeconomics*, 2nd edn. Ed. W. Breit and H. M. Hochman, New York: Holt, Rinehart and Winston, pp. 57–76.

Alchian, A. A., and W. R. Allen (1972) *University Economics*, 3rd edn. Belmont, Calif.: Wadsworth.

Arrow, K. J. (1951) *Social Choice and Individual Values*. New Haven, Conn.: Yale University Press.

Barker, Sir Ernest (1960) *Social Contract*. New York: Oxford University Press.

Baumol, W. J. (1982) 'Applied fairness theory and rationing policy', *American Economic Review* 72, 639–51.

Baumol, W. J. (1986) *Superfairness*. Cambridge, Mass.: MIT Press.

Buchanan, J. M. (1962) 'Politics, policy, and the Pigouvian margins', *Economica, New Series* 29, 17–28.

Buchanan, J. M. (1975a) 'Public finance and public choice', *National Tax Journal* 28, 383–94.

Buchanan, J. M. (1975b) *The Limits of Liberty*. Chicago, Ill.: University of Chicago Press.

Buchanan, J. M., and G. Tullock (1962) *The Calculus of Consent*. Ann Arbor, Mich.: University of Michigan Press.

Clarke, E. H. (1971) 'Multipart pricing of public goods', *Public Choice* 11, 17–33.

Coleman, J. S. (1966) 'The possibility of a social welfare function', *American Economic Review* 56, 1105–22.

Edgeworth, F. Y. (1881) *Mathematical Psychics*. London: Kegan Paul.

Elster, J. and A. Hylland (1986) *Foundations of Social Choice Theory*. Cambridge: Cambridge University Press.

Foley, D. (1967) 'Resource allocation and the public sector', *Yale Economic Essays* 7, 45–98.

Gordon, S. (1976) 'The new contractarians', *Journal of Political Economy* 84, 573–90.

Holcombe, R. G. (1983) 'Applied fairness theory: comment', *American Economic Review* 73, 1153–6.

Holcombe, R. G. (1985) *An Economic Analysis of Democracy*. Carbondale, Ill.: Southern Illinois University Press.

Mueller, D. (1967) 'The possibility of a social welfare function: comment', *American Economic Review* 57, 1304–11.

Nozick, R. (1974) *Anarchy, State, and Utopia*. New York: Basic Books.

Park, R. E. (1967) 'The possibility of a social welfare function: comment', *American Economic Review* 75, 1300–4.

Pattanaik, P. K., and M. Salles (eds) (1983) *Social Choice and Welfare*. Amsterdam: North-Holland.

Rawls, J. (1971) *A Theory of Justice*. Cambridge, Mass.: Harvard University Press.

Ricketts, M. (1981) 'Tax, theory and tax policy', in *The Political Economy of Taxation*. Ed. A. Peacock and F. Forte, New York: St Martin's Press, pp. 29–46.

Samuelson, P. A. (1954) 'The pure theory of public expenditure', *Review of Economics and Statistics* 36, 387–9.

Samuelson, P. A. (1955) 'A diagrammatic exposition of a theory of public expenditure', *Review of Economics and Statistics* 37, 350–6.

Samuelson, P. A. (1956) 'Social indifference curves', *Quarterly Journal of Economics* 70, 1–22.

Tideman, T. N., and G. Tullock (1976) 'A new and superior process for making social choices', *Journal of Political Economy* 84, 1145–60.

Varian, H. R. (1974) 'Equity, envy, and efficiency', *Journal of Economic Theory* 9, 63–91.

Yeager, L. B. (1985) 'Rights, contract, and utility in policy espousal', *Cato Journal* 5, 259–94.

7

Income and capital

G. C. Harcourt and G. Whittington

Irving Fisher (1930, p. 51[1]) described income as 'the alpha and omega of economics'. This may have been an exaggeration, but it was a forgivable one. Income is certainly a fundamental concept in economics. It features in basic microeconomic theory, when budget constraints are drawn on indifference curve diagrams to derive inferences about consumer choice which are fundamental to the analysis of market systems, and, at the macroeconomic level, national income is widely regarded as the most important single index of the prosperity of an economy. Associated with income is the concept of capital. The two concepts are so closely related both in theoretical analysis and in practical measurement that it is impossible to discuss one in isolation from the other. Despite Fisher's emphasis on income (which was intended to highlight a point in his own analysis rather than to disparage the importance of the concept of capital[2]) it is essentially a complementary concept to that of capital.

In view of the undoubted importance of both concepts, it is perhaps surprising that they receive only cursory and superficial treatment in the typical text on economics. Equally, in much work in applied economics, it is regarded as sufficient to use conventional rule-of-thumb measures of income or capital without due consideration for the subtleties of the underlying concepts or the strong assumptions which must be made if the practical measures are to be given a valid interpretation. The objective of this chapter is to give the reader an appreciation of these problems. The plan is as follows. Firstly, the concept of personal income and capital is introduced in section 7.1. The example of personal income and capital is used to explain the relationship between the two concepts and some of the fundamental theoretical difficulties in defining them. There is also a short discussion on income and capital as bases for taxation. In section 7.2 we turn to the application of the concepts of income and capital in the business sector. This has been an issue of great practical importance in recent years, which have seen a heated debate on accounting for changing prices (sometimes loosely described as 'inflation accounting', although relative prices can change even in the absence of pure inflation). In section 7.3 we turn to the macroeconomic theme of national income and capital. The section includes a discussion of the theoretical controversy surrounding the valuation of aggregate capital, as well as a brief account of how national income and capital are measured in practice. Finally, in section 7.4 some particularly important themes from the previous discussion are drawn out.

7.1 Personal Income and Capital

To the majority of the population, income probably means just what its name suggests, 'incomings' or cash receipts during a period. Thus, wages are income and so are dividends and interest received. The natural way to measure income would therefore seem to be to sum cash receipts for a period, with perhaps some adjustment to allow for changes in amounts owed or owing. This is indeed the view of income encouraged by tax laws, which usually, for very good practical reasons, stick as closely as possible to a receipts basis. It is also the way in which income is measured in many studies of consumer behaviour, e.g. in household surveys.[3] Capital, in this everyday world, is represented by an individual's wealth at a point in time: money, real property, personal chattels, investments and amounts due to be received ('debtors') less amounts owing ('creditors'). Changes in capital might be regarded as 'capital gains' which are separate from income, especially when they are not realized by sale; an obvious example is the appreciation in value of owner-occupied houses. This scenario for capital and the separation of capital from income is also consistent with the tax systems of a number of countries (certainly that of the UK) which tax 'capital gains' differently from income, or not at all. It is also consistent with many other legal and institutional arrangements, which probably reflect attitudes which are widely held in society, and which distinguish between income and capital in this way. An alternative view is the comprehensive income concept, as proposed by Simons (1938) for tax purposes: this includes all gains as income.

A view of income and capital similar (but not identical) to the popular cash receipts view was derived by Irving Fisher (1906, 1930) by a more sophisticated route. In Fisher's view, true income was the psychic pleasure enjoyed by an individual during a period. However, psychic income cannot be measured, so, as an observable alternative, Fisher proposed what he called 'real income' (i.e. consumption of real goods) which is 'measured by the cost of living' (i.e. the cost of consumption during the period). The latter concept is different from expenditure on consumption in the case of durable goods which are not consumed in the period in which they are purchased: the cost of the services consumed during the period represents the relevant charge for durable goods in the 'cost of living'. Additionally, Fisher recognized that the concept of income in everyday use is that described earlier, which he defined as money income, i.e. 'all money *received* which is not obviously, and in the nature of the case, to be devoted to reinvestment' (Fisher, 1930, p. 49). An important source of difference between 'money income' and 'real income' as defined by Fisher is that the former included savings (money income in excess of expenditure), whereas the latter included dissavings (expenditures in excess of money income).

Capital, in Fisher's scheme of things, has value only '*as a source of income*'. Its value is found by discounting future income to be derived from it, using the rate of interest as the discount rate. Capital gains are therefore not part of income but 'are merely capitalisation of future income'. This explains Fisher's emphasis on the relative importance of capital and income: income is of primary importance because capital would have no value if it did not ultimately give rise to benefits in the form of real income. However, it can be seen that the two concepts are essentially complementary: the real income would not accrue if the source (capital) did not exist. The dichotomy between the two is very clear in Fisher's elegant framework and it enabled him to clarify the consumer's problem of intertemporal choice under conditions of certainty, and the role of the rate of interest in determining that choice. It also led him to derive the policy prescription that taxes should be based on expenditure (as a proxy for 'real income') rather than comprehensive income (as advocated by Simons, 1938), on the ground that comprehensive income tax involved the double taxation of savings, once when they were initially made out of taxed income and a second time when the returns on investment were received.

Despite the theoretical elegance of Fisher's analysis, it suffered from a crucial deficiency in its refusal to regard savings as part of income. It thus ruled out a definition of income consistent with the common understanding of the word and substituted something different which already had a clearly understood name, consumption. As Kaldor commented, 'Fisher's approach has the virtue of yielding a simple and unambiguous result, but it does not accord with everyday notions on the subject; and in a sense, it only solves the problem by eliminating it' (Kaldor, 1955, p. 113). An alternative concept of income, which did include savings, was developed by the Swedish economists, notably Lindahl (1933). The alternative income concept proposed by Lindahl was income as interest. He argued that Fisher's own concept of capital, valued as a discounted sum of a future stream of returns, implies that capital should earn a normal rate of interest in each period, and that this interest should be regarded as income, irrespective of whether it is consumed or saved. True to the Swedish tradition, Lindahl also explicitly introduced uncertainty, by making a distinction between income anticipated *ex ante* at the beginning of a period, and income actually accruing *ex post* at the end of the period. Fisher's analysis, in contrast, had not dealt with uncertainty.

The Swedish approach was the basis of the celebrated discussion of income concepts by Hicks (1946), which is still the standard source of reference on the concept of personal income and its relationship to capital. Hicks's broad definition is of 'a man's income as the maximum value which he can consume during a week, and still expect to be as well off at the end of the week as he was at the beginning' (Hicks, 1946, p. 103). Thus, 'the practical purpose of income is to serve as a guide for prudent conduct'. In practice, this concept is difficult to measure and Hicks considers three 'approximations to the central meaning'. It should be noted that these are all *ex ante* concepts of income, based on expectations ('still expect to be as well off'), as must always be the case if the information is to be a guide to conduct.

Hicks's first approximation is that 'Income No. 1 is . . . the amount which can be spent during a period if there is to be an expectation of maintaining intact the capital value of prospective receipts (in money terms)' (Hicks, 1946, p. 104). Capital value is defined as the discounted present value of future receipts, so Hicks's Income No. 1 is consistent with Lindahl's view of income as interest: the amount which can be spent during the period will be the money rate of interest on opening capital. However, Hicks sees problems with this approach when interest rates are expected to change. In such a case, the maintenance of the money value of capital will lead to variations in income between periods, income being high when the rate of interest is high. Thus, maintaining money capital will not necessarily be adequate to maintain a constant level of potential money expenditure on consumption (if interest rates fall) and may maintain more than is necessary for this purpose (if interest rates rise).

In order to overcome the latter problem, Hicks proposed 'Income No. 2' as 'the maximum amount the individual can spend this week, and still be able to spend the same amount in each ensuing week' (Hicks, 1946, p. 105). This is equivalent to Income No. 1 when interest rates are expected to remain constant but, when they are expected to change, it allows money capital to be adjusted in such a way as to compensate for interest rate changes and allow a constant money expenditure on consumption. Hicks feels that this is 'a closer approximation to the central concept than Income No. 1 is'. In other words, when the criteria of consumption maintenance and capital maintenance conflict with one another, in Hicks's view the former should prevail. In this respect, Hicks follows Fisher in regarding the consumption flow as being of primary importance and capital as of subsidiary importance.

There is another refinement, however, which must be added to Hicks's income concept if it is to provide for the maintenance of *real* consumption in a period of changing prices. In order to deal with this problem, we have 'Income No. 3 . . . defined as the maximum amount of money which the individual can spend this week, and still expect to be able to spend the same amount *in real terms* in each ensuing week'. Obviously a similar modification could have been made to Income No. 1, defining the capital value to be maintained in real terms rather than in money terms, but Hicks did not pursue this possibility because he felt that consumption maintenance was nearer to his central concept. However, even Income No. 3 is only an approximation to the central concept, for two reasons. Firstly, we have the index number problem of defining what precise combination of goods constitutes 'real consumption', i.e. what weights should be applied to different commodities. Secondly, the definition is realistically couched in terms of *spending* but a formally correct definition would be in terms of *consumption*. The difference between the two arises from the existence of durable consumption goods. Estimating the consumption of durables does, of course, enter even Irving Fisher's comparatively simple definition of income as consumption, but it also adds complications to Hicks's definition and measurement of income.

Hicks's conclusion from this analysis of *ex ante* income is that the complexities of defining a measurable proxy for the central concept, combined with the essentially subjective nature of the concept itself (depending on the expectations of individuals), mean that 'we shall be well advised to eschew *income* and *saving* in economic dynamics. They are bad tools, which break in our hands' (Hicks, 1946, p. 107). However, this is in the context of an economic theory that is intended to explain the conduct of economic agents which must necessarily depend on their future expectations. Hicks points out that there are also three *ex post* concepts of income corresponding to the *ex ante* concepts discussed earlier and concedes that these are 'a useful measuring-rod for economic progress' (Hicks, 1946, p. 109). If anything, Hicks is overoptimistic about the accuracy of *ex post* measures. For example, he describes the *ex post* counterpart of Income No. 1 as 'not a subjective affair . . . it is almost completely objective' (Hicks, 1946, p. 109). In fact, there is a subjective element in the assessment of both closing and opening capital values. The valuation of closing capital depends upon the existence of a complete set of markets in competitive equilibrium which value it at a unique amount which is equal to the discounted present value of the future receipts to which it gives rise. When, in the next section of this essay, the measurement of business income is considered, it will be seen that this assumption is questionable. The valuation of opening capital in *ex post* income measurement gives rise to a difficulty to which Kaldor (1955) gives particular attention: it is necessary to calculate a revised value of opening capital which is not observable. This is the value of opening capital which would have obtained at the beginning of the period had the state of knowledge been the same as that which obtained at the end of the period. This recalculation of opening capital is necessary in order to identify windfall gains (or losses) which occur within the period as a result of the revision of expectations about future returns and interest rates. Such gains need to be separated from current income because they represent changes of expectations about future income, i.e. they are a revision of capital values rather than income.

Thus, all measurement of income and capital involves a degree of subjectivity, although it is reasonable to accept that *ex post* measurements of income are relatively less subjective than *ex ante* measurements. Moreover, it is important not to reject any form of measurement merely because it does not conform precisely to some theoretical ideal. Hicks approves of *ex post* measures of national income and also of business accounting measures which are 'rough approximations used by the business man to steer himself through the bewildering change of situation which confront him' (Hicks, 1946, p. 102). This draws attention to another important consideration: the appropriate concepts and measures of income and capital will depend very much on the purpose for which they are used.

Subsequent sections of this essay will consider the specific concepts of income and capital used in business income calculations (section 7.2) and in the measurement of national income and national capital (section 7.3). This section concludes with a brief discussion of the concepts used or advocated for the purposes of personal taxation.

Taxable Income and Capital

Fisher's advocacy of consumption as a basis both of income measurement and of direct taxation has already been discussed. The alternative concept, comprehensive income, was advocated strongly by H. C. Simons (1938). This included not only savings (thus making it closer to Fisher's 'money income' than to his 'real income') but also all gains of the period (hence the description 'comprehensive'). Thus, Simons would include windfall gains or 'capital gains' in taxable comprehensive income. This was perfectly legitimate from his point of view, because he was mainly concerned with ability to pay tax and reasoned that all gains enhanced ability to pay, irrespective of their source. Fisher, in contrast, was more concerned with efficiency, i.e. with avoiding distortion of the price system by taxes, and reasoned that the alleged double taxation of savings discriminated against savings and investment relative to immediate consumption. This illustrates how different income measures might serve different purposes. It should also be noted that both Fisher and Simons were aware that personal income (i.e. the flow of utility to the individual) is not fully captured in a stream of consumption expenditure or money income and that personal capital consists of more than the value of personal wealth in the marketplace. In particular, human capital is an important component of individual wealth which has since been explored more thoroughly by economists (notably at the University of Chicago, to which Simons belonged). However, psychic income and human capital raise measurement problems even greater than those already discussed, so that they are hardly likely to provide practical bases for direct taxation.

The issue of whether consumption or income should be the basis of direct taxation has continued to be aired since the days of Fisher and Simons. Kaldor (1955) wrote a powerful treatise in favour of expenditure taxation, based on his experience as a member of the UK Royal Commission on Taxation. He concluded that income not only is a difficult concept to define precisely (as Hicks also found) but also is extremely difficult to measure in practice; this reinforced his case for expenditure (which is less difficult to measure) as a tax base. Clearly, ease and objectivity of measurement are most important properties of a tax base, in order to prevent avoidance and evasion by the taxpayer.

The Meade Committee (1978) also considered the relative merits of income and expenditure as bases for direct taxation. Like Kaldor, it concluded that expenditure had practical advantages of measurement over comprehensive income. It also concluded that, because of the considerable range of savings and investment reliefs already given in the UK, expenditure tax, (i.e. excluding savings from the tax base) was closer to present UK practice than was income tax. The Meade Committee laid great stress on the need to remove the distortion in the capital market which results from the situation that different forms of saving and investment are accorded different tax treatments. It is notable that Fisher's 'double taxation of savings' argument against income tax did not feature strongly in the discussion. The reason for this is that economic theorists are now much more aware than in Fisher's day of the difficulties of deriving simple welfare implications in a world characterized by imperfect markets. Fisher's argument implicitly assumes that all markets are perfectly competitive and that taxes will therefore interfere with the optimal allocation of resources achieved by the price system. Once we consider imperfect markets, unequal taxation of different activities or commodities may actually serve to correct the consequences of market imperfections. Furthermore, the 'double taxation of savings' argument considers only one choice facing the taxpayer: that between present and future goods (i.e. the savings decision). In practice, direct taxation involves another choice, that between goods and leisure (i.e. the decision about the amount of work to do) and the latter commodity is usually untaxed. It is possible that a broadly based income tax, levied at a lower rate, might induce less distortion in the work decision than a more narrowly based expenditure tax levied at a higher rate (to obtain the same revenue). A readable and penetrating theoretical analysis of some of these issues is provided by Atkinson and Sandmo (1980).

Capital has also provided a basis for taxation, but to a lesser extent (in revenue terms) than income. The main reasons for this are twofold. Firstly, the valuation of personal wealth poses difficult problems when wealth includes items which are not readily marketable, and yet excluding such items would lead to inequities in the system. Secondly, there is the problem of liquidity. Taxes on accrued wealth may have to be met by realizing some of the wealth and this may involve breaking up valuable productive units such as farms or business firms; yet any special exemptions for these types of asset will lead to inequities and probably avoidance (e.g. wealthy people will invest in farms). Both these problems occur in the three main types of capital tax, but to a variable degree. The taxation of capital gains would suffer greatly from measurement problems if it were assessed on accrued rather than realized gains, because it would be based on the difference between two unreliable wealth measures. The accruals basis (which would, for example, be the logical basis to use if capital gains were included in a comprehensive income tax base) would also give rise to a greater liquidity problem than a realization basis. For these reasons, the UK Capital Gains Tax is assessed on a realization basis, but this means that it can be avoided by postponement of realization. The second type of capital tax is the inheritance or transfer tax. Here, the valuation problem is less severe than under an accrued capital gains tax because valuation is required only once, at the point of transfer, but the liquidity problem still arises because the transfer does not usually take the form of an open market sale. Thus, taxes of this type (such as the UK's Inheritance Tax) often include reliefs for business assets or agricultural property. The third type of capital tax is the wealth tax, levied annually on total wealth. This obviously raises the valuation problem, but it is not so severe as would be the case in measuring accrued capital gains because it is based on a total value of wealth rather than changes in wealth, so that valuation errors will not be so large proportionately. It also raises potential liquidity problems, but these depend upon the rate of wealth tax relative to the money rate of return on wealth, and on how the return on wealth is taxed: a wealth tax is obviously more severe if it is levied in addition to a tax on returns rather than instead of such a tax.

This brief discussion of taxation has been intended merely to give an indication of the part which income and capital can play in the tax base. Much fuller accounts of the issues involved are given by Kay and King (1986) and the Meade Committee (1978). However, this account has demonstrated that measures of income and capital are contingent upon the purposes for which they are used. Even for tax purposes, there is no unique measure of income or capital which will meet the needs of all tax systems, irrespective of the objectives of the system or the structure of the other taxes within it.

7.2 Business Income and Capital

The economic progress of a business is measured by the accountant in terms of both capital and income. Capital is measured in the balance sheet by summing the assets (debits) and deducting liabilities (credits) to leave a residual claim which is the proprietors' capital or 'equity' in the business at a single point in time. Income is measured over a period in the profit and loss account, which sums revenues and deducts expenses to leave a profit (or loss) attributable to the proprietors. The ratio of profit to proprietors' capital is the accounting rate of return, which is often used as an index of economic performance, although it is by no means the same thing as the economist's ideal measure of the rate of return.[4] Equally, the accountant's measure of assets or of proprietors' capital is not usually a current market valuation, still less the discounted present value of future receipts which would be the valuation preferred by many economists. Similarly, the accountant's measure of profit does not include all gains at current market values or allow for the maintenance of the market value of opening capital, as is implied by Hicks's Income No. 1 measured *ex post*. Thus, despite the superficial resemblance of the accountant's figures to the income and capital concepts proposed by economists, they fall really into Hicks's category of rough signposts to guide the business man, rather than ideal concepts.

The accountant's traditional procedure has been to use historical cost as the basis of accounting values, i.e. assets are valued at what was paid for them (with some pragmatic modifications) less, in the case of long-lived assets with finite lives, an allowance for depreciation, the amount of the original outlay which has now been used up (by being charged against profit) as a result of the effluxion of time. Thus, values in balance sheets do not produce current valuations of capital. The profit and loss account charges costs on a historical cost basis, so that depreciation of fixed assets and the cost of materials are not necessarily charged at their current cost at the time of sale. Conversely, the gains shown in the profit and loss account do not include unrealized appreciation in the value of assets during the period. Thus, the accountant's measure of profit does not correspond at all closely to the Hicksian ideal (in his *ex post* No. 1 measure) of consumption (which would be dividends distributed to proprietors or shareholders, in the case of a business firm) plus closing capital less opening capital.

The accountant's historical cost measures have always been rough approximations, but the period of rapidly changing prices since the early 1970s has made them look even rougher, so rough in fact that efforts have been made to improve them. There has been a debate in many countries as to the appropriate method of effecting improvements[5] and the chosen solution has varied with circumstances. In Latin America a form of general index adjustment has been adopted in a number of leading countries. This is known as constant purchasing power accounting (CPP). The essence of the method is to restate historical cost figures in current prices by applying the change in the general price index which has occurred since the historical cost was established. To take a very simplified example, assume that a speculator in gold spends £10,000 on gold at time 0 and still holds it at time 2. There are no other transactions. The general index is 100 at time 0, 110 at time 1 and 132 at time 2. Under the historical cost method traditionally favoured by accountants his balance sheets and profit figures will be as follows.

Historical Cost

Balance sheet

At time 0

	£		£
Proprietor's capital	10,000	Asset (gold), at cost	10,000

The balance sheet will be the same at times 1 and 2, since no transactions have taken place.

Profit

	Period to 1
Revenue	NIL
Expenditure	NIL
Profit	NIL

The same would apply in the period 1 to 2, because no transactions have taken place.

Under CPP the balance sheets would be restated as follows.

CPP

Balance sheets

At time t_0

	£		£
Proprietor's capital	10,000	Asset (gold)	10,000

At time t_1

Proprietor's capital $(10,000 \times 110/100)$	11,000	Asset $(10,000 \times 110/100)$	11,000

At time t_2

Proprietor's capital		Asset	
(11,000 × 132/110)	13,200	(11,000 × 132/110)	13,200

It will be seen that the CPP general index restatement affects both sides of the balance sheet equally in this case (the introduction of assets or liabilities of fixed money value would change this), so that the net income is unchanged from the historical cost case. Thus profit for each period is nil in our example. The adjustment to opening capital to allow for general inflation is in the spirit of Hicks's proposal for real income measures, but it is in the context of his No. 1 measure, capital maintenance, rather than Nos 2 and 3, consumption maintenance. The restatement of assets can be taken as a broad-brush general index attempt to revalue closing capital. Where there is pure inflation (all prices increase in the same proportion) this adjustment will be entirely successful, and it will be relatively more successful the greater the extent of pure inflation. This may explain the adoption of the CPP method in Latin America, where inflation rates are very high. In countries with lower rates of inflation and relatively high relative prices, we might expect more emphasis on recognizing specific price changes, and this has been the case especially in the English-speaking world.

The method of specific price change accounting which has gained practical support in both the UK and the USA (although it has recently ceased to be compulsory in both countries) is known as current cost accounting (CCA). The principle of CCA is to restate assets in terms of changes in their specific prices. In one form, used in the calculation of operating profit, it restates opening capital also in terms of specific prices, in order to reflect the maintenance of the operating capability of the firm. Thus, no capital gains will be recognized in the profit statement and, in our specific example, the profit will remain nil. If we assume that the price of gold in our example was 100 at time 0, 120 at time 1 and 150 at time 2, we shall have the following CCA balance sheets.

CCA

Balance sheets

£ £

At time 0

Proprietor's capital	10,000	Asset (gold)	10,000

At time 1

Proprietor's capital		Asset	
(10,000 × 120/100)	12,000	(10,000 × 120/100)	12,000

At time 2

Proprietor's capital	Asset
(12,000 × 150/120) 15,000	(12,000 × 150/120) 15,000

Thus the asset is now revalued at a more realistic assessment of its current value. However, proprietors' opening capital is also restated by an equal amount, so that no gain is shown for the period. The justification for this adjustment to opening capital is that the proprietor must maintain the operating capability of the business, i.e. its physical capacity. In this case, the actual amount of gold held by the proprietor is unchanged,[6] and in this sense he has made no gain.

The concept of capital maintenance has been the subject of much debate in the contexts of business income and also of national income. Hicks (1974) describes the adherents of physical capital maintenance as 'materialists'. The alternative view of capital is that it is not a collection of physical assets but a fund of purchasing power, representing command over goods and services in general. Hicks describes this as the 'fundist' view of capital, and it can be seen that this view could be associated with both the real and the money capital maintenance concepts described earlier. The historical cost method used money capital as the benchmark to be maintained before recognizing a gain, so that the fund in that case was defined in money units. The CPP method used real capital, defined in terms of constant purchasing power, as the benchmark.

It can be seen that we can combine revaluation of assets by specific price changes, as in the CCA case, with either of the 'fundist' capital maintenance concepts. Using money capital maintenance would involve leaving the proprietor's original capital at £10,000 in each period and treating the increment in value as a gain. Thus the balance sheet at time 1 would show an accrued gain of £2,000 (i.e. £12,000 minus £10,000) and that at time 2 would show an accrued gain of £5,000. The profit statement would show a gain of £2,000 in the first period (ending at t_1) and £3,000 in the second (ending at t_2). This type of accounting method was proposed by the Sandilands Committee (1975) in its statement of gains, which was one component of a proposed CCA system.

The latter proposal might seem adequate when the general price level is stable but unsatisfactory in periods of inflation. The real purchasing power adjustment to capital (used in the CPP system) can deal with inflation. Combining this with CCA asset valuation produces what is sometimes known as a 'real terms' system. In the case used above, this would produce the following results:

Real terms

Balance sheets

£   £

At time 0

| Proprietor's capital | 10,000 | Asset | 10,000 |

At time 1

Proprietor's capital   Asset
(10,000 × 110/100) 11,000   (10,000 × 120/100) 12,000
Real gain
(12,000 − 11,000)   1,000
                     12,000   12,000

At time 2

Proprietor's capital   Asset
(11,000 × 132/110) 13,200   (12,000 × 150/120) 15,000
Accumulated gain
(1,000 × 132/110)   1,200
Real gain of the
period
(15,000 − 14,400)   600
                     15,000   15,000

The income statements would be as follows:

Period 1 (t_0 to t_1)

£

Operating profit		NIL
Gain on holding asset	(£12,000 − £10,000 × 110/100)	1,000
Total real gains		1,000

Period 2 (t_1 to t_2)

Operating profit		NIL
Gain on holding asset	(£15,000 − £12,000 × 132/110)	600
		600

This method differs from the pure CPP and CCA methods illustrated earlier in so far as it reports the real gains on the asset, i.e. the amount by which its rise in price has exceeded the rise in the general price level. Whether this gain should be reported as part of profit or separately is a matter of some controversy. The format illustrated above follows the classical dichotomy proposed by Edwards and Bell (1961), who separate operating profit (calculated on a 'materialist' physical capital maintenance concept) from holding gains (calculated on a 'fundist' purchasing power capital maintenance concept).

Apart from the choice of capital maintenance concept and the question of whether holding gains should be separated from operating gains, there has also been controversy about the method of valuation to be adopted. Accountants traditionally cling to historical cost because it is supposed to be more objective than current value (having a transactions base) but even amongst proponents of current value there is controversy about the precise measure to be used. For example, there is a choice between four broad types of current market price: replacement cost, realizable value, discounted present value and value to the business (an eclectic measure which selects one of the other three bases according to rules derived from reasoning of an opportunity cost variety).[7] Within each of these broad methods, there are many variations.

Thus, the accountant has to choose between a bewildering variety of alternative methods of measuring income. It might be hoped that the earlier discussion of the analysis by Hicks and others would guide this choice. Unfortunately, it offers little guidance. The reason is quite simple. The accountant inhabits a real world which is characterized by uncertainty and imperfect and incomplete markets. Thus, replacement cost, selling price and other current values may well differ from one another, offering a choice of values, and income is an ill-defined concept. Beaver and Demski (1979) put this argument more fully and rigorously, and conclude that the role of accounting measures in such a world is not to provide a single unique measure of 'true' economic income, which does not exist, but rather to provide useful summarized information about a firm's economic progress. In other words, the accountant is a provider of Hicks's 'rough approximations, used by the business man'. However, this does not mean that some approximations are not less rough or more useful than others. What it does mean is that the choice of accounting measures will be contingent upon the precise needs of the user of the information and the circumstances of the business being described. It will not be determined uniquely by theoretical analysis of the concepts of income and capital under artificially idealized conditions.

7.3 National Income and Capital

In considering the concepts of income and capital at the level of the whole economy and in discussing the meaning and measurement of capital in particular, it is first useful to sketch two different views (or 'visions') of the accumulation process at work in capitalist economies. One view is derived from the work of the neoclassical economists of the nineteenth century, especially Walras, and comes to modern readers principally through the writings of Irving Fisher, as was pointed out in the discussion of income and capital at the levels of the individual and the business (see also Tobin, 1987). The alternative view has its roots more in classical political economy and especially in Marx. In its modern form it owes much to Sraffa's influence, to Keynes and his followers and to Kalecki and his followers, not least Joan Robinson whose own notable contributions were much influenced by Keynes and, more and more in her later years, Kalecki, and by Marx and Sraffa.[8]

In the Fisherian vision of the economy, the accumulation process is the outcome of the attempts by individuals to allocate the use of their resources over time, including borrowing and lending, so as to maximize their intertemporal utility from the resulting consumption streams. It is no accident that the two dominant theories of the consumption function (other than that of Keynes), namely, Friedman's permanent income hypothesis and Modigliani's life cycle hypothesis, have their origins in Irving Fisher's ideas. In the economy as a whole, therefore, the split between present and future consumption streams is seen as determined by the equality between the rate of time preference and the rate of interest at which the market for loans is cleared. Viewed thus, the dominance of consumption as the objective of economic life is brought out while both capital accumulation and the firm serve merely as vehicles through which the lifetime utilities of their owners are attained.

This view of the accumulation process incidentally provides a rationale for the use of an index of the general price level rather than indices of prices of specific assets for the estimation of capital to be maintained in the measurement of business incomes; for if firms are merely agents of the ultimate consumers (their shareholders, for example) and have no rationale of their own, rather than going concerns associated with particular assets and activities, then it is general purchasing power and *its* maintenance that is of primary importance, and the prices of particular assets and the value of particular activities are ultimately beside the point. Fisher's approach highlights the view that the economy originated for the benefit of the individuals who make it up and that the institutions that have developed are, on this view, but the means to this particular end.[9]

By contrast, the classical, Marxian and Keynesian view is that profit-making and accumulation are ends in themselves, ways of life forced on individual capitalists if they are to survive in the Marxian scheme, because this is what capitalists like or feel compelled to do (sometimes, in Keynes's view, for Freudian reasons). Thus, the activity of the economy is directed by the striving of the decision-making classes, especially with regard to accumulation, to achieve their own ends, rather than merely to serve those of consumers. Of course, one means of achieving their ends will be to satisfy consumer demands, but the latter are seen as principally socially determined and basically subordinate to the accumulation process. Thus, in Kalecki's writings, the constraint on consumption expenditure is mainly the size of the wage bill and what *it* derives from the interaction of desired accumulation and the distribution of income, which is itself determined by the differing saving propensities of the wage-earners and profit-receivers and the discretion which business people have concerning the price–money wage relationship. In Kaldor's work, though, the effective demand aspects disappeared for a while; accumulation and profit-making had first claim on the community's resources and the wage-earners, in effect, accepted the residual. Such a view is also in accord with the accounting convention that firms should be regarded as 'going concerns' and income and capital struck accordingly. This is hardly surprising, since the original development of double entry book-keeping and the rise of the capitalist mode of production went hand in hand. Nor is it surprising that, from this point of view, it is more appropriate to undertake inflation adjustments by using specific price indices so that, if the firm is to continue as a 'going concern', it must be able to measure its income in such a way that maintaining activity in *particular* activities is a possibility, should it wish to do so. Similarly, prices in the first tradition are conceptually indices of scarcity while in the latter they are indices of the difficulty of reproduction.[10]

The preceding sketches provide a perspective from which to view modern treatments of (and controversies about) the concepts of income and capital in the economy as a whole. They also help us to avoid unnecessary confusion which otherwise may occur (and often has). One of the first great insights into the working of capitalism was the recognition of the tendency in a system of free competition for rates of profit to be equalized in all activities. Such a tendency was common to Smith, Ricardo and Marx and, moving closer to the present day, to the first generation of neoclassical economists, especially Jevons, Marshall, Walras and Wicksell. It follows that, very early on, the concept, i.e. the meaning, of capital had to be explored and, complementary to it, the origin and the determinants of the size of profits, especially of the rate of profits in aggregate, to which ultimately the rates in each activity had to measure up. There was, as we would say now, both a macro and a micro aspect to the theories of profits and capital in both classical and early neoclassical theory. It is no accident, therefore, that Piero Sraffa, for example, in attempting his revival of classical political economy, consistently refers to the rate of profits and treats it as a macro concept – the ratio of the surplus, after wages and the means of production have been deducted from the gross product, to the means of production in the economy *as a whole* (e.g. in his circulating commodity model of part 1 of *Production of Commodities by Means of*

Commodities, Sraffa 1960). Ricardo and Marx also thought of the rate of profits as a macro concept; Ricardo in the *Principles* and Marx in *Capital* both looked for its origins and measurement in significant quantities of embodied labour-time, a view which has received its most rigorous statement in modern times in Sraffa's work. (This emphasis was first brought out most clearly by the late Ronald Meek when he discussed the similarity between Marx's exposition of this point of view and Sraffa's well-known expression $r = R (1-w)$, where r is the rate of profits, R is the maximum rate of profits and w is the wage measured in terms of Sraffa's Standard commodity (see, for example, Meek, 1967, pp. 175-8).) Such an approach continues to underlie the work of modern Marxists and of many in the post-Keynesian school to whom it is as natural as it is for the business people, whose behaviour and activities they are trying to understand, to think in terms of profits and capital. We mention this because in the other, more orthodox and mainstream, development such concepts have rather fallen out of favour. The emphasis there is on the problem of intertemporal prices, and rates of return, in so far as they appear at all, are regarded as derived concepts that are not of special or primary importance.

Yet that could not be said of the first generation of neoclassical economists who regarded it as an important task to explain what determines the *overall* rate of profits and to give meaning to capital as a whole, both because they saw this as an essential task of economic analysis and also, at least in some specific instances, e.g. J. B. Clark and the Austrians, as a counter to what they viewed was the pernicious influence of the labour theory of value. The latter, as every schoolchild ought to know, is primarily a theory of the origin and measure of profits in the capitalist mode of production, an analysis which has as a corollary a theory of the origin and measure of the pattern of relative prices of production. (It is certainly *not* the proposition that commodities exchange in proportion to their embodied labour values.)

Such a background allows us to put into perspective the modern debates in capital theory which concern the meaning, and not just the measurement, of 'capital'. They began in the public domain in 1953 (although there is evidence that Piero Sraffa was already posing disquieting questions for his Cambridge colleagues about these issues nearly 20 years before; see Harcourt, 1986, pp. 99), with Joan Robinson's question, in her 1953-4 article, about in what units K is measured.[11] The context of the question was, what meaning could be given to the notion of 'capital' as a factor of production within the neoclassical supply and demand framework? Why was there a need to do this? In the Fisherian approach it is argued that it is not necessary – that, with time preference and the rate of return over cost in its modern guise of the social rate of return on investment or saving (see Solow, 1963), we have no need to mention either 'capital' or 'its' marginal product. The answer is both simple and fundamental. *If* it is believed that there is a need to explain the rate of profits in the economy as a whole, and if it is believed that the intuitive insight of the supply and demand approach is that when we have relatively more of something its price is low and vice versa, *then* we need to know exactly what we mean by a quantity of capital, just as we need to know what we mean by a quantity of labour (measured in hours or by heads) and a quantity of land (measured in acres). That is, we need to have a *technical* unit in which to measure capital *as a whole before* the analysis starts, so that it must be measured in a unit which is independent of distribution and prices. Only then may we argue that relative quantities and accompanying marginal products are important determinants of relative prices and of the associated distributive shares.

Once stated like this, it becomes clear why, apart from the obvious fiction of malleable capital with its accompanying fanciful synonyms of leets, butter, Meccano sets (why not Lego?) and so on, it is impossible to find such a unit. For, as Marshall was one of the first economists to point out, even within the supply and demand framework, capital has at least two dimensions: funds, free capital seeking outlets in those areas which offer the highest expected returns; and hard objects, hostages to the uncertain fortunes of an unknown future once the investment has been made. In neither case is it possible to make much sense of it as a quantity measured independently of distribution and prices. (Joan Robinson argued that it could be given a limited meaning as a factor of production when measured as 'real' capital in terms of labour-time but that this measure, depending as it does on the rate of profits, is not independent of distribution and does not result in propositions about the sizes of the rate of profits and the wage rate which resemble traditional marginal productivity propositions.) It follows that the concept of the marginal product of capital which played a large role in discussions of the size and share of profits in the national income, as well as in many other areas of economic enquiry, ceases to be a coherent concept within the supply and demand approach.[12]

Of course, if we now approach the *concept* of capital from its classical roots, while there are difficulties with this approach too they are of a very different nature (see Garegnani, 1959, 1984). As Eagley (1974) pointed out, the concept of capital dominated classical economic thought and it had many dimensions. It received its fullest statement in Marx's major work – it is not an accident that all three volumes are called *Capital* – in which capital is represented as a circuit, both at the level of the individual firm and at the level of the economy. In these circuits the individual capitals continually change their form and are bound up with the social relationships which permeate both the sphere of production and the sphere of distribution and exchange. At each stage of the circuit there are possibilities that things will go wrong, from which arises the possibility of crises, but that is not our principal concern here. What we wish to concentrate on is capital as the key variable in the discussion of the creation, extraction, distribution and use of the surplus in capitalist economies. Marx himself emphasized the distinction between the processes at work in the sphere of production and those at work in the sphere of distribution and exchange. In the sphere of production the conditions of employment and production – the length of the working day and the intensity of work, the intricate details of the class war in the factories – were worked out in order to lay the foundations for the creation of a potential surplus over and above the means of production and variable capital goods, i.e. wage goods. Whether the potential was realized or not depended upon the conditions in the sphere of distribution and exchange, so that the funds advanced at the beginning of the circuits could be realized in greater sums than were started with, allowing not only reproduction but also expansion the next time around. In the modern versions, especially those associated with Kalecki and Joan Robinson (and also with Keynes and Kaldor, though not in as clear or as general a fashion), it is the capitalists' spending decisions, particularly their investment decisions, combined with the differing saving propensities of their class and the wage-earning class and the discretion which the capitalists have, in some sectors anyway, over the prices which they charge for their products, which determine how much of the potential surplus is in fact realized period by period. In telling this story, a vital condition has to do with what Marx called financial capital, namely, that capitalists as a class are not constrained in their spending decisions by their current incomes, as by and large wage-earners as a class are, because the former can always borrow from banks or on the stock exchange, as well as using their own accumulated retained profits from previous periods.

The modern developments of this approach have also concentrated on the structure of the interdependence of production and consumption, summed up in Sraffa's graphic phrase, production of commodities by means of commodities. In this framework, production is viewed as a circular process, in which commodities are classified according to whether they play a role in determining prices (in which event they are referred to as basics) or whether their prices are determined (so that they are referred to as non-basics). This description of production is contrasted with what Sraffa (1960, p. 93) regarded as the view of modern theory, or the dominant neoclassical paradigm, at least in its early days – that it is a 'one-way avenue . . . from "Factors of production" to "Consumption goods"'. Pasinetti, in particular, has developed Sraffa's ideas with his analysis of the concept of vertical integration which originated with Sraffa's ingenious concept of a subsystem.[13]

A subsystem is a thought experiment whereby from the conditions of production of the actual economic system a mini-system is constructed which has as its *net* product only one commodity (perhaps a unit of it, perhaps the amount that is in the net product of the actual system). The gross product of the subsystem contains in addition to this net product enough of this commodity and all other relevant commodities to enable the commodities used up as means of production in the production process to be replaced. Then the total amount of direct labour in each of the industries of the subsystem is the amount of labour needed directly and indirectly to produce this particular net product, as well as what Pasinetti has called the composite commodity requirement of a final good. (We have considered here a circulating commodity model but the device is a general one, applicable to joint production systems, including the case of fixed capital.) Moreover, we may now, through this rearrangement, view the production process as a series of 'notional' vertically integrated activities, one for each commodity. The total labour force employed in the economy may be 'redistributed' into its vertically integrated components which may be obtained from the subsystem corresponding to each commodity in the original net product. The same process may be repeated, as many times as we like, for the 'composite' commodity of each subsystem.

This way of looking at the production interdependence of the economy allows the analyst to pick up the physical aspect of the provision of capital goods through accumulation. The financial aspect of the process, as we have seen, is associated with Marx's circuits of capital, which start with money and move through commodities (including the purchase of the commodity, labour-power) and back to money again when the produced commodities are sold, so, it is hoped, realizing the money profit and turning the potential surplus available into an actual one, which will allow the repetition and possibly the expansion of the process.

National Income

One byproduct of the Keynesian revolution was the further development of a national accounting framework. Stone, along with Meade and with Keynes's blessing, pioneered these studies for the UK in the early days of World War II, and subsequently left his stamp on the collection and the unified classification of national accounting statistics at the international level (Stone, 1981). The welfare aspects of such measures are skilfully surveyed by Sen (1979), and the techniques employed in calculating them are explained by Stone and Stone (1977). However, what we wish finally to discuss here is the rather hybrid nature of the accounts in their Keynesian form because Keynes himself was caught, sometimes uncomfortably, between the neoclassical categories of his mentor, Marshall, and the classical, especially Marxian, categories of his contributions to the theory of employment where, quite unwittingly, he carved out for himself the path that

Marx had earlier followed; for a detailed account of these similarities, see Sardoni (1987). (We say unwittingly, for Keynes never made a close or detailed study of Marx's writings and was in fact rather contemptuous of his contributions, going so far as to say, when congratulating Robinson on her *Essay on Marxian Economics* (Robinson, 1942), that there 'is something intrinsically boring in an attempt to make sense of what in fact was not sense . . . that [Marx] had a penetrating and original flair but was a very poor thinker indeed'.)

Though Marshall regarded the development of economic analysis as an evolutionary process and said that his own work, with regard to the classical economists, was a continuation and extension of their analysis, in fact he radically departed from their categories. This was particularly so of the distinction between productive and unproductive labour which in Marx's work became the central clue to the source of the surplus, of profit and of further accumulation. The distinction was scrapped as incoherent by Marshall and the concept of surplus itself only lingered on in the vastly different context of consumer's and producer's surplus. As the national accounts reflect more Marshall's view, for they were developed for the purpose of welfare analysis and comparisons as well as for employment theory, their categories have not always been appropriate for the examination of the sources of longer-run growth and trends generally in modern capitalist economies. Or, at least, this has been the claim of some modern Marxist scholars who have endeavoured to re-estimate and reclassify the amounts and their classifications, the better to bring out the potential sources of future accumulation and to throw light on some of the recent problems of, for example, the US economy and its puzzlingly poor performance with regard to growth both overall and in productivity. Another purpose is to investigate whether there is in fact a long-run tendency for the rate of profits (as defined in the classical–Marxian sense) to decline (see, for example, Wolff, 1979, 1986, 1988; Weisskopf, 1979; Mosley, 1985, 1988). We mention these as interesting examples of the problems that arise when concepts bearing the same name have different meanings within different approaches – and no more so than with regard to those time-honoured concepts, capital and income, which have been with us since political economy began.

7.4 Conclusions

The preceding sections have touched upon a wide range of contexts in which the terms 'income' and 'capital' are used. It is not possible, except at the cost of gross superficiality, to *summarize* the earlier discussion and, indeed, the discussion itself was able to skim only the surface of many aspects of capital and income and merely refer to others (such as the welfare implications of national income measures). However, it is possible to draw some fairly simple *conclusions* from the discussion, because certain clear themes run throughout. These are as follows.

1 Income and capital are most certainly major concepts in economics. The variety of theoretical contexts and practical applications in which they occur should provide ample evidence of this.
2 These apparently simple concepts, which are often used in everyday language (and quite often by economists) without any thought that their meaning might be ambiguous, are in fact complex and subject to a wide variety of definitions.
3 Amongst the wide variety of definitions of capital and income, no single one is 'correct' in all circumstances. In terms of measuring business income there is no single 'bottom line' measure of profit, or net worth, of a business which will unambiguously measure its economic success over a period or its wealth at a point in time. The same is true at the individual level and at the national level, and it also applies to the use of the concepts in economic theory.
4 The selection of appropriate definitions of income and capital depends upon the precise context in which they are being used. Different definitions may be appropriate for different purposes, and, perhaps surprisingly and certainly contrary to popular belief, it is a sign of honesty rather than dishonesty if the accountant or the economist produces different measures of income or capital in different circumstances.
5 The concepts of capital and income are closely related. Income implies a concept of capital to be maintained before income is recognized, and capital derives its value as a source of future income (at least in the neoclassical model of economics).
6 There are two broad strands in the definition of capital and in the capital maintenance concept used in the definition of income. Hicks (1974) has described these as the 'materialist' approach (which views capital as a collection of specific objects) and the 'fundist' approach (which views capital as a fund of general purchasing power). However, it is important to avoid too facile a use of such broad classifications: few of the businessmen who espoused physical capital maintenance in the measurement of business income in the mid-1970s (as justification for tax reliefs in a period of inflation) would classify themselves as Marxists, although Marx also took a 'materialist' view of capital, as well as a 'fundist' one.

In conclusion, the chapter was intended to alert the reader to some important facets of the concepts of capital and income, without inducing total scepticism about the usefulness of these concepts. Certainly, if wrongly defined for the purpose, they fall into Hicks's category of 'bad tools, which break in our hands' (1946, p. 107), but the same is true to some extent of every concept in economics, and in other branches of knowledge.

NOTES

1 Page references in the text to papers reprinted in Parker, Harcourt and Whittington (1986) refer to the book rather than to the original source.
2 Fisher's classic book on the subject (1906) was, in fact, entitled *The Nature of Capital and Income*, which indicates his appreciation of the essential complementarity of the two concepts.
3 In practice, cash receipts may provide a good approximation to more sophisticated concepts of income for the majority of the population who have little personal wealth and rely on wages, pensions and other cash receipts for their livelihood. However, this statement has to be qualified by the observation that home ownership and the accumulation of pension rights are becoming increasingly important and widely distributed.
4 There has been considerable theoretical analysis of the relationship between accounting rates of return and the economist's concept of the internal rate of return, e.g. Harcourt (1965), Kay (1976), Fisher and McGowan (1983) and Edwards, Kay and Mayer (1987). The latter argue that the relationship between the two is closest when accounts are prepared according to the 'real terms' variant of current cost accounting (CCA), which is discussed later in section 7.2.
5 The international debate is surveyed by Tweedie and Whittington (1984). The alternative techniques are explained and illustrated numerically by Whittington (1983).
6 The example of a speculator in gold is not particularly well suited to the concept of operating capability: it is much easier to define operating capability in the case of manufacturing industries. However, this difficulty does illustrate the importance of the contingency view of choice of accounting method. Operating capability may be useful in describing certain types of firm, but not others.
7 The precise 'value to the business' rule is: select the lower of replacement cost and recoverable amount, where recoverable amount is the higher of net realizable value and discounted present value of future net receipts from maintaining present use.
8 It is also possible to discern these influences in the writings of Hicks; see Hicks (1975).
9 For an account of economists who have had doubts about this view, and of the implications for Fisherian results when present and future consumption are not the only arguments in the utility function, see Steedman (1981).
10 See Pasinetti (1986) for an account of this distinction and Cohen (1989) for some fundamental doubts as to whether either conception can survive the transplantation to a world of heterogeneous commodities.
11 'The production function has been a powerful instrument of mis-education. The student of economic theory is taught to write $Q = f(L,K)$ where L is a quantity

of labour, K is a quantity of capital and Q a rate of output of commodities. He is instructed . . . to measure L in man-hours of labour; he is told something about the index-number problem involved in choosing a unit of output; and then he is hurried on to the next question, in the hope he will forget to ask in what units K is measured' (Robinson, 1953–4, p. 81).

12 For Champernowne's attempt to salvage the traditional results by use of a chain index measure of capital and for why it is not successful, see Champernowne (1953–4), Harcourt (1972, pp. 29–34, 45) and Pasinetti (1969, especially the appendix, pp. 529–31).

13 See Sraffa (1960, appendix A) and Pasinetti (1973).

REFERENCES

Atkinson, A. B., and A. Sandmo (1980) 'Welfare implications of the taxation of savings', *Economic Journal* 90, 529–49.

Beaver, W. H., and J. S. Demski (1979) 'The nature of income measurement', *Accounting Review* 54, 38–46. Reprinted in *Readings in the Concept and Measurement of Income*. Ed. R. H. Parker, G. C. Harcourt and G. Whittington, 1986, Oxford: Philip Allan, pp. 167–78.

Champernowne, D. G. (1953–4) 'The production function and the theory of capital: a comment', *Review of Economic Studies* 21, 112–35.

Cohen, A. J. (1989) 'Prices, capital, and the one-commodity model in neoclassical and classical theories', *History of Political Economy*, forthcoming.

Eagley, R. V. (1974) *The Structure of Classical Economic Theory*. New York: Oxford University Press.

Edwards, E. O., and P. W. Bell (1961) *The Theory and Measurement of Business Income*. Berkeley, Calif.: University of California Press.

Edwards, J. S. S., J. A. Kay and C. P. Mayer (1987) *The Economic Analysis of Accounting Profitability*. Oxford: Clarendon.

Fisher, F. M. and J. J. McGowan (1983) 'On the misuse of accounting rates of return to infer monopoly profits', *American Economic Review* 73, 82–97.

Fisher, I. (1906) *The Nature of Capital and Income*. New York: Macmillan.

Fisher, I. (1930) *The Theory of Interest*. New York: Macmillan, pp. 3–35. Reprinted in *Readings in the Concept and Measurement of Income*. Ed. R. H. Parker, G. C. Harcourt and G. Whittington, 1986, Oxford: Philip Allan, pp. 45–65.

Garegnani, P. (1959) 'A problem in the theory of distribution from Ricardo to Wicksell', unpublished PhD dissertation, Cambridge University.

Garegnani, P. (1984) 'Value and distribution in the classical economists and Marx', *Oxford Economic Papers* 36, 291–325.

Harcourt, G. C. (1965) 'The accountant in a golden age', *Oxford Economic Papers* 17, 66–80.

Harcourt, G. C. (1972) *Some Cambridge Controversies in the Theory of Capital*. Cambridge: Cambridge University Press.

Harcourt, G. C. (1986) *Controversies in Political Economy: Selected Essays of G. C. Harcourt*. Ed. O. F. Hamouda, Brighton: Wheatsheaf.

Hicks, J. R. (1946) *Value and Capital*, 2nd edn. Oxford: Clarendon Press, pp. 171–81. Reprinted in *Readings in the Concept and Measurement of Income*. Ed. R. H. Parker, G. C. Harcourt and G. Whittington, 1986, Oxford: Philip Allan, pp. 102–10.

Hicks, J. R. (1974) 'Capital controversies: ancient and modern', *American Economic Review* 164, 307–16.

Hicks, J. R. (1975) 'Revival of political economy: the old and the new', *Economic Record* 51, 365–7.

Kaldor, N. (1955) *An Expenditure Tax*. London: Allen & Unwin, pp. 54–78. Reprinted in *Readings in the Concept and Measurement of Income*. Ed. R. H. Parker, G. C. Harcourt and G. Whittington, 1986, Oxford: Philip Allan, pp. 111–32.

Kay, J. A. (1976) 'Accountants, too, could be happy in a golden age', *Oxford Economic Papers* 28, 447–60.

Kay, J. A., and M. A. King (1986) *The British Tax System*, 4th edn, Oxford: Oxford University Press.

Lindahl, E. (1933) 'The concept of income', in *Economic Essays in Honour of Gustav Cassel*. Ed. E. Lindahl, London: Allen & Unwin, pp. 399–407. Reprinted in *Readings in the Concept and Measurement of Income*. Ed. R. H. Parker, G. C. Harcourt and G. Whittington, 1986, Oxford: Philip Allan, pp. 82–90.

Meade Committee (1978) *The Structure and Reform of Direct Taxation*. London: Allen & Unwin.

Meek, R. L. (1967) *Economics and Ideology and Other Essays*. London: Chapman and Hall.

Mosley, F. (1985) 'The rate of surplus value in the postwar US economy: a critique of Weisskopf's estimates', *Cambridge Journal of Economics* 9, 57–79.

Mosley, F. (1988) 'The rate of surplus value, the organic composition of capital, and the general rate of profit in the US economy, 1947–76: a critique and update of Wolff's estimates', *American Economic Review* 78, 298–303.

Parker, R. H., G. C. Harcourt and G. Whittington (eds) (1986) *Readings in the Concept and Measurement of Income*. Oxford: Philip Allan.

Pasinetti, L. L. (1969) 'Switches of technique and the "rate of return" in capital theory', *Economic Journal* 79, 508–31.

Pasinetti, L. L. (1973) 'The notion of vertical integration in economic analysis', *Metroeconomica* 25, 1–29.

Pasinetti, L. L. (1986) 'Theory of value – a source of alternative paradigms in economic analysis', in *Foundations of Economics*. Ed. M. Baranzini and R. Scazzieri, Oxford: Blackwell, pp. 409–31.

Robinson, J. (1942) *An Essay on Marxian Economics*, 2nd edn, 1966. Oxford: Blackwell.

Robinson, J. (1953–4) 'The production function and the theory of capital', *Review of Economic Studies* 21, 81–106.

Sandilands Committee (1975) *Inflation Accounting*, Report of the Inflation Accounting Committee, Cmnd. 6225. London: HMSO.

Sardoni, C. (1987) *Marx and Keynes on Economic Recession*. Brighton: Wheatsheaf.

Sen, A. K. (1979) 'The welfare basis of real income comparisons: a survey', *Journal of Economic Literature* 27, 1–45.

Simons, H. C. (1938) *Personal Income Taxation*. Chicago, Ill.: University of Chicago Press, pp. 41–58. Reprinted in *Readings in the Concept and Measurement of Income*. Ed. R. H. Parker, G. C. Harcourt and G. Whittington, 1986, Oxford: Philip Allan, pp. 91–101.

Solow, R. M. (1963) *Capital Theory and the Rate of Return*. Amsterdam: North-Holland.

Sraffa, P. (1960) *Production of Commodities by Means of Commodities*. Cambridge: Cambridge University Press.

Steedman, I. (1981) 'Time preference, the rate of interest and abstinence from consumption', *Australian Economic Papers* 20, 219–34.

Stone, J. R. N. (1981) 'The international harmonisation of national income accounts', *Accounting and Business Research* 12, 67–79.

Stone, J. R. N., and G. Stone (1977) *National Income and Expenditure*, 10th edn. London: Bowes and Bowes.

Tobin, J. (1987) 'Fisher, Irving (1867–1947)', in *The New Palgrave*, vol. 2. Ed. J. Eatwell, M. Milgate and P. Newman. London: Macmillan, pp. 369–76.

Tweedie, D. P., and G. Whittington (1984) *The Debate on Inflation Accounting*. London: Cambridge University Press.

Weisskopf, T. T. (1979) 'Marxian crisis theory and the rate of profit in the postwar US economy', *Cambridge Journal of Economics* 3, 341–78.

Whittington, G. (1983) *Inflation Accounting, An Introduction to the Debate*. London: Cambridge University Press.

Wolff, E. (1979) 'The rate of surplus value, the organic composition of capital, and the general rate of profit in the US economy, 1947–76', *American Economic Review* 69, 329–41.

Wolff, E. (1986) 'The productivity slowdown and the fall in the rate of profit, 1947–76', *Review of Radical Political Economy* 18, 87–100.

Wolff, E. (1988) 'The rate of surplus value, the organic composition of capital, and the general rate of profit in the US economy, 1947–76: reply', *American Economic Review* 78, 304–6.

8

The firm

Brian J. Loasby

A firm is a productive organization within an economy. Its activities, one might think, should therefore be explained by the interaction between its internal structure and its external environment; but that is not how economists normally proceed. Although economics is necessarily a study of system behaviour, the study is normally focused on one system and its elements, even though the system to be studied is embedded in a larger structure and its elements are complex systems in their own right.

This kind of simplification is far from unique to economics; but it does require some justification. The pragmatic justification is that it often seems to generate results which are corroborated by evidence; the epistemic justification is that the systems under study are highly decomposable (Simon, 1969). Thus it is argued that the internal structure and behaviour of a firm (or an animal, or a cell) is of minor importance in explaining the behaviour of a collection of firms (or animals, or cells), and that only aggregated features of the environment need be invoked in modelling that behaviour. Industrial economists treat each firm as a single decision-making unit within an industry; and although interactions between firms may be important, interactions between industries are not. The remainder of the economy sets the constraints, such as input prices and substitution elasticities for its products, to which an industry must conform; but these constraints are impervious to any action of the industry or its component firms. In this chapter, the firm's interior is generally treated as more problematic than its environment.

8.1 Enterprise and Progress

Adam Smith

It is the interior of the firm to which Adam Smith first draws our attention, and that in the second paragraph of chapter 1 of *The Wealth of Nations*. Smith's prime explanation of increasing productivity, and therefore of the growth of national income, is the division of labour, and the improvements in productive methods which it generates; and what Smith wishes to achieve in his famous example of the pin factory is to demonstrate the effects of a complete division of labour 'placed at once under the view of the spectator' (1976, p. 14). Thus the firm first appears as a principal agent of economic progress and as an organizational structure for coordinating specialized activity; as we shall see, these two features form the basis of Marshall's theory of the firm.

However, Smith is careful to point out that much beneficial specialization takes place between firms; indeed, a major aim of his treatise is to demonstrate that such specialized activities can generally be better coordinated by the market than by government regulation. His analysis thus implicitly raises the question why there should be two different schemes of specialization, within and between firms, matched with two different schemes of coordination, by managerial direction and the market; but this question had to wait 160 years for a theoretical answer.

A second implicit question lay dormant for more than a century. Since, according to Smith (1976, p. 31), the division of labour must always be limited by the extent of the market, any expansion of demand, 'though in the beginning it may sometimes raise the price of goods, never fails to lower it in the long run. It encourages production, and thereby increases the competition of the producers, who, in order to undersell one another, have recourse to new divisions of labour and new improvements of art, which might never otherwise have been thought of' (1976, p. 748). A universal assumption of falling long-run costs was bound to collide with the notion of a perfectly competitive equilibrium as soon as both notions could be precisely formulated; but we should notice that the cost reductions which Smith had in mind were not embodied in any readily accessible production function, but resulted from the development of new methods of production which could not be anticipated in any detail.

For Smith, competition was an essential part of that process of cost reduction; and its effectiveness depended not only on the absence of monopolistic restrictions but on individual attitudes and initiative. Though manufacturers and merchants welcomed profit, they were not all equally assiduous in seeking it. Few passages are better known than Smith's analysis of what is now called the agency problem in joint-stock companies (1976, p. 741); but he recognized that sole proprietors might have other interests too – the practice of slavery, which he regarded as clearly inefficient, was to be explained by man's love of domineering (1976, p. 388). Nevertheless, Smith argued that the process of competition would generally be effective in driving market price towards natural price (1976, pp. 73–5), as well as in generating a reduction in natural price as demand expanded, and he thus felt justified in conducting his analysis at the level of the industry. The prevalence of competitive processes allowed him to treat a market economy as a decomposable system, in which there was no need for a specific theory of the firm.

J. S. Mill

J. S. Mill (1965) greatly extended Smith's discussion of the effects of the division of labour, especially as it was applied within a single enterprise. He drew on Babbage's (1832) analysis of the advantages of large factories to produce a systematic treatment of economies of scale, and argued (1965, p. 133) that firms would tend to grow to the most efficient size. However, efficiency and profitability were not determined simply by the choice of technique, for Mill followed J. B. Say in recognizing the great variation between entrepreneurs in skill and situation. Profit 'depends on the knowledge, talents, economy, and energy of the capitalist himself, or of the agents whom he employs; on the accidents of personal connexion; and even on chance' (Mill, 1965, p. 406). Such variations are characteristic of a competitive economy – in Mill's, but not the modern neoclassical, sense.

However, Mill was well aware that competition could not be ensured simply by the absence of natural monopoly or legal restraint, for people who were free to compete might not wish to do so, but might rely instead on custom and usage (1965, p. 239). Such practices, which were common in retail trade (1965, p. 243), set bounds to economic analysis in Mill's view, for 'only through the principle of competition has political economy any pretension to the character of a science' (1965, p. 239). Mill's exposition of scale economies made the firm's internal organization of primary importance in determining costs of production; yet the commodity, not the firm, was the proper unit of analysis for economists, and, as with Smith, it was the force of competition which allowed each commodity to be analysed at the level of the industry rather than the firm.

Alfred Marshall

Marshall, too, wished to analyse the price and output of commodities at the level of the industry; and he wished to make use in his analysis of the concept of equilibrium between industry demand and supply. 'The history of the individual firm cannot be made into the history of an industry' (Marshall, 1961, p. 459); nevertheless the history of an industry cannot be understood without understanding the behaviour of the firms which compose it. Thus Marshall's industrial analysis is based on a much more elaborate discussion of the firm's structure and behaviour than is to be found in any of the subsequent equilibrium theories of the firm.

More emphatically than for Adam Smith, the firm is the principal agent of economic progress; and Marshall wishes to explain how this progress is brought about (Loasby, 1989, pp. 47–70). Marshall transforms Mill's recognition of the variation in 'knowledge, talents, economy and energy' between firms into a procedure for the discovery of new products and processes through the generation and trial of a variety of ideas (1961, p. 355). The interior of the firm is important not just for the coordination of specialized activities – the standard modern conception of the economic problem – but because the internal organization of a firm aids the development of knowledge (1961, pp. 138–9). But what most distinguishes Marshall from his predecessors, and from almost all his successors, is his concern for the firm's external organization (1961, p. 458) – its network of relationships with suppliers, customers and even competitors. This network not only helps provide the information which is needed to approach equilibrium but also forms a kind of invisible college which promotes the growth of industrial knowledge. The interaction between the firm's internal structure and its environment is crucial to Marshall's explanation of economic progress; yet it receives no formal analysis.

Marshall (1961, p. 241) extended Smith's central principle of the division of labour to a law of both biological and social evolution, which carried with it the need for closer integration of the specialized functions which emerged; and his law of increasing returns, which appears to have no limit other than the extent of the market, explicitly invoked improved organization as the means by which greater productivity is achieved (1961, p. 318). This improved organization might be external rather than internal, and Marshall gave proper emphasis to the contribution of external economies – notably in transport and communications (1961, pp. 674–5) – to nineteenth-century economic growth; but he had no wish to understate the importance of internal economies of scale, which Mill had discussed so extensively. However, he recognized the problem implicit in Smith's insistence that an expansion of demand always induces a fall in cost, for early in his own study of economics he had been impressed with Cournot's analysis of equilibrium (Marshall, 1961, p. x) – and in that analysis continually falling costs for a firm implied monopoly. But this conclusion Marshall had rejected as empirically false, and much of his detailed study of industry was intended to provide a theoretical rebuttal (1961, vol. II, p. 521).

This rebuttal was based on the importance of time and its irreversibility: like Marshall's explanation of economic progress, it was a theory of the firm, but not a theory of equilibrium. Lower-cost methods could not be plucked from a fully specified production set, but had to be worked out and applied; new customers had to be persuaded of the merits of the products on offer; and the firm's internal organization and trade connections had to be adapted to the new requirements. All this took time (1961, p. 500); meanwhile, those in charge of the firm were getting older, and perhaps losing some of their ability or motivation, and so the effort and attention required to achieve the results which were theoretically possible might not be forthcoming.

Marshall knew, quite as well as Mill, that business enterprise could not be guaranteed simply by the absence of restraints on competition; there were wide differences between people, and also, in Marshall's view, systematic differences over the life of individuals and the life of firms. The vigour of youth could outperform the routines of a mature business, despite the economies to which the latter had access (1961, p. 316). The life cycle of firms was no doubt a natural element in the application of Darwinian ideas, to which Marshall, like so many of his contemporaries, was much attracted; it also appeared to fit the pattern of industrial development which he had spent so much time observing.

As Marshall himself recognized in the sixth edition of *Principles* in 1910 (1961, p. 316), the growing importance of joint-stock companies with professional management was beginning to change the pattern; but he retained (1961, pp. 303–4), though in a milder degree, Adam Smith's doubts about the quality of performance which such organizations could be expected to achieve. The declining vigour of his own life cycle prevented him from dealing satisfactorily with the implications of the changing organization and ownership structure of firms, despite his interests in scientific management (Marshall, 1919, pp. 365–94); nor did he succeed in convincing his successors of the limitations of equilibrium methods for dealing with economic progress.

From Enterprise to Equilibrium

One of Marshall's theoretical concepts had unfortunate consequences (Loasby, 1989, pp. 71–85). Firms which passed through a cycle from birth to death clearly had no long-run equilibrium; thus such an equilibrium was to be explained in terms of industry demand and supply. Nevertheless, Marshall wished to emphasize that the history of an industry was the product of the actions and interactions of firms and of the people who managed them; therefore he introduced into his long-run analysis the concept of the 'representative firm' (1961, p. 317). This was mainly an expository device; but it had an analytical purpose as an indicator of the reasonable expectations of a potential new entrant. Thus the long-run equilibrium price had to be equal to the average (not marginal) costs of the representative firm in order to ensure a rate of new entry which just balanced the exit of dying firms. At any given time there might or might not be one or more firms which happened to display the characteristics of this representative firm; what was certain was that no firm could be expected to display those characteristics for long. But despite Marshall's warnings, the association of the representative firm with long-run equilibrium tended to conceal the transience of its representativeness.

This transience was further obscured by Pigou's (1928) formal presentation of what he called the 'equilibrium firm'. Pigou, like Marshall, wished to explain the long-run equilibrium of the industry, and he was careful not to claim that industry equilibrium entailed the equilibrium of any actual firm (1928, p. 239). He did not deny the possibility that some firms might be in long-run equilibrium, however – a possibility that Marshall's definition of the representative firm was designed to exclude. Thus his definition of industry supply price as equal to both the marginal and the average cost of the equilibrium firm (1928, p. 243) clearly focused attention on the firm's cost curves as the core of the analysis. It was now a very simple step from the proposition that the conditions of industry equilibrium could be conveniently represented by the device of an equilibrium firm to the proposition that industry equilibrium required its component firms to be in equilibrium too.

The step was attractive as well as simple, for Pigou showed (1928, p. 246) the equilibrium firm nestling in what is now familiar fashion at the lowest point of a U-shaped cost curve, held in place by the forces of competition: all that is missing is a horizontal demand curve. The idea that firms would tend to settle at their optimum size, as we have seen, is to be found in Mill's work (though not, of course, in Marshall's); Pigou's analysis could be interpreted to show that a strict regime of perfect competition – the conditions for which (and the limited relevance of which) had been systematically explored by Frank Knight (1921) – would ensure such a result. Moreover, Pigou's own examination of the economics of welfare (1920) had emphasized the desirability of this outcome. That this conception of equilibrium entailed the rejection of the tradition of economic progress that had run from Smith to Marshall seemed to bother very few economists.

8.2 The Firm in Equilibrium

Pigou had provided, without intending to, the model for the perfectly competitive firm; and thereby, equally without intent, he had extinguished Marshall's theory of the firm. But one significant relic of Marshall's theory remained: economies of scale. Though now changed out of recognition, from the result of improved organization consequent upon a growth of demand to opportunities for cost reduction which were there for the taking, these economies nevertheless seemed to be important. They had seemed important enough, indeed, for Pigou (1920) to advocate subsidizing industries with unexhausted economies of scale as an important means of increasing economic welfare. But unexhausted economies of scale posed another problem: how could they possibly be reconciled with the concept of perfectly competitive equilibrium? The question had been posed by Sraffa (1926), who was apparently unaware of Cournot's answer and failed – like many others – to understand Marshall's; Pigou's diagram of the equilibrium firm encapsulated it in a stark form.

Before making his recommendation to turn in the direction of monopoly, Sraffa (1926, pp. 540–1) had himself suggested a different way out: to assume that all firms in a competitive industry had constant costs. Now if one examines the specification of a perfectly competitive economy, especially as set out in an Arrow–Debreu system, with perfect knowledge, no resource monopolies and no transactions costs of any kind, it is very hard to see why the costs of any single producer should not be constant; since any technical economies can be shared out by multiple contracts: indeed, as we shall see, the principal difficulty is to find any reason for the existence of firms at all. But not everyone was willing to give up the idea that costs might vary with output. Moreover, the contemporary state of industry, especially in Britain, seemed to exhibit some unexhausted economies of scale – though these were not always distinguished from underemployed fixed factors. Thus some alternative to the perfectly competitive equilibrium apparently needed to be found – and it obviously had to be found at the level of the firm, since it was the unexplained constraint on the growth of its member firms which seemed to invalidate the perfectly competitive equilibrium of the industry.

Joan Robinson

In retrospect, the solution which was presented by Joan Robinson in 1933 appears to be an obvious development. Sraffa had pointed towards monopoly; and there was already a standard monopoly analysis with a falling demand curve which could clearly accommodate falling costs, provided only that they fell more slowly than demand. Moreover, Marshall had himself suggested that in certain circumstances a firm's rate of expansion would be constrained by the shape of its own demand curve, which could be very steep – though he was clearly thinking of adjustment processes, and certainly not long-run equilibrium (1961, pp. 287, 458). Joan Robinson simply ascribed monopoly demand curves to imperfectly competitive firms (1933, p. 50): by reinterpreting monopoly equilibrium in terms of marginal revenue – which seemed such a powerful discovery to those who made it – and combining this with Pigou's competitive requirement that price should be equal to average cost, she developed a closely argued analysis which clearly placed the new theory of the firm at the heart of microeconomics.

The firm of this new theory had nothing but the name in common with Marshall's firm. Despite Joan Robinson's claim (1933, p. 17) that it was 'very similar to the firms in the real world' it possessed neither internal nor external organization, being simply a fictitious person – an optimizing agent equipped with production function and demand curve who was fully constrained to a situationally determined equilibrium. Since this firm was supplied with all necessary data, there was no need for any organization to search for them. It is not at all clear why such a firm should have access either to economies of scale or to its own demand curve, though within the specification of the model it is clear that either requires the other for the determination of equilibrium.

In replacing an organized group of people by a fictitious individual, Joan Robinson made her own contribution to the general tendency to populate economic models with abstractions in order to increase analytical rigour. If, as is usual in neoclassical economic theory, the results of interest are those which apply to aggregates, such as commodities, productive services or economies, then the elementary units of analysis may perhaps be chosen for theoretical convenience; the firm is no more intended to be a real firm than the household is intended to be a real household. Neoclassical theory works best when individual agents are insignificant: why then should they not be fictitious? It is thus an understandable paradox that the admission of the firm to the core of economic theory coincided with the loss of interest in the firm as an organization.

Edward Chamberlin

Chamberlin's (1962) theory of monopolistic competition, which is normally amalgamated with Joan Robinson's theory in the textbooks, was different in both origins and implications. Chamberlin started not with economies of scale but with another item of unfinished Marshallian business: the recognition (Marshall, 1919, p. 397) that monopoly and competition 'shade into one another by imperceptible degrees: that there is an element of monopoly in nearly all competitive business: and that nearly all monopolies . . . would lose [their power] ere long, if they ignored the possibilities of competition, direct and indirect.' Chamberlin set out to include both competition and monopoly within a general theory; and though the search for zero-profit equilibrium drove him to a specification of long-run equilibrium (the tangency solution) which is formally identical with Joan Robinson's, he quite clearly regarded this as a limiting case, which required 'heroic assumptions' (1962, p. 82) about both the costs and the markets of individual firms. Though he never explored the consequences of relaxing these assumptions beyond recognizing (1962, p. 113) that monopoly profits would be scattered throughout any monopolistically competitive industry, he clearly did not believe that they would often be valid. Indeed, it has been strongly argued that Chamberlin regarded his equilibrium analysis as no more than a convenient instrument for analysing a process of competition in unorganized markets, in which firms had to search for customers and devise products which would satisfy unknown preferences (Robinson, 1971, pp. 33–4). Despite the sharpest differences in form, the spirit of Chamberlin's analysis seems remarkably close to that of Kirzner (1973), and might even be considered a precursor of Casson's (1982) theory of the market-making entrepreneur.

Chamberlin's explicit inclusion of product and selling costs as decision variables, though yielding little more than the conclusion that the formal conditions of optimization needed to be extended to cover them, seemed to promise an applicable theory, and Chamberlin provided the chief inspiration for the American tradition of industrial economics. Joan Robinson's principal contribution to this tradition was the association of any competitive imperfection with welfare losses – about which Chamberlin was sceptical from the first, since the elimination of apparent welfare losses required the elimination of some products (1962, p. 94). Her analytical apparatus, and its policy implications, tended to be preferred by textbook writers seeking a unified framework of equilibrium models.

The theory of the firm consequently became a series of exercises in constrained optimization, in which the firm was no more than a convenient device which allowed the specification of market structure to determine the outcome. This is Cournot's theory of the firm, which Marshall, after much consideration, had rejected as inadequate; but it was, and is, well suited to the standard definition of the economic problem as the allocation of given resources to meet given wants by the use of a given technology set. What it does not suit is the problem of generating and coordinating the discovery and application of knowledge.

Within its own terms of reference, the continuing and ineradicable difficulty with Cournot's method is its inability to yield a general theory of oligopoly. Chamberlin recognized that any specification of oligopolistic equilibrium depended on the pattern of expectations which was attributed to the firms concerned and furthermore that there was no uniquely rational pattern; oligopoly was thus not one problem but several (Chamberlin, 1962, p. 53). So it remains; for oligopoly has resisted all attempts at a general solution which could be derived from the standard axioms of formal theory. However, it has provided apparently limitless opportunities for the exercise of technical ingenuity in the formulation of economic games, which typically are resolved by the imposition of a Cournot equilibrium. Economists have nevertheless contrived to ignore the wider implications of this failure, which threatens their whole enterprise, for their axioms are incapable of handling any interdependent structure without the support of *ad hoc* assumptions – and all economies are interdependent systems.

Managerial Theories

Continuing failure to produce a unique situationally determined equilibrium for oligopoly presented an opportunity for another approach (Loasby, 1989, pp. 101–18). Baumol (1959) skilfully used his model of sales revenue maximization to demonstrate that an objective other than profit maximization was not only tractable but offered a new solution to the oligopoly problem. But his determinate solution depended on the simplest of all devices for handling oligopoly, that of ignoring interdependence entirely – in outcomes as well as expectations. A similar strategy was followed by both Williamson (1964) and Marris (1964) in developing models which were based on managerial utility maximization and growth maximization respectively. All three models assume significant scope for managerial discretion, and they are best regarded as alternative theories of monopoly which display the logical consequences of decisions to use monopoly profits in different ways within the firm. Their predictions differ from those of profit-maximizing models in interesting ways, though the empirical status of these predictions is still uncertain.

These managerial theories exemplify a simple, but effective, variation on the standard research strategy of conducting controlled thought experiments by varying the environment of a conventionally defined firm; in managerial theories the environment is held constant while the firm's objectives are varied. There are no other significant differences. The analysis still assumes the standard data of preferences, resources and technology in order to generate a clearly specified optimum; though Marris has a good deal of value to say about the management of product innovation his formal model does not incorporate any of the problems or uncertainties involved but assumes well defined opportunities and leads to a once-and-for-all choice of a growth strategy extending into the indefinite future. Nor are these theories managerial in the sense of exploring the specific problems of controlling a large and complex enterprise. Baumol invokes complexity, and the consequent need to simplify decision-making, as one of his arguments for ignoring interdependence in what otherwise appears to be a world of perfect information, and Williamson introduces the number of subordinates as a means of producing managerial satisfaction through salary and status; but that is all.

The firm is still as unified as a household – still a fictitious person. Though the separation of ownerhip from control helped to motivate these theories, it is unnecessary as a means of justifying the objectives postulated. Since Scitovsky's (1943) proof that profit maximization requires the attribution of a special – though not entirely implausible – preference function to the decision-maker there has been no logical basis for objecting to other preference functions in an owner-managed firm. Those explored in these three models are all perfectly reasonable possibilities for a sole owner, and indeed are as reasonable for the sole owner of a one-man business as for the sole owner of a giant corporation. Within the conventions of modern theory, large firms have to be invoked to provide the potential monopoly profits which alone give scope for discretion; but ownership is not crucial. By contrast, it seems hardly less true now than in Say's time that firms of any size or pattern of ownership may exhibit a wide range of profitability. To explain such a range, however, we need to go beyond the modern standard definition of the firm and its setting.

8.3 The Firm as Market

Nevertheless, the dominant tendency appears to be an ever more rigorous application of situational determinism (nowadays more usually labelled rational choice theory) to theories of the firm. It has been understood for a long time that perfectly competitive product markets leave only one viable option for a firm that wishes to survive, and for a rather shorter time that in these conditions the nominal objective is formally irrelevant since survival is the only question. Imperfect competition with unrestricted entry is equally compelling: indeed it was an important component of Joan Robinson's argument that imperfectly competitive firms had no way of avoiding the imposition of welfare losses on the economy – the only remedy was the imposition of an alternative economic system.

Oligopolistic and monopolistic product markets, however, are apparently more tolerant; thus they seem to offer scope both for a range of profit-motivated equilibria and for the satisfaction of other preferences. But within a general equilibrium system it may be misleading to consider one market on its own. Capital markets are always assumed to be highly competitive, and they provide an effective substitute for competitive product markets. Any firm which is failing to maximize its profits is necessarily also failing to maximize its market value (since this is effectively determined by the net present value of its expected stream of future earnings); it therefore presents an obvious profit opportunity to anyone who buys up the shares and imposes a profit-maximizing routine. Marris relied on the possibility of takeover to constrain the drive for growth in his managerial theory; but in order to allow the growth objective to produce some distinctive results he left the constraint loose. The strategy of varying managerial objectives within an otherwise conventional theory only makes sense if some opportunities for profit remain unexploited.

Unexploited profit opportunities, however, are incompatible with the neoclassical concept of equilibrium – especially as it is interpreted in Chicago. There is thus no need to invoke the threat of takeover, as Marris does. In modern finance theory, rational shareholders have no wish to direct businesses and each holds efficiently diversified portfolios; but this is no problem. Quite the contrary: the separation of management from control is another example of efficient specialization, and is efficiently coordinated by the market system. Management is best left to professionals; and professional managers maximize profits. This is not only because capital markets use all publicly available information and generate efficient mechanisms for monitoring managerial performance; the managerial labour market provides effective incentives for managers to demonstrate their productivity by increasing shareholders' wealth, and even to create added value by exposing any incompetence or misdirected zeal on the part of other managers. That is how managers maximize the return on their own human capital (Fama, 1980).

In this analysis we need nothing but profit maximization to explain the behaviour of firms, because no other choice criterion is viable. What is more, we need no special conception of a firm: each firm is simply the locus of a particular set of markets, which generates a network of optimal contracts. Theories of the firm are superfluous: the working of an economy can be explained in terms of market transactions between economic agents, who do not need to be further categorized. Since the sole purpose of economic activity is to satisfy consumers' preferences, firms are simply agents of consumers; given an effective means of controlling agents, we can confine our attention to the principals. The firm (like money) is superfluous.

Does anything happen within a firm which deserves any special attention? Alchian and Demsetz (1972) suggest one activity only: team-work, in which there is no straightforward market method for correctly rewarding (and thus motivating) the contributors to a non-separable production function. This apparent market failure is overcome by the creation of a special kind of market: contracts for the productive services of team members are centralized on a coordinator, who monitors the behaviour of team members, has the right to vary membership and is the residual claimant to the value of the team's output after contractual payments have been met. These arrangements ensure efficient production; and competition between potential coordinators ensures that team members are not exploited.

The firm is not a hierarchy. Alchian and Demsetz (1972, p. 777) insist that the coordinator neither possesses nor needs any authority over team members. 'The firm . . . has no power of fiat, no authority, no disciplinary action any different in the slightest degree from ordinary market contracting between any two people.' A firm is not an alternative to a market; it is simply a different way of structuring a market, the difference consisting solely in focusing the set of contracts on a central agent. The coordinator is a market-maker: outside firms the role of market-maker is either ignored or ascribed to the auctioneer (who needs no residual claims to motivate his efficient performance).

Alchian and Demsetz's problem of team-work hardly seems an adequate basis for explaining the organizations which we see today; but the role of specialist makers of markets may be more promising, as Casson (1982) has indicated. Fama (1980), however, abolishes the market-maker and relies on the mutual monitoring of all economic agents and the continuing search for advantage to ensure the efficient coordination of economic activities. The observed characteristics of firms are simply a veil which conceals the effective exchange of goods and services.

8.4 Transactions Costs

R. H. Coase

Any reconstruction of a theory of the firm must be based on a rejection, at least in part, of this vision of perfect and costless coordination. The simplest adjustment is that proposed by Coase (1937), who suggested that there were costs of using markets and that these costs could in part be avoided by substituting a relationship of continuing commitment to particular trading partners. Coase argued that the costs of using markets were likely to be particularly heavy for anyone who wished to arrange for a flow of production to meet a varying stream of demand, since this would entail frequent recontracting. He wrote before the theoretical emergence of contingent commodities, but it seems to be widely agreed that contingent commodities are likely to be particularly subject to what is usually called 'market failure'; thus the need to collect information about market prospects and potential contractors, and to negotiate contracts, may perhaps be accepted.

Now the suppliers of labour services might well be relatively indifferent about the products on which they exercised their skills – different lengths or diameters of pins, for example; thus there might be mutual advantage in a long-term contract by which workers agreed to make whatever kind of pins the owner of the pin factory should decide he wanted made, in return for regular wages. Thus one contract could replace a series, with consequent savings of transactions costs. The management of this new relationship, based on employment rather than the sale of products, also entailed costs, as Coase recognized; and the choice between them would therefore be determined, like other choices, at the margin. Coase thus at last proposed a means of answering the question implicit in Adam Smith's application of the principle of division of labour to the organization of production both within and between firms; and he did so in a way which extended the range of the analytical method which had been deployed by Cournot. Just as each firm's output was determined at the level which equated marginal revenue and marginal cost, so the scope of each firm's activities was curtailed at the point where the marginal costs of making and managing imperfectly specified contracts balanced the marginal costs of market transactions.

O. E. Williamson

Coase's analytical method was for many years regarded as a very effective way of using economic analysis to define its own limits – and, in the process, clearly locating the interior of the firm beyond those limits – rather than, as Coase himself suggested, as a means of explaining the variety of industrial structure which was rather casually assumed in the standard structure–conduct–performance analysis of the firm. Had it been so used, it might have qualified the usual welfare assessments, which took no account of transactions costs.

The subsequent transformation has been predominantly the work of one man, Oliver Williamson (1975, 1985, 1986). He has extended the idea of transactions costs from those of search and negotiation – effectively the costs of discovering an equilibrium which is implicit in the data – to incorporate elements which are less readily absorbed into neoclassical theory: bounded rationality, information impactedness and opportunism. With the aid of these elements he has sought to identify circumstances in which the information necessary to conclude a contract acceptable to both parties is unlikely to be obtainable, or where an initial contract, however acceptable in itself, is likely to produce serious inequalities in bargaining strength at the time of contract renewal, e.g. because one of the parties becomes locked into dependence on its contractual supplier or customer. The primary focus of Williamson's analysis of transactions costs is the extent of vertical integration: which stages in a production chain are likely to be linked by market contracts and which are likely to be brought under a single direction.

Williamson very reasonably emphasizes the ways in which his theory of industrial organization differs from standard neoclassical theory; yet in principle his extension of rational choice to include transactions costs (and even the moral hazard which is an important contributor to those costs) may be judged as compatible with neoclassical theory as the inclusion of information sets, which occurred over much the same time. Moreover, though Williamson recognizes that firms make mistakes, the logic of his argument that the choice of governance structures (market or hierarchy) is based on transactional efficiency drives his formal analysis towards the conclusion that the equilibrium pattern of industrial organization is ideal when it is appraised in relation to a correct and comprehensive specification of the opportunities and constraints.

Moreover, Williamson's justification of the multidivisional firm as the most effective means of ensuring profit maximization within a large and diversified organization brings him paradoxically close to Fama; whereas Fama declares that what is called a firm is simply a collection of markets, Williamson (1975, pp. 141–8) argues that a multidivisional firm organized into investment centres, which are under the financial control of a central office, constitutes a more efficient localized capital market than the general financial markets can provide. The principal reason that he gives is that much of the information which outsiders need for effective monitoring is known only to those being monitored, who are unlikely to disclose any part of it which might be used to their own disadvantage. Though this reason may often be valid, it should not be forgotten that similar difficulties are common within formal organizations. Despite Williamson's work, the relative difficulties, costs and advantages of making – and maintaining – markets within and between firms is a seriously underdeveloped area of economics.

Transactions costs, and the factors which produce them, have provided a very useful means of examining both the scope and the internal organization of firms; but, like any other method of analysis, Williamson's has its limitations. Though the choice between market and hierarchy, and the choice between alternative hierarchical structures, is governed by expectations of the consequences of that choice over a considerable period of time, it is inherent in his method that the analysis of those consequences precedes the choice, rather than following it. (Choice depends on expectations of the consequences, but, as usual when economists make use of expectations to explain rational choice, these are assumed to be well founded.) A decision to replace market relationships by an administrative structure is in this respect similar to the neoclassical alternative of a decision to conclude a set of contingent contracts, or to the derivation of an optimal strategy through a process of backward induction.

Yet the ideas on which Williamson has built his theoretical structure derive from a conviction that we have neither the knowledge nor the reasoning capacity to make such calculations possible. By Coase's argument, the creation of a firm signifies a decision not to try to anticipate the future but to attempt to manage it; and the work of Herbert Simon, whose influence Williamson gladly acknowledges, has emphasized the importance of procedural rather than substantial rationality. Transactions cost analysis appears to make the choice of administratively rational procedures itself a substantively rational choice.

8.5 Managerial Behaviour and the Growth of the Firm

It therefore seems desirable to complement transactions cost theory with some attempt to analyse the workings of boundedly rational managers in boundedly rational organizations, giving due attention to the effects of organizational structures on the procedures which are adopted. Though it may sometimes be helpful to regard product divisions as substantively rational investment centres, that is by no means all that they are. In a boundedly rational world, managerial discretion need not be attributed to monopoly; it is an inevitable result of limited knowledge, and of our limited ability to make use of what knowledge we think we have. Even if, to an omniscient observer, there are very tight long-run constraints, nevertheless if these constraints are not understood by managers, or by those seeking to control them, then managers will have substantial discretion for a time – even to make long-run decisions, though these may never come to fruition.

H. Leibenstein

Managerial discretion arising from imperfect knowledge provides the setting for Leibenstein's (1976) theory of the firm. Since no one knows the boundaries of a firm's opportunity set, how closely it is approached depends on individual behaviour. Managers do not share the objectives of shareholders, or indeed of their managerial superiors, and their contracts are necessarily incomplete. They have some choice in the direction, pace, quality, and duration of their efforts, and the way in which they exercise this choice is determined by their perceptions and their motivation. Their motivation within this discretionary range cannot be purchased within the market but arises within the organization, in part as a result of the attitudes and motivation of others. For Leibenstein, as for Cyert and March (1963), a firm is a coalition, and provided that it is meeting the aspirations of its members (in terms of on-the-job satisfaction, as well as income) there will usually be a general desire to preserve that coalition; this is likely to imply both minimum and maximum acceptable levels of effort. In order to explain performance (what Leibenstein calls the level of x-efficiency) it is therefore necessary to examine first the firm's external environment and then its internal environment – which, as students of management well know, may depend more on style than on structure.

Leibenstein has produced a theory of the interior of the firm which is notable among economic theories for its kinship to organizational psychology; but it has not had a great deal of impact. Economists do not generally like theories which allow agents to have discretion, for such theories neither yield clear predictions nor allow straightforward welfare assessments. We can rely on perfect competition to deliver Pareto-optimal allocations because in perfect competition no one has any discretion of any kind: its virtues derive from its isomorphism with a system of ideal planning. If we accept the arguments which have been advanced to invalidate the possibilities of discretion which underlie the managerial theories of the firm, then there is no difficulty in disposing of Leibenstein's analysis by the same methods. However, if we are prepared to accept the claims by Say, Mill and Marshall for a wide range of performance by firms in apparently similar situations – or even to pay some attention to the business press – then we may think that Leibenstein has something to contribute to our understanding of the firm. His theoretical structure may be used both to complement and to qualify Williamson's analysis, which is concerned with organizational structures but not the activities of management.

E. T. Penrose

A different route into the interior of the firm had been taken earlier by Mrs Penrose (1959). Her method of analysis was even less congenial than Leibenstein's, since it not only relied on managerial discretion but made no attempt to derive an equilibrium. Indeed, she argued that there was no general tendency for firms to reach an equilibrium size; at any moment there was a managerial limit on what each could encompass, but that limit continually receded, apparently for ever. Conventional economics has continued to recognize the existence of economies of scale, though few economists have been entirely comfortable with them. They help to determine the size of firms in particular branches of production, but there have been few attempts to explain the path by which firms might reach this technologically determined size. (This is no surprise in a subject where equilibrium is almost always the focus of attention.) For Mrs Penrose, in contrast, the path was all that could be examined; and the critical variable was not technology but management.

A rational reconstruction of the origins of her theory would focus on Coase and Marshall – though she makes no reference to Coase and only two footnote allusions to Marshall (who is then incorrectly identified in the index). Nevertheless the reconstruction is worth sketching. Coase, we recall, explained that coordination within a firm would be preferred when the costs of managing emergent events by the use of an administrative structure were judged to be lower than the costs of repeated contracting. There are ways of reducing both kinds of costs; we have already referred to the possibilities of organizing a market, but now let us concentrate on the costs of management. The establishment of rational procedures for identifying and handling problems may bring about substantial reductions in the costs of decision-making; and given enough relevant experience these procedures may be designed to reduce substantially the chance of mistakes. But experience is essential; and it cannot be rushed.

Moreover, within an organization of any size, decision-making, like other operations, offers scope for the division of labour. Each decision-maker may then develop appropriate procedures for economizing on the costs of making his own decisions. There are often a number of reasonably satisfactory ways of doing so; but it is important that members of a single organization make use of methods which are mutually consistent. The emergence of a consistent set of routines also takes time, as anyone with experience in an organization recruiting new members will know. Thus the members of an organization will need to learn their business and also to learn how to work together. But once the management system is working well, using familiar and effective procedures, its capacity is much greater than while it is being built. It must be remembered, however, that this capacity will be most effective – and in extreme cases, will only be effective – when applied to similar activities and using the same group structure: 'the resources with which a particular firm is accustomed to working will shape the productive services its management is capable of rendering' (Penrose, 1959, p. 5).

Since we are necessarily far removed from the world of omniscience, or even of well-defined probability distributions, the uses to which these created resources may be put depend on the perceptions of those who make the decisions (prompted, no doubt, by the perceptions of those who provide information or advice). Here again, the experience of the firm's managers may count for a great deal, though imaginative managers may see far beyond experience; whether what they see is a realizable future or a mirage may be very hard to decide before resources are committed. Resources and prospects – supply and demand – combine to create a firm's productive opportunity, which is both subjective and peculiar to that firm. Moreover, because every decision and the observation of its consequence provides new knowledge (even if this is no more than a corroboration of previously held beliefs), 'the productive opportunity of a firm will change even in the absence of any change in external circumstances or in fundamental technical knowledge' (Penrose, 1959, p. 56).

This picture of a firm as 'a pool of resources the utilisation of which is organised in an administrative framework' (Penrose, 1959, p. 149), which is continually evolving and is always in some respects unique, is of course thoroughly Marshallian. The major difference is that Marshall expected firms to pass into a stage of decline, whereas Mrs Penrose, having deliberately restricted her attention to firms that grow without seeking to explain why some do not, assumes that members of a growing firm will continue to be assiduous in putting their growing experience to its most effective use, never preferring to convert the potential increase in managerial capacity into organizational slack. Leibenstein offers some reasons why one might expect some preference for slack as potential productivity increases. If this preference becomes strong, the firm affected simply drops out of Mrs Penrose's analysis.

Marris's (1964, p. 113) discussion of Mrs Penrose's theory is misleading. 'She sees the firm as an administrative and social organisation, capable, in principle, of entering almost any field of material activity.' In very basic principle the firm has indeed such a potential; but once it begins operating it necessarily becomes specialized, because that is the only way in which it can keep its decision-making costs low enough to justify its existence as an alternative to a set of market transactions (or to a better-organized firm). Once its growth is under way, its product-market scope is conditioned – though not strictly determined – by its history. Penrosian firms may thus generate the characteristic patterns of Chamberlin's monopolistic competition. This limitation also explains how, in more turbulent times than those in which Mrs Penrose was writing, growth can turn into decline even if the desire for growth remains. Demand for the products to which a firm is well adapted may decrease, or radically different technologies may be introduced; and its special skills, like the special skills of individuals, may not be at all readily adaptable to other potential opportunities, particularly if the necessary readjustments threaten the established coalition.

R. R. Nelson and S. G. Winter

As a result of their activities and experience, Mrs Penrose's firms learn about their environment and how to cope with it efficiently. They do not create new technology; thus their contribution to innovation is through the diffusion of what has been created elsewhere. It may be argued, however, that improved methods of management are no less important factors in economic progress than improvements in material technologies: Schumpeter (1934) included organizational innovations in his list of entrepreneurial activities, and Chandler (1962) claimed that the introduction of the multidivisional corporate structure was a condition of the organized flow of product and process innovation which firms such as Du Pont have produced in the last 70 years. Improved products, improved processes and improved methods of management all contributed to Marshall's vision of economic progress, and all were generated in part by firms and the interaction, both competitive and collaborative, between them.

The role of the firm in a process of evolutionary change is the focus of Nelson and Winter's (1982) analysis. The intellectual heritage of that analysis includes all the theories we have considered which take seriously what happens within the firm. It includes the Marshallian emphasis (which, as we have seen, derives from Smith) on the firm as a prime instrument of economic progress, not least through the generation of new and useful knowledge. It recognizes the imperative, implicit in Coase's explanation for the existence of firms, for firms to improve the efficiency of their management processes in order to maintain, and perhaps enhance, their transactions cost advantages over coordination by market contract. It explains the growth of managerial capacity, on which Mrs Penrose's theory is built, by the emergence and continued evolution of routines, which, being boundedly rational and a product of an organization's internal as well as external history, necessarily 'give each firm its unique character' (Penrose, 1959, p. 75) and thereby ensure that tendency to variation which Marshall insisted was a chief cause of progress. The firm's environment is both a source of experience and a test of performance: 'the market system is (in part) a device for conducting and evaluating experiments in economic behaviour and organisation' (Nelson and Winter, 1982, p. 277).

Like Cyert and March and also Leibenstein, Nelson and Winter recognize that, without the comprehensive network of fully specified contracts assumed by Fama, the firm is a coalition, the maintenance of which should not be taken for granted, and which may be particularly threatened by attempts to change existing patterns of behaviour. Finally, they abandon the distinction which is fundamental to standard theory, and which persists (though with some qualifications) in these other theories, between production sets (which are data) and choices (which are acts); instead they treat both as routines. The administrative framework is included within the firm's resources; and, like other resources, it both enables and constrains.

8.6 Rational Choice Equilibrium or Organizational Process

A theoretical system may be regarded as a pool of analytical methods the utilization of which is organized in a conceptual framework; and this framework too both enables and constrains. Though there are many variations, it is possible to distinguish two distinct ways of conceptualizing the firm in economics. One is the fictitious person, who pursues clearly defined objectives (whatever they may be) by making rational calculations on the basis of exogenous data which are readily available – or which, in the limit, may be discovered by setting in motion the Bayesian clockwork. In these conditions, it is no great strain on credulity to imagine an internal structure of responsibilities, incentives and monitoring arrangements which justifies the assumption that what happens within the organization may be ignored in explaining its behaviour: the requirements for decomposing the system appear to be satisfied. Indeed, the problem may appear to be rather why there should be an administrative structure at all; and, as we have seen, the more thoroughgoing exponents of the principle of substantively rational choice believe that there is no reason for it. The firm is not only a fictitious person; it is invisible.

Coase's justification for the existence of firms has no basis in such a world. Transactions costs make it optimal to accept a degree of ignorance (if optimality can be defined in the presence of unknown data); and the establishment of a firm registers a commitment to the on-going management of events (though not, of course, without some attempt to foresee possibilities and make preparations to meet them). A firm is a learning system – at the least a system for learning how to manage, in a wider sense, a system for learning about resources, about technology and about markets. It is an instrument for the generation and application of knowledge, which is an evolutionary process. Its design affects its performance, by providing a framework for perception and interpretation which both enhances and restricts the potential for learning. It needs to maintain coherence (the analysis of which may provide scope for equilibrium ideas) but also to preserve flexibility: managerial discretion, like liquidity, is highly desirable – perhaps indispensable – for coping with emergent events. The firm (like money) is a substitute for knowledge of the future.

Economists, like other people, cannot foresee the future either of their economies or their subject. Both have developed in ways that were not anticipated 30 years ago. The intellectual and psychological attractions of an apparently closed system are familiar to us all. An open system is less comfortable; but it may provide greater opportunities.

REFERENCES

Alchian, A. A., and H. Demsetz (1972) 'Production, information costs and economic organization', *American Economic Review* 62 (5), 777–95.
Babbage, C. (1832) *On the Economy of Machinery and Manufactures*. London: Knight.
Baumol, W. J. (1959) *Business Behavior, Value and Growth*. New York: Macmillan.
Casson, M. (1982) *The Entrepreneur: An Economic Theory*. Oxford: Martin Robertson.
Chamberlin, E. H. (1962) *The Theory of Monopolistic Competition*, 8th edn. Cambridge, Mass.: Harvard University Press.
Chandler, A. D. (1962) *Strategy and Structure*. Cambridge, Mass.: Harvard University Press.

Coase, R. H. (1937) 'The nature of the firm', *Economica, New Series* 4, 386–405.

Cyert, R. M., and J. G. March (1963) *A Behavioral Theory of the Firm*. Englewood Cliffs, N. J.: Prentice-Hall.

Fama, E. F. (1980) 'Agency problems and the theory of the firm', *Journal of Political Economy* 88, 288–307.

Kirzner, I. M. (1973) *Competition and Entrepreneurship*. Chicago, Ill.: University of Chicago Press.

Knight, F. H. (1921) *Risk, Uncertainty and Profit*. Boston, Mass.: Houghton Mifflin.

Leibenstein, H. (1976) *Beyond Economic Man*. Cambridge, Mass.: Harvard University Press.

Loasby, B. J. (1989) *The Mind and Method of the Economist*. Aldershot: Edward Elgar.

Marris, R. L. (1964) *The Economic Theory of 'Managerial' Capitalism*. London: Macmillan.

Marshall, A. (1919) *Industry and Trade*. London: Macmillan.

Marshall, A. (1961) *Principles of Economics*, 9th (variorum) edn. London: Macmillan.

Mill, J. S. (1965) *Principles of Political Economy*. Toronto: University of Toronto Press.

Nelson, R. R., and S. G. Winter (1982) *An Evolutionary Theory of Economic Change*. Cambridge, Mass.: Harvard University Press.

Penrose, E. T. (1959) *The Theory of the Growth of the Firm*. Oxford: Blackwell.

Pigou, A. C. (1920) *The Economics of Welfare*. London: Macmillan.

Pigou, A. C. (1928) 'An analysis of supply', *Economic Journal* 38, 238–57.

Robinson, J. V. (1933) *The Economics of Imperfect Competition*. London: Macmillan.

Robinson, R. (1971) *Edward H. Chamberlin*. New York: Columbia University Press.

Schumpeter, J. A. (1934) *The Theory of Economic Development*. Cambridge, Mass.: Harvard University Press.

Scitovsky, T. (1943) 'A note on profit maximisation and its implications', *Review of Economic Studies* 11, 57–60.

Simon, H. A. (1969) *The Sciences of the Artificial*. Cambridge, Mass.: MIT Press.

Smith, A. (1976) *An Inquiry into the Nature and Causes of the Wealth of Nations*, 2 vols. Ed. R. H. Campbell, A. S. Skinner and W. B. Todd, Oxford: Oxford University Press.

Sraffa, P. (1926) 'The laws of return under competitive conditions', *Economic Journal* 36, 535–50.

Williamson, O. E. W. (1964) *The Economics of Discretionary Behavior*. Englewood Cliffs, N. J.: Prentice-Hall.

Williamson, O. E. W. (1975) *Markets and Hierarchies*. New York: Free Press.

Williamson, O. E. W. (1985) *The Economic Institutions of Capitalism: Firms, Markets, Relational Contracting*. New York: Free Press.

Williamson, O. E. W. (1986) *Economic Organisation: Firms, Markets and Policy Control*. Brighton: Wheatsheaf.

9

Productivity

David F. Heathfield

Economic progress is a central, continuing and little-understood aspect of Western civilization. It is so much part of our experience that it is practically taken for granted. And yet the world could be, and in places is, otherwise. Some societies seem to remain in fairly primitive steady states while others continue to 'progress' to higher and higher standards of living. Whether or not economic progress is a good thing is not at issue here – this chapter deals with the still somewhat hazy attempts at explaining it and this is where productivity comes in.[1]

The term productivity has taken a number of meanings in its long life and even today has a certain ambiguity. Essentially productivity governs the relationships between the output of goods and services and the inputs of land, labour and capital which are used to produce those goods and services. It has long been recognized that the output of goods per unit of land (or per unit of labour or per unit of capital) differs from place to place and varies with time. In some times and in some places an enormous quantity of crops can be grown on a small quantity of land (and with very little human effort) and in other places and in other times we have to work extremely hard merely to eke out a bare subsistence. These differences in output per unit of input are differences in productivity.

In early agrarian communities it was common to ascribe variations in productivity over time to the Gods, who controlled the weather, and, more prosaically, to ascribe spatial differences to differences in the type of soil available. Soil in the valleys (the 'bottoms') produced more per acre and more per man-hour than that further up the hillsides. To some extent then differences in productivity can be ascribed to differences in the quality of the inputs. An acre of land in one place is not the same thing as an acre of land elsewhere and one hour of labour by one man is not the same thing as one hour of labour by someone else (even when they appear to be exerting the same effort). The first explanation of productivity differences therefore lies in the heterogeneous nature of each input.

Notice that even if labour were perfectly homogeneous there would still be differences in output per man-hour simply because some labourers would be working on high-quality soil and others would be working on low-quality soil. Therefore to say that this labourer is more productive than that labourer is not necessarily to say anything about the relative merits of the two labourers.

A second reason for productivity differences arises even when all inputs are perfectly homogeneous. Consider two identical areas of land, one of which is required to support a large population and the other a small population. The workers of population 1 are in every way the same as those of population 2 but many more of them work the fixed quantity of land. We know from the law of diminishing returns that the output per acre in the heavily populated region will be higher than that in the less heavily populated region and likewise the output per man-hour in the densely populated region will be lower than that in the sparsely populated region. Thus factor productivities depend, at least in part, upon factor ratios. Factors have a higher productivity where they are relatively scarce even though each factor is perfectly homogeneous.

A third source of productivity differences arises even when factors are perfectly homogeneous and in equal ratios to each other. This source of productivity differences is due to differences in scale. If in one case there are 20 acres of land and 20 men and in the other case there are 200 acres and 200 men then the latter is said to be of larger scale than the former – in all other respects they are the same (i.e. the same type of land, the same type of labour and the same factor ratios). There is plenty of evidence to suggest that the productivity of both labour and land will be at least as great in the larger farm as in the smaller farm and will most probably be higher. There seem to be three reasons for this increased productivity.

First there is the 'dimension effect'. For example, to store a given volume of grain would require a barn of a certain size with a certain surface area. As the volume increases so does the surface area but by much less. For a wooden barn the shape of a cube of side n m the area to be covered (and painted) would be $5n^2$ and the volume of stored grain would be n^3. Thus for the smaller farm to store 1000 m^3 of grain would require them to produce and erect 500 m^2 of wood. For the larger farm (ten times larger), 10,000 m^3 of barn space would require about 2000 m^2 of wood. Thus the storage capacity has been increased tenfold but the material cost has increased only fourfold. If the large farm were split up into ten small farms the quantity of wood required to store their outputs of grain would rise from 2000 m^2 (for the one large farm) to 5000 m^2. This dimensionality effect seems to carry over to other aspects of production too.

Apart from the dimension effect, scale also affects productivity because of the so-called discontinuities in some factors of production. The examples of discontinuities are usually drawn from capital rather than from labour or land. The idea is that if a particular process requires a particular machine then the firm, whatever its size, must buy one even if it is used only once a month. Production could be greatly increased without exceeding the capacity of the one machine so that its cost can be spread over more and more units of output. Had the machine been 'continuous' then a small firm would be able to buy a small machine and work it to capacity, but discontinuity means that the machine is the machine and you either have it or you do not. Thus the output per machine in the large firm would be greater than that in a small firm, but such differences in productivity are due to the machine's being idle for long periods in the small firm – they are not due to any inherent superiority of the larger firm.

Neither the dimension effect nor the discontinuity effect is the primary cause of productivity rising with scale, however. Productivity was a theme of Adam Smith's *An Enquiry into the Nature and Causes of the Wealth of Nations* which was published in 1776 and emphasized an aspect of production quite different from that of his predecessors. According to Smith output per man-hour was greatly increased by the 'division of labour'. His well-known example of this was the famous pin factory. If individual workers manufactured pins on their own then each worker would produce at the most 20 pins per day. If, however, the task of making a pin were divided up into a number of small actions and one such action were given to one worker to perform then the output per day per worker would be 4,800 pins; an increase in output per head of 24,000 per cent.

A number of reasons are offered for this incredible increase. First, there will be much less time spent in moving from one task to the next. The worker who is straightening the wire, for example, will continue using pliers all the time and will not need to put down the pliers and pick up a file. Second, each worker can specialize in the task he can do best – the worker who can deftly straighten wire but is all fingers and thumbs when trying to file a point on the pin can concentrate entirely on straightening and completely avoid filing. And third, by carrying out the simple task over and over again workers become more and more proficient at that task. The greater the division of labour, the more these efficiencies can be reaped and the greater the productivity of each worker becomes.

The idea of the division of labour was emphasized by Smith in a way which was quite different from his predecessors but it would be wrong to think that he originated the idea. Lowry (1979) shows, for example, that Xenophon had a clear view of division of labour. Plato too was aware of the benefits of specialization but the emphasis seems to have been on the improved quality of the product rather than on the increased efficiency. The improved quality of work is achieved by exploiting each worker's particular aptitudes rather than by saving the worker's time.

The extent to which it is possible to engage in the division of labour depends on the size of the firm (or, more accurately, on the size of its market) and hence productivity increases with scale (on scale, see also Sraffa, 1926, and Silberston, 1972).

In his recent survey Gold (1981) argues that scale effects are not well understood either by economists or engineers. The dimension effect is admitted by him as a possible source of such economies but only in a very limited number of instances – no satisfactory argument has been advanced for generalizing it to other than storage and very similar types of production. The indivisibility argument also leaves much to be desired. It may well be that some machines can only be built to a certain size (or capacity) and until the firm is big enough to use the machine fully its factor inputs will rise by less than output. According to Gold this should lead to decreasing costs until the one machine is fully used and then, when the second machine is installed, costs will increase again as it will now be only partly used. This cyclical movement in costs as output increases is not what is meant by increasing returns to scale. There is also the point that the factor inputs should perhaps be measured not in terms of the quantity present but by the stream of services they provide. An idle machine should not therefore constitute an input (see the end of section 9.2).

Thus the first technical account of productivity (Smith's) appeared more than 200 years ago and contained not only the division of labour argument presented here but also the idea that the productivity of one factor (labour) depended upon the quantity of the other factors present (as outline above). These two effects, according to Smith, were not separate but inextricably linked.

Smith's view was that as the division of labour progressed tasks became more and more simple and so lent themselves to mechanical performance rather than manual performance. It would have been impossible for Smith's labourer to design a machine capable of producing a complete pin but it is not so difficult to design a machine capable of straightening a piece of wire.

> This great increase in the quantity of work, which in consequence of the division of labour, the same number of people are capable of performing, is owing to three different circumstances; first, to the increase of dexterity in every particular workman; secondly, to the saving of time which is commonly lost in passing from one species of work to another; and lastly, to the invention of a great number of machines which facilitate labour and abridge labour and allow one man to do the work of many. (Smith, 1981, p. 17)

Thus, according to Smith, the division of labour promotes, and is promoted by, the more and more extensive use of machinery. The division of labour leads to increases in the productivity of all factors, and the increasing use of capital will lead to further increases in the productivity of labour and land.

Pratten (1980) has followed up the pin-making example and quotes Babbage's (1833) estimate that pins per head per day in 1830 was 70 per cent above the level given by Smith. More modern processes (1980), in practice, have daily outputs per worker some 100 times greater than the 1830 estimate. (This makes no allowance for the shorter working day.) Pratten suggests that Smith overestimated the division of labour effect and ascribes much more of the improvement to capital and new types of machine. In this respect Pratten's arguments are similar to those of Gold. Marglin (1974) too argues that Smith overestimates the benefits of the division of labour. Marglin points out that time saving can indeed come about by requiring each worker to continue in one task without having to change tools but that can be done by keeping one worker on one task forever or by keeping him on it for a day – at any rate only long enough to render the set-up costs a negligible proportion of the total costs. (The real reason for the division of labour, according to Marglin, is that it enables the capitalist to maintain control over the labour force.)

Of the five foregoing sources of productivity differences, four (divine beneficence, the whims of nature, the dimensionality effect and the discontinuity effect) are free. That is, they occur without apparently incurring any cost. The remaining source of productivity differences, however, may involve some costs. As the division of labour progresses the labourer spends more and more of his working time on repetitive trivial unrewarding tasks. Smith was well aware of this and advocated the provision of public fairs and other divertisements to make the leisure time of labourers as interesting as possible. The main point is that the nature of work is changed and changed in ways which may not always meet with everyone's approval. If, when the input of labour is calculated, the disutility of each man-hour is allowed for as well as the number of man-hours, then it may well be that there is not quite so large an increase in productivity as was originally supposed. Thus there is the possibility of confusing increases in productivity with increases in factor inputs unless the measurement of those inputs is appropriate to the task on hand.

9.1 New Knowledge

Some 70 years after the publication of *The Wealth of Nations*, John Stuart Mill emphasized a rather different explanation of productivity growth. In his *Principles of Political Economy* (1976) he discusses production at some length and points out that the role of labour in production is simply to move things about so as to bend the forces and processes of nature to man's will.

> He moves a spark to fuel, and it ignites, and by the force generated in combustion it cooks the food, melts or softens the iron, converts into beer or sugar the malt or cane-juice, which he has previously moved to the spot. He has no other means of acting on matter than by moving it. Motion, and resistance to motion, are the only things which his muscles are constructed for. . . . But this is enough to have given all the command which mankind have acquired over natural forces immeasurably more powerful than themselves; *a command which, great as it is already, is without doubt destined to become indefinitely greater. . . .*
>
> Labour then, in the physical world, is always and solely employed in putting objects in motion; the properties of matter, the laws of nature, do the rest. The skill and ingenuity of human beings are chiefly exercised in discovering movements, practicable by their powers, and capable of bringing about the effects which they desire. (Mill, 1976, pp. 24–5; emphasis added)

The emphasis is added to draw attention to the idea that mankind's control over the forces of nature is great and is certain to grow. As it grows we shall make better use of our factors of production. We may learn about new materials, new products or new processes and by doing so we increase our productivity. This increased knowledge is what we now call technological progress or sometimes technical progress. Technology changes as we learn more and more about the laws of nature and thereby master nature itself. Some of this knowledge is new knowledge in the sense that it was unknown by anyone previously but some of the 'new' knowledge is only new in the sense that it has spread out from its originator to reach those who have only belatedly learnt it. There are then two problems: how is new knowledge found and how is it diffused?

As to the first of these we have already seen that according to Adam Smith some suggestions will come from the employed labour who will see better and easier ways of performing the trivially simple tasks which result from the division of labour. In more modern literature this is called *learning by doing* and will be taken up again later.

This is a rather casual way of progressing and can be augmented by the producer's devoting some of his factors of production not to the direct production of goods but rather to seeking new improved products and processes. This is called research and development (R & D) or 'applied' research.

A third source of new knowledge is somewhat less direct. John Stuart

Mill attaches enormous importance to the role of speculative thinking as a means of acquiring new knowledge and thence increasing productivity.

> In a national, or universal point of view, the labour of the savant, or speculative thinker, is as much a part of production in the very narrowest sense, as that of the inventor of a practical art; many such inventions having been the direct consequences of theoretic discoveries, and every extension of knowledge of the powers of nature being fruitful of applications to the purposes of outward life. . . . the modern art of navigation is an unforeseen emanation from the purely speculative and apparently merely curious enquiry, by the mathematicians of Alexandria, into the properties of three curves formed by the intersection of a plane surface and a cone. No limit can be set to the importance, even in a purely productive and material point of view, of mere thought. . . . intellectual speculation must be looked upon as a most influential part of the productive labour of society, and the portion of its resources employed in carrying on and in remunerating such labour as a highly productive part of its expenditure.
>
> (Mill, 1976, pp. 41–2).

This is what we would now call 'pure', as opposed to applied, research and it most certainly plays an important role in the explanation of the continuing generation of new knowledge.

As to the spread of knowledge out from its originator to the potential appliers of that knowledge there are again two points to be considered. The first problem is to explain the spread of knowledge. How do producers come to be aware of other people's discoveries and inventions? The second problem arises not from producers' being unaware of the new knowledge but from their unwillingness to use it. This reluctance comes about because not all improvements in productivity are freely and easily applied.

Although some new knowledge can be exploited very quickly, some can be exploited only after some new capital goods have been acquired. In the case of the steam engine, for example, the theory was known but could not be immediately applied to transport. It had to await the building of the steam locomotives, rolling stock and rail lines etc. Those producers who have gone to the trouble and expense of constructing canals are unlikely to view the building of a railway with any enthusiasm. To some extent then producers are trapped by decisions they have already made on investment and face the expense of constructing new capital goods if they wish to exploit the new knowledge. Thus the spread of knowledge and the adoption of new techniques are not always coincident. Application may well lag behind the spread of knowledge.

The first type of technological progress (using existing factors more efficiently) is called disembodied technological progress because it can be applied immediately using existing capital. The second kind of technological progress is called embodied technological progress because it is embodied in particular kinds of capital and the new knowledge cannot be exploited without new investment.

There are therefore four basic explanations of differences in and changes of the productivity of factors of production.

1 differing and changing factor qualities, i.e. factors are not homogeneous through time and space;
2 differing and changing factor combinations;
3 differing and changing scale when there are economies of scale; and
4 technological differences and technological change.

9.2 Measurement

Much lies behind these apparently simple notions and none of them lends itself to easy explanation or quantification. What we have, in the post-war literature, is a diversity of studies, some concentrating on the productivity of a particular factor, some concentrating on a particular source of productivity and one or two attempting a more general overall assessment of productivity. We shall begin with a fairly technical attempt at an overall measure of productivity. This is due to Solow (1957).

One way of representing these different sources of productivity change is with the production function. The production function is a mathematical expression describing the ways in which land, capital and labour can be combined to produce certain quantities of output. In general a production function may be written as

$$Q = f(L, K, N) \tag{9.1}$$

where Q is output, L is land used in the process, K is capital and N is labour. The usual assumptions are that

$$\frac{\delta Q}{\delta N} > 0 \tag{9.2}$$

$$\frac{\delta^2 Q}{\delta N^2} < 0 \tag{9.3}$$

$$\frac{\delta^2 Q}{\delta N \delta K} > 0 \tag{9.4}$$

The first of these states that labour N is productive so that output increases as more labour is added to the process. The second states that the increments in output induced by uniform increments of labour (with capital and land being fixed) get smaller and smaller the more labour there is. This comes immediately from the law of diminishing returns. The third states that the marginal product of labour increases as more capital is added to the process.

Conditions (9.2), (9.3) and (9.4) are expressed in terms of labour and capital but N and K can be replaced by any factor and the assumptions still hold.

These assumptions seem reasonable enough but are not statements about productivity. Productivity usually refers to the average output per unit of a factor input but the three assumptions above are couched in terms of marginal productivities. However, it is possible to infer something about productivity from these assumptions. Equation (9.1) can be re-expressed in terms of averages by dividing both sides by N say. Thus

$$\frac{Q}{N} = \frac{f(L, K, N)}{N} \tag{9.5}$$

$$\frac{\delta(Q/N)}{\delta N} = \frac{\delta Q/\delta N}{N} - \frac{Q}{N^2} \tag{9.6}$$

$$\frac{\delta(Q/N)}{\delta N} = \frac{\delta Q/\delta N - Q/N}{N} \tag{9.7}$$

The left-hand side of (9.7) is the rate of change of average labour productivity with additional labour. The right-hand side is the difference between the marginal and the average productivity of labour divided by N. Thus if the average product of labour is greater than its marginal product (9.7) is positive and the average will be rising with employment, i.e. rising with N. But since the marginal productivity (by assumption (9.2)) is falling, it must eventually become less than the average and thus the sign of (9.7) must become negative. Hence it must be the case that the average product of labour will fall as employment increases.

It must also be true that, since capital is productive (assumption (9.2)), then adding capital will increase output even when labour input is held constant. Thus the output per unit of labour will be increasing as more and more capital is added to the process. Factor combinations will therefore affect the productivity of individual factors as assumed above. As one factor is added to fixed quantities of other factors then the average product of the variable factor will decline but the average productivities of the fixed factors will rise.

The next question to address is not to do with factor combinations, which we shall now assume to be fixed, but with scale. What happens to average products if all factors are increased together?

From (9.1) we have

$$dQ = \frac{\delta Q}{\delta N} \, dN + \frac{\delta Q}{\delta L} \, dL + \frac{\delta Q}{\delta K} \, dK \tag{9.8}$$

$$dQ = \frac{\delta Q}{\delta N} N \frac{dN}{N} + \frac{\delta Q}{\delta L} L \frac{dL}{L} + \frac{\delta Q}{\delta K} K \frac{dK}{K} \tag{9.9}$$

But for pure changes in scale it must be the case that $dN/N = dL/L = dK/K = dF/F$. Hence

$$dQ = \frac{dF}{F} \left(\frac{\delta Q}{\delta N} N + \frac{\delta Q}{\delta L} L + \frac{\delta Q}{\delta K} K \right) \tag{9.10}$$

Now we know from Euler's theorem that the term in parentheses is equal to Q if $f(L, K, N)$ is homogeneous of degree one. Hence (9.10) becomes

$$\frac{dQ}{Q} = \frac{dF}{F} \tag{9.11}$$

The percentage change in output equals the percentage change in factor inputs so that doubling inputs doubles output too. That is, the production function has constant returns to scale. In this case there is no change in factor productivity as scale increases.

If, however, the function has increasing returns to scale then the proportional change in output will be greater than the change in factor inputs (since $Q < (\delta Q/\delta N)N + (\delta Q/\delta L)L + (\delta Q/\delta K)K$) and so the productivity of each factor will increase with scale.

If the function has decreasing returns to scale then the proportional change in output will be less than the proportional change in factor inputs and so the productivity of each factor will fall as scale increases.

Solow and many others assume constant returns to scale. This means that any change in factor productivity must be due to something other than scale changes and so eases the search for explanations. It also means that the adding-up problem is avoided.

In a profit-maximizing perfectly competitive world each factor receives its marginal physical product so that the real wage rate is the marginal physical product of labour and the total wage bill is the marginal physical product $\delta Q/\delta N$ multiplied by the number N employed, and so on for every factor. The term in parentheses in (9.10) is the sum of the factor rewards and, for constant returns to scale, exactly exhausts the total product (i.e. it equals Q). If there were increasing returns to scale then the sum of the factor rewards would exceed the total product.

This constant returns to scale assumption helps in another way too. Solow has only two factors: L, which represents a homogeneous labour input of unchanging quality, and K, which represents every other input.

The relation between these two inputs and their output does change over time, however, so that

$$Q = A(t)f(L, K) \tag{9.12}$$

where $f(L, K)$ is the production function as before and $A(t)$ represents the drift in the production function over time.

If (9.12) is differentiated with respect to time we have

$$\frac{dQ}{dt} = \frac{dA}{dt}\left[f(L, K) + \frac{\delta Q}{\delta L}\frac{dL}{dt} + \frac{\delta Q}{\delta K}\frac{dK}{dt} \right] \tag{9.13}$$

Dividing each side by Q yields

$$\frac{dQ/dt}{Q} = \frac{dA/dt}{A} + \frac{\delta Q}{\delta L}\frac{L}{Q}\frac{dL/dt}{L} + \frac{\delta Q}{\delta K}\frac{K}{Q}\frac{dK/dt}{K} \tag{9.14}$$

Now the left-hand side is the proportionate rate of growth of output with time; the first term on the right-hand side is the rate of shift of the production function with time, i.e. technical progress (this is shown in Figure 9.1); the second term is the proportional rate of change $(dL/dt)/L$ of labour input multiplied by the share $(\delta Q/\delta L)L/Q$ of output going to labour; and the third term is the proportional rate of change $(dK/dt)/K$ of capital multiplied by the share $(\delta Q/\delta K)K/Q$ of output going to capital.

Let the share of output going to labour be W_L and the share of output going to 'capital' be W_K, and let the rate of shift in the production function be a, the rate of growth of output be q, the rate of growth of labour be l and the rate of increase of capital be k. Equation (9.14) can be rewritten as

$$q = a + lW_L + kW_K \tag{9.15}$$

Solow's point is that if we know q, l, k, W_L and W_K (which we can know) then we can calculate a (the rate of technical progress) as the residual. Solow calculates a for the private non-farm sector of the American economy for the years 1909–49. His results are plotted in Figure 9.2. This graph shows that, with some small reverses, the trend in technical progress has been upward over time. The reversals are worrying since technical change – changes in knowledge – cannot strictly be reversed. How is it possible to 'forget' some things in 1940 which were known in 1939?

The rate of increase before 1930 seems to have been much less than that between 1930 and 1949. A, taken to be 1 in 1909, rose to about 1.2 by 1930 and to about 1.8 by 1949. The overall result for the whole 40 years is on average about 1.5 per cent per year.

The output per man doubled over that time; this is partly due to the shift of the production function (which according to the above figures accounts for 80 per cent of that 100 per cent increase). The remainder is due to the

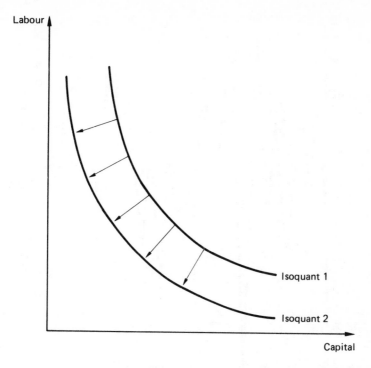

Figure 9.1 Isoquant moves towards the origin as technical progress
occurs.

increased capital per unit of labour. The latter may be thought of as
movements *around* the isoquant rather than movements of it.

The analysis so far is couched in terms of a fairly general production
function but in his article Solow goes on to investigate the form of
production function implicit in his results. Using his general function (9.12)
we have

$$Q = A(t)f(K, L) \tag{9.16}$$

If there are constant returns to scale then (9.16) can be rewritten as

$$q = A(t)f(k) \tag{9.17}$$

where $q = Q/L$ and $k = K/L$.

Dividing both sides by $A(t)$ we have

$$\frac{q}{A(t)} = f(k) \tag{9.18}$$

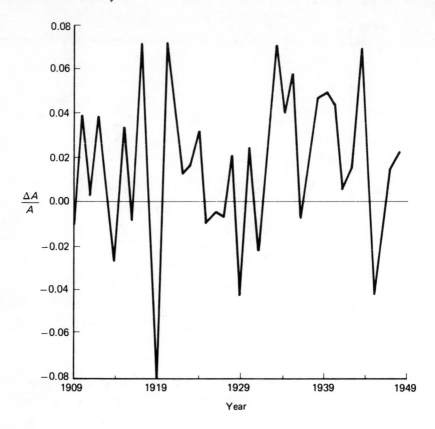

Figure 9.2 Year-on-year changes in productivity in US non-farm output, 1909–1949. *Source*: Solow, 1957.

Since Solow has data on q and k and since he has computed the value for A for each of the years he can use (9.18) to explore various forms of f. He tries five:

$$\frac{q}{A(t)} = \alpha + \beta k \tag{i}$$

$$\frac{q}{A(t)} = \alpha + \beta \log k \tag{ii}$$

$$\frac{q}{A(t)} = \alpha - \beta/k \tag{iii}$$

$$\log \left[\frac{q}{A(t)} \right] = \alpha + \beta \log k \tag{iv}$$

and

$$\log \left[\frac{q}{A(t)} \right] = \alpha - \beta/k \tag{v}$$

All have very high explanatory power (all have R^2 above 0.99) and there is little to choose among them. Solow marginally prefers (iv) which is the well-known Cobb–Douglas function, and that function is chosen here to illustrate the 'production function' approach to productivity measurement. Equation (9.19) is a Cobb–Douglas function with constant returns to scale, i.e.

$$Q = AL^{\alpha}K^{1-\alpha} \tag{9.19}$$

or, dividing throughout by L,

$$q = AK^{1-\alpha} \tag{9.20}$$

In this version of the function there is no technical progress since A is a constant. But if we are prepared to assume a uniform annual rate of technical progress, say n per cent per year, then (9.20) can be rewritten as

$$q = A_0 \exp(nt) \, k^{1-\alpha} \tag{9.21}$$

from which A_0, n and α can be found if we have observations of q and k (see Heathfield and Wibe, 1987).

Were we to estimate (9.21) using Solow's data we would estimate n to be about 1.5 per cent since that is the constant proportionate rate of technical progress found by his more direct measure.

The constant returns to scale Cobb–Douglas function can be specified by only one parameter (α) and, as we shall see, imposes rather severe constraints on the kind of technical progress we can measure in this way. However, it is well known and easy and economical to use.

Solow makes it abundantly clear that his analysis rests on a number of strong assumptions. He has assumed that technical progress was disembodied and that there were constant returns to scale, perfectly competitive product and factor markets, and a constant work-week for both factors. Furthermore the measure of output used is gross (rather than net) so depreciation of capital is not subtracted from the output figures and neither is there any correction for improvements in the quality of labour (or anything else for that matter).

Some of these assumptions arise from limitations of the data available. Others are necessary in order to separate movements *of* the production function from movements *around* the production function. One of these assumptions (constant returns to scale) has already been mentioned, but it has also been implicitly assumed that the technical progress affected both factors equally. It could have been the case that technical change affected only the productivity of one factor – or perhaps affected one factor rather more than the other. That is, technical progress may be labour saving, capital saving or neutral and Solow has assumed neutrality. He tested this assumption by investigating whether the rate of technical change was correlated with changes in factor ratios. He found no evidence of this and hence concluded that (at least with his data) technical change was neutral.

There are rather more rigorous definitions of the neutrality of technical change due to Hicks, Harrod and Solow. Technical progress is Hicks neutral when there is no change in factor ratios unless there is a change in factor price ratios. Technical change is Harrod neutral when there is no change in capital–output ratio unless there is a change in interest rate. Technical change is Solow neutral when there is no change in the labour–output ratio unless there is a change in the wage rate.

Thus if technical change were Hicks neutral it would improve the productivity of both labour and capital equally. If it were Harrod neutral it would improve the productivity of labour rather than that of capital. And if it were Solow neutral it would improve the productivity of capital rather than that of labour. These alternatives are shown in Figure 9.3.

These distinctions are perhaps better made by considering technical progress not as an independent term in the production function but as a term augmenting other factors. Thus for example the input of labour may be measured in efficiency units rather than in straightforward man-hours (and similarly for capital) so that

$$Q = A(t)f(L^*, K^*) \tag{9.22}$$

where L^* is the labour input in 'efficiency units' and is equal to $\exp(nt)\, L$, K^* is the capital input in 'efficiency units' and is equal to $\exp(mt)\, K$, L is the straightforward measure of labour input in man-hours and K is the straighforward measure for capital. Equation (9.22) indicates that the function, $f(L^*, K^*)$ will drift over time (owing to the term $A(t)$) as before and this will cause output to increase even when $f(L^*, K^*)$ is held constant. But in (9.22) output still grow even without the first term $A(t)$. This is because with actual man-hours and actual capital-hours (L and K) held fixed, the efficiency inputs (L^* and K^*) will continually increase – the first, at an annual rate of n per cent and the second at an annual rate of m per cent.

Equation (9.22) can then be rewritten as

$$Q = A(t)f\,[\exp(nt)\, L, \exp(mt)\, K] \tag{9.23}$$

To see what this means it is helpful to replace this general function with a specific function, e.g. the Cobb–Douglas function:

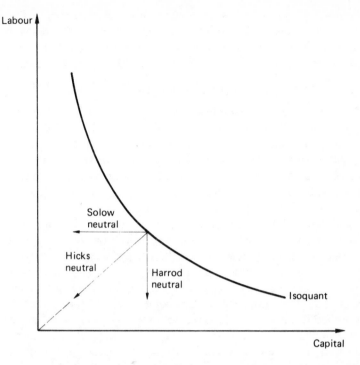

Figure 9.3 Neutrality of technical change.

$$Q = A(t) \, [\exp(nt) \, L]^{\alpha}[\exp(mt) \, K]^{1-\alpha} \tag{9.24}$$

It will be clear that (9.24) can be written as

$$Q = A(t) \, \exp[(n+m)t] \, L^{\alpha}K^{1-\alpha} \tag{9.25}$$

This is indistinguishable from the original form of technical progress and demonstrates that for the Cobb–Douglas case it is impossible to distinguish between Hicks-neutral, Harrod-neutral and Solow-neutral technical change. Thus the choice of the Cobb–Douglas function rules out the possibility of finding anything other than Hicks-neutral technical progress.

Other well-known functions do lend themselves to such distinctions. Consider for example the constant elasticity of substitution (CES) function

$$Q = \gamma[\delta K^{-\theta} + (1-\delta)L^{-\theta}]^{-1/\theta} \tag{9.26}$$

where γ is the efficiency parameter (similar to A in the Cobb–Douglas function), δ is the distribution parameter (similar to α in the Cobb–Douglas function) and θ determines the elasticity of substitution via $\sigma = 1/(1-\theta)$.

Technical progress can be introduced into this function in three ways. First, γ can be made a function of time so as to move the whole function. Second, K can be expressed in efficiency units (as above). Third, L can be expressed in efficiency units. If this is done (9.26) can be rewritten as

$$Q = \gamma_0 \exp(st)\{\delta[K \exp(mt)]^{-\theta} + (1-\delta)[L \exp(nt)]^{-\theta}\}^{-1/\theta} \tag{9.27}$$

Clearly s increases the productivity of both L and K equally – it is Hicks neutral. m increases the productivity of capital – it is capital augmenting and Solow neutral. n increases the productivity of labour – it is labour augmenting and Harrod neutral. Notice that if $m=n$ then the two factor-augmenting terms can be taken out of the term in braces and combined with the efficiency parameter. In this case technical progress will be identical with Hicks neutral.

It will be recalled that Solow assumed that technical progress was disembodied, i.e. it need not be embodied in a particular type of capital. This assumed disembodiment of technical progress is important since it allows the rate of technical progress to be independent of the rate of investment and furthermore allows the capital stock to be aggregated without reference to the age of each component. When technical progress is embodied it is necessary to know not only how many machines are in use but also the dates of their manufacture. Very old machines will have lower productivity than new machines; hence it is necessary to allow for capital of different 'vintages'. This question has been investigated by Salter (1969) who extended the idea of vintages beyond that of embodied technical progress.

Salter recognizes that not only is a particular level of technique embodied in items of capital equipment but so is a particular combination of factors. The production functions specified above allow any combination of labour and capital at any time so that should the price of labour increase relative to that of capital then the entrepreneur would shift out of labour into capital. This shift would be instantaneous and costless and hence the production function truly represents the range of factor combinations available to the entrepreneur. Salter's point is that this choice is open to entrepreneurs only at the point of buying a machine: once the machine is bought the choice is no longer open. This is the so-called putty–clay hypothesis. Before investment, capital is putty and can be moulded into any shape whatever. After investment, capital is clay and has been baked into a particular form which cannot be altered. This means that each vintage of capital reflects not only the technique available at the date of construction but also the relative factor prices at that date. The *ex ante* and *ex-post* isoquants are shown in Figure 4.4.

This distinction between putty and clay perhaps calls for a better use of terms. Assume first that there has been no technical progress but there has

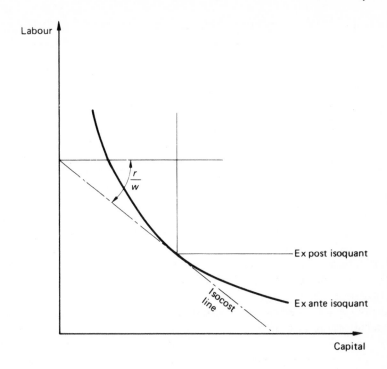

Figure 9.4 The putty–clay model.

been a once-and-for-all change in relative factor prices. The combination of factors will not immediately respond because the existing capital stock is not malleable – it is clay rather then putty. Eventually, however, the oldest machines will need to be replaced and this provides an opportunity to choose the 'best' combination of factors for the new machines. Slowly, then, as the capital wears out the combination of factors will move towards its new optimum. The choice of factor combination is called a choice of technology and it may be helpful to restrict the term 'technological progress' to movements of this kind, i.e. movements around the existing production function. This resticts the term 'technical progress' to reflecting movements of the production function. That is, technical progress measures the rate of change of the *ex ante* choice set – that facing the entrepreneur when buying new capital. Technological progress measures the rate at which actual technology changes as entrepreneurs seek to update existing capital. The most recent piece of capital embodies the latest and hence the 'best-practice' technology.

The gap between the best practice and the average is demonstrated by Salter with an example taken from the US blast furnace industry for the

Table 9.1   Gross tons of pig-iron produced per .nan-hour, 1911–1926

Year	Best-practice plants	Industry average
1911	0.313	0.140
1917	0.326	0.150
1919	0.328	0.140
1921	0.428	0.178
1923	0.462	0.213
1925	0.512	0.285
1926	0.573	0.296

years 1911–26 (table 9.1). As can be seen the best-practice output per man-hour has been steadily increasing although the rate of increase seems to have slowed slightly during the war years. (Recall that America did not enter World War I until 1917.) The average has also increased but not consistently since there was a fall between 1917 and 1919. This could reflect the fact that during wartime even old capital is brought into production and so the average is lowered. Of course these figures refer only to output per man-hour and so the best-practice data reflect factor substitution as well as technical progress. Similarly the average-practice figures reflect not only technological progress but also the changing range of vintages in use. Normally the range of vintages in use would grow steadily smaller and smaller as they all converged onto the best practice. This process of convergence would be upset by (a) the continual changing of what is best practice consequent on technical progress and on changes in relative prices and (b) sudden increases in demand which bring old machines back into play.

The range of vintages in use will certainly depend on wear and tear, i.e. physical depreciation. Machines do not last forever and even with no change in relative prices and in the absence of any technical progress there will be an annual turnover of machines. Physical depreciation, however, is not the only, nor the most important, cause of machine replacement. As the best practice moves further and further away from an existing vintage then so will that vintage become less and less profitable. More efficient machines will lower production costs – and hence prices – until the old machine can no longer produce at a profit even though it may still have a long physical life ahead of it. Similarly of course any fall in demand would reduce the price and squeeze out the less efficient machines (this is the reverse of what happened during wartime as above). This source of lay-off is called obsolescence and arises from economic rather than physical performance.

Much has been made of this by Scandinavian economists, especially Johanson (1972) who assumes strict clay ex post. The entrepreneur chooses a machine with a particular technology best suited to his expectations regarding future prices over the estimated life of that machine. The choice set he faces at this stage depends upon the current technical possibilities as portrayed by the kind of production function used above (Cobb–Douglas or CES). Once the choice is made the entrepreneur is stuck with that technology and will have a number of machines each with its own technology. The next decision the entrepreneur has to make concerns which of his machines it will be profitable to use and which he will leave idle. This will depend on the prices of inputs, the price of output and the technology embodied in each machine (see for example Heathfield and Wibe, 1987).

This view of the clay nature of capital is somewhat extreme in that some substitution, even *ex post*, is likely to be possible in many, if not all, cases. Furthermore there is almost certainly the possibility of disembodied technical progress. This, it will be remembered, does not depend on particular types of capital and may best be thought of as organizational improvements – as if existing machines can be rearranged or used in a novel way.

There is plenty of evidence that disembodied technical progress does occur. Perhaps the best-known example is that of a Swedish steel plant at Horndall. The plant was installed and operated at a certain level of productivity but every year thereafter the level of productivity increased. As people operated the plant they begin to understand it better and to see new ways of improving it. There appears to be no limit to this kind of technical progress. In the case of the Horndall plant the improvements continued for 40 years.

Since, for disembodied technical progress, there is no cost associated with its introduction, there is no reason to distinguish between technical change and technological change.

This source of increased productivity is interesting in that it suggests a possible explanation of the increased productivity. The Solow view simply takes technical progress as a residual. The production function approach makes it a function of time; it is as if the passage of time itself improves production. This is rather similar to Arrow's suggestion that technical progress is learning by doing (see Arrow, 1962). It is not so much the passage of time *per se* which increases productivity but the fact that we accumulate knowledge or know-how as we gain more and more experience of the tasks in hand. This may be proxied by accumulated output and/or accumulated investment (the latter is favoured by Arrow). The production function then becomes

$$Q(t) = \sum_{0}^{t} Q(t) f[L(t) K(t)] \qquad (9.28)$$

or

$$Q(t) = \sum_{0}^{t} I(t) f[L(t), K(t)] \qquad (9.29)$$

In each case the first term is a more reasonable explanation of shifts in the production function than the simple exponential time trends used previously. In equation (9.28), cumulative output appears and hence, the more the firm has produced, the more efficient it will be.

This association of productivity with output has led some writers to attribute the improved productivity to increasing returns to scale. This is a possible, though perhaps an unhelpful, use of language. Returns to scale, as usually defined, depend upon the current rate of production rather than on its history. Furthermore returns to scale are reversible: if a firm were to adopt a smaller scale of production – say by replacing one large plant by a number of small ones – then it would lose any returns to scale previously enjoyed. If cumulative output is used then there can be no reversal; productivity continues to increase whatever the rate of current output, until production ceases altogether (see Silberston, 1972).

Rather than relate technical progress to previous experience, some investigators have tried to enter knowledge itself as an input into the production function. This knowledge is in some respects like capital. It is a produced factor of production and the amount used should be susceptible to rational choice just like any other investment decision. The idea is that firms can actively seek appropriate knowledge by directing some labour into R&D. R&D expenditure can be measured and hence can be entered into a production function just like any other factor of production (see Nelson, 1959).

It is not quite like other factors, however. When a firm makes an investment in fixed capital it owns the capital and can control who uses it and how it is used. Similarly if it hires labour then, at least for those hours, no one else can use it. In the case of knowledge, however, the ownership and control question is much less clear. New ideas generated by one firm's R&D expenditure can sometimes be copied by its competitors at very little cost. Patent rights do help with this but there remain some interesting incentive problems (see Mansfield, 1965, and Dasgupta and Stiglitz, 1980).

One criticism of this expenditure approach to measuring knowledge is that R&D expenditure does not, in every case, prove successful. Research, by its very nature, is an uncertain activity with uncertain pay-offs; some projects are enormously successful and others fail to come up with any ideas at all. A more reliable measure of the output of the R&D departments is not the expenditure on them rather the number of patents issued. This also permits a market in technology (see Wilson, 1977, and Bosworth, 1980).

So far there has been little attempt to address the main empirical problems of work on productivity measurement. It has been assumed that capital data measure whatever is required of capital input, that labour data do likewise for labour and finally that output data correctly measure

Table 9.2   Output, input and productivity for the US private domestic
economy 1945–1965

	Output	*Input*	*Productivity*[a]
Initial estimates	3.49	1.83	1.60
Corrected for errors in			
Aggregation	3.39	1.84	1.49
Investment goods prices	3.59	2.19	1.41
Relative utilization	3.59	2.57	0.96
Aggregation of capital services	3.59	2.97	0.58
Aggregation of labour services	3.59	3.47	0.10

[a]Productivity = output/input.

output. All these have been questioned and, in the context of productivity measures, thoroughly investigated by Denison (1967) and Jorgenson and Griliches (1967) among others.

Abramovitz (1956), Kendrick (1961), Denison (1967) and Jorgenson and Griliches (1967) have all investigated the extent of productivity change over time and productivity differences among sectors and/or nations. All these authors have attempted to correct estimates of productivity for omissions and errors in measurement. As might be expected there is still no agreed view. Jorgenson and Griliches (1967) hold that almost all the apparent differences between some weighted combination of outputs and some weighted combination of inputs can be accounted for without resort to the 'residual' or technical progress. He offers the results shown in table 9.2.

The first estimates of total factor productivity (1.60 per cent per annum) is calculated using National Income Accounts figures and assuming that the input of each factor is proportional to the stock of it available. The first correction 'aggregation' arises from the argument that the weights used in aggregating the diverse items of output and inputs (Paasch or Laspeyres indices) induce biases in measure of growth. If, for example, the weights are the base-period values of the separate items to be aggregated, then as some items grow and others fall the constant weights will underestimate the effect on the aggregate of those items which have grown and overestimate the influence of those items which fall. Many writers suggest that the Divisia index provides a less biased measure of change (see Richter, 1966). The Divisia index is defined in differential form:

$$\frac{\mathrm{d}X}{X} = \frac{\mathbf{p} \cdot \mathbf{dx}}{\mathbf{p} \cdot \mathbf{x}}$$

where X is the index of quantity, $\mathbf{p}$ is the vector of prices and $\mathbf{x}$ is the vector of quantities. This index satisfies the time and factor reversal conditions and, provided that there are constant returns to scale and perfect competition, is independent of the shape of the time path over which dX is integrated to yield the change in the index between any two points in time.

This correction affects both output and input, reducing the measure of output and increasing the measure of inputs. These together reduce the residual from 1.60 to 1.49 per cent per annum.

The second correction, 'investment goods prices', arises from the argument that what is wanted for productivity analysis is the aggregate of capital using weights not based on the relative prices of new items of capital equipment but rather based on the relative prices of capital services. By this is meant the annual rentals which each item of capital attracts. This depends partly on the purchase price of a new piece of capital but also on the annual rate of depreciation, the rate of interest and capital gains. Clearly, even if the purchase prices of new capital goods remained unchanged over time, any change in the rate of interest or in depreciation would affect their annual rentals and it is the rentals which should be used to aggregate the items.

This argument also applies to consumer durable goods and hence this correction will again apply to both output and input measures. The result of using these new weights is to increase the values of the aggregates, and when this is done the the measure of output increases from 3.39 to 3.59 per cent per annum and inputs increase from 1.84 to 2.19 per cent per annum. Productivity falls from 1.49 to 1.41 per cent per annum.

The third correction arises from the fact that the number of machines and the number of men present do not determine output. The hours which each works and the intensity of their work has to be accounted for. The transformation from machines to machine hours is accomplished by measuring installed wattage and the annual electricity consumption – these together yield trend estimates of the duration and intensity of use of capital during the year. Labour input too is corrected for hours of work and effort. When these corrections are applied the input measure (output is not affected by this) increases from 2.19 to 2.57 per cent per annum and productivity is reduced from 1.41 to 0.96 per cent per annum.

The fourth correction recognizes that the capital services aggregate as previously outlined assumed equal tax rates on the various items so that the prices of their services depended only on capital prices, interest rates and capital gains. Since the concept of capital in these studies is so wide (it includes land for example) the assumption of equal tax rates is quite strong. When corrected for, the index of inputs rises from 2.57 to 2.97 per cent per annum and the productivity falls from 0.96 to 0.58 per cent per annum.

The final correction is an attempt to allow for the heterogeneous nature of labour. Different categories of labour are aggregated not simply by adding man-hours but by weighting each category according to its reward. This further increases the index of inputs from 2.97 to 3.47 per cent per annum and the productivity 'residual' falls from 0.58 to 0.10 per cent per annum.

The main thrust of the Jorgenson and Griliches paper is of course that measuring productivity as a residual means that it includes all the errors in measuring inputs and outputs. With sufficient work (and ingenious theory) this residual can be reduced to insignificance. Denison's conclusions are rather different from this. He makes fewer corrections than Jorgenson and Griliches and argues that about half the growth in output could not be explained in terms of factor inputs and hence constitutes the residual productivity change or technical progress. For a more recent attempt at applying this production function method to British manufacturing see Muellbauer (1984).

Productivity change seems to have been a continuing feature of Western economic and social history. The improvement of our material living standards has come to be expected – almost taken for granted – but it has not been without its reversals. By reversal, it is meant that the pace of productivity change is sometimes very high and at other times is comparatively slow. The real question is when will the trend end and why is it not smooth? This is partly a question of fluctuations in capacity utilization and partly a question of fluctuations in the rate of growth of capacity. The first is to do with 'cycles' like the trade cycle and the Kondratief cycle. The second is to do with productivity and is what concerns us here. The recent (1970s) slowdown has attracted much attention and for an attempt at explaining this world-wide slowdown in economic growth see Lindbeck (1983) and Giersch and Wolter (1983).

Most of what has gone before is to do with modelling how productivity changes with time. A considerable amount of work has also been done on explaining spatial disparities in productivity. One such explanation is closely linked with the time dimension of technical progress: since new ideas are being thought up all the time they will first be used by their discoverers and gradually knowledge of the ideas will spread to others and they will become progressively more and more widely used. This spreading out of the new idea will give a spatial aspect to productivity differences which will persist for as long as new ideas are coming forward. The proportion of firms using the new techniques follows a logistic S-shaped curve. At first the discoverer of a new process uses it; then firms close by, and other firms close to the second-phase users, and then other firms 'catch' the idea and the rate of adoption accelerates. Eventually of course most firms have 'caught' the idea and so the few remaining firms with high resistance to it are eventually conquered and it becomes common practice.

For obvious reasons this is called the epidemic model of technological diffusion (see Mansfield, 1969; Davis, 1979; and Stoneman and Ireland, 1983).

If one particular country habitually discovers things first then it is the world's technical leader and other countries will lag behind. This has led to the 'catch-up' hypothesis of spatial differences in productivity and in productivity growth. The follower countries will clearly be behind the leader and so have lower levels of productivity but, so the argument goes, the further they are from the technical 'frontier' the quicker they could improve, i.e. they have a long way to go before meeting the frontier and hence can move much faster than the leading country which can only improve at the rate of new discoveries. The USA was once the leading technical nation but has possibly now given way to Japan.

9.3 Conclusions

The notion of productivity is old and ambiguous. There seems to be a persistent belief in man's ability to continue to improve his material standard of living. This implies that we can produce more and more output without necessarily providing any more inputs. To some extent differences in output per man can be ascribed to the provisions of nature but nature is unlikely to offer a continually improving level of productivity such as we presume. The division of labour, economies of scale and the provision of more and more capital per man offer early explanations of continuing productivity growth but none is without its critics. The solution seems to lie in technical progress which is a measure of how our progressive understanding of the laws of nature grant us greater and greater command over nature. This enables us to make better and better use of labour (and our capital and land). Quite a lot of work has been done on this. We need to know how this knowledge comes about – is it by chance, by design or simply as a consequence of engaging in the act of production? This explanation of our increasing productivity is attractive in that it is limitless and, once won, is free and infinitely durable. Even so some have argued that this apparent ever increasing productivity is a result of incorrectly measuring inputs and outputs. This argument, though well made technically, seems so much at variance with our common experience that it is very difficult to accept. Most firms and most countries do seem to believe that the pursuit of knowledge pays off in a strictly material way whatever its other merits may be. In a materialistic world the explanation of productivity change is of major if not supreme importance.

NOTES

1 Useful surveys of the literature relating to this chapter are given by Blaug (1963), Gold (1981), Hahn and Matthews (1964), Kamien and Schwartz (1975), Kennedy and Thirlwall (1972), Kravis (1976), Nadiri (1970), Nelson (1959) and Puu and Wibe (1980).

REFERENCES

Abramovitz, M. (1956) 'Resource and output trends in the United States since 1870' *American Economic Review* 46 (2), 5–23.
Arrow, K. J. (1962) 'The economic implications of learning by doing', *Review of Economic Studies* 29, 155–73.
Babbage, C. (1833) *Economy of Machinery and Manufactures*. London: Knight.
Blaug, M. (1963) 'A survey of the theory of process innovations', *Economica* 30, 13–32.
Bosworth, D. (1980) 'Technological environment, market structure and investment in technological change', in *The Economics of Technological Progress*. Ed. T. Puu and S. Wibe, London: Macmillan, pp. 151–79.
Dasgupta, P., and J. Stiglitz (1980) 'Uncertainty, industrial structure and the speed of R & D', *Bell Journal of Economics*, Spring, 1–28.
Davies, S. (1979) *The Diffusion of Process Innovations*. Cambridge: Cambridge University Press.
Denison, E. F. (1967) *Why Growth Rates Differ: Post-war Experience in Nine Western Countries*. Washington, D.C.: The Brookings Institution.
Giersch, H., and F. Wolter (1983) 'Towards an explanation of the productivity slowdown: an acceleration–deceleration hypothesis', *Economic Journal* 93 (369), March, 35–55.
Gold, B. (1981) 'Changing perspectives on size, scale, and returns: an interpretive survey', *Journal of Economic Literature* 19, 5–33.
Hahn, F. H., and R. C. O. Matthews (1964) 'The theory of economic growth: a survey', *Economic Journal* 73, 779–902.
Heathfield, D. F., and S. Wibe (1987) *An Introduction to Cost and Production Functions*. Basingstoke: Macmillan.
Johanson, L. (1972) *Production Functions*. Amsterdam: North-Holland.
Jorgenson, D. W., and Z. Griliches (1967) 'The explanation of productivity change', *Review of Economic Studies* 34, 249–83.
Kamien, M. I., and N. L. Schwartz (1975) 'Market structure and innovation: a survey', *Journal of Economic Literature* 13, 1–37.
Kendrick, J. W., (1961) *Productivity Trends in the United States*. Princeton, N.J.: Princeton University Press.
Kennedy, C., and A. P. Thirlwall (1972) 'Technical progress: a survey', *Economic Journal* 82, 11–72.
Kravis, I. B. (1976) 'A survey of international comparisons of productivity' *Economic Journal* 86.
Lindbeck, A. (1983) 'The recent slowdown in productivity growth', *Economic Journal* 93 (369), March, 13–34.

Lowry, S. T. (1979) 'Recent literature on ancient Greek economic thought', *Journal of Economic Literature* 17 (1), 65–86.

Mansfield, E. (1965) 'Rates of return from industrial research and development', *American Economic Review* 55, 310–22.

Mansfield, E. (1969) *Industrial Research and Technological Innovation*. New York: W. Norton.

Marglin, S. A. (1974) 'What do bosses do? The origins and functions of hierachy in capitalist production', *Review of Radical Political Economics* 6 (2), 60–112.

Mill, J. S. (1976) *Principles of Political Economy*. Fairfield, Calif.: Augustus Kelly.

Muellbauer, J. (1984) 'Aggregate production functions and productivity measurement: a new look', Centre for Economic Policy Research Discussion Paper No. 34, November.

Nadiri, M. I. (1970) 'Some approaches to the theory and measurement of total factor productivity: a survey', *Journal of Economic Literature* 8, 1137–77.

Nelson, R. R. (1959) 'The economics of invention: a survey of the literature', *Journal of Business* 32, 101–27.

Pratten, C. F. (1980) 'The manufacture of pins', *Journal of Economic Literature* 18, 93–6.

Puu, T. and S. Wibe (1980) *The Economics of Technological Progress*. London: Macmillan.

Richter, M. K. (1966) 'Invariance axioms and economic indexes', *Econometrica* 34 (4). 739–55.

Salter, W. E. G. (1969) *Productivity and Technical Change*. Cambridge: Cambridge University Press.

Silberston, A. (1972) 'Economies of scale in theory and practice', *Economic Journal* 82, 369–91.

Smith, A. (1981) *An Enquiry into the Nature and Causes of the Wealth of Nations*. Indianapolis, Ind.: Liberty Classics.

Solow, R. M. (1957) 'Technical change and the aggregate production function', *Review of Economics and Statistics* 39, 312–20.

Sraffa, P. (1926) 'The laws of returns under competitive conditions', *Economic Journal* 36 (144), 535–50.

Stoneman, P., and N. Ireland (1983) 'The role of supply factors in the diffusion of new process technology', *Economic Journal, Conference Papers* 93, 65–77.

Wilson, R. (1977) 'The effect of technological environment and product rivalry on R&D effort and licensing inventions', *Review of Economics and Statistics*, 59 (2), 171–8.

10
The debt burden
Brian Hillier and M. Teresa Lunati

The issue of the burden of the national debt has a long and continuing history as a source of economic controversy. It concerns whether or not the burden of a public project may be shifted to future time periods or to later generations if the project is financed by the sale of public debt rather than by the immediate levying of taxes.

In this chapter the issues involved are discussed and some answers to the questions raised are offered. Much of the discussion below will hinge upon the use of formal or abstract theoretical models, and the approach adopted is primarily that of the economic theorist rather than that of the historian of economic thought. However, frequent references will be made to the work of some of the important contributors to the debate, so that the reader should be able to grasp the historical progress of the argument.

The organization of this chapter is as follows. Section 10.1 outlines the different definitions of debt burden adopted by writers in the area and proposes a justification of the lifetime utility concept used in the model here. Section 10.2 reviews the historical debate on the burden of the debt. In section 10.3 the basic framework of analysis, an overlapping generations model, is presented and some preliminary results concerning the effects of shifts from tax to bond finance for a given level of public expenditure are derived. The next section introduces private intergenerational transfers into the model and shows how the results are modified. Specifically it examines the particular conditions under which the method of financing is irrelevant, i.e. under which there is no debt burden. Section 10.5 looks at issues not covered by the formal modelling of the previous sections, and finally the last section offers some conclusions. The basic conclusion here is that the mode of finance of public expenditure does indeed generally matter.

10.1 Definitions of the Burden of the Debt

There are economists who argue that the national debt is no burden on the economy and that the real cost of government expenditure, no matter how financed, cannot be shifted, and there are those who take the opposite view. A third view sometimes expressed is that 'discussion of debt "burden" has become pointless, and that we should do better to devote our time to the study of particular situations in which the raising or retirement of debt is one of the possible means of pursuing a specified objective' (Wiseman, 1961, p. 181). In so far as this third view is arguing that what really matters is the determination of optimal government policy, it has much to commend it. The problem with this view, however, is that in coming to an opinion on optimal policy it may be necessary to know whether there is a debt burden or not.

Before proceeding any further it is necessary to define the concept of the burden of the national debt (in what follows, the phrases national debt, public debt and government debt are used synonymously).[1] Several definitions have been used in the past and it is important to distinguish between them in order to avoid confusion.

Simple No-debt Burden or Real Resource Measure

Some contributors to the debate seem prepared to admit no burden of the debt. Rather they examine the burden of a public project, which they define as the total amount of real resources withdrawn from the private sector at the time the project is undertaken. From this viewpoint then, internal debt, i.e. public debt sold to domestic residents, obviously cannot be used to transfer or shift the burden of the project to the future and the cost must be borne by the generation alive at the time the project is carried out. Such contributors, however, would usually concede that external debt, i.e. public debt sold to foreigners, may involve a transfer of the burden. In the words of Lerner,

> a nation owing money to other nations (or to the citizens of other nations) *is* impoverished or burdened in the same kind of way as a man who owes money to other men. But this does not hold for national debt which is owed by the nation to citizens of the *same* nation. There is then no external creditor. 'We owe it to ourselves'. . . . An *external* loan enables an individual or a nation to get things from others without having to give anything in return, for the time being . . . when he repays the debt he has to consume less than he is producing. But this is not true for *internal* borrowing . . . it does *not* enable the nation to consume more than it produces . . . the repayment of internal debt does not necessitate a tightening of the belt. (Lerner, 1948, pp. 256–7)

A similar argument was put quite dramatically by Samuelson: 'To fight a war now, we must hurl present-day munitions at the enemy; not dollar bills, and not future goods and services' (1958a, p. 651).

Lifetime Consumption

Whilst the above arguments seem eminently sensible under the above definition of 'burden', they are not so appealing under different definitions. Bowen, Davis and Kopf put forward a definition of

> the real burden of a public debt to a generation as the total consumption of private goods foregone *during the lifetime* of that generation as a consequence of government borrowing and attendant public spending. . . . Our preference for the lifetime of a generation as the unit of account is based on the proposition that people can and do forego consumption at a moment of time in order to be able to consume more later, and that to use the amount of consumption foregone at any one moment of time as some sort of index of the overall sacrifices made by a generation is misleading. (Bowen, Davis and Kopf, 1960, p. 702)

Such a definition allows for the possibility that, although a generation carrying out a governmental project must devote real resources to that project (which is the grain of truth in the arguments of Lerner and Samuelson and the like), this does not necessarily imply that lifetime consumption of that generation, or following generations, is unaffected by the mode of finance of the project. It is, in other words, possible that the real burden, now measured in terms of lifetime consumption, of a public project financed by public debt sales can be transferred from one generation to another when compared with the alternative, which is implicit in the definition given by Bowen, Davis and Kopf, of tax financing of the project.

Bowen, Davis and Kopf also introduced the useful distinction between a 'gross burden' and a 'net burden'. The 'gross burden' refers to the effects (in terms of lifetime consumption) of debt finance of a given public expenditure relative to the effects of tax finance of that given expenditure. The 'gross burden' then does not take 'into account the benefit that may result from the public expenditure' (Bowen, Davis and Kopf, 1960, p. 702). The 'gross burden' would seem to be the relevant concept for the burden of the debt debate to focus upon. As Buchanan put it:

> Although it is essential for sound analysis to consider both sides of a prospective fiscal operation . . . the two sides . . . must be kept conceptually distinct . . . [since] if the effects of public expenditure which is debt financed are attributed to debt creation, it is likely to be forgotten that the same results could possibly have been achieved by either tax financing or currency creation. (Buchanan, 1958, p. 29)

The concept of 'net burden' is not explicitly defined by Bowen, Davis and

Kopf but it can be taken to be the effects of a given public expenditure, however financed, relative to the effects of not carrying out that expenditure at all. Clearly, there could be a 'gross burden' but a 'net benefit' associated with a given public expenditure on a worthwhile project, whose benefits to a generation exceeded the costs borne by that generation associated with financing the project.

Lifetime Utility

Whilst the Bowen, Davis and Kopf definition of burden is an improvement on the first given above, a still different one is used in what follows below. Instead of defining real burden in terms of forgone lifetime consumption as they do, it may be better to go one step further and define the real gross burden of the debt to a generation as the effect on its *lifetime utility* of bond financing rather than tax financing a given public project. This new definition allows for taking into account the effects of a switch from tax to bond finance not only on lifetime consumption, but also on other variables such as lifetime labour supply and leisure enjoyment. Moreover it enables discussion of the optimal level of public good provision. It seems the most appropriate definition, since it looks at the overall welfare of an individual, rather than focusing on specific items.

Primary and Secondary Burdens

Two further definitional concepts worth noting are those of the primary and secondary debt burdens introduced by Buchanan (1958). The primary burden of the debt refers to the burden imposed directly on a generation by the taxes on it to cover the interest payments on, and/or repayment of, public debt. The secondary burden of the debt refers to the indirect effects on the behaviour of private-sector individuals of the tax payments, e.g. interest rate effects, capital stock changes and so on. The gross burden of the debt may be seen as consisting of the sum of the primary and secondary burdens.

10.2 Earlier Views on the Burden of the Debt

Before going on to the formal analysis of the next section it is interesting at this stage to look briefly at the historical progress of the debt burden debate and, especially, at how it has become tangled up in the macroeconomic debate about the merits, or otherwise, of deficit-financed government expenditure.

Ricardo's Analysis

The most famous early work on debt theory is that of Ricardo, who set out quite clearly the conditions under which bond financing of a public project would have equivalent effects to tax financing of that project. The Ricardian equivalence theorem, as it has come to be called, still has its adherents and still features in policy debate today. A succinct statement of the theorem has recently been offered by Davies:

> The theorem states the following. For any given level of public expenditure, it makes no difference to the level of nominal demand whether the government chooses to finance that level of spending wholly through taxation, or through a mix of taxation and public borrowing. Hence variations in the budget deficit do not alter the spending decisions of the private sector, even for a temporary period, and even if they make large differences to the disposable income of individuals and companies.
>
> How can this be so? According to the Ricardians, the secret is that the private sector is rational enough to realise that the act of running a government budget deficit, financed by the sale of bonds, is nothing more than a *postponement* of the need to raise tax . . . so taxes will eventually have to be raised to redeem or service bonds. Since people will instantly realise this, they will react to a rise in the budget deficit (and the bond issue) by increasing their savings to pay the expected higher level of taxes as the bonds are serviced. Total private spending therefore does not change. (Davies, 1985, p. 17).

Davies, however, does not himself adhere to the Ricardian equivalence theorem and noted that 'the stringency of the assumptions required to make it true has already been widely recognised among economists to be extremely implausible' (Davies, 1985, p. 17). The circumstances under which there will be no difference between the two methods of finance for the internal debt case were neatly set out by Houghton:

> People will be indifferent between tax finance and loan finance if the present value of discounted future tax liabilities under the loan scheme is equal to the value of present taxes under the tax scheme. For this to be the case it is required not only that the capital market be perfect so that those who prefer to pay taxes in the future rather than the present can do so by raising personal loans at the government's borrowing rate, but also that *either* people expect to live for ever, paying known taxes, *or* that they treat the known liabilities of taxpayers in the future as their own. If, compared on a present value basis, tax liabilities differ under the two schemes, their economic consequences may differ. (Houghton, 1970, pp. 297–8)

Ricardo himself recognized the stringency of the conditions necessary for the Ricardian equivalence theorem, and did not attach practical significance to it, so much so that Buiter and Tobin have argued that it should be called the 'non-Ricardian equivalence theorem' (Buiter and Tobin, 1979, p. 42).

The Classical Formulation

Buchanan has argued that a clear '"classical" formulation of public debt theory took shape only in the last two decades of the nineteenth century' (Buchanan, 1958, p. 105), and even then it was not universally accepted, as may be seen by the following quotation from the work of H. C. Adams (which Buchanan offers as one of the best formulations of the classical position):

> there are writers of respectability . . . who deny the inability of a people to meet within the year all necessary expenditures, and who refuse to assent to the time-honored argument that by a loan the burden of a war may be distributed. Such writers claim that the generation engaged in the contest must bear the burden of its expenses, that this burden can in no manner be bequeathed. . . . Although this latter conception of war expenditure does not appear to me to be quite accurate, it is yet based upon the manifest truth that each generation must subsist upon the product of its own industry. . . .
>
> Such a statement of truisms, however, is no final argument in favour of the taxing policy, nor does it meet fairly the claim of those who say that by means of loans the burden of a conflict may in part be thrown upon posterity . . . *they fail to understand the difference between capital expended in a war and the burden entailed upon the citizens* of a country by a war. (Adams, 1893, p. 24, quoted in more detail in Buchanan, 1958, pp. 106–7; italics added by Buchanan)

Adams and others believed that the burden of public expenditure could be shifted from one generation to another by means of debt finance and Buchanan argued that this was the dominant classical position by the turn of the twentieth century.

The Keynesian View

According to Mishan the view that the burden cannot be shifted replaced the classical formulation in Britain 'largely due to the efforts of Keynes and his followers . . . to such an effect that no inhibitions about the public debt being a burden on the economy remained to restrain the British government from, in fact, incurring huge budget deficits in its finance of World War II' (Mishan, 1963, p. 530). The swing of the pendulum occurred not only in Britain, but also elsewhere as indicated by the quotations from Samuelson and Lerner given above.

Clearly, in their fervour for deficit-financed fiscal policies, the Keynesians saw the debt burden argument as a potential counter-argument to be dismissed as quickly as possible. The Keynesian response was both unfortunate and illogical. Even if the effects of tax finance of public expenditure differ from those of loan finance of that expenditure, that need not negate the arguments in favour of a loan-financed increase in expenditure in a Keynesian context of involuntary unemployment. Under such circumstances, indeed, the employment-generating effects of the expenditure could be argued to be greater under loan finance than under tax finance if the former method is associated with higher private-sector expenditure. The Keynesians may thus have done nothing to strengthen their case for deficit-financed fiscal policy, but instead only served to confuse the difference between resources expended on a project and the burden on the generation carrying out that project, in a way similar to the writers attacked earlier by Adams.

The Modern Debt Burden View

The Keynesian 'new orthodoxy', as Buchanan called it, became the dominant orthodoxy until he began the counter-attack in 1958 and sparked off a new vigorous stage in the debate. The Keynesian view soon received further criticism from Bowen, Davis and Kopf (1960), Modigliani (1961) and others, but was supported by die-hard believers such as Lerner (1961) and Mishan (1963). The analysis to be presented in the following sections will offer support to the counter-attack led by Buchanan. It will show that, for one reason or another, the conditions for the no debt burden argument are so stringent for it to be of no empirical relevance. The results that follow below are almost entirely consistent with Bowen, Davis and Kopf's summary of their argument that 'while the resources consumed by a debt-financed public project must entail a contemporaneous reduction in private consumption, the issuance of government bonds permits the generations alive at the time the public project is undertaken to be compensated in the future for their initial sacrifice' (Bowen, Davis and Kopf, 1960, p. 703). The difference is that, using the lifetime utility measure adopted here, it is not necessary that consumption patterns change in order for the burden of public good provision to be shifted from one generation to another by switches in the mode of finance. The burden could, instead, be shifted via changes in work–leisure patterns.

The Rediscovery of the Ricardian Equivalence Theorem

Rather ironically, the no burden stance is now typically associated not with Keynesian economists (who seem to have been swayed by the arguments of Buchanan, Modigliani and others) but with those of a more monetarist or new classical persuasion. This twist in events is due largely to the work of Barro (1974) who restated the Ricardian equivalence theorem using more formal analytical techniques than had previously been applied to the topic. However, as the following sections will show, even in a neoclassical optimizing framework such as that used by Barro, the conditions necessary for the theorem to hold may be shown to be extremely stringent and there are monetarists and new classicists who are not prepared to accept it. Anyway, as far as the larger debate on macroeconomic policy is concerned the burden of the debt debate is only one of the issues; other important questions concern the role of the government in attempting to stabilize the economy at full employment and the existence and strength of automatic stabilizing forces.[2]

10.3 A Basic Neoclassical Model

In order to analyse whether, and how, debt finance shifts the burden of public projects from one generation to another relative to tax finance, this section presents a version of Samuelson's (1958b) overlapping generations model. In this model individuals have finite lives and, for the moment, are assumed to be purely selfish and to have no concern for any other individuals. It is easy to show that in this case there is a gross burden imposed on future taxpayers by debt financing of public projects. In section 10.5, the case where individuals are concerned about the well-being of their predecessors or heirs is examined. In this case, provided that there is a sufficient degree of altruism, successive generations may be connected by a chain of voluntary intergenerational transfers and, hence, under further particular circumstances, the Ricardian equivalence theorem may hold.

The Framework of Analysis

Consider, for simplicity, a model with only two generations, and assume that there are the same number P of people in each generation. Each individual lives two periods, which will be distinguished by the superscripts y (young) and o (old). Members of the first generation (subscript 1) are old in the same time period as that in which members of the second generation (subscript 2) are young. The members of each generation work only while young, and are all identical in terms of tastes and productivity. For the present it is assumed that each member of each generation faces a constant returns production function, with marginal product with respect to a unit of labour time equal to w units of output (all variables are expressed in real terms throughout, so that the price of goods may be considered to be unity). The effects of introducing productive capital into the model will be discussed after dealing with the simpler case where labour productivity is independent of the capital stock. Furthermore, it is assumed that output may be consumed as private goods while young, used to pay taxes or to buy bonds, or stored (with a fixed rate of appreciation of r) for consumption as private goods while old. Let the utility of the pth member of the ith generation be given by

$$U_{ip} = \alpha \ln c_{ip}^y + \beta \ln c_{ip}^o + \gamma \ln g + \delta \ln(\bar{n} - n_{ip}^y) \quad i = 1, 2 \quad (10.1)$$

$$p = 1, \ldots, P$$

where c_{ip}^y denotes consumption of private goods while young by a member of the ith generation, c_{ip}^o denotes consumption of private goods while old by a member of the ith generation, and g represents the aggregate provision of public goods by members of the first generation. All parameters are positive. It is also assumed that public goods neither appreciate nor depreciate, and enter into the utility functions of members of both generations in the same way. Finally, the maximum amount of labour-time available to a member of the ith generation while young is $\bar{n}$, and n_{ip}^y is the amount of that time actually spent working.

Debt versus Tax Finance

The above model may be used to show that for a given level of public good provision there is a gross burden imposed on members of the second generation by switching from tax to bond finance. Initially taxes are taken to be of the lump-sum kind, and discussion of income taxes is reserved until later.

Consider the debt finance case. The fixed level $\bar{g}$ of public good provision is financed by the sale of bonds to members of generation 1 while young, which are then redeemed with interest at the fixed rate $\bar{r}$ when the members of generation 1 are old. The bonds are redeemed by levying taxes t_2 on members of generation 2 while young. The interest rate $\bar{r}$ on bonds is enough to make generation 1 members indifferent between holding bonds b and storing private goods k_1, for their old age, and the aggregate public good provision is assumed to be met out of the bond purchases of generation 1 members at this rate of interest. It is also assumed that members of generation 1 cannot individually provide public goods themselves and believe that the aggregate public good provision is independent of their individual bond purchases. The alternative assumption, that individuals recognize that the amount of public good provision is not independent of their bond purchases (or tax payments), would not significantly affect any of the results, although it would affect the precise solutions presented in the tables below.

Under the present assumptions the problem facing members of generation 1 is to maximize the utility function (10.1) with respect to c_1^y, c_1^o, k_1, b and n_1^y subject to the following first- and second-period budget constraints:

$$wn_1^y = c_1^y + b + k_1 \tag{10.2}$$

$$(b + k_1)(1 + \bar{r}) = c_1^o \tag{10.3}$$

Since the individual is indifferent between holding bonds and storing private goods, the government can choose b, leaving the private individual to choose k_1 so as to optimize over total savings of $b + k_1$. Equations (10.2) and (10.3) may be combined to yield the lifetime budget constraint facing members of generation 1 under the debt finance case, as shown in table 10.1

Similarly, members of generation 2 maximize the utility function (10.1) subject to the following budget constraints:

$$wn_2^y = c_2^y + t_2 + k_2 \tag{10.4}$$

$$k_2(1+\bar{r}) = c_2^o \tag{10.5}$$

where the lump-sum taxes t_2 are used to redeem, with interest, the bond holdings of generation 1 members. As before, combining the first- and second-period budget constraints yields the lifetime budget constraint for a member of generation 2, as shown in table 10.1.

Comparing the lifetime budget constraints of members of generation 1 and 2 for the debt case, as shown in table 10.1, it is evident that the burden of the public expenditure is eventually placed on members of generation 2.

In contrast, in the tax finance case the public good provision is financed by lump-sum taxes t_1 on members of generation 1, and the burden is not shifted to generation 2. The lifetime budget constraints for this case are also shown in table 10.1, as well as the values for c_i^y, c_i^o, n_i^y and k_1 given by solving the optimization problems of each generation in each case, and so are values for b, t_1 and t_2.

It follows from the above discussion that members of generation 1 are better off under the debt case than under the tax case, and vice versa for the members of generation 2. This is confirmed by examining the solutions for consumption, when young and old, and labour supply; under the debt case the members of generation 1 work less and consume more in each period of life than under the tax case, whilst the reverse applies to

Table 10.1 Debt versus tax finance

	Debt case	Tax case
Generation 1		
Lifetime budget constraint	$wn_1^y = c_1^y + \dfrac{c_1^o}{1+\bar{r}}$	$wn_1^y = c_1^y + \dfrac{c_1^o}{1+\bar{r}} + t_1$
c_1^y	$\alpha\phi w\bar{n}$ [a]	$\alpha\phi(w\bar{n} - t_1)$
c_1^o	$\beta\phi w\bar{n}(1+\bar{r})$	$\beta\phi(w\bar{n} - t_1)(1+\bar{r})$
n_1^y	$(\alpha+\beta)\phi\bar{n}$	$[(\alpha+\beta)\bar{n} + \sigma t_1/w]\phi$
k_1	$\beta\phi w\bar{n} - b$	$\beta\phi(w\bar{n} - t_1)$
b	$\bar{g}/P$	–
t_1	–	$\bar{g}/P$
Generation 2		
Lifetime budget constraint	$wn_2^y = c_2^y + \dfrac{c_2^o}{1+\bar{r}} + t_2$	$wn_2^y = c_2^y + \dfrac{c_2^o}{1+\bar{r}}$
c_2^y	$\alpha\phi(w\bar{n} - t_2)$	$\alpha\phi w\bar{n}$
c_2^o	$\beta\phi(w\bar{n} - t_2)(1+\bar{r})$	$\beta\phi w\bar{n}(1+\bar{r})$
n_2^y	$[(\alpha+\beta)\bar{n} + \sigma t_2/w]\phi$	$(\alpha+\beta)\phi\bar{n}$
t_2	$(\bar{g}/P)(1+\bar{r})$	–

[a] $\phi = (\alpha+\beta+\sigma)^{-1}$.

members of generation 2.

Thus, while it is a truism to say that public good provision uses up current resources at the time it is carried out, this does not imply that the mode of finance of the public good is irrelevant. There is clearly a gross burden imposed on members of generation 2, and lifted from members of generation 1, by switching from tax to debt finance. The intuition is simple. Under the tax case, members of generation 1 produce the public good and receive no recompense from members of generation 2 for so doing. Under bond finance members of generation 1 still produce the public good but are, eventually, paid for doing so by members of generation 2. The simple Keynesian 'no debt burden' view is clearly misleading if the lifetime utility measure of burden is accepted. Members of generation 1 gain higher utility over their lifetime under debt rather than tax finance, since under the former case members of generation 2 must transfer resources to members of generation 1: it is this transfer of resources from one generation to another which makes tax and debt finance different and which creates the burden of the debt.

The gross burden so far is composed entirely of a primary burden imposed on those who finance the public good provision. Once productive capital is introduced into the model it is possible to show that a secondary burden is also imposed on the second generation by switching from tax to bond finance. Before examining such issues in any detail it may be useful to look at the concept of net burden using the current model.

Since the public good enters into the private individual's utility function (10.1), it is clear that the provision of public good g will tend to increase individual utility and that this may more than offset the decrease in utility imposed on those who finance that provision.[3] Thus, members of generation 1 will be better off under the debt case than under the case of no public good provision at all, since in the debt case they enjoy the public good but members of generation 2 pay for it. Furthermore, it is also possible that members of generation 1 are better off under the tax case than under the case of no public good provision (depending upon the amount of public good provision and the individual's utility function). Symmetrically, relative to the case of no public good provision, members of generation 2 are clearly better off under the tax case and possibly better off under the debt case (again, depending on the size of the public good provision and on the individual's preferences). Therefore, there may be a net benefit for each generation under either the tax or the debt case when compared with the no public good provision case.

Notice that if private individuals were allowed to provide public goods without government intervention, the *laissez-faire* equilibrium would involve an underprovision of the public good compared with the Pareto optimum, since individual optimization does not take into account the effects of individual provision of public goods on the welfare of the other members of society (see, for example, Cornes and Sandler, 1985). Thus, even in this case, members of generation 1 may be better off under the tax case than under *laissez-faire* if the government sets the level of public good provision appropriately, and they will be even better off if debt finance is used. Similarly, members of generation 2 will be better off under the tax case than under *laissez-faire* if that involves more public good provision given the assumption that they benefit from such provision, and they may still be better off under the debt case where they have to pay for the public good provision.

These arguments indicate that the government should not simply consider whether to use tax or debt finance for public good provision or to provide none at all, but should rather contemplate the optimum level of public good provision and the optimum mix of tax and debt finance to distribute the cost of financing it across generations. The solution to this problem will depend upon the government's and individuals' preference functions and on the physical constraints facing the economy. In other words, as Mishan put it, the 'real problem turns out to be an *allocative problem* – one of disposing of our resources over time' (Mishan, 1969, p. 84). Whilst consistent with Mishan's conclusion in this respect, the present analysis does not support the rest of his arguments which imply that there is no gross burden involved in the switch from tax to debt finance since 'the real sacrifice . . . has to be made currently' (Mishan, 1969, p. 74) when some public project is undertaken. This view is a *non sequitur*, and, indeed, if it were not it would imply that the decision to tax or debt finance some project would not be relevant to the allocative problem. Thus it may be going too far to say that 'politically persuasive terms such as "burden" . . . have no rightful place in the vocabulary of economics' (Mishan, 1969, p. 85). Rather it is correct to say that 'borrowing . . . may be used to secure intergeneration equity by passing on part of the cost of capital outlays to the future' (Musgrave and Musgrave, 1973, p. 603).

The Introduction of Productive Capital

Now consider the effects of introducing productive capital into the above model. The key idea here is that a substitution of loan for tax finance tends to reduce saving (excluding bond holdings) and, hence, investment. The effect of this is to reduce the size of the capital stock with which the next generation has to work and therefore to reduce the marginal product of labour in the next generation, as well as to increase the marginal product of capital (i.e. the interest rate). This imposes a secondary burden on the future generation which many argue will exceed the primary burden of paying off the debt. This point of view was expressed forcefully by Modigliani (1961) in a Keynesian framework, but it holds equally well in a neoclassical framework such as the one adopted here. Indeed, it is possible to see from table 10.1 that saving in the form of real capital k_1 is smaller for the debt case than for the tax case. In terms of the model underlying table 10.1 the size of k_1 does not matter to the second generation, but in models where k_1 affects the labour productivity of the second generation, such effects do impose a considerable secondary burden. Also notice that if public expenditure were zero so that t_1 would be zero in the tax case, then k_1 would be higher. This implies that, if the size of k_1 matters to the second generation, then even the tax case imposes some costs on the second generation compared with the zero public expenditure case. Thus, as Musgrave and Musgrave put it, 'burden transfer, therefore, occurs whenever generation 1, in transferring funds to the government, responds by reducing its capital formation in the private sector. This is the result whether this response is to paying taxes or to buying public debt' (Musgrave and Musgrave, 1973, p. 605). However, as Mishan noted,

> if we are prepared to talk of an additional 'burden' being suffered by future generations whenever we are led to consume some part of current output rather than accumulate it (and thus enable future generations to enjoy a larger stock of capital goods, and so increase their consumption), are we not entitled to talk of a 'burden' being imposed on the *present* generation when, instead, we reduce our consumption in favour of increased consumption by our grandchildren? (Mishan, 1969, p. 83)

Clearly, the answer to this question is that, as already noted, the real problem is an allocative one, concerning the optimal path of consumption over time. Until some political agreement on the shape of this optimal path is reached, 'we cannot legitimately pronounce any government policy as resulting in too much or too little consumption today or, for that matter, too much or too little consumption tomorrow' (Mishan, 1969, p. 85).

Finally, it should be noted that the above inverse relationship between the size of the stock of bonds and the capital stock is not robust to changes in the model. The introduction of factors such as risk and uncertainty or non-identical individuals may result in a positive relationship between the size of the bond stock and the capital stock. For example, if interest payments on bonds involve income transfers from poor taxpayers to rich bond-holders who have a higher propensity to save, then the income transfer could lead to greater aggregate saving and even a higher, not lower, capital stock.

10.4 The Model with Intergenerational Transfer Motives

It has been noted earlier that the Ricardian equivalence theorem requires, amongst other things, either that individuals expect to live for ever or that they treat the known liabilities of taxpayers in the future as their own. Since the present purpose is that of examining intergenerational redistribution, the overlapping generations model is a more appropriate tool for investigation than the infinite lives version.

In the overlapping generations model, the Ricardian equivalence theorem may hold if successive generations are linked by a chain of voluntary intergenerational transfers. Consider, for example, that people wish to make bequests to their heirs; then, as Ferguson put it,

> everyone who planned to leave a positive estate under tax finance may plan to leave an even larger estate under debt finance so that their

heirs can meet the additional tax liability. There is nothing in the use of bonds which will cause these people to increase their lifetime consumption. . . . Thus, the amount of . . . shifting depends upon the number of taxpayers in the initial generation who plan to leave no estate. Debt financing will in effect allow these people to leave a negative estate. (Ferguson, 1964, p. 226)

Barro's Debt Neutrality Theorem

In the model of the previous section the mode of financing public expenditure clearly has real effects. This view achieved dominance in the 1960s but was strongly attacked by Barro (1974). Barro revived the Ricardian equivalence theorem by using an overlapping generations model with intergenerational transfer motives. He shows that 'a substitution of debt for tax finance for a given level of government expenditure' has no real effects 'so long as there is an operative intergenerational transfer (in the sense of an interior solution for the amount of bequest or gift across generations)', since in this case 'current generations act effectively as though they were infinite-lived' (Barro, 1974, pp. 1096–7). In other words, Barro argues that the intergenerational redistribution of income associated with a switch from tax to bond finance for a given level of public good provision, which forms the basis for the gross burden in the discussion above, would be neutralized by offsetting changes in voluntary intergenerational bequests (a transfer from old to young) or gifts (a transfer from young to old) as long as there would have been such transfers before any financing policy change. As Barro puts it:

> if, prior to the government bond issue, a member of the old generation had already selected a positive bequest, it is clear that this individual already had the option of shifting resources from his descendant to himself, but he had determined that such shifting, at the margin, was nonoptimal. Since the change (from tax to bond finance) does not alter the relevant opportunity set in this sense, it follows that – through the appropriate adjustment of the bequest – the values of current and future consumption and attained utility will be unaffected. (Barro, 1974, p. 1103)

There will thus be no real effects caused by a switch from tax to bond finance (or by a change in the debt–tax mix) and hence no gross burden imposed on the second generation.

Barro's argument, however, only holds under certain circumstances; in particular it holds for models with non-distorting lump-sum taxes and breaks down when distorting taxes are used. Thus, whilst private intergenerational transfers are lump-sum payments which may be used to neutralize the effects of changes in lump-sum taxes, they cannot be used to offset the distortionary effects of non-lump-sum taxes which 'will affect private opportunity sets in ways that will not be neutralised by offsetting changes in private behaviour' (Buiter, 1979, p. 425). Rather surprisingly though, it is possible, when taxes are non-lump-sum, for members of generation 1 to be worse off under debt than tax finance. In such a case, bonds, in contrast with the standard view, appear to be negative net wealth.

Bequests in the Basic Model

The above arguments may be illustrated by introducing intergenerational transfer motives into the model by assuming that the utility of a member of generation 1 depends on his own private and public good consumption and work effort and also upon the attainable utility of his descendant in generation 2, where each member of generation 1 is assumed to have only one descendant. The utility function for a member of generation 2 is still given by equation (10.1) whilst that for a member of generation 1 is now given by

$$U_{1p} = \alpha \ln c_{1p}^{y} + \beta \ln c_{1p}^{o} + \gamma \ln g + \delta \ln(\bar{n} - n_{1p}^{y}) + \varrho U_{2p} \qquad (10.6)$$

where ϱ is positive and indicates the weight attached by an individual to the utility of his descendant, i.e. it represents the degree of altruism.

Assuming that each member of generation 1 knows the optimization problem facing his descendant, then he must solve his life-cycle optimization problem taking into account the behaviour and utility level of his descendant as a function of the bequest q he makes to him. The relevant comparisons for consideration of the gross burden issue may be made by examining table 10.2. The first column of the table relates to debt-financed provision of a given level $\bar{g}$ of public good with the debt redeemed with interest by lump-sum taxes on members of generation 2, whereas the second column relates to the same public good provision financed by lump-sum taxes on members of generation 1. The third and fourth columns similarly relate to debt or tax finance but the taxes are fixed-rate income taxes.

From the first two columns, since $t_2 = t_1(1 + \bar{r})$, then the outcomes for c_i^y, c_i^o and n_i^y will be the same under either tax or debt finance, and the bequest q can be shown to adjust to offset the switch from tax to debt finance; i.e. the value of q for the debt case is simply that of q for the tax case plus an amount to offset the tax payments which generation 2 members have to pay under bond finance. Strictly, this conclusion only holds if a positive bequest would be made under the tax case, and this will be the case if ϱ exceeds the value of $w\bar{n}/(w\bar{n} - t_1)(1 + \bar{r})$ shown in the row ϱ^*. If the degree of altruism is less than this critical value ϱ^*, then in the tax case no bequest would be made (ruling out the possibility of negative bequests) and the switch from tax to debt finance would hence allow an intergenerational transfer from young to old to occur, and there would be a gross burden placed on the young in making such a switch. The necessary ϱ^* condition varies from case to case, as shown in the table; for the debt case if ϱ exceeds the value shown in column 1 there would be a positive bequest, but a non-marginal switch from debt to tax finance could have real effects if ϱ were less than the critical value shown in column 2 (since the move to tax finance may cause a larger redistribution of income in favour of generation 2 than generation 1 would voluntarily undertake).

Thus the necessary conditions for the Ricardian equivalence theorem to hold are that there must be a sufficient degree of concern for the young generation by the older generation and that the old must take into account the future tax liabilities of the young. Similar results may be found for models with intergenerational concern running the other way or both ways (i.e. the young caring about the old as well as vice versa), and for models with productive capital.[4] However, it is crucial for the debt neutrality theorem that taxes be of the lump-sum kind which do not distort behaviour by affecting marginal conditions. This may be seen by examining columns 3 and 4 of table 10.2, which refer to proportional taxes on labour incomes.[5] For private-sector behaviour to be invariant with respect to debt or tax finance under income taxes it is required that the values of c_1^y, c_1^o, n_1^y, c_2^y, c_2^o and n_2^y in column 3 and column 4 be equivalent. This is not the case, as may be proved by first of all assuming that the n_1^y solutions in columns 3 and 4 are equivalent; if this is so then for the n_2^y solutions to be equivalent it is necessary that $t_2 = -t_1/(1 - t_1)$, which, since a sensible value for t_1 must be between 0 and 1, would then imply a negative value for t_2; but this would not make sense since t_2 must also lie between 0 and 1. Thus, when taxes are of the distorting kind, it is not feasible for the switch from tax to debt finance to have no real effects. However, whereas the standard textbook analysis, and that of the previous section, might argue that bonds are net wealth, and hence that the first generation feel better off under the debt case, this is not necessarily so since the future tax liabilities of the second generation are taken into account by the first-generation members. Indeed, if ϱ exceeds the critical value in column 4 then the switch to debt finance may (for given parameter values) cause a reduction in consumption and an increase in time spent working by members of generation 1 in order to finance bigger bequests to their descendants, who also consume less but work less too. It would seem then that in this case, far from the private sector's being indifferent to the mode of finance of public good provision, the tax-financed case might be better for both generations. Of course, as for the lump-sum tax case, if the bequest were not positive under the tax case then the switch to bond finance might be used to redistribute income

Table 10.2 Debt versus tax finance: the bequest case

	Lump-sum taxes		Income taxes	
	Debt case	Tax case	Debt case	Tax case
Generation 1				
Lifetime budget constraint	$wn_1^y = c_1^y + \dfrac{c_1^o+q}{1+\bar{r}}$	$wn_1^y = c_1^y + \dfrac{c_1^o+q}{1+\bar{r}}+t_1$	$wn_1^y = c_1^y + \dfrac{c_1^o+q}{1+\bar{r}}$	$wn_1^y(1-t_1) = c_1^y + \dfrac{c_1^o+q}{1+\bar{r}}$
c_1^y	$\dfrac{\alpha\phi[w\bar{n}(2+\bar{r})-t_2]^a}{(1+\bar{r})(1+\varrho)}$	$\dfrac{\alpha\phi[w\bar{n}(2+\bar{r})-t_1(1+\bar{r})]}{(1+\bar{r})(1+\varrho)}$	$\dfrac{\alpha\phi\bar{n}(2+\bar{r}-t_2)}{(1+\bar{r})(1+\varrho)}$	$\dfrac{\alpha\phi w\bar{n}[2+\bar{r}-t_1(1+\bar{r})]}{(1+\bar{r})(1+\varrho)}$
c_1^o	$\dfrac{\beta}{\alpha}c_1^y(1+\bar{r})$	$\dfrac{\beta}{\alpha}c_1^y(1+\bar{r})$	$\dfrac{\beta}{\alpha}c_1^y(1+\bar{r})$	$\dfrac{\beta}{\alpha}c_1^y(1+\bar{r})$
n_1^y	$\bar{n} - \dfrac{\sigma\phi[w\bar{n}(2+\bar{r})-t_2]}{w(1+\bar{r})(1+\varrho)}$	$\bar{n} - \dfrac{\sigma\phi[w\bar{n}(2+\bar{r})-t_1(1+\bar{r})]}{w(1+\bar{r})(1+\varrho)}$	$\bar{n} - \dfrac{\sigma\phi(2+\bar{r}-t_2)\bar{n}}{(1+\bar{r})(1+\varrho)}$	$\bar{n} - \dfrac{\sigma\phi[2+\bar{r}-t_1(1+\bar{r})]\bar{n}}{(1+\bar{r})(1+\varrho)(1-t_1)}$
q	$\dfrac{[\varrho(1+\bar{r})-1]w\bar{n}+t_2}{1+\varrho}$	$\dfrac{[\varrho(1+\bar{r})-1]w\bar{n}-\varrho(1+\bar{r})t_1}{1+\varrho}$	$\dfrac{[\varrho(1+\bar{r})-1+t_2]w\bar{n}}{1+\varrho}$	$\dfrac{[\varrho(1+\bar{r})(1-t_1)-1]w\bar{n}}{1+\varrho}$

ϱ^*	$\dfrac{1}{1+\bar{r}}\;1-\dfrac{t_2}{w\bar{n}}$	$\dfrac{w\bar{n}}{(w\bar{n}-t_1)(1+\bar{r})}$	$\dfrac{1-t_2}{1+\bar{r}}$	$\dfrac{1}{(1+\bar{r})(1-t_1)}$
b	$\bar{g}/P$	–	$\bar{g}/P$	–
t_1	–	$\bar{g}/P$	–	$\bar{g}/Pwn_1^y$
Generation 2				
Lifetime budget constraint	$wn_2^y+q=c_2^y+\dfrac{c_2^o}{1+\bar{r}}+t_2$	$wn_2^y+q=c_2^y+\dfrac{c_2^o}{1+\bar{r}}$	$wn_2^y(1-t_2)+q=c_2^y+\dfrac{c_2^o}{1+\bar{r}}$	$wn_2^y+q=c_2^y+\dfrac{c_2^o}{1+\bar{r}}$
c_2^y	$c_1^y\varrho(1+\bar{r})$	$c_1^y\varrho(1+\bar{r})$	$c_1^y\varrho(1+\bar{r})$	$c_1^y\varrho(1+\bar{r})$
c_2^o	$c_1^o\varrho(1+\bar{r})$	$c_1^o\varrho(1+\bar{r})$	$c_1^o\varrho(1+\bar{r})$	$c_1^o\varrho(1+\bar{r})$
n_2^y	$\bar{n}-(\bar{n}-n_1^y)\varrho(1+\bar{r})$	$\bar{n}-(\bar{n}-n_1^y)\varrho(1+\bar{r})$	$\bar{n}-(\bar{n}-n_1^y)\varrho\dfrac{(1+\bar{r})}{1-t_2}$	$\bar{n}-(\bar{n}-n_1^y)\varrho(1+\bar{r})(1-t_1)$
t_2	$(\bar{g}/P)(1+\bar{r})$	–	$\bar{g}(1+\bar{r})/Pwn_2^y$	–

[a] $\phi=(\alpha+\beta+o)^{-1}$.

towards the older generation and would have the standard non-neutral effects.

Thus, the Ricardian equivalence theorem requires, amongst other things, that taxes be of the lump-sum kind, and cannot therefore be expected to hold in the real world where taxes are predominantly non-lump-sum. This conclusion may similarly be extended to models where the intergenerational concern flows the other way (from young to old) or flows both ways.

The following section looks at extensions beyond the full-information neoclassical closed economy model used so far.

10.5 Extensions and Qualifications

The Open Economy

Those who argued that there can be no burden associated with internal debt (since the cost of public good provision must, in the internal debt case, fall on the generation alive when resources are diverted from private to public use) did not extend this argument to external debt. They argued that external and internal debt differ, since the former allows a nation to consume more than it is producing and to pay for it later. However, it has been argued here that such a view of internal debt is a *non sequitur*, and it can, in fact, be argued that internal and external debt have similar effects as far as the burden of the debt is concerned. The only difference is that, of course, external debt does allow a nation to consume more than it contemporaneously produces by borrowing from overseas, whilst internal debt does not. However, if there is a debt burden associated with internal debt, e.g. as in the analysis associated with table 10.1, then, similarly, there will be a debt burden associated with external debt. In contrast, if there is no debt burden associated with internal debt, e.g. because voluntary private sector bequests offset the redistribution of income from young to old implicit in debt finance, then, similarly, there will be no burden associated with external debt. A forward-looking and bequest-leaving older generation can foresee tax payments by the younger generation in repayment of external debt and adjust its bequests accordingly, just as for the case of internal debt, so long as taxes are lump sum.

Money

So far the analysis has been limited to a government using either taxation or debt finance, but it is also possible for the government to use a third method: money financing. In the real world money financing usually takes place via increases in deposits of the government at the central bank, but it is possible, without loss of generality, to consider money financing to involve currency issue to pay for public good provision. It should be noted that within a neoclassical framework it is difficult to explain why individuals should wish to hold money, since, in such a framework, there is no real role for a medium of exchange or means of payment (see Goodhart, 1975, ch. 1). However, within the overlapping generations model, this issue may be sidestepped by placing money in the individual's utility function (see, for example, McCallum, 1983), i.e. by arguing that holding money performs some other function, apart from being a store of value, such as a trans-action role. Introducing money in this way would not affect the conclusions which have been derived earlier. In other words, provided that taxes are lump sum, as long as intergenerational transfer motives are operative, marginal shifts between tax and debt finance for a given level of public expenditure and of money supply would still not have real effects.[6] Indeed, such shifts are 'strongly neutral', in the sense of Benninga and Protopapa-dakis (1984), i.e. both private consumption patterns and real cash balances remain unchanged after such a financing switch has occurred.

Shifts between debt and money finance or between taxes and money finance may, under similar conditions, result in 'weak neutrality', i.e. consumption patterns would remain unchanged but real money balances would adjust. Clearly, when money gives direct utility, individuals would not be indifferent to the latter shifts. More specifically, under either policy shift 'weak neutrality' requires that the real cost of holding money be constant, thus implying an adjustment in the nominal interest rate.

In particular, in the case of a shift from debt to money, i.e. an open market purchase where the real present value of taxes is by assumption kept fixed, the nominal interest rate would have to fall for individuals willingly to hold the new higher level of real cash balances. Moreover, the rise in the money–debt ratio would also imply a fall in the inflation rate (for a similar result see Sargent and Wallace, 1981). Not that the individual's welfare would be increased as a result of this policy.

However, a shift from taxes to money for a given level of public debt – which might be viewed as a shift in the backing of government bonds – while the real sector of the economy is again left unchanged would imply a use in the nominal interest rate, in the price level and hence in inflation rate. Thus, the individual's welfare would here be reduced owing to the reduced level of real money holding.

For further analysis of the effects on the economy of both shifts in the backing of bonds and open market operations, see Aiyagari and Gertler (1985) and Lunati (1987).

282   B. Hillier and M. T. Lunati

The Growing Economy

Barro's revival of the Ricardian equivalence theorem was couched in terms of whether or not individuals perceive bonds as net wealth, i.e. whether or not individuals discount the future taxes to be paid in servicing and redeeming the debt. If future (lump-sum) taxes are discounted then bonds are not net wealth, and the Ricardian equivalence theorem holds. Barro argued that this result depends upon the bond's being redeemed out of taxes at some known future date. In a growing economy where the rate of growth of the population exceeds the real interest rate on bonds, a policy designed to hold the per capita debt constant will entail more debt sales to the young generation than is necessary to finance the interest payments and redeem the debt held by the old generation. In this case bonds may be considered to be net wealth, and Barro acknowledged this to be a limitation on his neutrality result, although he argued in an exchange with Feldstein (1976) that such a situation was not consistent with rational utility-maximizing behaviour (see Barro, 1976), since it would imply private inefficient overaccumulation of capital relative to the optimum golden rule level.

Carmichael, however, has shown that 'the real effects of national debt are independent of whether or not individuals perceive the debt as net wealth. The correct question is whether or not changes in the level of debt force individuals into patterns of intertemporal consumption that they are unable to neutralize by adjustments in their portfolio behaviour' (1982, p. 202). He goes on to show that, provided that intergenerational transfers are operative in the same direction both before and after the policy action, 'individuals are able to undo the intertemporal allocation effects of a debt expansion by appropriate adjustment of their planned gifts or bequests. This holds even when the growth rate exceeds the interest rate, such that the debt constitutes an addition to the net wealth of the community' (p. 212). In the latter case, when the economy's growth rate is greater than the rate of interest, a bequest motive cannot be operative because it would require ϱ to exceed unity, which in turn may be shown to be inconsistent with a steady state equilibrium (see also Weil, 1987). However, an operative gift motive could restore the debt neutrality result. This 'extended neutrality theorem' holds both in the steady state when output, bond stock and population are all growing at the same rate, and also for the short run when the growth of the bond stock need not match the growth of population and output. However, yet again, such results depend upon the use of lump-sum taxes (or subsidies) and would not continue to hold if taxes were of the distortionary kind. Furthermore, McCallum has argued (in an infinite lives framework) that it is feasible to maintain a positive growth rate of real bonds per capita, but 'only if the growth rate is smaller than the rate of time preference' (1984, p. 132).

A final and related argument, which is widely supported, is that if the government attempts to hold tax rates, real expenditure and monetary growth at fixed values throughout the trade cycle, then endogenous adjustment of the bond stock to satisfy the government financing requirement would lead to explosive behaviour of the bond stock and an unstable economic environment (see, for example, Turnovsky, 1977; Christ, 1979; Scarth, 1980). This argument indicates that economists' concern about debt financing should focus on its implications for stability, as well as for debt burden. In this context, it is also often argued that stability requires the nominal interest rate to be below the growth rate of nominal income (see, for example, Bispham, 1986). For an early discussion on the issue of growth and the burden of the debt, see Domar (1944).

A Fix-price Keynesian Unemployment Framework

Thus far, a neoclassical market-clearing model has been used. Gale (1983, ch. 1) has considered the Ricardian equivalence theorem within the different context of a fix-price Keynesian unemployment model and has shown that the theorem may still hold provided that intergenerational transfers are operative. However, in the Keynesian framework the debt neutrality result turns out to be just one of several potential equilibrium outcomes; non-neutrality could just as easily occur if a tax cut yielded a Keynesian expansionary response through a self-fulfilling (entirely rational) expectation of an increase in wealth (discounted disposable income flow). According to Gale, this non-uniqueness of equilibria in a non-Walrasian framework provides 'a powerful, perhaps irresistible, critique of the Ricardian position' (1983, p. 73). However, as Rankin (1985) has pointed out, this non-uniqueness of Gale's model is found in an economy with only one asset, bonds, and the introduction of money eliminates the indeterminacy, with the neutral outcome becoming the only possible one (as long as the intergenerational transfer motive is operative, and taxes are lump sum).[7] Nevertheless, once the common technique of including money in the utility function is accepted, Rankin argues that bonds too should enter the utility function, since they too may provide some sort of liquidity services. In this case, non-neutrality will again result. This is not surprising. If bonds provide utility then a switch from tax to bond finance may be expected, *ceteris paribus*, to provide more utility and to have real effects even if intergenerational transfer motives are operative. This would hold equally well in a neoclassical framework as in the Keynesian one and, indeed, is parallel to the results on 'weak neutrality' noted for a shift between money and debt finance, or between money and tax finance, in the neoclassical model with money.

Uncertainty

The effects of uncertainty depend upon the way in which it enters the model. If taxes are lump sum, and there is no uncertainty about the relative tax burden but only about the aggregate level of future taxes, then the uncertainty in the individual's real tax burden associated with changes in the debt–tax mix or manipulation of the debt maturity structure would not in general affect individual behaviour. For example, a sudden and unforeseen increase in interest payments and the corresponding increase in tax liabilities would not involve any net shift in the risk composition of individual balance sheets in a world of homogeneous individuals.

However, if there is uncertainty about the relative burden of lump-sum tax payments, then the neutrality result need no longer hold and real effects may follow. In particular, when the allocation of the tax share is purely random, the net increase in the risk contained in household balance sheets due to a bond-financed tax cut may yield an ambiguous response of current consumption. In fact, as Barro has underlined (1974, p. 1115) the individuals' reactions might involve an increase in their desired total saving, as well as a portfolio shift away from more risky toward less risky assets – with the impact on the real rate of return on capital, and hence on capital formation, depending on which of the two responses dominates. However, as shown by Chan (1983), under certain conditions – which include a time-separable utility function and a non-increasing absolute risk aversion with respect to second period consumption – the first response would be the dominant one. Therefore, a shift from taxes to bonds, while increasing the individual's net risk, would imply a reduction in consumption and a rise in saving, so that bonds would have a negative wealth effect. It might be noted that this result reverses the common view – e.g. Tobin (1971) – according to which, in the presence of uncertainty about the relative tax burden, uncertain future liabilities might well be discounted 'more heavily' than the current tax cut, so that a shift from tax to debt financing would result in a net wealth effect. If, however, a positive correlation between individuals' tax liabilities and their incomes is assumed (with income taxes working, at least partly, as a public income insurance policy), then a bond-financed tax cut could imply a net reduction in the overall individual's risk. Opposite results to those described in the previous case would then follow, and thus bonds would be net wealth. For further and most recent research in this area, see Barsky, Mankiw and Zeldes (1986).

Imperfect Capital Markets and Liquidity Constraints

If public and private securities are imperfect substitutes, e.g. because government securities are less risky than private ones or because individuals have different discount rates, then the issue of public debt will have real effects. Furthermore, if some individuals under tax finance are liquidity constrained (unable to borrow to finance present consumption) then a switch from tax to bond finance might ease that constraint and allow them to consume more in the present at the expense of consumption in the future if they have to pay higher taxes later to finance the debt. In a perfect capital market individuals would have been able to borrow to effect this reallocation of consumption over time, while in an imperfect capital market the issue of bonds would be required to enable such reallocation to take place. In this respect, as Barro noted, 'government debt issue will increase net wealth if the government is more efficient, at the margin, than the private market in carrying out the loan process' (1974, p. 1095). For a further interesting discussion of such issues see Chan (1983); see also Drazen (1978) for a discussion of how imperfect capital markets and human capital may cause non-neutrality.

Heterogeneous Individuals

The above discussion of imperfect capital markets required the assumption of heterogeneous individuals with different discount rates, but there are several other ways in which heterogeneous individuals may prevent debt neutrality from occurring. For example, it was assumed in the analysis in section 10.4 of this paper that all individuals have one heir, but once it is recognized that individuals do not all have the same number of heirs then it can be seen that debt neutrality no longer prevails even if intergenerational transfers are operative. For instance, if some individuals have one heir and some two, then a switch from (equal per capita) lump-sum taxes on the older generation to bond finance with (equal per capita) lump-sum taxes on the younger generation in the future has redistributive effects on income across the one-heir or two-heir family types – the move to bond finance will imply that the two-heir family types finance a larger portion of the public expenditure (see Carmichael, 1982).

Transactions Costs

If there are real costs associated with collecting taxes (even of the lump-sum kind) or with selling bonds, such that it is not equally efficient to raise revenue by tax and bond issue, then, obviously, the real effects of tax or bond finance for a given level of public good provision will differ.

Merit Goods and 'Strategic' Bequests

If parents are concerned not with the maximum attainable utility of their children when making a bequest but rather with specific components of their children's consumption (merit goods) and can tie bequests to force their children to consume more, or less, of such goods, then debt neutrality will no longer hold. Equally, if parents gain utility directly from making a bequest or if they use promises of bequests to bribe their children into paying attention to them in their old age, then debt issue will be non-neutral (see Barro, 1974; Drazen, 1978; and in particular, for a discussion of strategic bequests, Bernheim, Shleifer and Summers, 1985).

10.6 Conclusions

It has been shown that in the absence of operative intergenerational transfer motives there can be a gross burden associated with the switch from tax to bond finance even in a neoclassical market-clearing model with lump-sum taxes. There is a burden of the debt associated with the intergenerational income transfer that bonds allow. This burden is much greater if productive capital is 'crowded out' by the use of debt rather than tax finance.

Arguments against the burden of the debt position have been of two kinds. One has been based upon the obvious *non sequitur* that public good provision uses up real resources at the time it is carried out, and therefore, no matter how it is financed, the generation that sacrifices those resources is the one that bears the burden. As seen above, this argument may be quite easily dismissed. The other, which is both more interesting and subtle, has been the Ricardian equivalence theorem, or Barro's debt neutrality theorem: individuals realize that eventually taxes must be paid to finance interest payments and redemption of bonds, so that, as long as intergenerational transfer motives are operative, individuals treat tax or bond finance as equivalent. Were this argument valid it would have the far-reaching conclusion that 'fiscal effects involving changes in the relative amounts of tax and debt finance for a given amount of public expenditure would have no effect on aggregate demand, interest rates, and capital formation' (Barro, 1974, p. 1116). However, it has been argued that the Ricardian equivalence theorem holds only in highly restrictive circumstances; most notably it requires homogeneous individuals with equal numbers of heirs, as well as the use of only lump-sum taxes. With respect to the latter crucial point even Barro is prepared to recognize that 'in the real world governments levy a variety of taxes, but none of them look like the lump-sum taxes in our theory' (Barro, 1984, p. 331). It seems, therefore, that real effects follow from changes in the relative amounts of tax and debt finance for a given amount of public expenditure: policy-makers' financing decisions do matter. The direction of the real effects, however, depends upon the nature of the economy and may only be determined by empirical research.[8]

NOTES

1 In reality public debt consists of various assets with differing characteristics in terms of interest rates, term to maturity (the length of time which must elapse before the debt is repaid) and so on, although for present purposes it will be useful to think of public debt as a single type of financial liability of the government.
2 For a lucid discussion of the wider macroeconomic issues see Brunner (1981).
3 For the welfare effects of public spending when it enters the utility function, see also Rankin (1987).
4 For a further discussion of the necessary conditions for intergenerational transfers in either direction see Drazen (1978), Carmichael (1982) and Hillier and Lunati (1987).
5 Note that when income taxes are used the government must calculate the correct tax rate required to finance a given level of public expenditure. This can be done if the government knows the labour supply solution n_i^y for the private-sector individuals, in which case it can adjust the tax rate to the point where total income tax receipts equal total public expenditure. For a discussion of the damaging effects of progressive wealth taxation on Ricardian equivalence, see Abel (1986).
6 Note, however, that money held until death may be viewed as a kind of bequest, and that this, obviously, affects the conditions necessary for there to be a bequest over and above such money holdings.
7 Rankin actually used an infinite lives framework, but this is akin to assuming operative intergenerational transfers in an overlapping generations model.
8 For an introduction to the empirical literature on debt neutrality see Bernheim (1987) and the references therein.

REFERENCES

Abel, A. B. (1986) 'The failure of Ricardian equivalence under progressive wealth taxation', *Journal of Public Economics* 30, 117–28.
Adams, H. C. (1893) *Public Debt*. New York: Appleton-Century-Crofts.
Aiyagari, S. R., and M. Gertler (1985) 'The backing of government bonds and monetarism', *Journal of Monetary Economics* 16, 19–44.
Barro, R. J. (1974) 'Are government bonds net wealth?' *Journal of Political Economy* 82, 1095–117.
Barro, R. J. (1976) 'Reply to Feldstein and Buchanan', *Journal of Political Economy* 84, 343–9.
Barro, R. J. (1984) *Macroeconomics*. New York: Wiley.
Barsky, R. B., N. G. Mankiw and S. P. Zeldes (1986) 'Ricardian consumers with Keynesian propensities', *American Economic Review* 76, 676–91.

Benninga, S., and A. Protopapadakis (1984) 'The neutrality of the real equilibrium under alternative financing of government expenditures', *Journal of Monetary Economics* 14, 183–208.

Bernheim, B. D. (1987) 'Ricardian equivalence: an evaluation of theory and evidence', in *NBER Macroeconomics Annual 1987*. Ed. S. Fischer, Cambridge, Mass.: MIT Press, pp. 263–303.

Bernheim, B. D., A. Shleifer and L. H. Summers (1985) 'The strategic bequest motive', *Journal of Political Economy* 93, 1045–76.

Bispham, J. (1986) 'Growing public sector debt: a policy dilemma', *National Westminster Bank Quarterly Review*, 52–67.

Bowen, W. G., R. G. Davis and D. H. Kopf (1960) 'The public debt: a burden on future generations?' *American Economic Review* 50, 701–6.

Brunner, K. (1981) 'The case against monetary activism', *Lloyds Bank Review* 139, 20–39.

Buchanan, J. M. (1958) *Public Principles of Public Debt*. Homewood, Ill: Irwin.

Buiter, W. H. (1979) 'Government finance in an overlapping generations model with gifts and bequests', in *Social Security Versus Private Saving*. Ed. G. M. von Furstemberg, Cambridge, Mass.: Ballinger, pp. 395–429.

Buiter, W. H. and J. Tobin (1979) 'Debt neutrality: a brief review of doctrine and evidence', in *Social Security Versus Private Saving*. Ed. G. M. von Furstemberg, Cambridge, Mass.: Ballinger, pp. 39–63.

Carmichael, J. (1982) 'On Barro's theorem of debt neutrality: the irrelevance of net wealth', *American Economic Review* 72, 202–13.

Chan, L. K. C. (1983) 'Uncertainty and the neutrality of government financing policy', *Journal of Monetary Economics* 11, 351–72.

Christ, C. (1979) 'On fiscal and monetary policies and the government budget constraint', *American Economic Review* 69, 526–38.

Cornes, R., and T. Sandler (1985) 'The simple analytics of pure public good provision', *Economica* 52, 103–16.

Davies, G. (1985) *Governments Can Affect Employment*. London: Employment Institute.

Domar, E. D. (1944) 'The "Burden of the Debt" and the National Income', *American Economic Review* 34, 798–827.

Drazen, A. (1978) 'Government debt, human capital and bequests in a life-cycle model', *Journal of Political Economy* 86, 505–16.

Feldstein, M. (1976) 'Perceived wealth in bonds and social security: a comment', *Journal of Political Economy* 84, 331–6.

Ferguson, J. M. (1964) 'Temporal utility and fiscal burden', in *Public Debt and Future Generations*. Ed. J. M. Ferguson, Raleigh, N.C.: The University of North Carolina Press, pp. 219–28.

Gale, D. (1983) *Money: In Disequilibrium*. Cambridge: Cambridge University Press.

Goodhart, C. A. E. (1975) *Money, Information and Uncertainty*. London: Macmillan.

Hillier, B., and M. T. Lunati (1987) 'On Nash versus Stackelberg strategies and the conditions for operative intergenerational transfers', *Scottish Journal of Political Economy* 34, 91–6.

Houghton, R. W. (1970) 'Taxes v. loans', in *Public Finance*. Ed. R. W. Houghton, London: Cox & Wyman, pp. 297–8.

Lerner, A. P. (1948) 'The burden of the national debt', in *Income, Employment and Public Policy: Essays in Honor of Alvin H. Hansen*. Ed. L. A. Metzler et al., New York: W. W. Norton, pp. 255–75.

Lunati, M. T. (1987) 'Backing of government bonds and open market operations: real equilibrium in a production economy', Discussion Paper No. 127, IRISS–ISER, University of York.

McCallum, B. T. (1983) 'The role of overlapping-generations models in monetary economics', in *Money, Monetary Policy, and Financial Institutions*, Carnegie-Rochester Conference Series on Public Policy 18. Ed. K. Brunner and A. H. Meltzer, Amsterdam: North-Holland, pp. 9–44.

McCallum, B. T. (1984) 'Are bond-financed deficits inflationary? A Ricardian analysis', *Journal of Political Economy* 92, 123–35.

Mishan, E. J. (1963) 'How to make a burden of the public debt', *Journal of Political Economy* 71, 528–42.

Mishan, E. J. (1969) *Twenty-one Popular Economic Fallacies*. London: Penguin.

Modigliani, F. (1961) 'Long-run implications of alternative fiscal policies and the burden of the national debt', *Economic Journal* 71, 730–55.

Musgrave, R. A., and P. B. Musgrave (1973) *Public Finance in Theory and Practice*, 2nd edn. New York: McGraw-Hill.

Rankin, N. (1985) 'Debt neutrality in disequilibrium', in *Advances in Monetary Economics*. Ed. D. A. Currie, London: Croom-Helm, pp. 17–40.

Rankin, N. (1987) 'Disequilibrium and the welfare-maximising levels of government spending, taxation and debt', *Economic Journal* 97, 65–85.

Samuelson, P. A. (1958a) *Economics: An Introductory Analysis*. New York: McGraw-Hill.

Samuelson, P. A. (1958b) 'An exact consumption-loan model of interest with or without the social contrivance of money', *Journal of Political Economy* 66, 467–82.

Sargent, T. J., and N. Wallace (1981) 'Some unpleasant monetarist arithmetic', *Federal Reserve Bank of Minneapolis Quarterly Review* 5, 1–17.

Scarth, W. M. (1980) 'Rational expectations and the instability of bond-financing', *Economics Letters* 6, 321–7.

Tobin, J. (1971) *Essays in Economics: Macroeconomics*. Amsterdam: North-Holland.

Turnovsky, S. J. (1977) *Macroeconomic Analysis and Stabilization Policy*. Cambridge: Cambridge University Press.

Weil, P. (1987) 'Love thy children. Reflections on the Barro debt neutrality theorem', *Journal of Monetary Economics* 19, 377–91.

Wiseman, J. (1961) 'The logic of national debt policy', *Westminster Bank Review*, 8–15.

11

Liquidity

M. K. Lewis

'Liquidity' is one of the most widely used terms in economics. From a present-day vantage point, the origins of the term appear clear enough. There would seem to be little reason to disagree with Sir John Hicks's (1962) contention that it is a Keynesian word. As supporting evidence we can cite Hicks's (1935) paper in which the word liquidity first makes its appearance in the context of a discussion of Keynes's *Treatise on Money* (1930).[1] Contemporaneous non-British accounts suggest different origins. Neuman (1935) makes no reference to Keynes, nor indeed do Makower and Marschak (1938). Neuman instead looks to Fisher (1930). All four writers define liquidity by reference to Menger's concept of *Absatzfahigkeit*, translated in 1892 as 'saleability' (Menger, 1892) and later as 'marketability' (Menger, 1950; Streissler, 1973). There are also antecedents in the literature of money and banking, where the idea that banks should confine themselves to 'self-liquidating paper', which forms the basis of the real bills doctrine, can be traced back to Adam Smith and his contemporaries (Mints, 1945).

Nevertheless, Keynes, more than anyone, brought the concept of liquidity from the monetary literature into the mainstream of economics. By 1949, to judge from McKean (1949), Hart (1949) and Goodwin (1949), it would seem that liquidity was firmly entrenched as part of the 'Keynesian addition to accepted ideas' (Goodwin, 1949).

In the two decades after 1936, attention was focused upon the novel features of the analysis: liquidity preference (especially the 'liquidity trap') and under-full-employment equilibrium, and liquidity preference versus loanable funds as explanations of interest rate determination. The next decade saw the high-water mark of liquidity in economic discussion on a number of levels. In the UK, the Radcliffe Committee (1958) contended that 'it is the whole liquidity position that is relevant to spending decisions', emphasizing 'raising funds by selling an asset or by borrowing' as an alternative to 'money in the bank'. Articles in the Federal Reserve Bulletin in 1961 ('Liquidity and Public Policy') and 1963 ('Recent changes in liquidity') show the similarity of thinking in policy circles in the USA. The theoretical bases for these views came from the work of Gurley and Shaw

(1955, 1956, 1960), Sayers (1960), and the 'Yale School', led by Tobin (1963) and Tobin and Brainard (1963), which sought to 'dethrone' money from its position in economic analysis. Empirical studies of the demand for monetary assets were called 'liquidity functions' (Bronfenbrenner and Mayer, 1960; Gurley, 1960) and liquid assets functions (Kreinin, 1961; Christ, 1963; Feige, 1964). A number of studies examined the liquidity preferences of banks (Meigs, 1962; Frost, 1966; Morrison, 1966), while liquidity premiums in the term structure of interest rates were studied by Kessel (1965), Conard (1966) and Cagan (1969). Problems of international liquidity were almost continually under discussion.

During the 1970s interest in liquidity receded. Floating exchange rates killed off discussion of international liquidity. At a domestic level, there was some swing back to the view that a quantity of 'money' can be identified and possesses a special significance amongst a spectrum of liquid assets which saw the widespread adoption of money supply targets in the formulation of economic policy. Textbooks quietly substituted 'demand for money' for 'liquidity preference'.

The 1980s has seen a revived interest in liquidity, especially of banks and financial markets, and a return to some old themes. Coinciding with the increased incidence of bank failures, economists have looked again at liquidity creation by banks, and the factors which lead to bank runs. They have also dusted off some old solutions (100 per cent reserve banking, 'free' banking, commodity standards) and proposed new ones (mutual fund banking, alternative transactions media) which would have the effect, in Simmons's (1947) terminology, of 'making money more like other things'. At the same time, growth of trading in financial markets has stimulated a re-examination of the working of markets. What has been called 'market microstructure theory' (Cohen et al., 1986) has moved beyond the perfect auction markets of Walrasian analysis, with free information, free transactions, free storage and transport, to examine the role of financial 'middlemen' in supplying search, inventory management and, in the process, liquidity services. It also examines the way in which market organization contributes to the liquidity of markets. Liquidity, or rather the lack of it, is one reason for 'missing markets' and explaining why the range of markets actually in operation falls short of that implied in Arrow–Debreu models. Here again the emphasis upon institutions, market conditions and economic states travels down the path originally begun by Marschak and Makower and Marschak in 1938 and indeed Keynes in his 'forgotten' chapter 17 of *The General Theory* where he wrote:

> The conception of what contributes to 'liquidity' is a partly vague one, changing from time to time and depending on social practices and institutions. (1936, p. 240)

It is in the context of social practices and institutions that we begin our examination of liquidity.

11.1 Wealth and Liquidity

Suppose that we wanted to add up a nation's wealth. We would presumably make a listing of items such as the following:

	£ billion
Agricultural and other land	39.3
Buildings and works	445.9
Dwellings	595.2
Cars, ships and aircraft	26.8
Plant and machinery	247.3
Producer stocks	89.8
Intangible assets	107.1
Net claims on overseas	78.9

These figures are in fact estimates made in May 1987 by the Central Statistical Office (Bryant, 1987) of the national wealth of the UK at the end of 1985, amounting to £1630.3 billion.[2]

Of the tangible assets listed above, 24.1 per cent were attributed by the Statistical Office to the UK public sector, 31.6 to the business sector and 44.3 per cent to the personal sector. Ultimately, however, the wealth, whether allocated to the personal or business sector, is owned by individuals. Furthermore, if we regard the State as simply representing the collective wishes of the inhabitants of the country, the ownership of all wealth can be seen as residing with individuals. Yet a person can be regarded as wealthy without holding any of the assets above. Most households own houses, cars and other consumer durables but few are direct owners of buildings, equipment and stocks of producer goods. Instead, they hold claims which do not even rate a mention in the stocktaking above: currency, building society and bank deposits, national savings certificates, insurance policies, pension rights, and shares in corporations. These are financial assets which take the form of claims against other individuals, institutions or governments. Financial liabilities are also incurred by the personal sector, mainly in the form of loans for house purchases and for other purposes. It is primarily amongst this collection of financial assets and liabilities that one would look when considering the concept of 'liquidity'.

Consider the contrasts between real and financial assets. Most real assets, other than land and natural resources, are produced as part of the output of trading enterprises and governments either in one's own or other countries. They are tangible goods which derive their value from a capacity to yield a stream of goods and services in the future. A financial asset, in contrast, is a title or promise to payment at some time in the future, and arises when someone lends funds to another entity. Each financial asset necessarily has two dimensions to it: one is the entitlement to payment expected by the holder of the asset; the other is the liability of the borrower who issued the asset. Here we run into problems of double counting which troubled earlier writers (see Machlup, 1966). On a strict netting out, the financial claims wash out when aggregated. What remain are the tangible assets listed above, owned ultimately by individuals and households even if indirectly held by the government on their behalf. Nevertheless, 'though on a balancing of assets and liabilities neither [borrower nor lender] is any "richer" than before, *something has been added . . .* and economists have got into the habit of referring to this something as "liquidity"' (Sayers, 1964, p. 4).

What has been added is the process of delegation inherent in the indirect ownership of the productive real assets. Individuals delegate management to financial institutions and governments – which lie between them and the ultimate constituents of wealth. Control is delegated to financial intermediaries in part because, through specialization, they are able to acquire and use information more efficiently than individuals and households. This information, at least in principle, enables the intermediaries to select and undertake better investments and to monitor their performance at lower cost than would be the case if individuals themselves acquired the tangible assets and managed the investments. Delegation occurs also because the complex network of intermediaries opens up choices to individuals and households which do not exist in the aggregate.

Neoclassical economics often treats capital as a malleable quantity (Meccano sets, jelly, clay) which can be added to or subtracted from marginally, and costlessly and timelessly, to any value desired.[3] Similarly, the textbook models of perfect competition or perfect contestability view assets as highly flexible in use with free entry to and exit from markets. Some assets do conform to these views by virtue of being able to be transformed relatively costlessly in physical form. Producers may hold stocks of, say, raw cotton in preference to stocks of finished cotton goods because the raw cotton can be converted physically into a range of alternative end-products (Marschak, 1949). Such stocks possess the attribute of *physical liquidity*. In this context, 'liquidity' (as opposed to 'frozenness') alludes to the ability of liquid bodies to be freely transformed into other forms. It is one aspect of Makower and Marschak's (1938) characteristic of 'plasticity'.

Most capital goods are durable objects that take time to construct and wear down. There is a considerable degree of real asset specificity which serves to reduce the flexibility of asset use. Specificity may arise for a number of reasons, e.g. because of high set up and relocation costs, because of the limited range of alternative uses for some assets and because production facilities are often designed with particular customers in mind. Such assets are marked by *physical illiquidity*, because their form cannot be changed freely. For example, capital can be withdrawn from shipping, at little cost, no more rapidly than the port facilities, dockyards and boats wear out. It can be transferred into roads no more quickly than trucks can be built and roadways constructed.

In contrast, an individual can generally shift from a relatively small holding of shares in shipping lines to those of road transport just as soon as a broker on the stock market can be contacted and the sale and purchase orders executed. By virtue of this *market liquidity* (Hirschleifer, 1972), an individual can also consume wealth much more quickly than the nation as a whole. Cash or bank deposits can be realized readily. Ordinary shares or bonds can be sold off or used as backing for loans, enabling an individual to augment current income for consumption. Leaving aside external borrowings, these options do not exist for the nation, which can consume specific capital goods only by not devoting the resources needed over time for their maintenance or replacement. Yet the superstructure of financial markets enables entire generations to sell off or transfer their accumulated wealth to the next generation.

By enabling people to hold wealth in forms which can be changed at will and consumed readily, the network of financial markets creates an illusion. The capital assets which ultimately back up the financial assets issued do not generally have the same characteristics. One household's assets can be consumed or changed in character with little loss in value, only as long as the great majority of other holders of wealth do not also seek to consume their holdings or alter the form of ownership. One small holder of an ICI share, for example, can liquidate his or her holdings with little loss, but all holders cannot do so. Similarly, one holder of a bank deposit can encash his or her balance, but not all depositors can do so at the same time. When acting in unison, the opportunities open to all wealth-holders to consume their assets and change their form are no different from those of the country as a whole.

This contrast between market liquidity and physical illiquidity, i.e. between the fluidity and flexibility of individual wealth and the rigidity of the composition of wealth in the aggregate, is what we mean by 'liquidity'. It is in the spirit of both Hicks (1974) and Simmons (1947). Hicks defined liquidity as 'flexibility':

> though there are many kinds of flexibility which are relevant to economic decisions, there is one that is outstanding. It is the flexibility

that is given by the market. A firm which acquires a non-marketable asset – say a new factory, designed and equipped for its own particular purpose – has committed itself to a course of action, extending over a considerable time, with a fairly narrow band of subsequent choices attached to it. It has 'given hostage to fortune'. The acquisition of an easily marketable asset, on the other hand, can easily be revoked. There is not the same diminution of flexibility; the firm is in a position that is almost as flexible, after the acquisitions, as before it. That, I suggest, is precisely what we mean by saying that the marketable asset possesses liquidity. (Hicks, 1974, pp. 41–2)

This is the idea pursued later by Jones and Ostroy (1984). Earlier, Simmons had referred to an asset which possesses liquidity as

> a bearer of options. . . . A person holding money and certain other assets, securities and non-specified commodities is 'endowed with a wide range of freedom as to time and kind of outlays'. (1947, p. 34)

The fact that these options rest on a fallacy of composition – or, if preferred, an 'illusion'[4] or 'confidence trick'[5] – means that they are sustained by confidence on the part of wealth-holders that they will be sustained. Without this confidence, the vast majority of holders will not refrain from simultaneously seeking to exploit the flexibility of financial assets, so that net demands for liquidation in the economy as a whole will not be small and regular. It follows that liquidity is necessarily subjective: conditioned by the attitudes, expectations and psyche of actual and potential market participants.

Just as there are marked differences between the individual and society as a whole in the ability to consume and rearrange wealth, there are also differences in the accumulation of wealth. Whereas social saving occurs mainly through the accumulation of tangible assets, saving by individuals can take the form of acquiring a wide variety of assets. In particular by enabling long-term investments to be financed by short-term funds, the network of markets and intermediaries performs what has been called an 'act of magic'[6] and both permits and solves the two main problems arising from the division of labour between savers and investors – problems which come about because the objects of exchange are contingent promises which must be acceptable to both savers and investors.

A person acquiring a contingent promise of future payments faces a moral hazard which underlies the distinction that Keynes made between borrowing risks and lending risks:

> Now the first type of risk is, in a sense, a real social cost, though susceptible to diminution by averaging as well as by an increased accuracy of foresight. The second, however, is a pure addition to the

cost of investment which would not exist if the borrower and lender were the same person. (1936, pp. 144–5)

As noted by Stigler (1967) the 'pure addition' comes about because of information costs – costs of acquiring knowledge about borrowers and overseeing their performance during the course of the loan. This risk will be avoided if those who save themselves undertake the investment: internalization of market transactions clearly reduces search, haggling, trading and information costs.[7] There would also be no problem if we could assume away default risk and/or costs of evaluating default risks – as is often done in theoretical models. Most usually the lender seeks refuge from lender's risk mainly by requiring that the loan be secured by assets of greater value than the amount of the loan. This excess – the borrower's equity in the collateral – provides a margin for costs of disposition and losses on realization. Some of the assets pledged as collateral may need to be in 'liquid' form. One of the explanations for the US practice of compensating balances – the requirement that those borrowing from banks maintain demand deposits equal to some proportion of the outstanding loan – is that they serve as part collateral for loans.[8]

Consequently, in order to secure lender's savings, an investment programme requires the dedication of a part of an investor's own current or past savings, with some portion used to maintain or acquire liquid balances. The extent of the liquid backing for indebtedness was used by McKean (1949) to define the 'illiquidity' of debt.

In similar vein, Farmer (1988) argues that liquidity is needed by a firm to secure supplies from workers and other contractual partners in circumstances when the value of the firm is unknown to them. In his model, the firm monetizes part of its assets by a bank loan and holds money balances in effect as a bond to shield suppliers from the risk of possible bankruptcy. This arrangement implies that, unlike the suppliers, the bank is privy to the information needed to evaluate the firm's worth. Possible reasons are examined in section 11.3. In Farmer's model, the bank trades access to information for a loan which appears on its balance sheet. Equally it could issue a performance bond and guarantee the firm's behaviour directly – one aspect of 'off-balance-sheet' banking.

Separation of savings from investment raises other questions about the character of the financial claims created. Preferences of borrowers and lenders need to overlap sufficiently so that there is some common ground upon which negotiations about the precise form of the contract can take place. A feature of tangible investment is the long gestation period: time is required for the investment to come to maturity and realize the high return expected. Capital goods frequently embody technologically irreversible processes and yield saleable services only when combined with other productive factors. In the absence of markets in which output can be sold forward and factor inputs bought forward, expectations of profit may not be fully realized. Borrowers undertaking investment may wish to borrow for relatively long terms so as to pace out the repayments with the flow of expected returns from the project, issuing long-term debentures or mortgages. Other borrowers may be so uncertain about future income and costs from the project that they prefer to borrow in a form which does not commit them to specific repayments, issuing shares and equity claims.

Lenders have preferences which typically do not coincide with those of potential borrowers. By lending funds, the saver is indicating a willingness to give up some present goods and services in return for a larger amount of goods in the future. But there are a great many uncertainties in life, and the saver may wish to retain discretion as to when the future consumption actually takes place. Without forward markets the prices at which future consumption will take place are not known with certainty, and spending opportunities may arise which are too good to miss. Savers may desire flexibility simply because they are uncertain about their future preferences (Kreps, 1979). In order to keep their options open, savers desire liquidity. But their choices are limited by the sort of securities which borrowers issue. Some compromise must be struck: either the saver must hold a long-term debt issued by the borrower, the borrower must accept frequent refinancing of short-term claims preferred by the lender, or there is some middle ground sought at a cost which may inhibit many potential lenders and borrowers from entering the market.

These two problems – pertaining to security and liquidity respectively – are seemingly distinct, but in fact are closely intertwined in two respects. Savers' concerns about the safety of their funds lent to investors, we have noted, come about in large part because it is costly to make themselves better informed about the characteristics and the prospects of the borrowers. Often the experience and knowledge acquired with the passing of time is an important teacher. Yet by locking themselves into inflexible long-term loans, lenders pass up the opportunity actually to benefit from new information signals. Thus lenders' risk puts a premium on liquidity.

At the same time, if the network of financial markets succeeds in its task and alters savers' perception of the security and accessibility afforded by the financial assets which they hold, then they are less likely to seek extensive collateralization of loans. Investment in consequence will be more highly levered. These perceptions have implications also for the liquidity demands of investors. Borrowers faced with the possibility that they will be pressed for payment of debts or early repayment of loans must take steps to augment liquidity or face distress sales of assets. Liquidity concerns of lenders hence add directly to the burden which illiquidity imposes upon the borrowers. Market arrangements which can simultaneously satisfy savers' needs for liquidity with lenders' desire for illiquidity (e.g. by guaranteeing refinancing of short-term debt) can reduce the lenders' liquidity demands.

The amount of liquidity sought by borrowers and lenders from the financial markets can be analysed by means of the usual marginal analysis. Failure to maintain adequate liquidity can be costly. Extra borrowings may have to be made at high interest rates to pay emergency bills, desirable consumption needs may have to be deferred, and new information and bargains passed up. These risks of illiquidity due to uncertainties about future contingencies, investment opportunities and spending needs can be 'insured' against but at a cost. Holding liquid assets is a direct cost to borrowers, since they must issue additional debt, presumably at higher yields, in order to secure the assets. For lenders, the cost comes in terms of income forgone by not holding higher-yielding assets. These benefits and costs must be balanced out to determine the optimal extent of 'liquidity insurance'.

In figure 11.1 we envisage wealth-holders choosing amongst assets according to these two characteristics of expected return and liquidity:

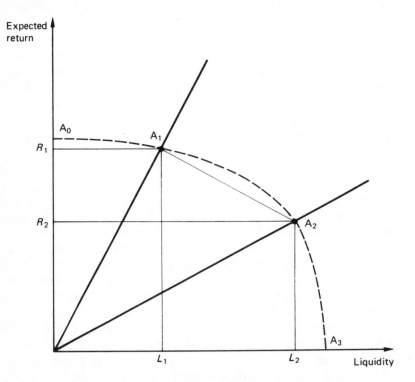

Figure 11.1 Representation of liquidity preferences.

essentially a variant of the Tobin–Markowitz expected return–risk analysis in which risk comes from illiquidity. It borrows from Lancaster's (1966) suggestion that consumers make choices not so much between commodities but between alternative bundles of characteristics incorporated in the commodities. This idea of needs and characteristics was pioneered earlier for assets by Makower and Marschak (1938) who classified assets in terms of their contribution to the attributes of lucrativity (profitability) and safety.

It is assumed initially that two assets A_1 and A_2 are available. Each is represented by a line through the origin, and the points A_1 and A_2 show, on some objective measure, the expected return and liquidity services which can be obtained from spending a unit of value (pound, dollar) on each asset. A_1 offers high yield and low liquidity, while A_2 offers low yield and high liquidity. If these are the only assets available, the choices are bounded by the coordinates at A_1 and A_2 (and linear combinations of the two assets). More generally, following Neuman (1935), we can expect market arrangements to provide a more or less continuous spectrum of assets ranging from zero return and full liquidity (A_3) to the highest yield on the asset with complete illiquidity (A_0) as shown by the broken line. Transactors would then choose assets along this opportunity locus according to their marginal rate of substitution between the two characteristics.

Assets combine a number of characteristics and we have yet to define specifically what various writers have meant by liquidity. However, the choices in figure 11.1 are no different in principle from other types of decision-making. Hicks (1974) points out that the concept of flexibility can be applied to military strategy, with a commander choosing between keeping his forces in a central position awaiting further information or committing them to battle where he anticipates the enemy to be concentrated. Mundell (1968) argues that the economic principles of scarcity and choice are basic to *all* conscious action. Irreversibility and the closing off of options, central to illiquidity, can be applied to other matters. One can accordingly suffer a liquidity shortage of time, i.e. a temporal liquidity problem. Similarly, a business may lack liquidity with respect to stocks of goods (inventories) and run into bottlenecks of production and declining product quality standards.

What is perhaps different about liquidity problems of the usual kind is the range and complexity of the social institutions which have developed out of the different preferred habitats of savers and investors to provide market liquidity. The flexibility that savers seek over the timing of future spending is achieved in two ways.

First, secondary markets in the financial claims allow an individual holder of, say, a ten-year bond to dispose of it prematurely. This is the traditional way in which markets for debt instruments permit the financing of long-term investments by short-term funds. In recent years the transformation has been reversed by the development of financial instruments (such as note issuance facilities) which convert short-term claims into guaranteed long-term financing for investment.

Equity markets undertake the same transformation. Each person buying shares may have the intention of making the funds available only for a temporary period. Or, even if intending to provide the funds for a longer term, the person may wish to hold the option of withdrawing them at short notice. Nevertheless, in the eyes of the firm which issues the share capital, the funds can be looked upon as a stable amount of long-term funding which can be invested in intangible illiquid assets. That is, from the viewpoint of the borrower the claim is physically illiquid (frozen). Liquidity rests on the fact that borrowers and lenders view the same asset in quite different terms.

Markets can provide liquidity only as long as transactors differ with respect to their endowments and the contingencies under which they operate. If everyone's situation and attitudes were the same, there would be no double coincidence of wants allowing pairwise trading to take place, and market liquidity would not differ from physical liquidity. This precondition is diluted, but not eliminated, by the activities of specialized market-makers and 'liquidity substitution' centres (Neuman, 1935) (such as financial intermediaries), which is the second way in which flexibility is achieved.

Financial intermediaries operate also by altering the characteristics of claims from lenders' and borrowers' viewpoints and, as such, augment the hierarchy of portfolio choices about expected return, risk and efforts of administrating and monitoring assets provided by the direct control of assets (A_0), holding equities (A_1), debt securities (A_2) and cash (A_3). Here we have one explanation for the phenomenon of financial innovation, in that new claims change the mix of characteristics so as to occupy a previously vacant space. In this way, the proliferation of claims reduces the gaps between claims and completes the market.

To illustrate, unit trusts (mutual funds) buy shares, pool them to diversify risk and then resell units or shares in the total diversified portfolio. Substitution of a single contract with the trust for the individual shares enables diversification and professional investment guidance to be built in, while a market can be established for the units themselves. People are thus provided with risk, liquidity and administrative choices which differ from those of the underlying shares, filling in the gap in the characteristics 'space' between A_1 and A_2.

Depository institutions and insurance companies go further. Life insurance companies package together savings via unit trust and bonds with protection against death while offering minimum guaranteed as to the value of the portfolio. They conduct an internal capital market in the various securities pools, typically offering policy holders the option to switch from one pooled fund to another. Like insurance companies, banks and other deposit-taking institutions offer explicit guarantees as to the redemption value of savings and enable those investing in real assets to obtain the type of longer-term funding which they prefer, while meeting savers' liquidity needs.

Section 11.3 concentrates on two of these institutional arrangements to provide for liquidity, namely the markets for securities and liquidity creation by banks. But first, what is meant by 'liquid' is clarified in section 11.2.

11.2 Characteristics of Liquid Assets

In examining the definitions of liquidity used in the literature, a number of common elements can be traced. In order to examine these elements we classify assets in terms of a number of characteristics, under the headings *marketability, realizability, maturity, reversibility, divisibility, predictability* and *plasticity*.

Marketability

By *marketability* is meant that ease and speed with which the 'value' of an asset can be realized – essentially Menger's concept of saleability. Makower and Marschak (1938) refer to an unpublished paper by Hasler which depicted the ease with which an asset can be sold in a diagram in which the axes measure 'prices that can be fetched' and 'various waiting intervals'. Figure 11.2 is constructed along these lines.[9]

At any moment in time an asset will have a certain market value P_t^*, by which is meant the *maximum* amount of cash that can be obtained by selling or otherwise liquidating the asset at that particular time, if the seller is allowed to make all useful prior preparation for the disposal of the asset and if conditions in the market remain unchanged during the sale. Determination of an asset's value is thus a conceptual exercise in which market conditions are assumed to be put into suspension. Makower and Marschak define this value (which they call 'future price') in terms of a perfect market. 'Saleability is the reciprocal of the difference between an asset's actual present price and the price it would have at present if the market in which it may be sold in the future were perfect' (1938, p. 302). Limited marketability arises from imperfections in the future market. A meaning of the value of an asset perhaps more in line with Menger's idea of an 'economic price' is provided by Lippman and McCall (1986). They con-

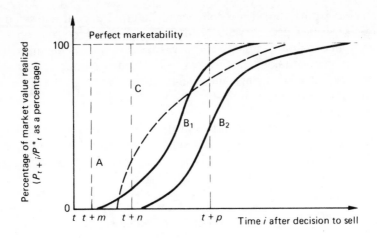

Figure 11.2 Marketability and realizability of assets.

ceive of an asset's value in terms of a setter's optimal search over time amongst offers to buy which have random arrival dates. Imperfect marketability in this case is due to insufficient time to carry out this search.

In these terms cash is perfectly marketable and is shown in figure 11.2 by a horizontal line at 100 per cent of value, indicating that, no matter how recent is the decision to sell, its full value can be realized in *terms of cash*. Amongst assets, the 'market for cash is more nearly perfect than for other assets' (Makower and Marschak, 1938, p. 306), and information about its attributes does not need to be sought out by market participants. For other assets there is some delay, however short, before they can be turned into cash. The line A at time $t + m$ represents the situation of assets such as savings deposits which can be fully realized as soon as the depositor gets to the branch or ATM of an institution or after the term of notice elapses and listed shares which can be sold at current value as soon as the broker is notified and effects the sale. Curves B and C depict the general case for tangible assets such as houses, durable producer and consumer goods and shares in private companies where time must be allowed to find a buyer and organize the market before the full value can be realized. If a unit of the asset is disposed of beforehand, an actual price P_t which is less than P_t^* can be expected to be realized. There are varying degrees of imperfect marketability, but no completely unmarketable asset to contrast with perfect marketability. Failure to realize anything no matter how long the time allowed for the asset's disposal is means that it has no value and its marketability – measured by the ratio P_{t+i}/P_t^* – relative to elapsed time i is simply underlined. Disposal in this case need not be limited to sale, for the asset can be assigned as security for borrowings.

Limited marketability is attributed in the earlier literature (Menger, Marshall, Neuman) to the narrowness and thinness of the market. Factors mentioned include a small number of potential transactors, their limited purchasing power, a large number of units sold, taxation provisions and social and political constraints upon trading. Scarcity of buyers at short notice and infrequency of trading mean that quick sales require acceptance of less than full market value of the asset. The newer literature (Hirschleifer, Orr, Lippman and McCall) shifts the emphasis to information deficiencies. Knowledge may be lacking as to the characteristics of the asset, the attributes of other transactors or the terms and conditions of the contract of sale. Where the spread of information about these is slow and imperfect, time must be allowed to elapse after the decision to sell before the full value can be obtained.

These are largely alternative descriptions of manifestations of the nature of the commodity being traded. Those things which are 'in universal demand', 'capable of being easily and exactly described', 'durable' and for which 'their value is considerable in proportion to their bulk' (Marshall, 1920, p. 326) will have a deep and geographically widespread market. Assets which have a limited number of uses, are one of a kind and perishable and do not lend themselves to transporting will, in contrast, lack marketability. Correspondingly, those assets for which the costs of information are low and the likely gains from search are immediate are ones which are generally demanded, standardized, storable and portable. Bonds and securities issued by the major governments and large public companies most readily meet these requirements, and for them the relevant market is the world. Custom-built housing, special-purpose equipment and bulky and perishable goods lie at the other extreme.

Realizability

Since an asset's marketability is an attribute which is defined by a functional relationship between the price ratio P_{t+i}/P_t^* and the time i taken for disposal, and not by a single value, it follows that no unique ordering of assets according to marketability is generally possible. This is the position illustrated in figure 11.2 where the curves for the two imperfectly marketable assets B and C cross. One way to obtain a simple ordering would be to compare the percentage realizations for a particular time available for disposal ($i = n$ or $i = p$ in figure 11.2). An asset's *realizability* can consequently be defined as the percentage value realized in cash after some specified interval of time. The remainder of the marketability distribution, which may effectively be the whole for those assets that cannot be liquidated prior to maturity dates in excess of the time interval, is referred to as *maturity*.

Some writers on liquidity appear to have realizability rather than marketability in mind. A difficulty with the former is that the curves relate to the sale of one unit of the asset and for some assets the price realized is far from independent of the number of units sold. An asset's ranking in terms of realizability will thus depend on the transaction's size. Figure 11.2 shows the hypothetical relationship between P_{t+i}/P_t^* and i for asset B when the size of transaction increases such that the larger the number of units sold (this number is greater for B_2 than for B_1), the less is the price realized for a given time to disposal. Even the seller of a well-known security on a well-organized exchange may find that the price immediately quoted for relatively large blocks is unfavourable compared with the price which can be obtained after some delay.

Divisibility

Some assets can be sold off only in large job lots and in that respect can be thought of as indivisible. The size of the smallest unit in which dealings can take place in an asset is an important determinant of the flexibility of an asset in exchange, and is referred to as *divisibility*. Cash is for most purposes fully divisible although this is not true of individual denominations, such as was the case with the old $1,000 note in the USA. At the other end of the scale, money market paper sold in minimum denominations or job lots is not divisible.

Reversibility

Liquidity is sometimes defined by reference to the difference between buying and selling prices or 'bid' and 'ask' prices as quoted in many organized markets. This price spread reflects the degree of perfection and the organization of the markets concerned, for in a perfect market all buyers pay the same price and all sellers receive the same price and there is no margin for market-making; buying and selling prices are equal. Nevertheless, while due to market imperfections, the spread reflects an asset property distinct from marketability. For example, shares in mutual funds (unit trusts) are readily saleable, but administrative fees front-loaded into the acquisition price can result in a bid–ask spread which can be as much as 13 per cent (although market-makers normally operate at 5–6 per cent). We refer to this attribute as *reversibility*.

Reversibility refers to the discrepancy in value between the contemporaneous acquisition and realization of an asset. Suppose that an asset is acquired and then immediately sold. Reversibility is measured by the realized amount relative to the contemporaneous acquisition price. For new cars, sold after driving out of the showroom, the difference is considerable. For cash, there is only the time and effort involved. The extent of the discrepancy depends on transactions costs broadly interpreted as brokerage, commission, insurance, time and effort, information uncertainties, and so on.

Even assets which exhibit perfect marketability – such as cash and other monetary assets – suffer from some degree of irreversibility owing to the presence of trading costs. Whereas no assets are completely unmarketable, for all practical purposes some are fully irreversible. Contributions to pension schemes which cannot be transferred to anyone else or encashed or borrowed against are an example. For most assets the transfer or adjustments costs which result in imperfect reversibility are both fixed and variable. The former consist of fixed service charges for time and trouble involved which are independent of the size of the transaction. Commission and administration charges which are levied proportionately to the value of the assets traded, as in the bid–ask price spread, are examples of variable transfer costs. Both types feature in studies of the transactions demand for money (e.g. Baumol–Tobin analysis).

So far illiquidity has been attributed to 'thin' markets, deficiencies of information and transactions costs. All are related. Thin markets and incomplete information make for illiquidity since transactors must devote time and efforts searching each other out. These 'frictions' give rise to intermediation of trading through middlemen (brokers, agents, financial institutions) who undertake the search and information-gathering (Rubinstein and Wolinsky, 1987). It is the time-consuming nature of search which makes the middleman's function worthwhile, yet the activity finds reflection in the transactions costs incurred by buyers and sellers when using the intermediation services.

Predictability

The next characteristic – *predictability* or capital certainty – is also widely cited as contributing to liquidity. An asset may be highly marketable in the sense that a holder can realize the asset's full value easily and speedily, but that market valuation (i.e. the future positions of the 100 per cent line in figure 11.2) may be far from predictable in advance. An asset's predictability or capital certainty is the extent to which its value in terms of cash can be predicted at future dates. Cash and deposits which are guaranteed as redeemable in terms of cash are fully predictable, as long as there is no risk of the institution's defaulting on the promise. Shares have imperfect capital certainty since stock market valuations in general and the fortune of particular firms can change. Government bonds are predictable at issue and on redemption; in between their value can fluctuate owing to interest rate variations. Value here is in monetary terms. The assumption implicit in this definition is that people are making purchases with money and that over the time span relevant for their transactions they are interested in ensuring redeemability of the assets in nominal terms. It presupposes a high degree of monetary stability.

Plasticity

A final attribute is Marschak's (1938) property of *'plasticity'*. He defines the plasticity of an asset as 'the easiness of manoeuvring into and out of various yields after the asset has been acquired' (p. 323). The yield of an asset consists of all the receipts and costs occasioned by the ownership of the asset over a specified interval of time, and these flows take the form of receipts of interest, dividends, rights, goods and services along with carrying costs like insurance, repairs and maintenance. The total return to the holder is the algebraic sum of the yield and the appreciation or depreciation in market value (capital gain or loss) over the interval of time.

Since the particular service flows entailed by ownership of the different types of assets take many forms, the marketability, divisibility, reversibility and predictability of the receipts and carrying costs themselves constitute properties of the asset. For example certainty of return is part of Jones and Ostroy's definition of liquidity and assets differ in the predictability of their total return. Yields which take the form of flows of cash receipts or of readily transformable intermediate products are more marketable than yields which take the form of specialized services or finished goods which must be consumed directly by the owner of the asset. This in turn contributes to the marketability of the asset itself.

By the term 'plasticity', Marschak had in mind that 'yields cannot be stocked or exchanged' so that 'flows of amounts consumed' (i.e. yields) can be rearranged only by 'buying and selling assets in the market' (p. 313). For Marschak, the plasticity of yields amounted to the saleability or marketability of the assets which generate the flow of consumable services.

This is an aspect that has been transformed in recent years by innovations in financial techniques. A ready market now exists world-wide whereby streams of coupon interest payments or receipts in one currency or basis can be exchanged into another currency or basis. For example, current and future fixed coupon interest obligations can be traded for floating rate interest streams. Coupon interest in one currency can be exchanged into another currency. These exchanges can be effected without having to alter ownership of the underlying assets or renegotiate either the original instrument or its covenants.

With the development of these markets for interest rate and currency 'swaps', a new distinction has emerged between financial and tangible products. Both, we have said, can be regarded as bundles of characteristics. Once physical products are produced, the characteristics can be altered only by transforming the asset in production or by trading the asset. The latter used to be the case for financial products. Now the attributes of financial products can themselves be unbundled and separately exchanged.

Nature of Liquidity

High marketability, realizability, divisibility, reversibility and predictability have featured, in varying combinations, in the definitions of liquidity that appear in the literature. No one has incorporated *all* these characteristics in a definition, although a good case can be made for doing so. Liquidity provides flexibility, and flexibility comes from markets which allow assets to be converted readily into other assets. An asset is acquired at one date and resold later in exchange for the goods required. The vehicle asset must have a good secondary market, be reversible and, since all purchases may not occur at the one time, be divisible. Uncertainty about the terms of trade between the asset and the good in the future is reduced if the vehicle asset is expected to have a low price variability in terms of the desired goods. Marketability, reversibility, divisibility and predictability would all seem relevant attributes in the definition of what constitutes a liquid asset.

Models of liquidity preference usually focus upon one of these attributes to the exclusion of the others. A wealth-holder's portfolio selection is simple if all assets are fully predictable, marketable, reversible and divisible: the portfolio offering the highest return will be chosen. If one asset promises a higher rate of return, the entire wealth will go into that asset irrespective of whether wealth is being accumulated for the near or distant future, as the portfolio can be changed at any time. The Tobin–Markowitz models single out imperfect predictability of asset returns as one reason to deviate from that simple strategy. But the assets under consideration in these models are assumed to be fully marketable, reversible and divisible, and hence equally suitable in other respects to serve as temporary stores of purchasing power. Theories of the transactions demand for money change the concept of liquidity from the absence of uncertainty with respect to the future value of assets to the absence of inconvenience. But in concentrating upon the impact of asset exchange costs on portfolio decisions they ignore not only unpredictability of yields on the assets but also other sources of market imperfections (low marketability, divisibility), including incomplete information about current and future earning prospects.

To emphasize one attribute to the exclusion of the other is mistaken. Liquidity summarizes a collection of characteristics which may be present to varying degrees in various assets. The concept is multidimensional and not measurable in any definite way. It is also subjective since marketability and predictability depend on evaluations by individuals of future conditions in the markets for particular assets.

Predictability and Liquidity

Certainty of price and marketability are the two attributes which are most frequently seen as contributing to liquidity. Hicks saw 'certainty of expected value' as sufficient in itself to define liquidity. Lippman and McCall, in contrast, explicitly reject predictability in favour of marketability alone, arguing that liquidity is about the breadth and efficiency of the market for a particular asset – defined as 'many transactions per day of a homogeneous asset' – and not about 'safety' (p. 47). Safety does not feature in their search model which has sellers maximizing a utility function which is linear in the pay-offs, so abstracting implicitly from risk aversion and a seller's characteristics – hence their contention that predictability is overly concerned with adverse outcomes or downside risk and as such ignores the possibility of favourable outcomes (i.e. upside risk). An alternative position, expressed here by Newlyn (1962), holds that an individual suffering capital depreciation will 'lose what we may loosely describe as "intra-marginal" units of wealth; if on the other hand he enjoys capital appreciation he will gain "extra-marginal" units of wealth; it follows from the principle of diminishing marginal utility of money that the satisfaction lost by depreciation will be greater than that gained by an equal appreciation' (p. 53).

Lippman and McCall also ignore that predictability and marketability are closely related. An asset is likely to be more marketable, the more certain its expected value is. Creation of a futures market for an asset, for example, which improves information about its future price, seems likely to enhance its marketability in spot transactions. Conversely, marketability improves predictability by reducing the variance of market prices around the market-clearing value (Telser, 1981).

Furthermore, while 'liquid' assets traded on organized markets are normally distinguished by a large volume of transactions, there is no necessary connection. Even if few transactions took place on a given day in the stock of, say, BP, the price of the stock would be well known and the stock would remain readily saleable.

Finally, we query whether liquidity can be defined at all meaningfully in terms of the time expected to sell an asset under an optimum search rule which ignores other sellers' actions. An individual's ability to search for an exit from a crowded room in the dark will differ if everyone else is also trying to rush to the exit.

Moneyness and Liquidity

A number of writers have equated liquidity with 'moneyness'. The relationship envisaged between the two is often two way: money is the most liquid of all assets, and the most liquid assets come to be accepted as money. So long as marketability, predictability etc. are designated in terms of cash, money must definitionally be liquidity *par excellence*. The case for basing marketability upon cash rests on the two-stage exchanges which take place in a monetary economy whereby good *j*, say, is initially exchanged for money and money is then exchanged for good *i*. Marketability relates to the speed and ease of the first exchange, and it follows that the switching costs can be avoided when money itself is the initial good. Money also ranks highly in terms of reversibility and divisibility. The question mark concerns predictability. Full value means cash value and, as Okun (1981) wryly observes, the finding that money can be instantaneously and costlessly realized as money is no more remarkable than the expectation that the full peanut-value of peanuts can be realized immediately. Ultimately the purpose of wealth accumulation is to ensure command over future goods and services, i.e. the peanut-value of money matters. The longer is the time interval involved, the greater is the importance of predictability in real terms. When there is considerable doubt about the future purchasing power of money, and a wide divergence between capital certainty in real and monetary terms, liquidity preference is in effect inverted. 'The whole question of liquidity then takes on quite a different aspect, and money ceases to be the asset to which liquidity preference attaches' (Robinson, 1952).

Those assets which are liquid seem likely to evolve as 'money'. How this evolution occurs is a question which is not addressed in modern-day theories of money. The overlapping generations model (McCallum, 1983) simply ignores money as a medium of exchange: money serves solely as a store of value. The cash-in-advance model (Clower, 1967; Kareken and Wallace, 1980) imposes a means of payment exogenously. In Menger's (1892) analysis, in contrast, assets destined for acceptability as money are distinguished by their superior saleability (marketability). Traders discover that certain commodities are more marketable than others and are willing to hold more marketable ones for use in exchange. Others come to accept them in trades not because of their use in production but because of their marketability and value in exchange. The assets become more marketable and valuable as their demand as a medium of exchange increases relative to their non-monetary demand.[10]

In order to qualify as candidates for this process, the assets should possess certain attributes such as stability of value, ease of transport and identification, durability, divisibility and ease of storage and ready saleability, i.e. the characteristics we have associated with *liquid assets*. It is tempting to argue that assets which are highly marketable, reversible, divisible and predictable evolve as money, so that liquidity confers moneyness. The difficulty with this line of reasoning is that an asset which lacks these attributes would soon acquire them should it become accepted as a medium of exchange. Moneyness would confer liquidity.

The ultimate test of moneyness is acceptability by the public, although the social consensus which leads to acceptability as money is, in common with many other social phenomena (legal norms, social conventions, clothing, language), far from fully understood. Moneyness is in essence a pure illustration of consumer sovereignty: whatever is considered as good as money becomes money.

Some contend that *only* money is liquid; for example Simmons (1947), 'there are no liquid assets aside from money, unless there is a central bank' so 'that only a central bank can create liquidity' (p. 36); and Davidson (1978): 'In this era of central banks, it is their decisions and activities that ultimately provide the liquidity of any ongoing monetary economy' (p. 62). In order to examine their contentions we must examine the market arrangements that are important for the liquidity of non-cash assets.

11.3 The Provision of Market Liquidity

Financial markets, like markets for commodities, take a wide variety of forms. Some markets are highly organized, dealing in a large quantities of relatively standardized commodities or instruments. Markets for bonds, shares, commercial paper, foreign currencies, interbank deposits, futures and option contracts are of this type. Liquidity in these markets comes from two sources. One is the set of rules governing the *organization of the market*, whether made by formal exchanges (stock market, futures exchange) or due to market conventions which have grown up informally, as in the foreign exchange and Eurocurrency markets. The other source of liquidity comes from the real world counterparts of Clower and Leijonhufvud's (1975) conceptualized *trade coordinator*. Clower and Leijonhufvud envisage that markets need for their smooth operation not a Walrasian auctioneer but a central coordinator of trading activity, gathering information and, most importantly, maintaining inventories of the goods traded so as to provide order over time in market prices. Coordination of trading activity and stabilization of prices in the highly organized markets is carried out by the *market-makers* – specialists, dealers, exchange members – who provide financial middlemen services.

Not all financial markets are of the highly organized character discussed above. Mortgages, consumer finance and commercial and industrial loans, for example, have characteristics and collateral specific to the borrowers concerned. They are frequently of a 'one-off' nature with terms and conditions negotiated directly between parties to the contract. Describing these classes of differentiated transactions as 'markets' is a useful, but simplifying, abstraction to denote the domains in which the transactions are negotiated and prices determined (Tobin, 1987). What justification we have for treating them as unified comes largely from the activities of *banks and other financial intermediaries* which are the principal makers of these markets. They provide the coordination of information and trade, and they are the suppliers of liquidity services to the informal financial markets.

Market Organization

Many aspects of market organization are deliberately designed to enhance the liquidity of market transactions. The way in which futures markets structured is an excellent illustration (Telser, 1981). Other aspects of markets, e.g. the development of information services, reflect a complex interactive process by which the organization of the market is induced by, and in turn induces, an increase in market liquidity (Burns, 1979). In this respect, a number of workers have observed that liquidity is 'self-reinforcing ' (Economides and Siow, 1988; Goodhart, 1989).

Futures markets are deliberately organized so that scale economies can be applied to forward transactions. A forward contract is tailor-made to suit the two parties involved, and a transactor needs to be acquainted with the specification of the contract, the honesty, competence and other characteristics of the other transactor, and the avenues available to enforce the agreement. A futures exchange standardizes a forward contract by determining times of trading, terms of the contract, number and time of monthly maturity dates, volume of asset per contract, mode of operation, conditions of membership of the exchange, rules for enforcement and magnitude of margin requirements. As a result, all contracts of the same maturity date are perfect substitutes for one another.

Standardization of the terms and conditions of the futures contracts is an information-saving device that makes it easier to ascertain the quality of the traded instrument. The exchange itself centralizes information and establishes in effect a Clower (1969) '*trading post*', at which buyers and sellers are able to gather at predetermined times. Open and competitive bidding by means of open outcry is best confined to expert members who trust each other to honour commitments and can trade quickly at a low cost. Assets with a low degree of risk of default are likely to be more marketable than those whose future delivery is less certain. Backing of the clearing house of the exchange for all exchange-traded contracts shifts default risk from individual parties to the clearing house itself.

These are features deliberately introduced to widen trading in each market instrument. Increased volumes of trading generate larger demand for market information and make investments in affiliated services worthwhile. Market news reports, communications facilities, inspection, grading and ratings services all seem likely in turn to expand trading, enhance marketability, narrow bid–ask spreads and reduce the variance of prices across trades and exchanges.

This self-reinforcing character of liquidity accounts for some observed features of markets. The desire to trade in markets characterized by ready marketability, high reversibility and low variance of price seems likely to lead to limitations upon the number of instruments traded, clearly evident in futures markets, and militate against the establishment of new markets. Some markets may go 'missing' because they are starved of liquidity (Economides and Siow, 1988). Increased liquidity in one market seems likely to enhance trading activity in related markets. Markets may be related geographically (e.g. foreign exchange trading in different time zones), by the substitutability of assets (Treasury bills and commercial paper) or in terms of the same assets at different trading dates (spot and futures). Development in turn of these related markets will make the first market even more liquid (Burns, 1979). Finally, a tendency for large markets to draw custom from the smaller ones and gain further in liquidity, so reinforcing the centripetal forces at work, is readily observable in international financial transactions.

Market-making

Prices are set in some organized markets by means of auctions. A feature of the tendering system used for the sale of Treasury bills and Treasury bonds in many countries is that, once the terms of the auction are set, the sellers remain passive while the buyers determine the price of the quantity offered for sale. This passivity is eminently suited for the sale of government securities, but not for private markets in which sellers may want to haggle with the buyers.

Haggling does feature in the oral auctions (open outcry or double auctions) which occur on futures markets whereby many bids and offers are called out simultaneously and deals are struck on the spot. For reasons noted above, in order to succeed this method of setting prices needs a considerable volume of trade and a regular flow of orders onto the market-place, so as to ensure the maintenance of market liquidity. A regular flow onto futures markets is ensured by the seasonal ups and downs of agricultural and manufacturing production while liquidity comes from restricting both the number of contracts traded and the number of floor traders. Heavily traded securities on the New York Stock Exchange continuously auctioned on the dealing floor approximate the open outcry pits of futures exchanges. These methods are less well suited to markets in which offers to buy and sell arrive intermittently. In these markets, transactors must decide whether to strike a deal on present terms or hold off and observe market trades and otherwise search out information about prospective market conditions. Not only is this search costly but transactors must bear the risk that market prices move adversely in the interim. In the terminology of Demsetz (1968), transactors lose the benefits of 'immediacy'.

In these markets, temporary prices are instead set by market-makers, who buy up securities from the mass of sellers and on-sell them to the buyers, normally at a higher price. Some middlemen, such as the specialists in the New York Stock Exchange dealing in the less actively-traded stocks and market-makers in the UK gilt-edged market, are obliged to quote, on demand and in most trading conditions, continuous and effective two-way prices at which they stand committed to deal. In other markets, market-making is an entrepreneurial response by market participants who are prepared to take a position on their own account. Other market participants are willing to deal with them because buy and sell orders are executed more or less immediately. In offering this 'on demand' service to transactors the market-maker needs to be well informed about potential transactors and market conditions. They must also be prepared to absorb securities into their own holdings to buffer short-run disparities between demand and supply. If at any point there is an excess supply temporarily in the market, the market-maker will purchase assets for his own account at the bid price. In response to a temporary excess demand, sales will take place out of stock at the asking price.

By acting as residual buyers and sellers in the market, the market-makers provide liquidity services in a number of ways. Transactors do not themselves need to acquire information about the availability of the securities; the market-makers in effect provide fast information for a fee, lowering search and transfer costs. Holding inventories of the asset to absorb imbalances in demand and supply enables market-makers to 'break lots', narrow the price changes between sales and thus contribute to the stability of market prices. From the viewpoint of potential participants, the market-makers provide immediate marketability, ready reversibility, divisibility and 'insurance' against fluctuations in price due to the irregular flow of transactions onto the market. They also offer another insurance facility, for payment to them for these services occurs only if the transaction is successfully completed. By levying brokerage fees and demanding an ask price in excess of bid (the bid–ask spread), market-makers insure transactors against the risk that any costs otherwise incurred in entering the market and searching for a trade will not be wasted. They guarantee that the transaction will be carried out at a satisfactory price.[11]

When providing liquidity services for a fee, market-makers incur various costs and take on certain risks.[12] Real resource costs are incurred by market-makers when acting as repositories of information and processors of orders, i.e. when acting as *brokers*. These include the labour cost of dealers and back room staff, cost of communications equipment, cost of clearing and record keeping, rent, membership fees and costs of obtaining a seat on the exchange etc. Holding costs come from the inventories needed by market-makers to offer 'on demand' facilities to transactors. Two sets of inventories are in fact needed, one of the assets dealt in so as to meet customers' immediate purchase orders, the other of money held or borrowed in order to take up unforeseen sales, and market-makers must recover from the difference between bid and ask prices the borrowing costs and opportunity costs of capital tied up in these stocks.

The major risk facing the market-making firm is of a change in the underlying price of the security when holding a long or short position. A fall off in demand will see transactors sell to the market-maker, which in turn must sell off the accumulated stocks at the new (lower) price or build up risks which its capital cannot sustain if purchases continue while the price continues to fall. These risks derive from the market-maker's inability to judge market trends correctly or failure to adjust bid–ask prices quickly enough in response to altered market conditions, or from the market-maker's trading with people who possess better information about the factors prompting the revaluation of the security (the insider information problem).[13]

Market-making firms, in common with many other intermediaries in financial markets, are able to reduce these costs and mitigate the risks in a number of ways; through scale economies in operation, by pooling of risks and by adopting the appropriate mix of flexi- and fixed-price responses.

Making a market in a security involves handling considerable amounts of information – about those companies the securities of which are being transacted, general economic and financial conditions, actual and prospective market participants – and the properties of information and search activities are an important determinant of the real resource costs of market-making firms. Institutions are confronted with current and prospective demands and supplies of funds arising from various sources. Suppose the institution is conducting random searches of funds sources and that there are a finite number of potential sources of funds per period, of which only a small proportion will turn out to be actual sources. By expending a given amount of resources on monitoring a subset of potential sources, the intermediary will, on average, locate a particular number of actual sources. As more resources are spent the mean number of actual locations found per pound may not alter but the variability of locations found per period will tend to fall. The relatively smoother flow of information about prospective suppliers and demanders so realized will show up as a narrower bid–ask spread reflecting the lower risk in matching up orders at profitable spreads. This scale economy is directly analogous to the reserve asset management principles which underlie the operation of financial intermediaries such as banks and savings institutions.

Market-makers' exposure to adverse price movements associated with their positions in specific assets can be offset by diversifying inventory holdings. Long positions in one asset can be set against short positions in others as long as the assets have independent fates, exploiting the standard principles of risk pooling. As the institution expands beyond the original subset of markets and takes positions in extra securities, however, it must monitor more and more assets with which it is less familiar. Hence the benefits of diversifying independent risk must to some extent be balanced against skills in processing information which may be enhanced by specializing in a limited number of securities.

Positions in one market can also be offset in other markets where, as in the case of the stock market, for example, futures and options markets exist for the assets traded. On the New York Stock Exchange, stocks can be bought and sold either on the floor of the exchange, through specialists, or 'upstairs' across the trading desks of the investment banks, in which dealers search out counter-parties or take securities onto their own books. They are prepared to make a market and supply immediacy, because use of stock index futures or options contracts enables a floor to be put under holding losses while the parcel of stocks is being 'warehoused'. For instance, a dealer can hedge against price falls by selling index futures contracts; should prices fall, the profit made from closing out the futures position with a buy order would offset the loss incurred on the stocks. The ability to shift risk between markets in this way implies that the markets for stocks, stock index futures and options effectively form one market, and position-takers in all three can be looked upon as combined risk-bearers.

Position-taking risks can also be reduced by operating with smaller stocks. The only mechanism by which inventories can be adjusted is through the attainment of market clearance at a different price. In response to the excess supply considered earlier, the market-maker needs to decrease buy–sell quotations so as to encourage expected demand and discourage supply. Markets in which trading volumes are large and sensitive to fluctuations in demand and supply, such as those for actively traded shares on the stock market, will be flexi-price markets because in such volatile conditions the market-makers will be reluctant to build up large positions entailing large risks. In other markets where trading is thin and sporadic, and the arrival of new information about the 'true' value of the asset is slow and infrequent, prices are adjusted more slowly. By providing a continuous market for such securities, the market-maker eliminates the wide short-term price swings which would otherwise occur with each transaction. When the market-makers infer from an altered pattern of trading orders that conditions may have changed and new information is arriving more rapidly, prices will be adjusted more frequently.

Market-makers' insurance against fluctuations in price and the market-ability they offer to would-be sellers thus illustrates the phenomenon of 'fair-weather' liquidity (Simmons, 1947). Dealers' ability to take securities onto their books and restrain the magnitude of price falls is limited by their capital base. Faced with a preponderance of sell orders and a build up of open positions, dealers would move down their quoted prices. Economic theory suggests that trade in speculative markets, *even when new information arrives*, can arise only if (rational) traders have differences of opinion,[14] and such unusual market conditions may be characterized by a general belief that prices must fall. When no buyers are elicited, market-makers would drop prices further and restrict quotations to the minimum allowable parcels which can be traded.[15] Asset prices can fall sharply with few actual deals being struck as market-makers mark down prices to limit exposures. Worse, during a period of rising prices, market-makers are likely to build up inventories of securities in the expectation of reselling later on a rising market, so boosting trading profits. This practice enables them to keep ask–bid spreads low, enhancing marketability and stimulating trading activity in good times. In bad times, customers' excess of selling orders is likely to be augmented by market-makers' attempts to liquidate their own positions, causing prices to decline further.

Trading halts and various other 'circuit breakers' have been recommended for the stock market in such circumstances, mainly to allow information to be disseminated more widely, hopefully drawing potential buyers into the market (see Brady Commission, 1988; Greenwald and Stein, 1988; Miles, 1988). But the possibility that trading will be suspended may merely encourage traders to 'jump the gun' and trigger the circumstances which bring trading to a halt. The simple 'fact of life, so apparent in October [1987, is] that markets have a limited capacity to absorb massive one-sided volume' (Brady Commission, 1988). Indeed, the Commission advocated restriction of trading precisely to formalize this fact and serve as a reminder of the 'illusion of liquidity'.

The argument here must be that traders were encouraged to buy on a rising market in the mistaken belief that they could insure or unload their portfolio quickly when the upward trend turned.[16] This illusion undoubtedly did contribute to the overvaluation of shares and the severity of the subsequent fall, but restrictions which could hamper liquidity in normal times and, by disconnecting the futures and cash markets, reduce risk-bearing capacity in abnormal times seem unhelpful.

Activities of banks

Banks are also repositories of information; they offer 'on demand' services to customers and 'insure' them against fluctuations in the market prices of assets. While they are major participants in organized markets, their major economic function, we argue, is to act as the market-makers in the informal financial markets referred to earlier.

Market-makers need to monitor the performance of entities whose securities are being inventoried, but dealers in the organized securities markets are unwilling to keep track of the activities of the many small firms which might turn out to be occasional minor borrowers. For their part, the firms are often reluctant to release publicly the information needed for markets issues of securities, which in any case is costly to provide. Banks' role as financers for small enterprises is shaped by the characteristics of the market for information. Because of the moral hazards inherent in the separation of savings from investments which gives rise to the information asymmetry between insiders and outsiders – the lender's risk noted in section 11.1 – a prospective lender needs to be given full details of the prospects of the investment project. Provision of this information by the investor involves him in the risk that the knowledge advantage he has may be given away in the process. 'The entrepreneur needs the lender, but once the lender has the information he no longer needs the entrepreneur' (Casson, 1982, p. 211). Banks have evolved to resolve this potential conflict of interest.

Banks establish a reputation for handling such knowledge responsibly. A relationship is formed with the customer in which the bank is provided with a regular flow of information which it voluntarily undertakes not to exploit in competition with the customer. Instead, the information is 'internalized' in the bank's investments in the customer's business. It is also in the nature of information that much of it is generated as a byproduct of other activities. In the case of banks, their provision of payment services enables them to be in touch with potential borrowers and build up a profile of their suitability for loans. That information is also privileged and can best be utilized by taking a position in the securities of the firm. Unlike market-makers, banks take a position by writing special contracts with the firms concerned. These contracts are designed with covenants and collateral to overcome lenders' risks, but also reflect the other liquidity services offered by banks.

We are used to thinking of banks as a collection of assets and liabilities, or a balance sheet. The conception preferred here is of banks as a collection of contracts. These contracts are the means by which the informal financial markets simultaneously satisfy savers' need for liquidity with lenders' desire for illiquidity. Divergences in preferences like these constitute an obstacle to trade's taking place, and the market solution is for banks (indeed financial intermediaries generally) to issue contracts to borrowers and lenders which differ from those which would be exchanged on the organized markets. Differences in these contracts define what is meant by the familiar description that financial intermediaries 'create liquidity'. For example, borrowers from banks are able to obtain funds for longer periods and depositors lend for shorter periods than would occur in the absence of banking. Depositors can make a claim against the bank 'on demand' in the circumstance of being short of cash.

As market-makers, banks can be visualized as purchasing securities from borrowers of funds and reselling them to lenders of funds with insurances and guarantees added: the 'insurance premium' for this service is covered in the bid–offer spread (i.e. the interest rate margin) and service charges.[17] Banks' guarantees go much further than those of other market-makers. In the organized markets, dealers guarantee predictability during execution of the trade in the sense that securities can be purchased (sold) at a better price than might otherwise be the case, but thereafter the risk of adverse price movements is passed on to the wealth-holders. This is not so with banks, for they continue to guarantee full predictability of value. Despite holding assets which individually have some risk, banks assure depositors that their funds can be realized at full capital value. While holding large portfolios of securities which cannot be sold individually, banks offer depositors the option to withdraw or transfer balances on demand or at short notice. On the other side of the balance sheet, borrowers from banks are insured against interest rates on their loans fluctuating daily, despite variations each day in the bank's cost of funds. Banks assure borrowers that loans will not have to be repaid within the period over which the funds are committed.

These are features of the contracts which appear on the balance sheet. In their off-balance-sheet activities,[18] banks provide for customers' liquidity needs by note issuance facilities and discount commitments – both contractual contingent obligations – whereby they guarantee the continuance of funding over periods as long as ten years to buy the notes which cannot be placed at the interest cost specified in the underwriting contract. Through activities such as bill acceptances, standby letters of credit and other financial guarantees, banks 'guarantee' payment of a customer's liability to a holder of its debt should the customer default. Although the initial incidence of the fee charged for this service is on the bank's customer (the borrower), the ultimate effect of lower yield is equivalent to the holder of risky (higher-yieding) paper paying a premium to the bank, in terms of forgone interest, for insurance against default. This is precisely equivalent to a depositor accepting an insurance policy from a bank in lieu of uninsured income from securities traded on the organized markets.

Banks are able to offer these guarantees in part because of their access to privileged information about loan prospects (discussed above), in part by employing an appropriate mix of fixed–flexi price strategies according to the characteristics of the markets (retail, wholesale, international) in which they operate, but mainly by taking advantage of economies of scale in the management of reserves of capital and money. A bank must be able to convince depositors that, despite having an asset portfolio composed of (at least partly) risky assets, its deposit liabilities can be redeemed at full value. This is achieved by a buffer stock of shareholders' funds which absorbs losses due to default on assets or capital losses on unanticipated security sales. Not all loans fail for the same reasons and, as long as there exists imperfect correlation in the fate of the different loans and investments, having a large and diversified range of assets allows risk of default to be pooled and reduced. Each depositor may hold the option of conversion into cash on demand but has no idea when the need may arise. When large numbers of liquidity options are combined and large numbers of loans are pooled, regularities emerge which enable banks to guarantee the spendability of their assets while making a profit.

When diversifying across independent risks of loan default and deposit variability, the principle of risk pooling relies on increases in the scale of bank portfolios, but the pooling can be within the firm or across firms. In the case of a large bank or one with an extensive branch network, the pooling occurs within the banking firm. This is the usual situation in retail banking. In wholesale or international banking, characterized by large-valued transactions, interbank funds markets and syndication of loans enables the pooling to occur outside the firm but within the group of banks. Liquidity is created by the banking system as a whole.

Bank Failure and Loss of Liquidity

An individual bank may fail to meet its contractual obligations to provide liquidity services for a number of reasons. First there is the inherent riskiness of the set of earning assets chosen by the bank and the contingent commitments it has undertaken. These risks reflect default possibilities and/or variability in the market price at some expected selling date of assets it holds or may be forced to acquire. Second, there are the additional risks created by the composition of the asset portfolio as between earning assets and reserves. Holding a low reserves–earning assets ratio may lead to liquidation costs if deposit outfows are large and unexpected sales of assets are required. Third, banks are very highly geared and, the lower is the equity–deposit ratio, the less likely it is that the promised returns to depositors and holders of contingent liabilities can be met out of the uncertain value of the assets and contingent claims held.

Experiences in the 1980s have demonstrated unequivocally that bankers do engage in 'risky business'. But a consistent theme in banking is the vulnerability of even well-managed banks to a 'bank run'. The problem lies in the form of the deposit contract and the unstated premise whereby the deposit of funds in an institution providing liquidity services relies upon a particular form of behaviour from other depositors. Specifically, a demand deposit contract provides investment in illiquid assets packaged together with 'insurance' for the depositor that liquidity is available if required. That insurance package is viable only if some small fraction of depositors demand liquidity. In the normal run of events it will be possible to estimate that fraction and provide for liquidity needs. However, while a depositor's demand for liquidity will depend normally on external factors (the standard hazards of life), it may also be prompted by concerns about the behaviour of other depositors and solvency of the bank. Should a change in the behaviour of other customers be expected to occur, it becomes sensible to withdraw funds.

In Diamond and Dybvig's (1983) model, now the classic analysis, a bank has a 'good' and 'bad' equilibrium. A three-period horizon ($T = 0, 1, 2$) is envisaged with investing choices governed by a productive process that returns R greater than one unit in $T = 2$ of the sole consumption good but only one unit if accumulation is interrupted at time $T = 1$. Portfolio choices must be made at time $T = 0$ while consumption needs are revealed later depending on whether the investor–consumer turns out to be a type 1 or type 2 person. Autarky can be improved upon by a bank which writes a deposit contract enabling type 1 people to consume C_1 and type 2 people to consume C_2 where $1 < C_1 < C_2 < R$. This payout is the 'good' equilibrium. A situation in which type 1 consumers withdrawing deposits at time $T = 1$ are joined by type 2 people is a 'bad' equilibrium because when all seek to withdraw deposits at time $T = 1$ the promised value of deposits plus interest cannot be met from the liquidation value of bank assets.

This change in behaviour (whether actual or expected) of depositors imposes an externality on the others, since any costs of liquidating a part of the asset portfolio to meet withdrawals are met by the remaining depositors rather than by those withdrawing funds. To avoid that externality, customers join the run, thereby aggravating the problem for those left.[19]

Observing difficulties at one bank, depositors at other banks are unable to assess whether the problem is specific to that bank or common to a wider set of financial institutions. They may reassess the soundness of the other banks or simply fear, for whatever reason, that the run may catch hold. Once depositors lack confidence that their liquidity needs will be met, banks may be unable to make good their promises to repay deposits at face value. Nor will they be able to make good their provision of illiquidity to borrowers by continuing to supply funding over the period of the loan. When, instead, premature repayment is demanded, the borrowers may not be able to obtain alternative funds on the same terms, and perhaps not at all, from other institutions.

Solutions to the Problem of Bank Runs

One solution (not considered by Diamond and Dybvig) is for banks to have shareholders willing to commit sufficient assets as collateral so that depositors are assured that their claims can be met.[20] The difficulty here is that collateral is normally not pawned but mortgaged, and recourse to courts of law is needed for the assets to pass into the hands of debtors, a process which is both uncertain and slow, and unlikely to reassure depositors with consumption needs pending. In fact, banks probably came into existence because of the inefficiency of the law in enforcing debts (Hicks, 1969).

In Diamond and Dybvig's model, banks hold illiquid capital assets. It used to be argued that banks should confine themselves to 'self-liquidating' loans (e.g. trade bills) on the grounds that deposits can be repaid from the receipts of maturing assets.[21] That would be so only if other bankers expanded their loans. A universal move to run down loans would see distress sales of assets, distress savings of funds and the calling in of debts which marks 'foul-weather' liquidity.[22] Ideas that banks hold 'shiftable' assets, i.e. assets sold on strong and active organized markets, suffer from a similar fallacy of composition.[23] Marketable securities are shiftable only if the majority of holders simultaneously refrain from attempts to liquidate them, so avoiding large one-sided selling pressures.

Diamond and Dybvig's suggestion is that banks can defend themselves against runs simply by suspending convertibility of deposits into cash. One way is for the redemption of deposits 'on demand' to be made optional at the discretion of the bank. Currency could also be allowed to trade at a premium relative to deposits, so imposing a penalty on those wishing to encash deposits: this was the method used by the New York Clearinghouse prior to the establishment of the Federal Reserve System. Finally, banks could unilaterally renege on contractual commitments to customers and close their doors: the solution commonly used by banks confronted by runs in earlier times. All impose costs on depositors in the form of unwanted and unpredictable losses of liquidity. None may bolster confidence in banks.

Since confidence has the characteristics of a public good, in most countries communal arrangements (central banks, industry support schemes, government deposit insurance schemes) have been introduced to maintain confidence in the banking system and thus sustain the liquidity of bank contracts. These might be thought to be analogous to the clearing houses which guarantee the fulfilment of futures contracts by members and thereby ensure the liquidity of futures contracts. There are two major differences. Just as the liability of a bank is constrained by its cash reserves, so also are the liabilities of the clearing house limited by the commodities pledged for delivery in settlement of futures commitments. But, unlike a bank, there need not be a tight relationship between the two, for it is always possible (and in fact usual) to reverse a futures position by an offsetting transaction prior to maturity. This reversal is at prices currently prevailing, not the original ones, so that the illiquidity risk translates into a price squeeze (Telser, 1981).

Second, any system which guarantees the performance of market participants runs into the moral hazard problem, for the willingness of the beneficiaries of the guarantees to take risks may increase. In order to limit risk, members of a futures exchange must deposit money with the clearing house as a reserve against possible losses. They must also keep margins of cash as a percentage of the value entailed in the transaction, and these cash margins must be adjusted in line with changes in market prices of futures. Members of the exchange, in turn, levy cash margins against their customers. These margins raise the cost of carrying a position in a contract and thus act to curb exposures. In contrast, bank regulatory authorities do not possess (or choose not to implement) a flexible margining arrangement.

Many of the proposals to solve the 'problem of bank liquidity' can be seen as attempts to move the mechanisms for bank safety closer to the example of private clearing houses. A popular suggestion is the substitution of risk-based for flat rate insurance premiums presently paid for government deposit insurance. In effect, this is sought as a means of flexibly 'margining' bank risk exposures, but difficulties have been found in devising formulae free of potential abuse.[24] Risk-based capital requirements, however, are being introduced.

Others argue that banks go too far in the guarantees and see a solution to the problem of bank safety in terms of fundamental reforms to the nature of banks and banking contracts. Bank runs occur because deposits are repaid on a 'first-come first-served fixed-price' basis, so that any concern that a bank cannot maintain a fixed price for deposits in the face of declining asset values makes it sensible for depositors to withdraw balances immediately. This incentive would diminish if instead banks operated like mutual funds, valuing and redeeming all deposits in line with the current market value of assets.[25] By marking deposits to market, liquidity squeezes would be converted into price squeezes, as occurs on the organized markets.

'Mutual fund banking', as the proposal is called, is an interesting idea but it ignores that there are good reasons why banks have taken on their present form. A strong desire exists among many depositors in terms of their liquidity preferences to hold claims which give full nominal guarantees. Over the time period relevant for transactions decisions, predictability in money rather than real terms presumably saves on calculation and decision-making costs. For mutual-fund-type accounts to be acceptable as transactions accounts, relatively low price variability is likely to be required. In order to ensure little price variability, backing in the form of liquid marketable assets would have to be held,[26] in sharp contrast with traditional bank advances to individuals and firms for which no deep secondary markets exist. They do not exist because only those with access to the same privileged information supplied to the bankers would be in a position to evaluate the securities' intrinsic market worth. The problem of bank liquidity cannot be solved by dispensing with banks' distinctive information services.

11.4 Conclusions

Indirect ownership of wealth is perhaps the most distinctive feature of modern developed economies. Individuals and households ultimately own the real assets, but delegate control through a network of markets. A central position in these markets is occupied by the market-makers. They, and not the auctioneer of economic theory, are the coordinators of trade. In the financial markets, both formal and informal, market-making intermediaries such as banks, dealers and specialists provide the 'market liquidity' which simultaneously satisfies the liquidity preferences of savers with the desire for illiquidity on the part of those investing in tangible wealth.

Liquidity in most of the definitions employed is found on examination to rest on a 'confidence trick'. Nevertheless, while illusory, the promise of flexibility afforded by the network of markets is important as it reduces the costs of having specialized positions in production and trade and lowers the risk premiums demanded to hold illiquid securities, so encouraging wealth-holders to invest more than they otherwise would in tangible inflexible assets. Those whose interest does not lie at all in holding illiquid assets may nonetheless contribute indirectly to their acquisition.

Markets can be thought of as like concertinas. When confidence is high, demand and supply shift out and markets offer considerable flexibility. When expectations are reversed, markets concertina in as both supply and demand contract. In the latter circumstances, the creation of liquidity by market intermediaries, so important for the working of markets in good times, becomes fragile. Banks and other market-makers in their normal operations are exposed to market risks of various kinds and structure their activities to limit their openness to losses. Risk pooling, diversification of portfolios and the utilization of economies of scale in holding inventories of securities and money are all part of those strategies. It is precisely in the nature of such activities that they provide insurance to the institutions only against 'normal risks'. Any attempt to protect themselves against abnormal risks like a bank run or liquidity crisis would mean forgoing normally profitable business in order to hold large inventories of securities and money, and competitive forces can be expected to lead financial institutions to make insufficient allowance for such possibilities when they set prices.

In order to ensure that the transformation of short-term liquid savings into long-term inflexible investments can continue without interruption, institutions group together in collective arrangements and receive government support. Governments, of course, cannot alter the nature of the tangible illiquid assets which lie at the end of the transformation process. It is merely the case that in a crisis governments are better able to sustain the confidence necessary for the 'illusion of liquidity' to continue.

NOTES

1 Presley (1988) contends that 'liquidity preference came initially from Hicks, and not from Keynes' (p. 11), but he is referring more to the breadth of the theory in Hicks's 'A suggestion for simplifying the theory of money' (1935) than to its genesis.
2 In line with national accounting conventions, consumer durables are excluded, being counted as consumption expenditure in their year of acquisition, while difficulties in measurement led the statisticians to omit any calculation of the value of assets of national resources, such as coal and oil, which are still in the 'ground', and also the value of the skills and expertise embodied in the labour force, i.e. human capital.
3 See Harcourt (1972) for a survey and critique.
4 The Brady Commission (1988) refers to the 'illusion of liquidity'.
5 The description is by Moore (1968).
6 This is the expression used by Baumol (1965, p. 3).
7 The advantages of internalizing market transactions are considered by Casson (1982, ch. 10).
8 The other explanations (see Gilbert, 1977) are that compensating balances allow banks to increase the return on loans and that they are required so that banks can pay implicit interest on demand deposits. (The latter explanation, however, seems to suffer from the fact that the holding of the balances is enforced rather than made willingly.)
9 Pierce (1966) and Moore (1968) construct curves with these axes.
10 See O'Driscoll (1985) for a recent account.

11 This argument belongs to Casson (1982).

12 Beginning with Demsetz (1968) a number of workers have examined the costs and risks of market-making in organized markets. Goodhart (1989) gives a recent survey.

13 The core idea here is that a market-maker faces an 'adverse selection' problem because those informed traders ('insiders') who possess non-public information know more about the true worth of the firm's securities than either the dealers or other traders ('outsiders'). Market-makers are bound to lose money to those trading on the basis of superior information, and the losses must be recovered from the bid–ask spread.

14 A number of authors have demonstrated that in a speculative market consisting of fully rational traders with identical prior information there will be a no trade equilibrium (Rubenstein, 1975; Milgrom and Stokey, 1982; Varian, 1985). Ways around the 'no trade theorem' are to suppose that there are irrational traders, trade due to hedging, or different prior beliefs. Given the assumptions, the latter must be due to differences in opinion not information, so that people interpret the same news differently.

15 In the London Stock Exchange the minimum sized quotation that dealers are obliged to post is 1,000 shares, and this is the bargain that many dealers posted immediately after 19th October 1987. Usually dealers quote offers in parcels up to 100,000 shares.

16 The Brady Commission reports that portfolio insurance models typically require the sale of 20 per cent of stocks or stock index futures when the market declines by 10 per cent. Portfolio managers seeking to follow such strategies came to the New York Stock Exchange on Monday, 19 October 1987, with $8 billion of stocks which their models said should already have been sold, but which they had been unable to sell in previous trading. This created immediate selling pressure.

17 The conception of banks as insurers is explored by Haubrich and King (1984), Lewis and Davis (1987) and Lewis (1989).

18 Surveyed by Lewis (1988).

19 Goodhart (1985) and Freeman (1988) also examine the potential fragility of the banking system. Dowd (1989) provides a critical survey of the literature.

20 In Diamond and Dybvig's model the distinction between depositors and shareholders is blurred, and I am indebted to Kevin Dowd for suggesting this possible market solution.

21 This is the basis of the so-called 'real bills doctrine'. See Mints (1945) for an examination of the historical development of the doctrine.

22 The term is due to Simmons (1947).

23 This was first pointed out by Whitney (1934).

24 Hirschhorn (1986) and Murton (1986) survey the literature and issues.

25 Mutual fund banking is examined by Goodhart (1989) and O'Driscoll (1985).

26 In this respect, mutual fund banking is essentially 100 per cent reserve banking where the reserves comprise highly marketable and predictable securities.

REFERENCES

Baumol, W. J. (1965) *The Stock Market and Economic Efficiency*. New York: Fordham University Press.

Brady Commission (1988) *Report of the Presidential Task Force on Market Mechanisms*. Washington, D.C.: US Government Printing Office.

Bronfenbrenner, M., and T. Mayer (1960) 'Liquidity functions in the American economy', *Econometrica* 28, October, 810–34.

Bryant, C. G. E. (1987) 'National and sector balance sheet 1957–85', *Economic Trends* 403, May, 92–119.

Bryant, R. C. (1981) 'Bank collapse and depression', *Journal of Money, Credit and Banking* 13 (4), November, 454–64.

Burns, J. M. (1979) *A Treatise on Markets*. Washington, D.C.: American Enterprise Institute.

Cagan, P. (1969) 'A study of liquidity premiums on federal and municipal government securities', in *Essays on Interest Rates*. Ed. J. M. Guttentag and P. Cagan, New York: National Bureau of Economic Research, pp. 107–42.

Casson, M. (1982) *The Entrepreneur. An Economic Theory*. Oxford: Martin Robertson.

Christ, C. F. (1963) 'Interest rates and "portfolio selection" among liquid assets in the US', *Measurement in Economics: Studies in Mathematical Economics and Econometrics*. Ed. C. F. Christ, Stanford, Calif.: Stanford University Press, pp. 201–18.

Clower, R. W. (1967) 'A reconsideration of the microfoundations of monetary theory', *Western Economic Journal* 6, 1–9.

Clower, R. W. (1969) *Monetary Theory*. Harmondsworth: Penguin.

Clower, R., and A. Leijonhufvud (1975) The coordination of economic activities: a Keynesian perspective', *American Economic Review* 65, May, 182–8.

Cohen, K. J., S. F. Maier, R. A. Schwartz, and D. K. Whitcomb (1986) *The Microstructure of Securities Markets*. Englewood Cliffs, N.J.: Prentice-Hall.

Conard, J. W. (1966) *The Behavior of Interest Rates – A Progess Report*. New York: National Bureau of Economic Research.

Davidson, P. (1978) 'Why money matters: lessons from a half-century of monetary theory', *Journal of Post-Keynesian Economics* 1 (1), Fall, 46–70.

Demsetz, H. (1968) 'The cost of transacting', *Quarterly Journal of Economics* 82, February, 33–53.

Diamond, D. W., and P. H. Dybvig (1983) 'Bank runs, deposit insurance and liquidity', *Journal of Political Economy* 91 (3), 401–19.

Dowd, K. (1989) *The State and the Monetary System*. Oxford: Philip Allan.

Economides, N., and A. Siow (1988) 'The division of markets is limited by the extent of liquidity', *American Economic Review* 78, March, 108–21.

Farmer, R. E. A. (1988) 'What is a liquidity crisis?', *Journal of Economic Theory* 46 (1), October, 1–15.

Feige, E. L. (1964) *The Demand for Liquid Assets: A Temporal Cross-Section Analysis*. Englewood Cliffs, N.J.: Prentice-Hall.

Fisher, I. (1930) *The Theory of Interest*. Reprinted 1961, New York: A. M. Kelley.

Freeman, S. (1988) 'Banking as the provision of liquidity', *The Journal of Business*, 61 (1), January, 45–64.

Friedman, M., and A. J. Schwartz (1970) *Monetary Statistics of the United States*. New York: National Bureau of Economic Research.

Frost, P. (1966) 'Bank's demand for excess reserves', unpublished Ph.D. dissertation, University of California, Los Angeles.

Gilbert, A. (1977) 'Effects of interest on demand deposits: implications of compensating balances', *Federal Reserve Bank of St Louis Review*, November, 8–14.

Goodhart, C. A. E. (1985) *The Evolution of Central Banks*. London: Suntony-Toyota International Centre for Economic and Related Disciplines, London School of Economics.

Goodhart, C. A. E. (1989) *Money, Information and Uncertainty*, 2nd ed. London: Macmillan.

Goodwin, R. M. (1949) 'Liquidity and uncertainty – discussion', *American Economic Review* 39 (3), May, 199–201.

Greenwald, G., and J. Stein (1988) 'The task force report: the reasoning behind the recommendations', *Journal of Economic Perspectives* 2 (3), Summer, 3–23.

Gurley, J. G. (1960) 'Liquidity and financial institutions in the postwar period', Study Paper No. 14, material prepared in connection with the study of employment, growth, and price levels for consideration by the Joint Economic Committee Congress of the United States. Washington, D.C.: Government Printing Office.

Gurley, J. G., and E. S. Shaw (1955) 'Financial aspects of economic development', *American Economic Review* 45, September, 515–38.

Gurley, J. G., and E. S. Shaw (1956) 'Financial intermediaries and the savings–investment process', *Journal of Finance* 11, May, 257–76.

Gurley, J. G., and E. S. Shaw (1960) *Money in a Theory of Finance*. Washington, D.C.: The Brookings Institution.

Harcourt, G. C. (1972) *Some Cambridge Controversies in the Theory of Capital*. Cambridge: Cambridge University Press.

Hart, A. G. (1949) 'Liquidity and uncertainty: assets, liquidity and investment', *American Economic Review*, 39 (3), May, 171–81.

Hartley, P. R. (1988) 'The liquidity services of money', *International Economic Review* 29 (1), February, 1–23.

Haubrich, J. G., and R. G. King (1984) 'Banking and insurance', Working Paper No. 1312, National Bureau of Economic Research.

Hicks, J. R. (1935) 'A suggestion for simplifying the theory of money', *Economica*, 2, 1–9.

Hicks, J. R. (1962) 'Liquidity', *Economic Journal* 72, December, 787–802.

Hicks, J. R. (1969) *A Theory of Economic History*. Oxford: Clarendon.

Hicks, J. R. (1974) *The Crisis in Keynesian Economics*. Oxford: Blackwell.

Hirschhorn, E. (1986) 'Developing a risk-related premium structure', in *Proceedings of a Conference on Bank Structure and Competition*. Chicago, Ill.: Federal Reserve Bank of Chicago.

Hirschleifer, J. (1972), 'Liquidity, uncertainty and the accumulation of information', in *Uncertainty and Expectations in Economics. Essays in Honour of G L S*

Shackle. Ed. C. F. Carter and J. L. Ford, Oxford: Blackwell, pp. 136–47.

Jones, R. A., and J. M. Ostroy, (1984) 'Flexibility and uncertainty', *Review of Economic Studies* 51, 13–32.

Kareken, J. H., and N. Wallace (1980) 'Introduction', in *Models of Monetary Economies.* Ed. J. H. Kareken and N. Wallace, Minneapolis, Minn.: Federal Reserve Bank of Minneapolis.

Kessel, R. A. (1965) *The Cyclical Behavior of the Term Structure of Interest Rates.* New York: National Bureau of Economic Research.

Keynes, J. M. (1930) *A Treatise on Money*, 2 vols. London: Macmillan.

Keynes, J. M. (1936) *The General Theory of Employment, Interest and Money.* London: Macmillan.

Kreinin, M. E. (1961) 'Analysis of liquid ownership', *Review of Economics and Statistics* 43, February, 76–80.

Kreps, D. M. (1979) 'A representation theorem for "preference for flexibility"', *Econometrica* 47 (3), 565–77.

Lancaster, K. J. (1966) 'Change and innovation in the technology of consumption', *American Economic Review* 56 (2), 14–23.

Lewis, M. K. (1988) 'Off-balance sheet activity and its regulation', in *The Management of Bank Assets and Liabilities.* Ed. J. S. G. Wilson, London: Euromoney Publications, pp. 161–204.

Lewis, M. K. (1989) 'Banking as insurance', in *The Future of Financial Systems and Services.* Ed. E. P. M. Gardener, London: Macmillan.

Lewis, M. K. and K. T. Davis (1987) *Domestic and International Banking.* Oxford: Philip Allan; Cambridge, Mass.: MIT Press.

Lippman, S. A., and J. J. McCall (1986) 'An operational measure of liquidity', *American Economic Review* 76, March, 43–55.

McCallum, B. T. (1983) 'The role of the overlapping generations model in monetary economics', *Carnegie-Rochester Series*, 18, pp. 9–44.

Machlup, F. (1966) 'The fuzzy concepts of liquidity, international and domestic', *International Monetary Economics.* London: George Allen & Unwin.

McKean, R. N. (1949) 'Liquidity and a national balance sheet', *Journal of Political Economy* 57, 506–22.

Makower, H., and J. Marschak (1938) 'Assets, prices and monetary theory', *Economica* 5, August, 261–88.

Marschak, J. (1938) 'Money and the theory of assets', *Econometrica* 6, 311–25.

Marschak, J. (1949) 'Role of liquidity under complete and incomplete information', *American Economic Review* 39, 182–95.

Marshall, A. (1920) *Principles of Economics.* London: Macmillan.

Meigs, A. J. (1962) *Free Reserves and the Money Supply.* Chicago, Ill.: University of Chicago Press.

Menger, K. (1892) 'On the origin of money', *Economic Journal* 2, 239–55.

Menger, K. (1950) *Principles of Economics.* Trans. J. Dingwall and B. F. Hoselitz, Glencoe, Ill.: Irwin.

Miles, D. (1988) 'An appraisal of stock markets circuit breakers', Discussion Paper No. 0030, LSE Financial Markets Group.

Milgrom, P. R., and N. Stokey (1982) 'Information, trade and common knowledge', *Journal of Economic Theory* 26, 17–27.

Mints, L. W. (1945) *A History of Banking Theory in Great Britain and the United States*. Chicago, Ill.: University of Chicago Press.

Morrison, G. R. (1966) *Liquidity Preferences of Commercial Banks*. Chicago, Ill.: University of Chicago Press.

Moore, B. J. (1968) *An Introduction to the Theory of Finance*. New York: Free Press.

Mundell, R. A. (1968) *Man and Economics*. New York: McGraw-Hill.

Murton, A. J. (1986) 'A survey of the issues and the literature concerning risk-related deposit insurance', *Banking and Economic Review* 4 (6), September–October, 11–20.

Newlyn, W. T. (1962) *Theory of Money*. Oxford: Clarendon.

Neuman, A. M. (1935) 'The doctrine of liquidity', *Review of Economic Studies* 3 (1), October, 81–99.

O'Driscoll, G. P. (1985) 'Money: Menger's evolutionary theory', Research Paper No. 8508, Federal Reserve Bank of Dallas.

Okun, A. M. (1981) *Prices and Quantities: A Macroeconomic Analysis*. Oxford: Blackwell.

Orr, D. (1970) *Cash Management and the Demand for Money*. New York: Praeger.

Pierce, J. L. (1966) 'Commercial bank liquidity', *Federal Reserve Bulletin* 52, August, 1093–101.

Presley, J. R. (1988) 'Sir John Hicks: contribution to monetary theory', in *Pioneers of Modern Economics in Britain*. Ed. D. Greenaway, London: Macmillan.

Radcliffe Committee (1958) *Report of Committee on the Working of the Monetary System*. London: HMSO.

Robinson, J. (1952) 'The rate of interest', *Econometrica*. Reprinted in J. Robinson, *The Rate of Interest and Other Essays*. Oxford: Blackwell, pp. 246–65.

Rubinstein, M. (1975) 'Security market efficiency in an Arrow–Debreu economy', *American Economic Review* 65, 812–24.

Rubinstein, M., and A. Wolinsky (1987) 'Middlemen', *Quarterly Journal of Economics* 101, August, 581–93.

Sayers, R. S. (1960) 'Monetary thought and monetary policy in England', *Economic Journal* 280, December, 710–24.

Sayers, R. S. (1964) *Modern Banking*, 6th edn. London: Oxford University Press.

Scitovsky, T. (1969) *Money and the Balance of Payments*. Chicago, Ill.: Rand McNally.

Simmons, E. C. (1947) 'The relative liquidity of money and other things', *American Economic Review, Supplement* 37, 308–11.

Stigler, G. J. (1967) 'Imperfections in the capital market', *Journal of Political Economy* 75 (3), June, 287–92.

Streissler, E. W. (1973) 'Menger's theories of money and uncertainty – a modern interpretation', in *Carl Menger and the Austrian School of Economics*. Ed. J. R. Hicks and W. Webber, Oxford: Oxford University Press, pp. 164–89.

Telser, L. G. (1981) 'Why there are organized futures markets', *Journal of Law and Economics* 24, April, 1–22.

Tobin, J. (1963) 'Commercial banks as creators of "money"', in *Banking and Monetary Studies*. Ed. D. Carson, Glencoe, Ill.: Irwin, pp. 408–19.

Tobin, J, (1987) 'Financial intermediaries', in *New Palgrave Dictionary of Econ-*

omics. Ed. J. Eatnell, M. Milgate and P. Newmann, London: Macmillan, pp. 340–8.

Tobin, J., and W. C. Brainard Ed. J. Eatwel, M. Milgate and P. Newman, (1963) 'Financial intermediaries and the effectiveness of monetary controls', *American Economic Review* 52 (2), May, 383–400.

Varian, H. R. (1985) 'Differences of opinion in financial markets', CREST Working Paper, March, No. 87–23, University of Michigan.

Whitney, C. (1934) *Experiments in Credit Control: The Federal Reserve System.* New York.

12

Unemployment

David A. Collard

Unemployment is more of a key experience than a key concept. The experience of losing a job and wishing but not being able to obtain a job at a wage equal to (or even a little below) the going rate is a concrete enough experience. But unemployment as an economic concept is soon seen to be somewhat fuzzy around the edges. When is unemployment voluntary and when is it involuntary? When is it a social problem and when is it a normal part of transitional adjustment? As becomes clear below, there is much scope for debate about the meaning and definition of unemployment. In this chapter there is space enough to deal with only some of the issues. In section 12.1 the extent and nature of the problem in context is set, with unemployment emerging as very much an aspect of a formally structured industrial society. In section 12.2 two periods in which orthodox and unorthodox views on unemployment clashed, Ricardo versus Malthus and Pigou versus Keynes, are examined. In section 12.3 the contribution of Keynes to this and the related macroeconomic literature are considered. In section 12.4 the various attempts that have been made to *explain* wage rigidity as the main cause of (voluntary or involuntary?) unemployment, including efficiency wages and implicit contracts, are summarized. In section 12.5 we trace the demise of the Phillips curve and the rise of the concept of the 'natural rate' of unemployment and look to hysteresis as a source of demand management optimism. Section 12.6 very briefly considers the role of technological change in bringing about unemployment. The chapter finishes by welcoming a revival of interest in the analysis of unemployment as simply one manifestation of the old-fashioned business cycle.

12.1 Extent and Nature of the Problem

The figure for so-called 'open unemployment' in developing countries is not particularly helpful. For the Asian countries it varied between 4 and 7 per cent in 1985: urban unemployment in Latin America was under 4 per cent in Brazil but over 20 per cent in Bolivia and Nicaragua (International Labour Organisation, 1987). Of those people in employment in Latin

America over 30 per cent were in the 'informal sector' where unemployment is technically zero but low earnings and underemployment are endemic. In India the organized sector accounts for only 10 per cent of the non-agricultural labour force. In all countries, developed and developing, unemployment and poverty are associated with one another. But in developing countries the *primary* problems are poverty and distribution: the adjustment is taken up by underemployment in the rural areas and among rural workers who have migrated into the cities – open unemployment is merely the tip of an iceberg. With real wages at or near subsistence there is, of course, little possibility of expanding employment by downward wage flexibility.

For a considerable time the phenomenon of unemployment in Europe presented similar difficulties of definition. Routh (1986), in an admirably sweeping historical study, refers to the 'mass of workers or underoccupied people present at the birth of the industrial revolution [who] were not seeking jobs because there were no jobs to be sought' (p. 25). For him unemployment proper started with the industrial trade cycle. Thus 'troughs' in employment in the UK occurred in 1879, 1886, 1893, 1904, 1914, 1920 and 1932. From 1938 the unemployment figure was about 12 per cent for the whole of the post-war period, right up to the late 1970s, it fluctuated moderately within the range 2–4 per cent. But from the mid-1970s onwards unemployment increased dramatically, regaining its 1938 level by the early 1980s. One of the major tasks of a theory of unemployment is to explain the dramatic fall in unemployment in the late 1930s and the dramatic rise in the late 1970s.

Table 12.1 indicates three major features of unemployment in the 'developed market economies' – the very high percentage rate, the importance of long-term unemployment and the importance of youth unemployment.

Unemployment rates in Western Europe and the UK are high both historically (the rate for Western Europe was 2.5 per cent in 1970) and in comparison with Japan and the USA. The disadvantages of such high rates of unemployment are almost too obvious to be stated and so only a brief restatement is offered here.

1 Involuntary unemployment brings with it a substantial reduction in real income for the households concerned. Such individual household losses reflect, when added up, the loss of output to 'society' resulting from unemployment. That this is a 'bad thing' is contentious only if one believes that unemployment is an essential part of technical progress and the business cycle – then it is simply 'lost output'. Even when employment eventually recovers and overtakes its initial level that output has, nevertheless, been 'lost', not merely displaced in time. Of course, if it is truly the

Table 12.1 Three features of unemployment

	Labour force unemployed (%) (1987)	Labour force unemployed for over 1 year (%) (1986)	Youth unemployment (%) (1987)
UK	13.0	41.4	20.8
USA	6.8	8.7	12.0
Western Europe	11.0	45.4[a]	21.3[b]
Japan	3.4	17.2	6.0

[a]Germany, Italy, France.
[b]Four countries.
Sources: International Labour Organisation, 1987; OECD, *Employment Outlook*.

case that unemployment is the inevitable price of economic progress there is still no argument at all for allowing the unemployed to pay it. Indeed the argument for a high basic minimum income would be greatly strengthened.

2 In the UK and Western Europe a large proportion of the unemployed have been out of work for a year or more. There are various implications of this historically high figure. Firstly it draws attention to the dual nature of the labour market: the long-term unemployed are 'outsiders' whose interests will not be taken into account by the 'insiders' conducting wage negotiations. Secondly, because they have no influence on wage negotiations (except perhaps as some sort of Marxian 'reserve army') special measures to help them will have little or no effect on the rate of inflation of money wages. By the same token Layard and Nickell (1987) conclude that 'once we take account of the fact that the long term unemployed have only a minor impact on wages, we find that, in the long run, the inflation-reducing effects of extra unemployment decline rapidly as unemployment rises' (p. 146). Thirdly, the long-term unemployed will contribute to the hysteresis effect (see below) whereby high unemployment rates now drive up equilibrium unemployment rates in the future. It happens in this case because their potential productivity and income earning power diminish as their unemployment experience lengthens.

3 Similarly, youth unemployment is almost everywhere nearly twice as high as unemployment in general. This is partly due to the increased cohort sizes of school leavers and partly due to increased female participation rates. It is clearly undesirable that the costs of fighting inflation should be borne disproportionately by the rising generation: less magnanimously the rest of us may be disturbed at the prospect of poor achievement and crime. This said, the youth unemployment figure probably gives a false impression of the burden borne by the over-fifties, many of whom have taken voluntary redundancy or early retirement and thus face substantially lower lifetime earnings streams than they might reasonably have anticipated.

4 Regional imbalances are also accentuated by unemployment. Thus in February 1988 the percentage unemployment rate for males ranged from 7.0 per cent in East Anglia through 10 per cent in the East Midlands and 15 per cent in the north-west to over 21 per cent in Northern Ireland (*Employment Gazette*, February 1988). It is unrealistic to hope that such disparities will be eliminated by labour mobility for, apart from the destruction of social relationships, those workers in depressed regions contemplating movement elsewhere would also face large capital losses (reflecting of course reduced expected earnings streams in the regions).

Even this very brief survey of the extent and nature of unemployment suggests two important conclusions for policy.

1 Unemployment is an economic and social evil and policy-makers should do all they can to reduce it, short of generating substantial increases in the rate of inflation.
2 To the extent that unemployment proves to be 'necessary', either to fight inflation or to allow technical progress and dynamic growth, its costs should be borne more fairly by age groups, by worker categories and by regions.

Whether or not unemployment is to any great extent involuntary has enormous implications for policy. If it is, if there is 'system failure', and increase in aggregate demand is called for; but if not, if there is simply labour market failure, the remedy lies in adjustment of prices and wages. The division here is broadly between Keynesian policies (fiscal and/or monetary expansion) and classical policies (removing obstacles to labour-market adjustment). But the conflict is not quite as sharp as that because the majority of Keynesians concede that *if* real wages *really were* sufficiently flexible downwards involuntary unemployment would be eliminated. That is why much of the modern literature has concentrated upon labour-market rigidity.

12.2 Orthodoxy and Dissent

In this section two interesting episodes in the history of economic thought on unemployment which serve to bring out some of the key issues are looked at very briefly. They are the disputes between Malthus and Ricardo in the early nineteenth century and between Pigou and Keynes in the 1920s.

Malthus and Ricardo

The Ricardian view, which became the orthodox classical view, was that employment could never be caused by a deficiency of demand because savings would be channelled into investment through the capital markets: hence Ricardo's observation (following Smith) that

> to save is to spend, as surely, as what he (Malthus) exclusively calls spending. (1951, p. 449)

Malthus never satisfactorily out-argued Ricardo on this central point but his approach is of great interest because of his use of the concepts aggregate supply and aggregate demand. This mirrored his value theory which was based on supply and demand rather than cost of production. Anticipating the argument that was to be used to such powerful effect by Keynes over a century later, Malthus saw the forces on the supply and demand sides as quite separate forces which would only by chance be equal. In response to Ricardo he introduced an 'investment opportunities' type of argument to put a brake upon the demand side.

> Almost all merchants and manufacturers save in prosperous times, much more rapidly than it would be possible for the national capital to increase, so as to keep up the value of the produce. (1951, p. 432)

Here Malthus, frequently represented as siding with the landlord class, expounded the merits of unproductive consumption. It is clear from Keynes's essay on Malthus (Keynes, 1951) that he thought highly of Malthus's attempt to articulate a theory of deficient demand just as he thought highly of other 'precursors' of *The General Theory* (including Mandeville and J. A. Hobson). The general thrust of the classical position, with the exception of J. S. Mill's brilliant essay 'Of the Influence on Consumption of Production' (Mill, 1844), was that Malthus was simply in error (as Ricardo had said). The new classical school similarly believes that Keynesian theory is itself in error. From that standpoint Keynes was simply the last and greatest of the underconsumptionists.

Pigou and Keynes

Of the post-Marshallian but pre-Keynesian economists A. C. Pigou made by far the most distinguished contribution to the analysis of unemployment in a series of works from *Unemployment* (1913), through *Industrial Fluctuations* (1927), *The Theory of Unemployment* (1933) and *Employment and Equilibrium* (1941), to his *Retrospective View* (1950). Casson (1983) groups Pigou with H. Clay and E. Cannan in emphasizing structural unemployment due to real wage rigidity. This was certainly a major element in Pigou's work and whole sections of his books are taken up with such issues. But for the present purpose it is interesting that, for Pigou, the demand function for labour as a whole fluctuated over the cycle. The fluctuations need not, of themselves, cause unemployment but would do so if accompanied by real wage rigidity. Pigou viewed increases in demand in a time of recession as a permissible device but only because it led to a fall in real wages which could not be achieved directly. It should be noted that Keynes himself did *not* envisage the demand for labour schedule (the real marginal product schedule) as moving around the cycle but rather as determined entirely physically by the production function.

Because the labour-demand schedule was of such central importance to Pigou he gave great attention to the measurement of its elasticity: the greater the elasticity, the less the reduction in real wages required to sustain full employment (or equivalently the larger the increase in employment consequent upon a reduction in real wages). Pigou guessed (1933, p. 88ff.) that the elasticity with respect to real wages was about −3 and that with respect to money wages about −1.5. Keynes, in contrast, insisted that the elasticity of demand for labour as a whole could not be a central part of unemployment analysis and that his own apparatus of aggregate demand had to be used instead. The confrontation between Pigou and Keynes over this matter has been well documented in Keynes's *Collected Writings* (1973, vol. 5) and is described by Collard (1981).

Could anything be done about unemployment apart from real wage reduction? In principle, yes: the authorities could take action to moderate shifts in the demand for labour over the cycle, but Pigou feared that in practice they would try to keep demand too high *throughout* the cycle thus causing inflation, moreover inflation at an increasing rate. He suspected that increases in government investment, aimed at reducing unemployment, could only work by indirectly lowering real wages – through 'friction, bamboozlements and so on' (Howson and Winch, 1977, p. 65). The famous controversy over *The General Theory* appears superficially to have been a classic confrontation between *system failure* and *labour-market failure*: yet it was not quite so, for Pigou never confined his analysis to the labour market. For him the accompanying monetary regime was always relevant. Furthermore, Pigou, unlike most of Keynes's older contemporaries (and certainly unlike Robertson), accepted effective demand as a tool of analysis and incorporated it into his own work – in particular in his brilliant late work *Employment and Equilibrium* (1941).

12.3 Keynes

For the last 50 years the macroeconomics of unemployment has been developed in the shadow of Keynes. The importance of Keynes's *The General Theory* from the standpoint of this chapter is that it was an attempt to build a coherent economics of *system failure*. It was therefore important for Keynes to dismiss at the outset the notion that unemployment could be eliminated by a reduction in the real wage: this was done in chapter 2 of *The General Theory*. While Keynes agreed that labour must be on its demand curve (marginal real value product equals real wage) it need not be on its supply curve (real wage need not equal the marginal disutility of effort). Workers would sometimes be willing to offer more labour than required at, or a little below, the prevailing real wage. Very well, the classical economist would reply, lower the real wage and supply will once again equal demand.

Anticipating such a retort Keynes argued that workers could not, in effect, bring about a reduction in their real wage. There were two separate arguments involved here, both to do with the fact that workers negotiated money wages, not real wages. The first argument was about relative earnings: as workers had to negotiate *money wages* they could not hold back their demands unless they had a firm understanding that other groups of workers would do the same. Otherwise they might lose relative to others. The second argument was about the wage–price nexus. A change in the money wage would change what Keynes called the 'wage-unit': a fall in money wages would lower the wage-unit and, depending on the mark-up, lower prices. So real wages would fall far less than money wages had fallen and the necessary fall in money wages would be very large indeed, probably unacceptably large. Taking these two arguments together, decentralized money wage bargaining could not deliver the real wage adjustment required for 'classical' theory to work. A third, subsidiary, argument, deployed in chapter 19, was that the redistribution of income implied by a fall in real wages would lower aggregate demand: this may indeed be true but was no advance on the earlier 'underconsumptionist' argument.

In a sense these arguments (or at any rate the first two of the three) are simply a sophisticated restatement of the labour-market failure case. And they do come up against the awkward fact that Keynes insisted on labour's being on its demand curve which, as the real marginal product curve, was determined by the production function. So employment and real wages would definitely vary inversely with one another. This proved to be an embarrassment in that it implied that the real wage would behave counter-cyclically, falling in the boom and rising in the slump: it also implied that, with technology and the capital stock given, increased employment *could only* be achieved if the real wage was somehow driven down. This had been precisely Pigou's argument about 'bamboozlements': was the whole business of raising aggregate demand simply a devious way of effecting a real wage reduction? And if it was, would rational workers not eventually thwart the policy by increasing their money wage demands?

It must be stressed, therefore, that for Keynes the employment–real-wage relation was almost incidental. He switched the focus away from the labour market and labour-market failure to effective demand and system failure. The condition that real wage equals marginal product moved to the wings: to the centre of the stage came the 'condition that output *and* employment are determined by effective demand. Given this switch in emphasis any reduction in money wages can only affect employment via effective demand, i.e. (in a closed economy without government) by an increase in consumption and/or investment expenditure. This was the essence of Keynes's attack on Pigou's *Theory of Unemployment*: to a very great extent Keynes had not so much destroyed the labour-market failure case as switched the grounds of the debate.

Keynes's essential argument was presented in chapter 3 of *The General Theory*. It was given great prominence by Keynes himself and, in the present writer's view, still represents what is of central importance in the book. Keynes distinguished between consumption, a passive item in expenditure which merely depended upon income, and investment, an active element which depended upon the expectations and hopes of business. That the one item is labelled 'consumption' and the other 'investment' is less important than that one is passive and the other active – the fact that some investment is routine and some consumption in the nature of investment expenditure is not important. So much for aggregate demand. Aggregate supply, however, depends on the 'proceeds' (for which read, roughly, profits) expected by business. These proceeds will depend upon expected output or income.

The famous 'Keynesian cross' or 45° diagram has therefore to be seen as depicting a fixed-point theorem. Given Keynes's assumptions about the consumption function there will be some level of income which 'maps into' itself. This level may or may not be at full employment income. If it is not, an upward shift in investment (or an increase in government expenditure) is indicated.

The General Theory is notorious for the number of loose ends it leaves. The book is less good at explaining why the standard mechanism for moving to full employment will not work: the reasons given for lack of real wage adjustment have already been discussed. Another obvious mechanism, this time to allow saving and investment to adjust to one another without the necessity of income changes, is the interest rate. This mechanism, Keynes argued, was flawed by a 'liquidity trap' which ensured that interest rates could fall no lower once bond prices had reached the maximum expected. The liquidity trap arose from Keynes's very specialized theory of bond holding which depended on 'speculative' holders of money taking clear (but different) views about the normal level of interest rates. There is little empirical evidence for a liquidity trap and, in any case, it could not arise in more modern 'portfolio' theory. A final automatic mechanism (which Keynes allowed for to a minor degree) was the 'real balance effect' (Patinkin, 1965) whereby a price fall would increase real balances and therefore effective demand. In so far as a fall in effective demand and in employment is usually accompanied by a price fall, the real balance effect provides a mechanism for moving back towards full employment. This mechanism features prominently in modern accounts, even in popular textbooks (Begg, Fischer and Dornbusch, 1987) and was clearly not sufficiently heeded by Keynes.

Taking all these points together it cannot be said that Keynes convincingly rebutted all the mechanisms whereby the classical result could reassert itself – real wage adjustment, interest rate adjustment and the real balance effect. The central insight of effective demand remains but the supporting structure is weak and liable to crumble if examined too closely. If there is any truth at all in the doctrine of inadequate effective demand it would be a gross caricature of Keynes's unemployment theory to model it as simply neoclassical economics plus the special assumption of rigid money wages. This would certainly generate some unemployment which would be involuntary as far as the individual worker was concerned but 'voluntary' with respect to labour as a whole. In effect this was the line adopted by subsequent theorists. It became customary in economics textbooks of the 1960s to model the Keynesian outcome as merely a special case (the rigid wage case) of neoclassical economics. No longer a 'general' theory, it was to be subsumed in the orthodox approach. Thus (see Friedman, 1968) one could choose whether to take output as given (the classical case) or wage rates as given (the Keynesian case).

Given this framework the natural question to ask is why wages do not change. It is surely not sufficient simply to *assume* that they do not without providing a supporting theory of how the labour market works. Even Keynes took great care to *explain* real wage rigidity in his system, though it did not provide (in his view) the central reason for unemployment. The following sections offer various explanations for wage rigidity.

12.4 Wage Rigidity and Unemployment

Quantity-constrained Equilibrium

The quantity-constrained equilibrium approach does not so much explain involuntary unemployment as classify it. Like rigid prices, rigid quantities are imposed, as it were, from the outside. Quantity constraints make themselves felt as follows. Households plan to sell certain quantities of labour, given their preferences and wage rates, and to receive such-and-such an income. From this expected income they will plan such-and-such a level of expenditure: this is usually referred to as the household's *notional* expenditure on goods. But now suppose that the households are constrained in the amounts of labour they can offer. They will then not be able to achieve their notional demands for goods but will have to make do instead with a lower *effective* demand. This is clearly in the spirit of Keynes and yet makes sense of the consumption function which is a highly unsatisfactory notion when incomes are choice variables for individuals (Barro and Grossman, 1976).

If households are unable to sell all the labour they wish at the going constellation of prices and wages there is an excess supply of labour. Households are stuck on the 'short side' of the market: there is unemployment. What is happening in other markets? In neoclassical general equilibrium theory excess supply in one market has to be balanced by excess demand in another, say the goods, market. Should this be the case we have what is known as *classical unemployment* (Muellbauer and Portes, 1978). The remedy is that goods have to be dearer and labour cheaper. A much more dramatic case is that of *Keynesian unemployment* where there is excess supply in the labour market *and* in the goods market. Firms are unable to sell all the goods they would wish to at the present price constellation, just as householders are unable to sell their labour. If this is so it is natural to look at measures for raising effective demand rather than relying on the relative prices of labour and goods. Thus one could try to raise effective demand directly through fiscal policy.

The reason why the quantity-constraint approach does not 'explain' unemployment is that it does not offer a convincing explanation of how the constraint can persist. In particular, why does the real wage not adjust so as to bring notional and effective demands together? Why do firms not take action in face of *their* quantity constraints? These conundra are not reasons for abandoning the approach which is a highly promising one: the approach merely requires an additional and convincing rationale for why firms should feel themselves to be demand constrained.

Monopoly: Parallel Revolutions Converge

The line of argument which explains involuntary unemployment in terms of either quantity constraints or price rigidities immediately invites a link with market imperfection – if only with the famous 'kinked' demand curve (Sweezy, 1939). Yet it is interesting that neither of the main progenitors of the 'revolutions' in macroeconomics and microeconomics in the 1930s, Robinson (1933) and Keynes (1936), had any doubt that the revolutions were totally separate ones. Mrs Robinson was particularly clear on this point:

> if there was full employment under competition, in equilibrium conditions, there will be full employment under the monopolists. (1933, p. 310, n. 1)

Keynes also made it clear, particularly in reaction to a comment of Ohlin (Keynes, 1973, p. 190) that his theory of effective demand was not tied to any particular form of competition. More recently, however, it has come to be accepted that it is impossible to explain the constraints that give rise to Keynesian macro results without recourse to theories of imperfect or monopolistic competition (Chamberlin, 1933).

Starting from the kinked demand curve where (with constant costs) changes in demand will generate changes in output but not price, a weaker generalization is that price changes by less than output (Benassy, 1976). Hahn (1978, 1984) has developed a more sophisticated series of models in which firms make correct conjectures about their demand schedules once they encounter some output constraint. In closely related models (Grandmont and Laroque, 1976; Diamond, 1982) firms' conjectures about future levels of demand become important. Equilibrium output is then a function of expected output so the outcome is analogous to the 'fixed point' of the Keynesian cross discussed in section 12.3. Attempts to carry the analogy of monopolistic output restriction straight across to macroeconomic unemployment have not yet been entirely successful, though interesting attempts have been made by Hart (1982) and Snower (1983). Hart achieves his result mainly by the assumption of only one produced good and Snower achieves his by allowing any firm to be representative. Either assumption ensures the automatic carryover of the micro 'underemployment' result to macroeconomics. There can be little doubt that the key to resolving this set of problems is going to be found somewhere in the link between monopolistic competition and macroeconomics. This is an exciting area of research that promises rich dividends.

An interesting early bridge across the two parallel revolutions was constructed by Kalecki (1936–7, 1938) who linked investment with the degree of monopoly. Investment is determined by lagged profits and, given the mark-up of prices over wages, income adjusts so as to keep savings equal to investment. From an initial equilibrium an increase in the mark-up leads to an increase in unemployment. Kalecki's linking of microeconomics and macroeconomics is frequently referred to but the approach has never been absorbed into the orthodoxy, mainly because of Keynes's dominance. From the modern standpoint the great disadvantage of the theory is that it leans heavily on fixed coefficients and makes little use of prices. Few, therefore, have crossed the Kaleckian bridge.

Implicit Contracts

An ill-fated though ingenious explanation of unemployment was pioneered by Bailey (1974) and Azariadis (1975). The starting point is the familiar observation that wages fail to respond to booms and slumps as competitive theory would have them do. With inelastic labour supply wages ought to adjust so as to take all the strain; but they obstinately refuse to do so, leaving much (or even most) of the adjustment to employment. On the assumption that workers are more risk averse than profit-maximizing firms it is possible to show that rational firms and individuals would reach an understanding (an 'implicit contract') whereby workers would receive a constant wage regardless of boom or slump conditions. Owing to risk aversion, workers are assumed to be prepared to accept *less* than their mathematical expectation of earnings: this enables the transaction to be advantageous to the firm as well. In effect workers are paying an insurance premium to the firm in good times so as to be able to receive the implicit contract wage in bad times. If implicit contracts are at all widespread wages will be 'rigid' and the familiar pattern of employment over the cycle is explained.

It is also possible to attempt an explanation of unemployment more directly. At low wage levels some workers will find it attractive to take leisure and/or engage in household production particularly if unemployment benefit or insurance is available. This may be embodied in an implicit contract of the form: 'lay me off if the slump wage goes below £100; above that, pay me an invariant wage of £150 over the cycle'. Thus lay-offs may be embodied in the implicit contract itself. But this is not as exciting as it appears to be, because such unemployment would have occurred anyway, even in a spot market. So in either case workers would have voluntarily chosen some unemployment. The only difference is that they chose it *ex ante* but may regret it *ex post* under implicit contracts when the implicit contract wage is still notionally available: in a spot market there is no notional alternative wage rate available.

The difficulties of the whole approach become more evident once one allows for incentives for truth-telling. Azariadis and Stiglitz (1983) show that while there is no problem in the 'first-best' case there may be incentives for the firm (having more information than the workers) to tell lies: to say, for example, that there is a market slump when there is in fact a boom. The problem is one in 'principal–agent' theory and it is possible to set initial conditions which ensure that firms have no incentive to cheat. Unfortunately the 'doctored' equilibrium may turn out to give either more or less than first-best employment depending on workers' preferences between wages and hours. Figure 12.1 illustrates the difficulty.

A and B indicate iso-profit lines in the boom and slump respectively and a and b the full first-best implicit contract equilibrium. But the equilibria need not be at a or b: if they are not there is an incentive to lie which may be remedied by setting the slump wage and hours at e. So if the indifference curves touched the iso-profit lines at, say, a and d there would be underemployment at e while if they touched at a and c there would be

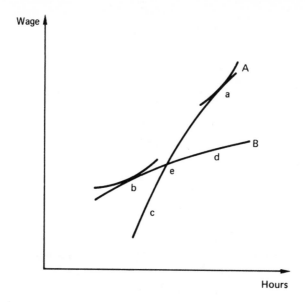

Figure 12.1 Implicit contract equilibria.

overemployment at e. This is embarrassing for a theory which started out as an explanation for involuntary unemployment. The saving grace of this whole line of development is that it has given a major impetus to the analysis of labour-market contracts.

Efficiency Wage Models

The basic idea behind 'efficiency wage' explanations of unemployment is a very simple one, though some of the models are themselves rather complex. All that is required is that labour productivity is higher at higher wage rates. As long as this is so, there will be a wage – the efficiency wage – above the competitive wage $\tilde{w}$, which maximizes profit. This is illustrated in figure 12.2 where the efficiency wage is w^*: even if there is unemployment u firms will not find it profitable to offer a lower wage.

The beauty of the efficiency wage argument is that, though wage is now above the competitive level ($w^* > \tilde{w}$) and there is unemployment, it is nonetheless 'equilibrium' unemployment. Whether such employment is voluntary is debatable as there is usually a secondary labour sector in which all workers could obtain employment at a lower wage rate; so in a sense their unemployment is voluntary.

A spirited defence of efficiency wage models against this and other criticisms is to be found in a valuable survey by Akerlof and Yellen (1986). Why should firms persist in paying above competitive wages? There are

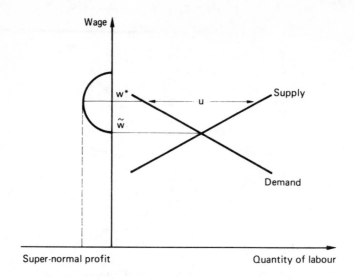

Figure 12.2 Efficiency wages.

several reasons. Firstly (Shapiro and Stiglitz, 1984), the efficiency wage will discourage 'shirking' because the worker now has more to lose by being dismissed. Secondly (the argument is similar to that already given for shirking), the efficiency wage will reduce costly turnover. Thirdly, and this is a much weaker argument, less efficient workers will reveal themselves by offering to work at lower wage rates. Fourthly, sociological arguments may be used (Akerlof, 1982) to show that the payment of efficiency wages can lift group morale and, with it, group productivity. The case against efficiency wage models rests on the possibility of alternative institutional devices. The most serious possibilities are (a) bonding, whereby the individual would lodge a bond with the firm and forfeit it upon being discovered shirking, (b) seniority, which provides an 'upward tilt' in earnings, and (c) differential payments during training. In short, the efficiency wage is an extremely crude device and probably inferior to a number of possible alternative arrangements. For a good account of these alternatives see Malcomson (1984). This whole line of investigation is another example of a theory which has advanced our understanding of labour contracts without necessarily helping towards an 'explanation' of unemployment.

Provisional Conclusion

Of the approaches considered in this section the quantity-constrained equilibrium approach merely restates the problem, the monopolistic competition approach is not yet sufficiently rigorous, the implicit contract approach is consistent with too wide a range of employment outcomes, and the efficiency wage hypothesis has to battle with alternative arguments. What they have in common is that unemployment arises because real wages, for some reason or other, fail to adjust to their competitive equilibrium. If they were allowed to do so there would be *some* real wage at which full employment was secured. The persistence of rigidity is perhaps not as puzzling in practice as it seems to be in theory. In the real world many labour contracts are made for quite long periods (because each side invests large amounts of human capital) and contracts also overlap (not all contracts are made at the same time). It is therefore not very surprising to find that wages are relatively rigid. However, unions and employers do not normally negotiate real wages but money wages and it is to the relationship between money wages and inflation that we turn in the next section.

12.5 The Phillips Curve, Rational Expectations and the Natural Rate

It has been known for a long time that employment and money wages and prices move pro-cyclically. Phillips (1958) drew on a long series of historical data, from the mid-nineteenth century onwards, to demonstrate a reasonably robust statistical relationship between the percentage rate of unemployment and the percentage increase in money wages (the rate of money wage inflation). The relationship soon became known as the Phillips curve and suggested the possibility of a policy 'trade-off' between unemployment and inflation. Formally, and assuming that policy-makers dislike both unemployment and inflation, they could select that point on the Phillips curve which minimized their 'loss function'. The curve also suggested that a zero rate of inflation (strictly of money wages, though it came to be accepted of prices too) could be achieved at some positive rate of unemployment. This rate of unemployment, the rate at which inflation was zero, was to become known as the 'natural rate' of unemployment. In the meantime, however, it seemed that any target level of unemployment could be attained provided that one was prepared to accept the (relatively modest) inflationary consequences. More recently better relationships have been found between the rates of change of the rate of wage inflation and the rates of change of the unemployment rate (Grubb, 1986). The relationship discussed in this paragraph has then to be treated in terms of rates of change of variables rather than the variable themselves.

During the 1960s it became clear that employment reductions could be 'purchased' only by larger and larger price inflation (a turn of events that had been correctly predicted by Pigou). An important modification was therefore proposed by Phelps (1967) and by Friedman (1968). Their argument was that once a given rate of money wage inflation comes to be expected it will already be incorporated in wage bargaining and the output decisions of firms. Only *unexpected* inflation will actually alter behaviour. Thus the *expectations-augmented* Phillips curve postulated a relationship between employment and the *difference between* actual inflation and anticipated inflation. Governments could therefore reduce unemployment only by increasing the rate of inflation above that expected. As economic agents (trade unionists, consumers) became used to higher rates of inflation still higher rates would be required to generate reductions in unemployment. To attempt to reduce unemployment below the natural rate, then, is to pursue a will-o'-the-wisp. This led Friedman to assert that there was no long-run trade-off between unemployment and inflation: the long-run Phillips curve was vertical. There could indeed be a short-run trade-off because economic agents formed their expectations 'adaptively' and could to some degree be 'fooled' by the authorities.

The monetarist case was that the authorities should abandon their attempts to reduce unemployment below the natural rate and, instead, simply aim to control the rate of inflation. This was to be achieved by controlling the rate of increase of money supply. It would be possible to return to zero inflation by gradually reducing the rate of growth of the money supply to the trend rate of growth of productivity. A much more dramatic development than this relatively moderate monetarist approach was the rational expectations view which was worked out for the macroeconomic case by Lucas (1972). On this view rational economic agents will not make *systematically* false forecasts: they will make errors but their errors will be randomly distributed about the correct figure. If such a view is married with the view that departures from trend output can be explained only by price 'surprises' then the way is open to show that no trade-off is possible *even in the short term*. Consider the following very simple model.

$$u = u^* - a(p - p_e)$$ the expectations-augmented Phillips curve
$$p = p_0 + bm$$ inflation mechanism
$$m = m_0 + c(u - u^*)_{-1}$$ monetary policy rule
$$p_e = p + \varepsilon$$ rational expectations assumption

where p_e is expected inflation, u is the unemployment rate, p_0 is trend expected, u^* is the natural rate, m is the rate of increase in the money supply, m_0 is the trend increase in the money supply and ε is a randomly distributed error term.

Under rational expectations individuals perceive that the authorities will increase the money supply whenever u deviates from u^*: they are therefore able to make accurate predictions (with a random error) of the price inflation rate. Policy presents no surprises so evidently unemployment is given by $u = u^* - a\varepsilon$ where $a\varepsilon$ is random. Unemployment varies randomly around the trend or natural rate. Any systematic policy aimed at reducing unemployment *must* be ineffective in so far as it is perfectly anticipated. The most important proposition to come out of rational expectations is this *policy ineffectiveness* proposition which is devastating in its simplicity. If the policy *is* systematic it cannot be effective: if it is *not* systematic it is hardly a policy.

The ineffectiveness proposition applies to monetary and fiscal policy, the standard apparatus of demand management. It does not apply to the natural rate u^* itself which may be affected by *supply-side* policies. The single supply-side factor which has been most discussed in the UK and the USA is the level of unemployment benefit as a proportion of earnings in work. This is given approximately by $b/(1-t)wh$ where b is the level of benefit, t the average tax rate, w the wage rate and h standard hours. The higher the replacement rate, the less attractive it will be to move out of unemployment into work. An appropriate supply-side policy for reducing unemployment would appear to be to reduce benefit rates and/or tax rates and indeed an avowed aim of the reform of social security introduced in 1987 was to treat poverty in work more generously than poverty in unemployment (Collard, 1985) – by, for example, increasing child payments under the Family Income Supplement Scheme relative to those under unemployment or social security. More crudely, one could simply reduce b. Most reforms of this type tend to fall heavily on the poor but if attention is confined to the effect on unemployment itself the key figure is the *elasticity* of the duration of unemployment with respect to benefit reduction. Unfortunately economists differ over the size of this crucial elasticity. Minford (1983), using the Liverpool model, produces a value of 2.8 while Layard and Nickell (1984) estimate the elasticity at 0.7. (An elasticity of 1.0 would mean that a 1 per cent benefit cut would lead to a 1 per cent reduction in unemployment duration and, if the flow into unemployment remained the same, a 1 per cent reduction in unemployment itself.) The difference appears to be mainly accounted for by the more elaborate analysis of wage rates in Nickell's analysis: Nickell's value is, in any case, much more plausible (Minford, 1984; Nickell, 1984). As for the replacement rate itself it is really quite low for the longer-term unemployed and workers with families: they have no incentive to remain unemployed and a benefit cut would simply mean a cruel cut in their income levels. Supply-side policies of this sort cannot be dismissed but they must be carefully judged on the basis of evidence rather than by myths.

Layard and Nickell have provided some already much quoted estimates of the contribution of various factors to the increase in the *natural rate* of unemployment from 7.63 per cent in the period 1975–9 to 9.07 per cent in the period 1980–3 (see Layard and Nickell, 1986, table 11). The contributions, in percentage points, were as follows: employers' labour taxes, 0.69; benefit replacement rate, −0.15; unions, 1.25; oil production, −1.73; competitiveness, −0.17; mismatch, 0.77; and incomes policy 0.78. It is of particular interest that the benefit replacement rate actually fell over the period and so could in no way be responsible for the increase in the natural rate. Note also that the incomes policy figure indicates that the natural rate might have been 0.78 lower had such a policy been in operation.

Thus the policy ineffectiveness proposition is intended to apply to the demand side, not to the supply side. But is the proposition correct? Casual empiricism suggests that governments are still able to increase their support by manipulating aggregate demand at election times (Hudson, 1985). Under the policy ineffectiveness proposition this tactic should fail. At a theoretical level the most important consideration is asymmetric information: the policy-maker is likely to have more, and better organized, information than the typical economic agent. It is primarily in the organization and use of knowledge, rather than in its mere possession, that the authorities will have an advantage, for the key economic indicators are now very widely available. One would not need to throw much dirt into the new classical machinery to make it seize up. It is not very difficult to show that *even with rational expectations* a contingent policy rule (i.e. a rule that varies with circumstances) may be superior to a fixed rule (e.g. a constant money expansion rule). On this see Buiter (1981) and Attfield, Demery and Duck (1985).

The thrust of monetarist and new classical interpretations of the Phillips curve is that demand management actually makes matters worse: it delivers *higher* inflation but is doomed to return to the natural rate of unemployment. A quite separate line of argument for caution in demand management is due to Malinvaud (1980, 1984). Here the emphasis is on appropriate relative factor prices. His account (rather simplified here) is that demand management leads to levels of real wages which are 'too high' and levels of real profit which are 'too low'. The twin effects of this are that capital is substituted for labour in the longer term and that investment in new plant (which depends partly on profits and profit expectations) is at a lower rate. In more old-fashioned terminology there is less 'capital-widening' and more 'capital-deepening'. Both effects will lead to a lower demand for labour and to either a lower natural rate or a lower long-run real wage or both. Thus while Malinvaud accepts that the short-run elasticity of employment with respect to real wages may be low (perhaps −0.2) the *longer-run* elasticity will be much more negative (perhaps −2.0).

The natural rate or its modern equivalent the non-accelerating inflation rate of unemployment (NAIRU) is therefore not immutable: it may change in response to policy or in long-run response to factor price maladjustment.

There are also reasons for believing that the natural rate may not be unique: many researchers (see Cross, 1988) have discovered hysteresis effects, i.e. the natural rate depends upon previous levels of unemployment. It is useful to think of hysteresis as shifting the Phillips curve *horizontally* over time (not vertically as in the case of inflationary expectations): there is, as it were, an *unemployment-augmented* Phillips curve. The extent to which the curve will shift depends upon the shape of the unemployment hysteresis function about which little is known. Purely to illustrate the possibilities, the function is shown in figure 12.3 as a simple S shape within upper and lower bounds $u^*_2 2$ and $u^*_2 1$ for the natural rate. Thus starting from a Phillips curve 0, policies to reduce inflation could eventually lead to curve 2 while policies to reduce unemployment could lead to curve 1. The normal Phillips curve result then breaks down for there will be a range of 'natural rates' to choose from, each consistent with unchanging inflation.

The superficial evidence for hysteresis is indeed rather strong. Until recently many commentators would have put the NAIRU at around 8–9 per cent (Layard and Nickell, 1986), but in the UK the rate of inflation has been steady in the range 3–5 per cent for the last two years and unemployment has remained obstinately at around 12 per cent. It is difficult not to feel that the apparently high NAIRU must, in some measure, be due to the demand restriction of earlier years. To the extent that the hysteresis hypothesis holds, the prospects for a positive demand management policy are much better than recently believed.

12.6 Technological Unemployment

One of the factors most commonly blamed for unemployment is technical change. Mainstream economics has not on the whole been sympathetic to this view because superior methods are bound to increase real income and will probably increase employment too, eventually even if not in the short run. Yet the view persists that technical change is an important cause of unemployment. The general thrust of the classical view was that 'machines' had beneficial effects on employment and so perhaps the exceptions to this general rule deserve most discussion. Until the third edition of the *Principles* (Ricardo, 1951, ch. 31), Ricardo took the general view that machinery could have no adverse effect upon employment. A dissenting view had been put by Barton (1817) and was to receive early 'mathematical' treatment by Tozer (see Collard, 1968).

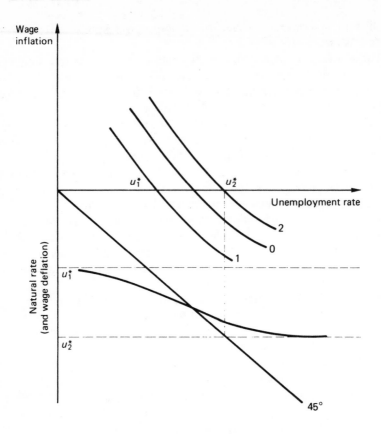

Figure 12.3 Hysteresis and shifts in the Phillips curve.

At the risk of oversimplification, a labour-saving technical change could be seen as a hiccup or perturbation in the smooth growth of labour demand: after the disturbance, demand would grow faster than before and so eventually the economy would catch up with its former growth curve and overtake it. Thus, under capitalism, with labour-saving technical progress there could be relatively short periods of involuntary unemployment.

In Marx's economic analysis with no technical change the demand for labour would outstrip supply and force up the relative real wage (reduce the rate of exploitation of labour), but the rate of exploitation could not fall below a certain level if accumulation was still to take place. However, with technical change the 'organic composition of capital' (*roughly* the capital–labour ratio) would rise, leading to relative surplus population and the industrial reserve army (see Marx, 1972, and Brewer, 1984) whose size would increase or decrease according to the stage of the cycle. The workers sucked in and then disgorged during this process constituted what Marx called the *floating* surplus population. This corresponds to the conventional industrial work-force. But his other categories are of interest: they are the *latent* surplus population in rural areas and the *stagnant* reserve army of, for example, *domestic* workers. The main focus was on the floating surplus population.

Technical change was not to be given such a major role again until Schumpeter's (1939) analysis of the cycle, based upon innovation. On Schumpeter's view booms come about because of a cluster of innovations: they are an essential part of the process of accumulation. It is not, of course, necessary to this view that scientific advances or even inventions are bunched in this way: all that is required is that profit-seeking capitalists find it profitable to follow one another once a burst of innovations begins. Schumpeterian innovation also plays a major role on more modern discussions of so-called 'long swings' in economic activity, the analysis of which has enjoyed something of a comeback since the crises of the late 1970s and early 1980s (see Freeman, 1983). Unemployment occurs in the long down swing because old industries and old technologies have slowly to give way to new: the pattern of relative prices and wages has to adjust; labour has to move geographically and/or learn new skills. Except for the dominant role of technology in the Schumpeterian story the unemployment which arises during the cycle really occurs because relative prices and wages fail to adjust quickly enough. The *underlying* explanation is then not very different from that offered by Pigou. All that is required is that the system experiences a shock of some sort (it need not be technical innovation) and that prices do not adjust so as to bring about the new equilibrium at once. The same would be true of any major relative price dislocation, e.g. the return to gold in 1925 at an excessively high parity which made UK export prices too high and required lower UK money wages and/or employment. This is broadly the view which has long been put by Hayek: it is a very simple but very persuasive view. Unemployment, according to Hayek, arises because of a 'distortion' in relative prices which may *only* be corrected by a change in prices. It *cannot* be corrected by manipulating aggregate demand in the Keynesian manner. If the authorities do pursue a Keynesian policy for an extended period the ultimate adjustment, when it comes, has to be very much more severe than it would otherwise have been.

It is not necessary to accept the whole Hayekian view in order to agree that technical change is essential to economic progress and requires painful adjustment. The precise course of technical change and its consequences for particular types of labour are largely unpredictable: the state of the art in forecasting these matters is still primitive and mechanical using fixed

352   *D. A. Collard*

input–output coefficients (e.g. Leontief and Duchin, 1986). Yet the distributional consequences of technical change can in fact be planned for. An ideal solution would be a version of Meade's scheme (Meade, 1964) for a 'social dividend' (now often referred to as a 'basic income'). Though social dividend types of proposal have been well known since the early 1940s, Meade's innovation was to use them so as to prevent the extremely unequal distribution of the fruits of technology. In his scheme the real wage would be determined competitively and produce full employment; but income would be made up only partly of the real wage, the rest being an equally distributed 'dividend' which would, of course, increase with technical progress. As it happens this function of the social dividend complements the other function commonly claimed for it, that it protects the poor while retaining the incentive to work.

12.7 Conclusions

Unemployment is indeed one of the key concepts in economics – even though there are still major difficulties in defining and measuring it. *Involuntary* unemployment is undoubtedly a major social evil and has not yet been defined out of existence. To be sure there are many forms of unemployment which may be defined as voluntary:

choice of leisure rather than work;
choice of leisure now rather than leisure later;
search for a better job offer;
the demand for an 'excessive' wage;
an implied consent to temporary lay-offs.

But it is difficult to imagine that such voluntary unemployment can underlie the very dramatic rises in unemployment which took place in the inter-war period and from the late 1970s. To explain these and the social hardship which comes with them is a major obligation. The most widely accepted explanation would be to combine exogenous shocks with labour-market rigidity: the unemployment which results is then voluntary in so far as it could be eliminated with sufficient downward flexibility in real wages. This line of explanation keeps everyone (apart from the unemployed) happy in that the outcome is essentially a new classical one but with Keynesian short-term features. Yet one remains unhappy about it. It is a pity that macroeconomics, following Keynes, became so cut off from earlier studies of the business cycle and it is encouraging to see a revival of interest in thinking about the business relationship over the cycle between output, prices, money wages and unemployment, all in the context of technical change and financial crises, is almost certainly the best way forward.

REFERENCES

Akerlof, G. A. (1982) 'Labour contracts as a partial gift exchange', *Quarterly Journal of Economics* 102, 543–69.

Akerlof, G. A. and J. L. Yellen (1986) *Efficiency Wage Models of the Labour Market*. Cambridge: Cambridge University Press.

Attfield, C. L. F., D. Demery and N. W. Duck (1985) *Rational Expectations and Macroeconomics: An Introduction to Theory and Evidence*. Oxford: Blackwell.

Azariadis, C. (1975) 'Implicit contracts and underemployment equilibrium', *Journal of Political Economy* 83, 1183–202.

Azariadis, C., and J. E. Stiglitz (1983) 'Implicit contracts and fixed price equilibria', *Quarterly Journal of Economics* 48, 1–20.

Bailey, M. N. (1974) 'Wages and employment under uncertain demand', *Review of Economic Studies* 41, 37–50.

Barro, R., and H. Grossman (1976) *Money, Employment and Inflation*. Cambridge: Cambridge University Press.

Barton, J. (1817) *Condition of the Labouring Classes*. Ed. J. H. Hollander, 1934, Baltimore, Md.

Begg, D., S. Fischer and R. Dornbusch (1987) *Economics*, 2nd edn. New York: McGraw-Hill.

Benassy, J.-P. (1976) 'The disequilibrium approach to monopolistic price setting and general monopolistic competition', *Review of Economic Studies* 43, 69–81.

Brewer, A. A. (1984) *A Guide to Marx's Capital*. Cambridge: Cambridge University Press.

Buiter, W. (1981) 'The superiority of contingent rules over fixed rules in models with rational expectations', *Economic Journal* 91, 647–70.

Casson, M. (1983) *Economics of Unemployment: An Historical Perspective*. Oxford: Martin Robertson.

Chamberlin, E. H. (1933) *The Theory of Monopolistic Competition*. Oxford: Oxford University Press; Cambridge, Mass.: Harvard University Press.

Collard, D. A. (ed.) (1968) *J. E. Tozer: Mathematical Investigation of the Effect of Machinery* (1838) New York: Augustus and Kelly Reprint.

Collard, D. A. (1981) 'A. C. Pigou 1877–1959', in *Pioneers of Modern Economics*. Ed. D. P. O'Brien and J. R. Priestly, London: Macmillan.

Collard, D. A. (1985) 'Social security and work after Fowler', *Political Quarterly* 56, 361–73.

Cross, R. (1988) *Unemployment, Hysteresis and the Natural Rate Hypothesis*. Oxford: Blackwell.

Diamond, P. (1982) 'Aggregate demand management in search equilibrium', *Journal of Political Economy* 881–94.

Freeman, C. (1983) *Long Waves in the World Economy*. London: Butterworth.

Friedman, M. (1968) 'The role of monetary policy', *American Economic Review* 58.

Grandmont, J. M., and G. Laroque (1976) 'On temporary Keynesian equilibrium', *Review of Economic Studies* 43, 53–67.

Grubb, D. (1986) 'Topics in the OECD Phillips curve', *Economic Journal* 96, 55–79.

Hahn, F. H. (1978) 'On non-Walrasian equilibria', *Review of Economic Studies* 45, 1–17.

Hahn, F. H. (1984) *Equilibrium and Macroeconomics*. Oxford: Blackwell.

Hart, O. (1982) 'A model of imperfect competition with Keynesian features', *Quarterly Journal of Economics* 47, 109–38.

Howson, S., and D. W. Winch (1977) *The Economic Advisory Council 1930–49*. Cambridge: Cambridge University Press.

Hudson, J. R. (1985) 'The relationship between government popularity and approval for the government's record in the UK', *British Journal of Political Science* 15, 165–86.

International Labour Organisation (1987) *World Labour Report*, vols 1, 2, 3. Oxford: Oxford University Press.

Kalecki, M. (1936–7) 'A theory of the business cycle', *Review of Economic Studies* 4, 77–97.

Kalecki, M. (1938) 'The determinants of distribution of the national income', *Econometrica* 6, April, 97–112.

Keynes, J. M. (1936) *The General Theory of Employment Interest and Money*. London: Macmillan.

Keynes, J .M. (1951) *Essays in Biography*. London: Rupert Hart-Davis.

Keynes, J .M. (1973) *Collected Writings*, vols XIII and XIV. Ed. D. Moggridge, London: Macmillan.

Layard, P. R. G. and S. Nickell (1985) 'The causes of British unemployment', *Bulletin of National Institute of Economic and Social Research*, February, 62–85.

Layard, P. R. G. and S. Nickell (1986) 'Unemployment in Britain', *Economic Supplement* 53 (210 (S)), 5121–70.

Layard, P. R. G. and S. Nickell (1987) 'The Labour Market', in *The Performance of the British Economy*. Ed. R. Dornbusch and R. Layard, Oxford: Clarendon.

Leontief, W. and F. Duchin (1986) *The Future Impact of Automation on Workers*. Oxford: Oxford University Press.

Lucas, R. E. (1972) 'Expectations and the neutrality of money', *Journal of Economic Theory* 4, 103–24.

Malcomson, J. (1984) 'Work incentives, hierarchy and internal labour markets', *Journal of Political Economy*, 486–507.

Malinvaud, E. (1980) *Profitability and Unemployment*. Cambridge: Cambridge University Press.

Malinvaud, E. (1984) *Mass Unemployment*. Oxford: Blackwell.

Marx, K. (1972) *Capital*, vols I–III. Moscow: Foreign Languages Publishing House.

Meade, J. E. (1964) *Efficiency, Equality and the Ownership of Property*. London: Allen & Unwin.

Mill, J. S. (1844) *Essays on Some Unsettled Questions of Political Economy*. London: J. W. Parker.

Minford, P. (1983) 'Labour market equilibrium in an open economy', *Oxford Economic Papers* 35, 202–44.

Minford, P. (1984) 'Response to Nickell', *Economic Journal* 94, 954–9.

Muellbauer, J., and R. Portes (1978) 'Macroeconomic models with quantity rationing', *Economic Journal* 88, December, 788–821.

Nickell, S. J. (1984) 'Review Article of "Unemployment: Cause and Cure"', *Economic Journal* 94, 946–53.

Patinkin, D. (1965) *Money, Interest and Prices: An Integration of Monetary and Value Theory*. New York: Harper & Rowe.

Phelps, E. S. (1967) 'Phillips curve, expectations of inflation and optimal unemployment over time', *Economica* 34.

Phillips, A. W. (1958) 'The relation between unemployment and the rate of change of money wages in the UK 1861–1957', *Economica* 25, November, 283–99.

Pigou, A. C. (1913) *Unemployment*. London: Home University Library.

Pigou, A. C. (1927) *Industrial Fluctuations*. London: Macmillan.

Pigou, A. C. (1933) *The Theory of Unemployment*. London: Macmillan.

Pigou, A. C. (1941) *Employment and Equilibrium*. London: Macmillan.

Pigou, A. C. (1950) *Keynes's General Theory: A Retrospective View*. London: Macmillan.

Ricardo, D. (1951) 'Notes on Malthus', in *The Works and Correspondence of David Ricardo*, vol. II. Ed. P. Sraffa, Cambridge: Cambridge University Press.

Ricardo, D. (1951) 'Principles of Political Economy and Taxation', in *The Works and Correspondence of David Ricardo*, vol. I. Ed. P. Sraffa, Cambridge: Cambridge University Press.

Robinson, J. (1933) *The Economics of Imperfect Competition*. London: Macmillan.

Routh, G. (1986) *Unemployment: Economic Perspectives*. London: Macmillan.

Schumpeter, J. A. (1939) *Business Cycles*. New York: McGraw-Hill.

Shapiro, C., and J. E. Stiglitz (1984) 'Equilibrium unemployment as a worker discipline device', *American Economic Review* 74, 433–44.

Snower, D. (1983) 'Imperfect competition, underemployment and crowding out', *Oxford Economic Papers* 35, 245–70.

Sweezy, P. M. (1939) 'Demand under conditions of oligopoly', *Journal of Political Economy* 47, 568–73.

13

Equilibrium and explanation

Huw Dixon

This chapter is a personal treatise on the method of equilibrium in economics. The problem posed by this topic is that there is no general *concept* of equilibrium: rather, there is a method of equilibrium analysis that is employed in most of economics. Thus, the subject of enquiry is as diverse as economics itself. The chapter is therefore a compromise between a discussion of the general method of equilibrium itself, and an examination of its various manifestations in particular economic models. A resolution of the tension is sought by a detailed examination of the models that seem to form the core of standard undergraduate and graduate courses. This method itself is further justified by the belief that most economists' 'concept' of equilibrium is born early on in their career – indeed, in the opening lectures of an introductory course.

Since there are so many different types of economic models with diverse preoccupations, the selection reflects personal whim and current fashion. Ten or 20 years ago, these factors would have indicated different topics: most notably capital theory and the associated issues raised by growth theory would have been central to any discussion of equilibrium. Consideration of these issues has been omitted mainly because they were well aired at the time.

In this chapter, attempts have also been made to steer clear of technicalities. Although technicalities sometimes enable a more precise expression, they all too often embroil us in details so that we lose the more general perspective. More importantly, the technicalities often add little or nothing to the basic equilibrium concept employed. Lastly, to avoid long-winded caveats and qualifiers, sweeping generalizations are used. The arguments should be seen as expressing a point of view, and it is certainly accepted that there are many other possible interpretations of particular models.

At its most general, we can say that 'equilibrium' is a method of solving economic models. At a superficial level, an equilibrium is simply a solution to a set of equations. However, there is more to it than that. Whilst economists rarely argue over how to solve equations, they do argue over whether a particular solution represents a 'real' equilibrium or not. What is at stake is the economist's view of economic agents and the market.

Equilibrium method has come to play a central role in explanation in economics. In this it differs from other sciences, where disequilibrium states are also the object of explanation. What then is the role of equilibrium in the process of explanation in economics: how do economists explain? The remarks in this chapter are restricted to theoretical economics. Very generally, economic explanation consists of two levels. At the first level, the *microstructure*, the economist posits the behaviour of the elements of the model. In most microeconomics, the basic elements of the model consist of agents (e.g. firms and households), whose behaviour is explained and understood as some form of constrained optimization. The agent maximizes some objective function (utility, profit) subject to some constraint (budget, technology). This constrained maximization is in effect the model of individual economic rationality. In other cases, the microstructure might simply take the form of directly postulating a behavioural relationship – as for example in Keynes's consumption function. At the second level, the *macrostructure*, the individual elements of the model are put together. (The method of equilibrium consists precisely in putting together the elements in a consistent manner in solving the model.)

This dual level of explanation is best exemplified by the most common equilibrium employed in economics: the competitive equilibrium. The microstructure consists of households who maximize utility subject to a budget constraint, and firms that maximize profits subject to a technology. The microstructure is summarized by demand and supply curves. At the macro level, we put these elements together using an equilibrium concept: in the case of competitive equilibrium, we have trade occurring at the price which equates demand with supply. Actual trades equal desired trades, and demand equals supply. The theory of the competitive market (price theory) can then be used to explain prices by relating them to individual behaviour through the market equilibrium. Thus, for example, changes in the cost of inputs can be seen as altering firms' supply decisions, and hence shifting the supply curve. This will then lead to an alteration in the equilibrium price.

Equilibrium thus plays a central role in the enterprise of explanation. Parts of the model are put together and, through the application of a particular equilibrium concept, the model comes to life. Once alive, economists see what it looks like, examining the model for properties of interest (is it Pareto optimal? how does it compare with other models?). Sometimes the models are made to 'dance' through the method of comparative statics, twitching from one position to another. The economist has real or imagined properties he wishes to explain: if the model displays them, he exhibits the model as an explanation. The crux of the explanation is: 'everyone is doing as well as they can (microstructure): when everyone is doing as well as they can, X happens (equilibrium or macrostructure)'.

This is seen as explaining phenomenon X. It is rather as if an inventor has an idea, constructs a machine and proudly exhibits its performance. For the economist, however, the machine remains an idea on paper. (A notable exception is Phillips's water model of the Keynesian income–expenditure model. This, however, is still a representation.)

Given the role of equilibrium in the process of explanation, what can be said of it in general? Perhaps the main discussion of 'equilibrium' occurs for most economists in introductory textbooks. This tends to be geared to the demand–supply model and the Keynesian income–expenditure model. We shall discuss these in detail in the next section. However, three basic properties of equilibrium in general are proposed.

P1, The behaviour of agents is consistent.
P2, No agent has an incentive to change his behaviour.
P3, Equilibrium is the outcome of some dynamic process (stability).

These properties are illustrated for the demand–supply and income–expenditure models in table 13.1.

The importance of these properties is by no means equal or uniform. In particular, the stability property P3 is often played down, since it is almost impossible to provide a coherent account of stability in economics. P2 is the key to constructing convincing economic equilibria: if a rival economist can point out that some agent can do better than he does, then the equilibrium model presented is cast into doubt. It is thus necessary to look more closely at how equilibrium consists in agents' having no incentive to alter their behaviour. In section 13.1 the three basic equilibria employed in economics are examined. Particular issues are discussed in subsequent sections: disequilibrium analysis (section 13.2), information (section 13.3) and time (section 13.4).

13.1 The Three Crosses

In this section we examine three different equilibria which are central and paradigmatic to economic analysis. First, we shall explore the competitive equilibrium, which forms the foundation of price theory and dominates the syllabus of most undergraduate economics courses. Second, we shall consider the income–expenditure equilibrium which forms the foundation of macroeconomic analysis, giving as it does the notion of the multiplier. Thirdly, we shall consider the Cournot–Nash equilibrium: this is the standard model of oligopoly and is chosen to represent the game-theoretic approach to equilibrium. Each of these equilibria has a central role in the teaching of economics: each is represented by a simple two-dimensional

Table 13.1 Equilibrium properties

	Demand–supply	*Income–expenditure*
P1	Demand equals supply	Income equals expenditure
P2	Actual trades equal desired trades	Planned expenditure equals actual expenditure
P3	*Tâtonnement*	Multiplier

diagram in which the equilibrium is represented by the intersection of two functions (invariably drawn as lines in textbooks). Hence each is a cross borne by the student, named after its creator (or some approximation thereto). The competitive equilibrium has two lines, one sloping up and one down, sometimes called the Marshallian cross; the income–expenditure equilibrium has two upward-sloping lines and is sometimes called the Keynesian cross; the Cournot–Nash equilibrium has two downward-sloping lines and for consistency is called the Cournot cross. The three crosses are depicted in figure 13.1.

As we shall see, although these three equilibria lie at the centre of the discipline of economics, they are very different, and in some sense contradictory, or at least incommensurable.

The Marshallian Cross

The idea of competitive equilibrium stems from the vision of the market acting as an invisible hand, the price mechanism bringing into balance the two sides of the market – demand and supply. As a formal idea it surfaces in its modern form in Marshall's *Principles* (1890). The equilibrium is represented in figure 13.2. The demand curve D slopes down; it represents the amount that households would like to buy at a given price. Thus at price P^0 demand is X'. The demand curve is derived under the assumption

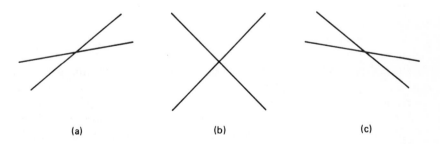

(a)   (b)   (c)

Figure 13.1 Three crosses: (a) Keynesian; (b) Marshallian; (c) Cournot.

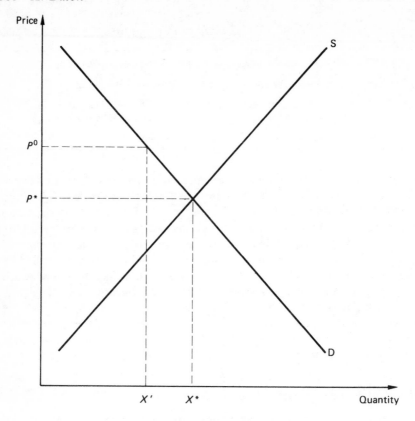

Figure 13.2 Supply and demand.

that households are *price-takers*: they treat prices as exogenous, unaffected by the action of any individual household. Under the assumption of price-taking behaviour, households have a linear budget constraint, from which they 'choose' the utility-maximizing combination of goods. The demand curve in a particular market represents the utility-maximizing quantity of the goods as the price varies (holding other prices etc. constant under the *ceteris paribus* assumption).

The supply curve S is also derived under the assumption of price-taking behaviour: it represents the quantity that firms wish to supply at each price. Profit-maximizing firms will choose the output which equates marginal cost with price; hence the supply function is simply the summed marginal cost functions of firms in the market, and is upward sloping due to the assumption of diminishing marginal productivity of labour or diminishing returns to scale. The demand and supply curves represent the microstructure of the market.

In figure 13.2 the supply and demand functions are put together. The competitive equilibrium occurs at the intersection of the two lines, with resultant price and quantity (P^*, X^*). Why is this seen as an equilibrium? The argument was outlined above in terms of the three properties P1–P3. At the competitive equilibrium the amount demanded equals the amount supplied (P1); desired trades equal actual trades (P2); at any non-equilibrium price there will be excess supply or demand which will tend to lead to a movement in price towards equilibrium – the *tâtonnement* process (P3).

Let us focus on P2, the notion that agents have no incentive to change their actions in equilibrium. What exactly do firms and households 'do' in a competitive equilibrium, and how might they do something else? In one sense the answer is obvious: firms and households exchange and trade; firms produce output which households consume. So it might be thought that, in evaluating the competitive equilibrium, we might consider whether firms or households might want to alter their production or consumption. For example, suppose that a firm reduces its output so that, in terms of figure 13.2, supply reduces from equilibrium X^* to X'. What will happen? This raises the general problem of specifying non-equilibrium behaviour in any model. There are at least two possibilities: first, that the price remains at P^*, and a reduction in supply simply leads to excess demand $X^* - X'$; second, that the reduction in supply leads to a rise in price to P^0. In the first case, the firm's behaviour simply leads it to produce at a point where price no longer equals marginal cost, thus reducing its profits. Hence the firm has no incentive to deviate from its competitive output. However, in the second case there will in general be an increase in profits: the reduction in output will increase price (even if only by a very small amount), which may result in an increase in profits (and certainly will result in an increase in profits if the reduction in output is small). In this case, then, the competitive outcome is not an equilibrium from the point of view of P2. This illustrates the strength of the price-taking assumption: not only is it vital to define the competitive outcome (in the sense that it defines the demand and supply functions), but it is also crucial to the notion that a competitive outcome is an *equilibrium* in the sense of P2, since it ties down out-of-equilibrium outcomes.

If we turn to P3, the competitive outcome is also seen as the outcome of the *tâtonnement* price adjustment process. There is a central paradox underlying the notion of price adjustment. How can we explain changes in price in a model in which all agents treat prices as given? One approach is to invent a third type of agent in the economy: the auctioneer. Walras based his idea of the auctioneer on the 'market-makers' of the French Bourse. The auctioneer is the visible, if imaginary, embodiment of the invisible hand. He has no economic involvement in the market: no mention is made of his objectives or constraints. He just adjusts prices in response to excess supply and demand. The story is very simple; the auctioneer calls out some arbitrary prices, agents report their desired demands and supplies, and the auctioneer raises prices where there is excess demand and lowers them where there is excess supply. If and when prices attain the competitive prices and there is no excess demand, the auctioneer waves his flag (or blows his whistle) and everyone then goes ahead and trades at the competitive price: households consume and firms produce. No trade or consumption is allowed before the competitive price is reached. Hahn and Negishi (1962) suggest an alternative 'non-*tâtonnement*' process which allows for *trading* at disequilibrium prices, but not consumption. Otherwise, the story is similar. The competitive outcome can then be seen as the outcome of this dynamic process of price adjustment by the auctioneer. However, it is not clear what has been gained by inventing a fictional price adjustment process to justify the competitive outcome. Perhaps all this means is that, if prices respond to excess demands and supplies, then price will eventually settle down at the competitive level. But it does not tell us *why* prices respond to excess demand or supply.

Textbooks adopt a slightly different approach. Competitive equilibrium is usually introduced and explained to students in an introductory economics course. Whilst the competitive model is later developed and extended, there is often little or no thought as to what it all means. The textbook writers therefore require an intuitive, plausible and convincing story. They argue that if price exceeds P^* then there will be excess supply (as in figure 13.2 at P^0): therefore firms will want to cut prices. Below P^*, there is excess demand and prices will be bid up by consumers or raised by firms. When supply equals demand, everyone can buy or sell what they want to at P^*, and so no one will want to change price. This story may be convincing, but it is certainly not correct. Whilst it is true that prices may well change in the desired direction in response to excess demands and supplies, it is not generally true that prices will come to rest at the competitive level. Take the case where firms set prices. If the market price exceeds the competitive price there will be excess supply: firms would like to sell more, and will be rationed by some mechanism to sell less than their profit-maximizing trade at that price. By undercutting the other firms by a little, any one firm can therefore attract customers from its competitors and expand sales to its desired supply at only a slightly lower price. Similarly, if there is excess demand, although the firms are able to sell as much as they want, they can increase profits by raising prices. Thus, one might expect a situation where a non-competitive price would move towards the competitive price. There is a serious conceptual issue here: in the case of undercutting, the 'price war' will never get anywhere – since price is usually modelled as a real variable, the undercut may be arbitrarily small (see Dixon, 1988a).

However, the real issue is whether or not the competitive price itself is an 'equilibrium': will firms wish to continue setting the competitive price when and if they have arrived there? In general, the answer is no (see Shubik, 1958; Dixon, 1987). Firms will want to raise price at the competitive equilibrium (see Dixon, 1987, theorem 1). The reason is simple. At the competitive price, firms are on their supply function: price equals marginal cost. This can only be optimal for the firm if the demand curve it faces is actually horizontal. But if the firm raises its price (a little), it will not lose all its customers since, although consumers would like to buy from firms still setting the competitive price, those firms will not be willing to expand output to meet demand (their competitive output maximizes profits at the competitive price). Those customers turned away will be available to buy at a higher price. Thus if a firm raises its price above the competitive price, it will not lose all its customers but only some of them, and so it will face the downward-sloping residual demand curve depicted in figure 13.3. Since it faces a downward-sloping demand curve, marginal revenue is less than price: hence at the competitive price and output (point a), marginal cost exceeds marginal revenue and the firm can increase profits by raising price (to P' in figure 13.3). This argument rests on an upward-sloping (and smooth) marginal cost function; in the standard Bertrand case of constant marginal cost, of course, it is in the interest of firms to continue setting the competitive price. However, the Bertrand case is not at all robust, since a slight deviation from constant marginal cost destroys the competitive equilibrium.

The standard textbook story of competitive price adjustment just does not stand up to closer scrutiny. The basic problem is the contradiction between an equilibrium concept based on price taking and the notion of agents (firms or households) setting prices. Indeed, it has proven very difficult to provide a coherent account of competitive equilibrium which allows for individual agents to do anything other than choose demands or supplies at given prices. This does not mean that many minds have not put their ingenuity to solving this puzzle (see Dubey, 1982; Simon, 1984). However, one can but marvel at the baroque intricacies needed to provide a suitable clothing for the classical simplicity of the original competitive edifice.

What are we left with? We shall return again to the Marshallian cross. However, at this stage one is tempted to say that the competitive outcome does not represent an 'equilibrium' at all. This is in a sense surprising since, for most undergraduates, competitive equilibrium is 'the' equilibrium. Certainly, for a couple of generations of academic researchers, the Arrow–

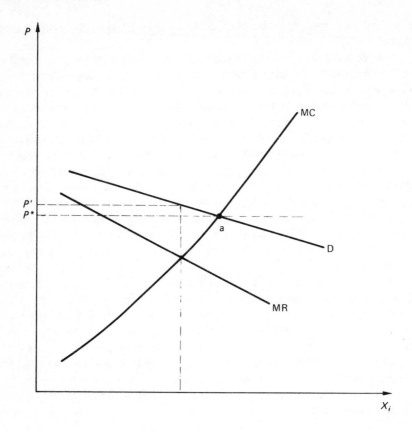

Figure 13.3 Non-existence of competitive equilibrium.

Debreu incarnation of the Marshallian cross held an almost ineluctable fixation. Debreu's *Theory of Value* was published in 1959. The best minds of a few generations travelled the more arcane regions of 'general competitive analysis'. It is the fate of each generation's passion to seem unnatural to its successors. Perhaps the seduction lay in the panoply of technique needed to analyse the model: it was, after all, Debreu who established real analysis at the preferred language of economists. On the conceptual level, however, whether one looks at the competitive outcome as the fixed point of some mapping or the intersection of supply and demand makes little or no difference. Nonetheless, if we look closely at the Marshallian cross it seems difficult to give a coherent account of equilibrium in terms of either P2 or P3. The central contradiction is that, whilst price plays a central role in competitive analysis, no agent (excepting the fictitious) has any direct control over the price. Thus it makes little sense to say either that no one has any incentive to deviate from the competitive outcome or that the price will adjust towards the competitive price.

This does not mean that the competitive outcome is not useful, despite not being an equilibrium. It can be seen either as an ideal type, a (possibly unattainable) benchmark, or an approximation to a non-competitive market. For example, since a competitive market has the desirable efficiency property of Pareto optimality, governments may wish to make non-competitive markets behave more like competitive markets (e.g. as in the regulation of natural monopolists). Or again, under certain circumstances a non-competitive market may behave almost like a competitive market: for example, under certain assumptions the Cournot equilibrium 'tends' to the competitive outcome (see below) as the number of firms becomes large. This means that a Cournot market with many firms can be approximated by its 'limiting case', the competitive outcome. However, that being said, it seems wrong to view the competitive outcome as an equilibrium at all (except perhaps under certain well-specified cases).

The Keynesian Cross

The Keynesian cross represents the equilibrium of the income–expenditure relationship developed by Keynes (1936) and is represented in textbooks by the 45° line diagram developed by Samuelson (1948). The microstructure here consists of simple behavioural relationships. First, expenditures are divided into 'autonomous' (i.e. uninfluenced by income) and 'induced' (i.e. influenced by income) expenditures. Investment and government expenditure are usually seen as autonomous, consumption as induced. A basic behavioural postulate is made about the relationship between income and consumption expenditure: higher income leads to higher expenditure, and furthermore the proportion of income spent falls with consumer income. The macrostructure of the model consists of putting together these two types of expenditure (autonomous and induced) and allowing income to adjust to ensure 'consistency' between income and planned expenditure. In figure 13.4 income Y is on the horizontal axis and expenditure is on the vertical axis. Total planned expenditure is consumption plus investment $I + C(Y)$. The 45° line represents the locus of equality between income and expenditure. At Y^* in figure 13.4, planned expenditure equals planned income, since $I + C(Y^*)$ intersects the 45° line.

Why is Y^* seen as the equilibrium outcome? Again, look to introductory textbooks for the answer. Since at Y^* planned expenditure equals income, and in terms of equilibrium property P2, agents have no incentive to change behaviour. At incomes other than Y^*, there will either be an excess of planned expenditure over income ($Y > Y^*$) or the opposite ($Y < Y^*$). Given the income–expenditure identity, something has to give (this is

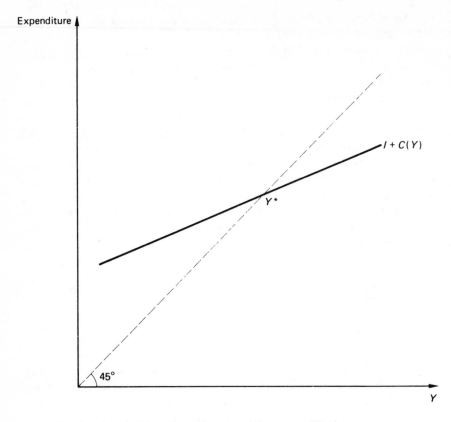

Figure 13.4 Income–expenditure equilibrium.

variously explained in terms of forced saving by consumers or undesired inventory charges by firms). It needs to be noted that there is no derivation of the consumption function from some constrained maximization, and so no 'explanation' of planned consumption, which is itself a datum of explanation. Furthermore it is an *aggregate* consumption function. It is not clear how we can make sense of behaviour changes by any individual, or consumers in general, and how we might judge the effects of any change. Thus P2 is very weak here.

However, the 'stability' equilibrium property P3 plays a much larger role in our understanding of the income–expenditure equilibrium. The driving force behind the equilibrium, the pump propelling the circular flow of income, is the multiplier process, which reflects the combination of a behavioural assumption (income generates expenditure through the consumption function) and an identity (income equals expenditure). One can view the equilibrium outcome Y^* as being generated by the following story. In the beginning there is just autonomous expenditure (for simplicity, say investment I). This generates income, in the sense that the act of 'expending' involves a transfer of money from the spender to the vendor (this is the income–expenditure identity). This income then generates consumption through the behavioural assumption that planned consumption depends upon income. As all economics students know, the end result of this infinite income–expenditure series is precisely income Y^*. This stability story is easily adjusted to allow for any 'initial' income.

If we consider the multiplier story underlying the Keynesian cross, we can see it is much more convincing and credible than the *tâtonnement* story. In one sense the multiplier process can never happen: it would take forever for the infinite geometric series to occur in real time and the process would run into serious problems of the indivisibility of currency. However, it is a process that we can observe, and the logic of geometric series implies that even a few iterations will move income close to Y^*. For example, when a foreign firm invests in a depressed region, it hires workers who spend money, shops open to serve them and so on. The *tâtonnement* is not observed. Whilst we see prices changing, there is no direct reason to believe that they come to rest at competitive levels. It is very important to note the contrast in emphasis between the Marshallian and Keynesian crosses in their emphasis on P2 and P3. Because the income–expenditure model has little microstructure to flesh out the issue of incentives to alter production or consumption, the explanatory emphasis shifts to the stability issue as embodied in the dynamic multiplier process underlying the equilibrium.

As a final comment, I do not believe that the Keynesian cross model is something of only archaeological interest in the history of macrocononic thought. It underlies most macroeconomic models in the determination of nominal income. The behaviour of real income is of course a different matter, which depends (usually) upon what happens in the labour market.

The Cournot Cross

The fact that Cournot published his *Recherches sur la Théorie Mathématique de la Richesse* in 1838 is remarkable. It pre-dates neoclassical economics by at least some 40 years, providing an analysis of duopoly that forms the basic model used in industrial organization, and is introduced as the oligopoly model in micro texts. More remarkable still, it introduced the basic equilibrium concept of modern game theory: the Nash equilibrium. For these reasons it is perhaps the archetypal model underlying current-day economics, just as Walras reincarnated as Debreu underlay the economic theory of a previous generation.

The basic idea of the Cournot–Nash equilibrium is very simple. Firms choose outputs, and the market clears given those outputs. The key step here is to invert the market demand function: rather than treating household demand as a function of price, price is seen as a function of firms' outputs. This mathematical inversion has significant economic implications. In the standard homogeneous good case, it imposes a single market price on the good. Thus there is not a separate price for each firm's output, but a common market price which each firm can influence by altering its output (see Dixon, 1988b, for a more detailed analysis).

If we stick to the homogeneous goods case, let there be n firms $i = 1, \ldots, n$, with individual outputs X_i, summing to total output X. Market price P is then a function of X:

$$P = P(X) \tag{13.1}$$

We can write each firm's profits U_i as a function of the outputs $\mathbf{X}$ chosen by each firm (where $\mathbf{X}$ is the n-vector of each firm's outputs).

$$u_i(\mathbf{X}) = X_i P(X) - c(X_i) \tag{13.2}$$

where $c(X_i)$ is the firm's cost function. A Cournot–Nash equilibrium is defined as a vector of outputs $\mathbf{X}^*$, where each firm's output X_i^* yields higher profits than any other output X_i given the outputs of other firms X_{-i}^* (where X_{-i}^* is the $(n - 1)$ – vector of outputs of firms other than i). Formally, at equilibrium X^*,

$$U_i \left(X^*_i, X_{-i} \right) \geq U_i(X_i, X_{-i}) \tag{13.3}$$

for all feasible outputs X_{-i} (usually any positive $X_i = 0$). There may of course be multiple equilibria or no equilibria: however, we shall proceed as if there is a single Cournot–Nash equilibrium.

The Cournot–Nash equilibrium is therefore almost completely defined in terms of equilibrium property P2. At equilibrium, no firm has an incentive to change its behaviour *given* the behaviour of others. Unlike in the competitive or Keynesian cross equilibria, what happens if one agent deviates from equilibrium is precisely defined. In the Cournot case, there is a function relating the outputs chosen by each firm to their profits (equation (13.2) above). In general game-theoretic terminology firms choose strategies (output) to maximize their pay-offs (profits), given the strategies of other firms. The Nash equilibrium is central to non-cooperative game theory, and its use is spreading through economics as it evolves beyond more traditional competitive or macroeconomic frameworks. The attraction of the Cournot equilibrium is that it is self-enforcing, since no one has an incentive to defect from it. Furthermore, if everyone expects a Nash equilibrium to occur, they will play their Nash strategy.

This is illustrated by the Cournot cross. The Cournot–Nash equilibrium is usually taught using the concept of a 'reaction function' (or, as others prefer, a 'best-response' function). Each firm's reaction function gives its profit-maximizing output given the outputs of the other firms. In the case of duopoly, firm 1's reaction function is derived by solving

$$\text{max}X_1 \ X_1[P(X_1 + X_2) - c(X_1)]$$
$$X_1 = r_1(X_2)$$
(13.4)

This tells us firm 1's best response to any output that firm 2 might choose. Similarly, for firm 2, $X_2 = r_2(X_1)$. Under standard assumptions, each reaction function is downward sloping with an (absolute) slope less than unity. In plain English, if firm 1 were to increase its output by one unit, the other firm's best response would be to reduce its output, but by less than the initial increase in firm 1's output. The Cournot cross is depicted in figure 13.5. The Cournot–Nash equilibrium occurs at point N, where the two reaction functions cross. Only at N are both firms choosing their profit-maximizing output given the output of the other firm.

What of the issue of stability in the Cournot model? The usual textbook story is that, starting from some disequilibrium position, the firms take turns to choose outputs. At each step, the firm chooses its output to maximize its profits given the output of the other firm (i.e. it moves onto its reaction function). In terms of figure 13.6, starting from point a we follow the arrows: firm 1 moves first to its reaction function, firm 2 moves to its reaction function and so on. This process will 'converge' to the equilibrium at N: although the firms will never reach N, they will get closer and closer (in mathematical terminology, the outputs converge uniformly to N but do not converge pointwise). An alternative adjustment process that is harder to depict is simply to have the firms simultaneously adjust to each other's output for the previous period. Assuming that technical 'stability' restrictions are met by the reaction functions, the Cournot–Nash equilibrium can be seen as the outcome of some dynamic process (P3).

However, rather like the *tâtonnement*, the Cournot adjustment process lacks credibility. The crucial weakness is that, at each step, the firms behave myopically: they choose their output to maximize their current profits given the output of the other firm, but ignore the fact that the process specifies that the other firm will adjust its output in response. In short, it is only sensible to treat the other firm's output as given at the Nash equilibrium.

This line of thought gives rise to the idea of allowing firms to have *conjectures* about each other's responses. Suppose we start at the Cournot–Nash equilibrium N. Suppose that firm 1 alters its output to X' in figure 13.7. What would firm 2's best response be? One is tempted to say that firm 2 would move along its 'reaction function' to X'_2. However, this will not be so in general if firm 2 envisages firm 1 making a subsequent response (since

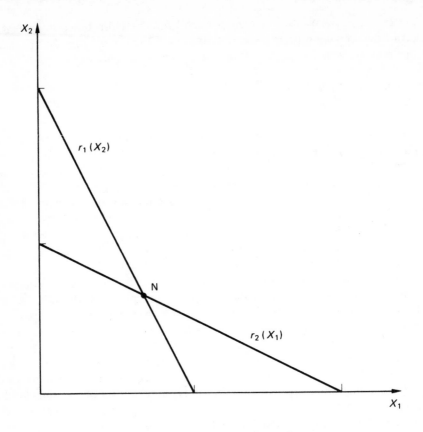

Figure 13.5 Cournot oligopoly.

X_2' is the best response treating X' as given). Thus the issue of how firms respond to each other is rather convoluted: each firm's response depends on how the other firm will respond to it, which depends on what the other firm thinks that the first firm thought. . . .

However, if we alter the firm's conjectures, we not only alter the process of adjustment, but also the equilibrium itself. The reason for this is that in taking output decisions firms will take into account the other firm's response, rather than treating the other firm's output as given as in the Cournot–Nash equilibrium.

The nature of conjectures can be very general, allowing for the initial position and the size of the change. For example, firm 1's conjecture about firm 2's output could give X_2 as a function K of X_1 and the initial situation (X_{10}, X_{20}):

$$X_2 = K(X_1, X_{10}, X_{20})$$

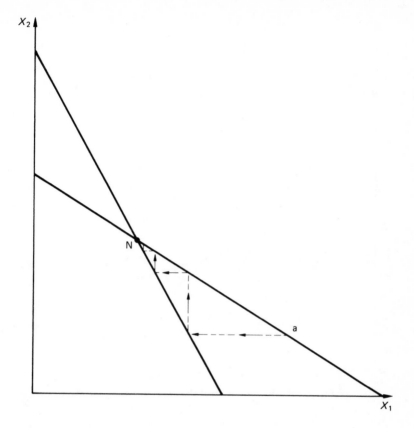

Figure 13.6 Convergence to Cournot equilibrium.

A much simpler (and more common) form of conjecture is to restrict firms to a specific form of conjecture – namely a proportional response which is invariant to initial position. This restricts firms to constant conjectures z about dX_j/dX_i, called 'conjectural variations'. In a symmetric equilibrium with two firms and a homogeneous product this results in the price–cost equation

$$\frac{P - c'}{P} = - \frac{1 + z}{ne}$$

where z is the conjectural variation, c' is marginal cost and e is industry elasticity of demand. If $z = -1$, each firm believes that industry output is constant, since the other firm reduces its output to offset an increase in firm 1's output exactly. In this case $P = c'$ – price equals marginal cost – and we have the competitive outcome. If $z = 0$ we have the Cournot outcome

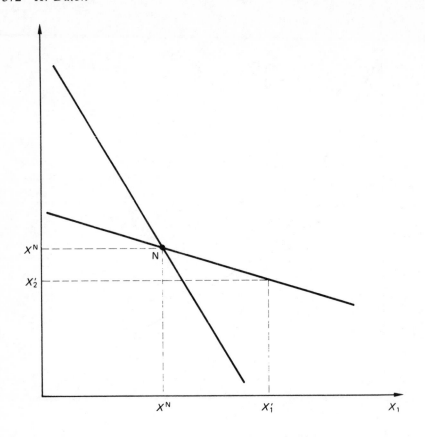

Figure 13.7 Deviations from equilibrium.

(firms believe the other's output is constant). If $z = +1$ then the price–cost margin equals $-1/e$, which is the collusive or joint profit-maximizing outcome. Industrial economists often use the conjectural variation model of Cournot oligopoly because just a single parameter (conjectural variation z) can capture the whole range of competitive behaviour from perfect competition ($z = -1$) to collusion ($z = +1$). The crucial point to note is that the nature of the equilibrium depends crucially on the conjectures firms have about out-of-equilibrium behaviour.

Thus the issue of whether or not firms have an incentive to deviate from equilibrium or not (P2) depends on how they conceive of disequilibrium. This causes problems for stability analysis in the Cournot model: if we allow firms to be aware of the fact that they will respond to each other out of equilibrium, then in general there is no reason for them to treat each other's output as given in equilibrium. The 'myopia' of the adjustment process is crucial for its convergence to the Cournot–Nash equilibrium at N rather than at some other point.

Current sentiment, taking its cue from game theory does not view the conjectural variations approach with esteem. There are perhaps two main reasons for this. First, the Nash equilibrium is seen as the only sensible equilibrium concept to employ. There is no question of being 'out of equilibrium': rational players would never play any but the Nash equilibrium strategies. Any other choice of strategies would involve one firm or the other being off its best-response function and hence able to do better. No players who recognized each other as rational would play anything but the Nash strategy. Second, on the issue of adjustment, it is currently popular to argue that the conjectural approach attempts to capture dynamics in a static 'one-off' model. If we want to understand the responses of firms to one another over time, we need to have a fully specified dynamic model in which time is explicitly present. In game-theoretic terms, this means dealing with (finitely or infinitely) repeated games, which allow firms to react to (and anticipate) each other. In the conjectural approach, the firm simply considers a range of simultaneous possibilities (different values of its own output with the corresponding conjectures about the other's output).

Under the influence of modern game theory, many economists would reject the importance of traditional 'stability' analysis, and with it equilibrium property P3. Equilibrium is to be purely defined in the form of consistency (P1) and in terms of the incentive to play equilibrium strategies given the other player's strategies (P2). There is a price to be paid for this approach of course, i.e. the notion that we must at all times be in equilibrium. This creates some problems, particularly in repeated games which we shall discuss in section 13.4.

Comparing the Marshallian and Cournot crosses, we can see that, whereas the Marshallian cross is ill conceived and defined as an equilibrium, the Cournot cross is well defined in the sense that it is clear on what firms do and how the incentive to deviate from equilibrium is specified. This has led many economists to see the Cournot–Nash approach as a way of rationalizing the Walrasian approach. The basic idea is to see the Walrasian equilibrium as the limit of the Cournot–Nash equilibrium as the number of firms in the industry becomes infinite or, – more precisely, – as the market share of each firm tends to zero. In this sense, the Walrasian outcome can be seen as an approximation to the 'true' Cournot–Nash equilibrium if there are many firms. The argument here is simple. The Walrasian equilibrium is based on the notion of price-taking behaviour, which means that firms treat marginal revenue as equal to price. Under Cournot competition marginal revenue is less than price since, as the firm increases output, the price falls. The extent to which the firm's marginal revenue is less than price depends upon the firm's elasticity of demand e_i which in turn depends upon its market share s_i and the industry elasticity e:

$$e_i = \frac{PP'}{X_i}$$

$$= \frac{X}{X_i}\frac{P}{X}P' = \frac{1}{s_i}e = ne$$

where P' is the slope of the market demand curve. If the market share s_i is very small, then we would expect the firm's elasticity e_i to become very large. If the firm's elasticity becomes very large, then marginal revenue becomes closer to price (recall that price taking is often described as having a 'perfectly elastic' or horizontal demand curve). Thus the behaviour of a Cournot–Nash equilibrium with many firms will be close to that of a Walrasian equilibrium.

An Evaluation

We have explored three different equilibria which lie at the heart of economics. To what extent do they embody a common equilibrium methodology? At the most superficial level, they do. We identified the three equilibrium properties P1–P3 that are often put forward and which seem to encapsulate the general view of equilibrium. All the equilibria possess these three properties in some sense. However, when we look at the equilibria closely, we can see that there are tensions and inconsistencies between both the equilibrium properties themselves (more specifically P2 and P3) and the equilibria. The inconsistency between P2 and P3 arises because of the nature of economic explanation. The tension between different types of equilibria arises because of substantive differences in their vision of how the economic world is conceived.

Let us first address the tension between P2 and P3, a problem that arises in both the competitive and Cournot equilibria. At the heart of this tension lies the problem of explanation. The behavioural model of agents in the microstructure gives rise to the state of the macrostructure. In equilibrium, these two are consistent. Out of equilibrium, they are not. Thus the behavioural model which defines the equilibium may not be suitable out of equilibrium. Most importantly, it may lead agents to behave suboptimally out of equilibrium, which makes explanation of such behaviour difficult for economists. This problem occurs when we consider P2 and P3: both involve some consideration of both equilibrium and disequilibrium states. In evaluating P2, we consider what happens when agents deviate from equilibrium behaviour, so moving away from equilibrium; in stability we analyse the equilibrium state as the outcome of a sequence of disequilibrium states ('outcome' in the sense of limit, end-point or destination).

The tension between P2 and P3 arises because the equilibrium behaviour used to define equilibrium under P2 seems inappropriate for analysing stability P3. The argument can be put briefly as follows.

1 Equilibrium is defined (partly) by behavioural postulates X.
2 In analysing stability (P3), the reason that the economic system moves towards equilibrium is that agents adjust their behaviour. Thus the driving force of the move towards equilibrium is the response of agents to their mistakes.
3 If agents adapted their behaviour to the disequilibrium situation, the motion of the economic system would differ and, most importantly, it might lead to a different equilibrium. In particular, behaviour Y which is appropriate in disequilibrium may not be consistent with the equilibrium defined by behaviour X.

This tension is present in both the Marshallian and Cournot cross equilibria. In the competitive cases, the equilibrium behaviour employed under P2 is price-taking behaviour. This makes reasonable sense in equilibrium (agents are indeed able to buy and sell as much as they wish), but, in analysing stability, P3, the assumption of price-taking behaviour becomes silly – prices change in response to excess demand, and agents are unable to realize their desired trades. The presence of excess demands drives the *tâtonnement* process, and the presence of excess demands reflects the fact that agents are making mistakes in some sense. Were they to adapt their behaviour to disequilibrium, the resultant end-point might be different from the competitive equilibrium. In the Cournot case we illustrated this argument using conjectural variations.

To turn to the second issue, each of the equilibria embodies a different vision of the economic world. In the competitive world we have individual agents responding to price signals which they receive from an impersonal market. They do not see their own actions influencing anything or anyone but themselves. In the Cournot game-theoretic world, although agents act indenpendently, they see that their own pay-offs (profits, utility) depend upon the other agents' actions as well as their own (and that their own actions influence others). There is no 'invisible hand' or price mechanism to coordinate activity across the economy. Rather, each agents acts in his own self-interest, ignoring the effect of his actions on others. In the Keynesian cross model, there are no individuals as such. Attention is focused on impersonal aggregates which are driven by their own laws rather than through any very specific modelling of individual action.

13.2 Disequilibrium and Equilibrium

The analysis of disequilibrium poses great problems for economic explanation. Whilst it is not plausible to maintain that every market and agent is at all times in equilibrium, economists have very little to say about what happens out of equilibrium. This is because equilibrium itself lies at the heart of economic explanation. There is a sense in which economists cannot explain out-of-equilibrium phenomena. If we recall the structure of explanation in economics, it rests on two levels: microstructure, where agents' behaviour is specified (usually as the outcome of constrained optimizations); and macrostructure, where the parts are put together into a whole by the use of an equilibrium concept. Putting these two levels together, we can explain: 'everyone is doing as well as they can (microstructure); if everyone is doing as well as they can, then this happens (macrostructure)'. The equilibrium concept thus relates the properties of the whole (be it macroeconomy, general equilibrium system, market or firm) to behaviour and motivation of the individual agents or parts.

The problem of disequilibrium analysis is that it is not an equilibrium, so that by definition the desired behaviour of agents is not consistent and in some sense their actions are not the best they could take. In essence, explanation of disequilibrium involves the explanation of a mistake. In a theory based on formal rationality (as opposed to procedural rationality), it is difficult to explain mistakes. With a procedural model of rationality, the explanation of a mistake can consist in showing that (in a particular instance) the procedure generating choices and actions is wrong. With a formal notion of rationality, there is no reference to the procedure: the decision is linked directly to the basic conditions of the problem, and there is no room for explaining the mistake. This difference is perhaps best illustrated by the contrast between adaptive and rational expectations in the context of the Lucas supply curve. With adaptive expectations, there is a procedure generating the expectations of agents in the economy; it may be a good or bad procedure depending on the behaviour of inflation. Whether it is a good or bad procedure, it can explain why agents may make systematic mistakes under certain circumstances (e.g. if inflation accelerates). With rational expectations, however, there can in principle be no explanation of how people make systematic mistakes. Indeed, that people make systematic mistakes would in itself be a refutation of the rational expectations hypothesis. Thus the formal notion of rationality employed by most economists is rather ill equipped to deal with disequilibrium.

This point is perhaps best illustrated by looking at disequilibrium in a competitive market. Although more of an allegory than a serious explanation of what happens, we can consider the *tâtonnement* process. Suppose that the price is above the competitive price. Supply exceeds demand, so that desired trades are 'inconsistent' (equilibrium property P1 is not satisfied). The price is falling, so 'price taking' is not appropriate. As to the issue of whether or not agents are doing as well as they can, that depends on how what goes out of equilibrium is specified. The traditional *tâtonnement* story gets around this by saying that there is no trade: in effect nothing happens. In the Hahn–Negishi (1962) story, trade occurs out of equilibrium: the Hahn–Negishi condition states that all agents have the excess demand of same sign. This means that only one side of the market is unable to meet its desired (or 'target') trades at the disequilibrium price. In terms of figure 13.2, this means that at P^0 those demanding the good are able to obtain their desired trades, whilst suppliers will in some sense be 'rationed' (more about this later). Thus actual trades will be given by X_0. The rationale for the Hahn–Negishi condition is that markets are 'efficient': if there is someone who wants to buy and someone who wants to sell, they will find each other. If the Hahn–Negishi condition were violated, then there could be agents on both sides of the market unable to trade. Clearly, there must be a sense in which those unable to realize their desired trade could do better. In terms of figure 13.2, the rationed suppliers could cut their price: again, the price-taking assumption is not appropriate out of competitive equilibrium. The basic assumptions about the behaviour of economic agents (demands and supplies are derived by treating prices as given, and there are no constraints on trades) are not consistent unless they are assumptions of competitive equilibrium. Or, to put it another way, agents display no 'disequilibrium awareness' in Fischer's (1981) terminology; they behave as if they were in equilibrium even when they are not.

One response to this is to extend the model to allow agents to behave in a fundamentally different and appropriate manner out of equilibrium. For the case of competitive price adjustment, Fischer (1981) has attempted the non-*tâtonnement* process in this way. The resultant model is extremely complex and unwieldy (the author contemplated submitting an equation in his model to the *Guinness Book of Records* for the longest ever Lagrangean, p. 290n.). This is not the place to discuss whether or not this attempt was successful. However, even if successful, it would simply come close to defining a new equilibrium for when prices are adjusting to the competitive equilibrium rather than studying disequilibrium itself.

This illustrates the fundamental problem posed by disequilibrium: the explanation is either unsatisfactory or it leads to the definition of a new equilibrium. The best illustration of this is the literature on fix-price 'disequilibrium' models.

In the 1960s, workers on the reinterpretation of Keynes (Clower, 1965; Leijonhufvud, 1968) argued that Keynesian macroeconomics was incompatible with Walrasian equilibrium, and that phenomena such as rationing and the income–expenditure process arose from 'false trading' at non-competitive prices. Unless prices were seen as adjusting instantaneously to their Walrasian values, microeconomics would need to be revised to take account of trading 'in disequilibrium'. The response of economists in the 1970s was to pursue they study of *disequilibrium* by defining a new sort of *equilibrium*, fixed-price equilibrium, the main contributions being by Barro and Grossman (1971), Benassy (1975) and Malinvaud (1977). The study of fixed-price equilibria adopted the basic notion of price-taking from the Walrasian approach, but made prices *exogenous* (rather than trying them down to the market-clearing level). The basic task was to provide a consistent and coherent account of trade at 'disequilibrium prices'. In Walrasian microeconomics, agents believe that they can buy or sell as much as they wish at the given price. Out of competitive equilibrium this is inappropriate, and so a new economic variable was introduced – the quantity or rationing constraint. The notion of *effective demand* was specified as the demand which (in the household's case) maximizes utility *given* the quantity constraints that it faces in other markets. Thus if a worker is unable to sell his labour (there is an excess supply of labour), this will restrict his demand for consumption goods. Similarly, if a firm cannot sell all it would like to at the current price, then its demand for labour will be influenced. This is the essence of the 'spillover' effect: if an agent is unable to realize his trades in one market, it may affect his demand or supply in other markets. In the eyes of the 'reinterpretation of Keynes' school, this was the very essence of the multiplier process and the income-expenditure feedback, which meant that quantities (rather than just prices, as in the Walrasian case) entered into demand functions.

By introducing a rationing regime into the market process, and allowing rationing constraints to influence individual agents' decisions, the fixed-price approach was able to reconcile the microstructure of the model with the macrostructure. In essence, at non-Walrasian prices, demands and supplies do not equalize; agents are unable to realize their desired trades (macrostructure). Recognizing the constraints on trade, agents revise their desired trades to take these into account (microstructure).

Thus the analysis of competitive 'disequilibrium' led to the invention of a new type of 'non-Walrasian' equilibrium. The analysis of 'disequilibrium' did not lead to a genuine disequilibrium analysis. Rather the logic of economic explanation led to the generation of another equilibrium concept. In this case, fix-price equilibria are a *generalization* of Walrasian equilibria: a Walrasian equilibrium is merely a fix-price equilibrium where agents face no (binding) rationing constraints.

Given the real disequilibrium analysis is to some extent incompatible with standard economic explanation and rationality, to what extent is economics possible without equilibrium? To see what economics looks like without equilibrium, it is salutary to look at one of the few economic models to reach textbook popularity which did not employ the equilibrium method. The example I have chosen is Kaldor's growth model (see Jones, 1975, pp. 146–9, for a concise exposition of Kaldor, 1957). The central issue in Harrod's growth model was the possible divergence of the 'warranted' growth rate (which equates planned saving and planned investment) from the 'natural' growth rate (determined by demography, technological progress etc.). Kaldor's microstructure consisted of the differential savings propensities out of wage and profit income. Thus savings were influenced by the distribution of income between wages and profits. Rather than employ an equilibrium concept in his model, Kaldor used a 'stylized fact': namely that there had been full employment in post-war European economies. Kaldor argued that the distribution of income between wages and profits would adjust to maintain consistency between the warranted and natural growth rates. Thus a feature of the macrostructure was employed to tie down the distribution of income (to 'close the model'), rather than an equilibrium concept. This explanation is viewed as odd because it works backwards: rather than deducing macro properties from individual and market behaviour, it deduces the distribution of income across wages and profits from the macrostructure. Indeed, Modigliani and Samuelson went so far as to say 'If you can believe this, you can believe anything' (1966, p. 234). The equilibrium methodology is so ingrained in economists' minds that they will not be convinced by non-equilibrium explanations.

13.3 Information and Equilibrium

Until now we have been considering only 'full-information' models, where agents have a given information set including all the relevant information for them to take decisions. In the 1970s there was a blossoming of interest in exploring the implications of imperfect information for economic behaviour and equilibrium. Perhaps the earliest interest was in the 'search' models of unemployment in the late 1960s. In these models, agents have imperfect information about prices (wages), e.g. what prices (wages) a particular firm is offering. Search models of unemployment modelled the response of the unemployed to this problem: do they take the next job offered to them at a particular wage, or will they continue to search and incur the cost of further unemployment? The general solution to this problem was the 'reservation wage' rule: the unemployed continue searching until they are offered at least their 'reservation wage'. However, these were not *equilibrium* models, since there was no explanation of the initial distribution of wage offers. Why should firms offer different wages to the same worker or type of worker? However, the model was nonetheless very influential, not least in its influence on Friedman's formulation of the natural rate hypothesis (Friedman, 1968). We shall take Spence's (1974) signalling model as our archetypal imperfect information model. This had a tremendous impact at the time, and introduced the fundamental distinction between separating and pooling equilibria which has proved to be so important.

The standard approach to imperfect information is to presume that if agents do not know the true value of X_1 they have some subjective probability density function for X, $f(X)$, in effect treating X as a random variable. Spence took the case of worker productivity, where there was asymmetric information so that, whilst workers knew their own productivity, firms did not. For example, let worker productivity X take discrete values, being either low or high (X_L, X_H respectively). Suppose that it is not possible to test directly for productivity. Whilst the employer might not know the actual productivity of an individual worker, it might have a subjective belief about the probability that the worker is high productivity (q) or low productivity ($1 - q$). Assuming that firms are risk neutral and minimize costs, they will be willing to offer workers their expected productivity EX:

$$W = \mathrm{E}X = qX_H + (1 - q)X_L \tag{13.5}$$

The wage offer depends upon both the subjective probability q and the values (X_L, X_H). If we take the latter as given, what is the 'equilibrium' value of W and q?

This raises an issue about beliefs in economic models. Given that beliefs are not 'tied down' by the truth (there is not full information), how do we explain agents' beliefs? We shall consider this issue in this section and the next. However, there now enters the notion of *epistemological* rationality. The agent is presumed to have (in some sense) the 'best' beliefs given the information available. 'Best' here usually means statistically optimal. An agent's beliefs are then explained by saying that they are (in some sense) statistically optimal. 'Best' in this context means something completely different from the notion of 'best' in the theory of rational choice, where it means the choice which yields maximum utility given the constraints faced. Different notions of rationality are employed in explaining beliefs and explaining consumption or production decisions. The key point is that beliefs are not chosen to maximize utility. It may increase my utility if I believe that I am Napoleon: however, that is not a 'rational' belief. Let us first define economic rationality: it is an *instrumental* rationality in which choices are made merely as a means to an end (utility or profit). If we were to extend economic rationality to beliefs, people would choose beliefs so as to maximize their utility. The belief that I am Napoleon might then be perfectly rational (indeed, not to believe I am Napoleon might be to involve some suboptimality). When beliefs clearly do matter in that they directly affect well-being (in some sense), economic rationality can be used to explain beliefs. However, in most economic models, beliefs do not enter the utility function of households directly. Debreu's households might be deist, pantheist or atheist; they might believe in general relativity or be creationists.

When explaining beliefs, however, a different notion of rationality is employed by economists. Let us take the example above of the firm hiring workers of unknown productivity. In equilibrium, is there any restriction to be placed on the firm's subjective probability q? The usual constraint suggested is that *in equilibrium* the belief is 'confirmed'. In the case sketched above, suppose that the objective (i.e. population) proportion of high-productivity workers is q^*. Then we require that $q = q^*$: the subjective probability equals the objective probability. Assuming that the firm employs a large number of workers, the average productivity of workers the firm employs is

$$\bar{X} = q^*X_H + (1 - q^*)X_L \qquad (4.2)$$

for the firm's beliefs are only 'confirmed' if

$$EX = \bar{X}$$

requiring that $q = q^*$. If the firm's subjective probability differs from the population proportion, then the average productivity of the work-force differs from what the firm expects.

If $q^* > q$, workers would (on average) be more productive, and vice versa. In the statistical sense, the firm would have an 'incentive' to revise its beliefs if X deviated from EX. 'Incentive' here is used not in its standard economic sense but in a statistical sense that the optimal estimator of the population parameter would be different. Economists often tend to confuse the language and concepts of economic and statistical rationality. This is probably because both can be expressed mathematically as an optimization. However, the fact that in one case it is utility (or profit) to be maximized and in the other it is the likelihood (or some such statistical criterion) to be maximized makes the two rationalities completely separate and incommensurable.

In most economic models, this incommensurability does not give rise to any incompatibility. However, I will give an example of when economic and epistemological rationality are incompatible. Let us return to the example of Cournot–Nash equilibrium which we explored in section 13.1. In figure 13.8, the Cournot–Nash equilibrium occurs at N: firm 1 is choosing its profit-maximizing output given the other firm's output X^N. In effect, firm 1 believes (or expects) firm 2 to play X^N, and chooses its best response. Furthermore, in equilibrium this belief is confirmed: if firm 1 produces X^N,

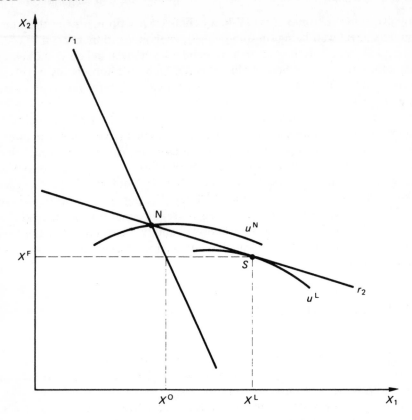

Figure 13.8 Where ignorance is bliss.

it is firm 2's best response to produce X^N. However, suppose that firm 1 believed that firm 2 was producing X^{Oh}: its best response would be X^L. If firm 1 stuck to this belief, firm 2 would (eventually) produce X^F, its best response to X^L. This is the standard 'Stackelberg' or 'leader–follower' equilibrium with firm 1 the 'leader' producing X^L, and firm 2 the follower producing X^F. Is this an equilibrium? In one sense it is: firm 2 is choosing its best response to X^F; firm 1 is choosing its best response to the output it believes firm 2 to be producing, namely X^O. The problem is that firm 1's beliefs are not correct: X^O does not equal X^F. If we require firm 1's beliefs to be correct, in addition to both firms' choosing their best response, there is only one possible outcome – the Nash equilibrium at N. In terms of its pay-off (economic rationality), the firm does better to have incorrect beliefs at (X^L, X^F): it loses no profits by the fact that its beliefs about the other firm's output are incorrect (X^O differs from X^L), but clearly it gains profits by being the Stackelberg leader as a result ($u^L > u^N$). However, most economists would not maintain that this was an equilibrium: the firm would have an 'incentive' (in the sense of epistemic rationality) to revise its beliefs about the other firm's output. Thus the firm (it is argued) will change its beliefs about X_2, so that the Stackelberg point (X^L, X^F) is not an 'equilibrium'. Thus despite the reduction in profits caused by the change of belief, epistemological rationality dictates that the belief cannot be maintained in equilibrium. There is thus a clash of rationalities, which are in this instance incompatible.

In this clash of incommensurable rationalities, economists let epistemological rationality overrule economic rationality. Even though the Stackelberg leader's delusion is profitable, he is not allowed to maintain his belief in the presence of clear evidence to the contrary. Thus we can add a fourth equilibrium property to our list:

P4, in equilibrium, agents have no incentive to alter their beliefs,

where 'incentive' is interpreted in the strictly epistemological sense, not the economic sense of P2. In the case of the simple example of firms hiring workers, P4 requires that subjective beliefs are 'confirmed', i.e. that $q^* = q$. In more complicated models, where X is a continuous variable, the beliefs might be subjective probability distributions, and P4 might require beliefs about mean, variance and possibly higher moments to be correct.

Having explored the new notion of rationality introduced to tie down beliefs in equilibrium with imperfect information, we can move on to examine perhaps the most important type of such equilibria: signalling equilibria (as introduced by Spence, 1974).

Suppose that we take the case where the firm hires workers of unknown quality, taking the model introduced earlier in this section. In equilibrium, we argued that the wage offer would equal the average productivity X of workers. This is called a pooling equilibrium, because both low- and high-productivity workers are pooled together (i.e. they are treated the same, and receive the same wages). In the full-information case, high-productivity workers would obtain their full marginal product X_H, low-productivity workers would obtain X_L. Thus the high-productivity workers do worse in the pooled equilibrium ($\bar{X} < X_H$) than in the full-information case, and low-productivity workers do better. There is thus an incentive for high-productivity workers to 'signal' their ability to their prospective employer. Very simply, a high-productivity worker can signal his ability if he can do something which a low-ability worker is unwilling or unable to do. This signalling activity need have no direct causal relationship with the workers' productivity. All that matters is that the high-productivity workers have lower costs of undertaking the activity. It has long been recognized that education is used as a 'screening' device by employers to sift applicants.

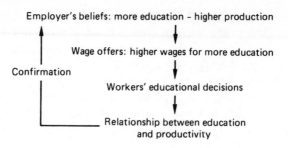

Figure 13.9 A signalling equilibrium.

Whilst education may sometimes have little direct or vocational content, it can be seen as enhancing the general ability of the educated. However, Spence (1974) abstracts from this, and focuses purely on the signalling element.

The essence of a signalling equilibrium is a circular relationship between the beliefs of agents and their behaviour. The essence is that the beliefs induce behaviour which confirms these beliefs. Thus, in the context of Spence's model, employers have a belief about the relationship between education and productivity (higher education is related to higher productivity); this causes firms to offer higher wages to more educated workers; this sets up the incentives workers face to obtain educational qualifications; workers' decisions about education determine the *actual* relationship (if any) between education and productivity. There is an equilibrium if the employer's beliefs are confirmed (P4 is satisfied). Figure 13.9 is a schematic representation.

The crucial feature of the equilibrium is that the *costs* of signalling (being educated) differ with productivity. More specifically, higher-productivity workers must have lower 'signalling' costs – in this case they must have lower costs of achieving a given level of education. The reason for this is that otherwise (given that the firm's wages are related to education) the low-productivity workers would also find it in their interest to obtain higher educational qualifications, so that the firm would offer them higher wages (in the belief that they were high-productivity workers). This is often called the 'incentive compatibility' constraint. The idea is that, in equilibrium, each different type of worker has the appropriate incentive to behave appropriately to its type. Thus, in the above case, the two types of worker differ by productivity. Suppose that the employer believes that low-productivity workers have no education, whilst those with y^* units of education (a B. A. degree) are high productivity. This wage offer might therefore be

$$W = \begin{cases} X_H & y \geqslant y^* \\ X_L & y < y^* \end{cases}$$

Assuming that there is no intrinsic value to education, workers will either choose no education ($y = 0$), or $y = y^*$ to get the higher wages. Workers will undertake the education if and only if the cost is less than the extra wages obtained. 'Incentive compatibility' requires that it is in the interest of high-productivity workers to obtain their B. A. (for them, the cost of attaining y^* is less than $X_H - X_L$); low-productivity workers, on the other hand, would find it too costly to obtain a B. A. (the cost of attaining y^* is greater than $X_H - X_L$). In the signalling equilibrium (if it exists), the two types of workers are *separated*: the incentives are such that they reveal their true type through their behaviour. When this occurs, there is said to be a *separating* equilibrium. If the employers beliefs were different, there could be a *pooling* equilibrium: if the employer believed that there was no relationship between education and productivity, he would offer the same wage regardless of education; no one would become educated, and thus the employer's beliefs would be confirmed.

In this type of equilibrium with asymmetric information and signalling, there is a very intimate relationship between economic incentives (P2) and the confirmation of beliefs (P4). However, it must be noted that in Spence's model the treatment of beliefs is very rudimentary, which results in multiple equilibria. The possibility of multiple signalling equilibria is easily illustrated using the educational signalling model. Following Spence, suppose that high-productivity workers have a cost $y/2$ of achieving education level y:

$$X_H - y/2 \geqslant X_L \tag{a}$$

$$X_H - y < X_L \tag{b}$$

Condition (a) states that, given y, it pays the high-productivity worker to invest in education (cost $y/2$), to obtain extra income $X_H - X_L$; condition (b) states that this is not so for the low-productivity worker, who has to invest more effort and resources to obtain y. Both (a) and (b) will be satisfied if

$$X_H - X_L \leqslant y^* \leqslant 2(X_H - X_L) \tag{c}$$

Thus, if the employer's beliefs about the 'critical' level of education y^* are in the interval (c), then there will be a separating equilibrium with workers' activity so as to confirm the employer's belief. There is thus a continuum of equilibria. Is there any sense in which one can sensibly rank the equilibria?

Suppose that the employer and workers are economists and understand

Spence's model. Then the employer will understand the incentive constraints (a) and (b). He will deduce that anyone undertaking a level of
education greater than $X_H - X_L$ must be a high-productivity worker: there
is no way that a low-productivity worker would conceivably want to
undertake a course of education that would cost more than the possible
extra earnings. Thus, if we consider the equilibria with $y^* > X_H - X_L$, they
involve an unnecessary cost in the form of education in excess of the
minimum required. It has been argued (Cho, 1987) that these equilibria
will not be 'stable'. A high-productivity worker can educate below y but
above $X_H - X_L$ and still single himself out as being high productivity. Thus
with 'sophisticated' knowledge about the way the model works, the equilibrium with the minimum amount of signalling necessary to separate types
is the most plausible (in the above case, $y^* = X_H - X_L$).

13.4   Time and Equilibrium

The passing of time is a central feature of human experience. It plays a
central role in much economic activity, since production takes time and
consumers have to decide how to spread their consumption and labour
supply over their (uncertain) lifetime. Yet, all the three equilibria studied
in section 13.1 were in a fundamental sense static equilibria. They were
equilibria in a timeless world, or at most equilibria at a point in time which
is unconnected to the past or future. How does our conception and
evaluation of equilibria alter when we allow for time?

First, consider the Walrasian equilibrium. If we introduce time into the
picture, there are two fundamentally different ways of conceiving of
equilibrium. First is the Arrow–Debreu model, which sees the earth as a
large market-place and world history as the working out of contingent
contracts. Second is the notion of temporary equilibrium, which sees
history as a *sequence* of transitory equilibria. We shall deal with these two
ideas in turn.

Competitive general equilibrium theory explores the issue of the existence and characterization of competitive equilibrium in an economy with
an arbitrary number of markets. For example, these might be seen as
corresponding to n basic commodity types (bananas, nuts etc.). As such,
the model is timeless. We can then ask how time can be brought into a
timeless model. This can be done by a logical exercise of dating commodities. Suppose that the world lasts T periods $t = 1, \ldots, T$. We can call a
banana at time t a particular commodity, to be different from a banana at
time s (where s is not equal to t). Rather than having n markets, we will
now have nT markets, corresponding to the n basic commodity types over
T periods. This is depicted in figure 13.10 where time proceeds from left to

Time ⟶

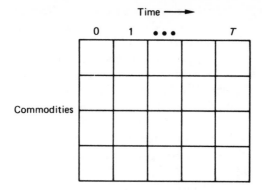

Figure 13.10 Arrow–Debreu markets.

right, each row representing a commodity type, and each column a date.

A particular square represents the market for a particular commodity i at a specific date t. Each market has a price P_{it}. Consumers will derive utility from the consumption of all nT dated commodities, which they will maximize subject to a budget constraint reflecting relative prices. Thus a household can as much sell an umbrella in the year 2000 for a corset in the year 1901 as it can exchange a banana for a nut in 1990.

In a certain sense, then, introducing dated commodities and their corresponding markets and prices into the abstract notion of competitive general equilibrium enables time to be included in the model. This is a purely logical exercise, however. What would the Arrow– Debreu world be like to live in? Competitive general equilibrium occurs at a list of prices – one for each market – at which demand equals supply in each market (or, more generally, there is no excess demand). The key feature is that there is *simultaneous* equilibrium across markets. In the full Arrow–Debreu world, prices across history need to be simultaneously determined. Prices across time need to be determined together outside the historical process itself. Following the great religious texts, we can place that which is beyond time at some notional beginning of time. Thus we can imagine that at the beginning of time the souls of all the world's population-to-be assemble in a large building (let us say the Albert Hall). The auctioneer would cry out a long vector of prices covering each commodity over world history. A *tâtonnement* process would occur, until every market was in equilibrium, whether for second-hand skins in 200 BC or microwave ovens in 2000 AD. Once equilibrium had been reached, the final prices would be struck. The souls of the future world would then dissolve from the Albert Hall to return to the unmanifest, each with a contract. This contract would tell them the prices of each commodity at every time, and their trades. Time would then begin, and souls would become manifest as people and live their allotted lives. History would simply be the working out of the original contract: each day economic man would look at his contract, and carry out his pre-ordained trades (as would economic woman). Economists have competing views as to whether this world would last forever ('infinite horizon' with T infinite), or whether the world would end after some period T. In the latter case, others have argued that perhaps, the world having ended, the whole process would begin again: perhaps the same souls involved in the infinite repetition of the same history, or different souls subject to the same laws. Alas, econometrics remains powerless to adjudicate on this issue. Clearly, the Arrow–Debreu world has little in common with our own world.

A more realistic vision of world history is given by the temporary equilibrium approach. This has the advantage that price formation is historically situated. It also has the advantage that each day that economic man wakes up he does not know what is going to happen. The basic vision in its simplest form is to *truncate* the Arrow–Debreu model. At time t, we can differentiate between *spot* markets, which are markets for goods to be traded at time t, and *futures* markets, which are for goods to be traded in date sequence to t. An extreme form of temporary equilibrium is to assume that the economy is rather like an adolescent punk – all spots and no future. Thus at any time there would be a market for each basic commodity, but no markets for future commodities. Suppose an infinitely lived household wishes to sell its 200 BC sheepskin to buy a 1990 AD microwave. Whereas in the Arrow–Debreu world this can be done directly at the Albert Hall in year 0, in a temporary equilibrium sequence economy the transaction is more difficult. The sheepskin would have to be sold in 200 BC and exchanged for money (or some other store of value). The money could then be held as an asset until 1990 AD arrives, when it is handed over for the microwave. The reverse transaction is rather more difficult: without a futures market for microwaves, our household would have to persuade the then equivalent of a bank manager to provide it with a bridging loan until the microwave sale in 1990 AD. This should prove no problem with perfect information and perfect foresight. However, if money balances are constrained to be positive (i.e. no borrowing), then the absence of this futures market might prevent the purchase of the sheepskin in 200 BC.

'All spots and no future' is an extreme form of temporary equilibrium. There might be some futures markets allowed (e.g. in financial assets or chosen commodities). In the above example, our household could then trade in these futures markets to finance the sheepskin purchase, e.g. by selling future money for current (i.e. 200 BC) money. This is in effect borrowing the money to buy the sheepskin.

World history here is a sequence of temporary equilibria. Unlike the

Arrow–Debreu world, markets unfold sequentially, rather than all at once. From the household's point of view, rather than there being one big intertemporal budget constraint spanning world history, there is a separate budget constraint for each point in time (or, with uncertainty, for each state of nature at each point in time). At any one time, all the consumer 'observes' are current prices in the markets in which the consumer trades. Whilst the consumer will of course base his current consumption decisions on what he thinks may happen in the future, the absence of futures markets gives him little or no indication of what future prices might be. This contrasts with the Arrow–Debreu story, where all prices for all time are known in the Albert Hall. This of course raises problems of intertemporal coordination. Taking our previous example, if the ancient Briton wishes to exchange his sheepskins for a future microwave, he will have to save (i.e. hold money). This act of saving transmits no direct signal to the microwave manufacturer to invest in order to provide for the eventual demand. This contrasts with the Arrow–Debreu story, where this is all sorted out in the Albert Hall. The absence of futures markets thus poses a decisive problem for coordinating economic activity over time, a problem first highlighted by Keynes (1936) and also highlighted by his subsequent reinterpreters (e.g. Shackle, 1974; Liejunhufvud, 1968; *inter alia*). The first 'fundamental theorem' of welfare economics – which states that any competitive equilibrium is Pareto optimal – is only generally valid in the Arrow–Debreu world: in a temporary equilibrium sequence economy the problem of intertemporal coordination is almost insuperable.

Although the Arrow–Debreu and temporary equilibrium approaches seem so different, economic theorists have taken pains to demonstrate that their outcomes need not be so different. With perfect foresight, for example, the history of the world (in terms of prices, consumption and so on) will look the same as if history had started in the Albert Hall. Whilst it might be reasonable to assume that infinitely lived households have perfect foresight, it is less appealing in the case of mortal households. The assumption of perfect foresight assumes that each and every agent can work out the equilibrium prices over time. This destroys the appealing notion of 'decentralization' by the price mechanism. Rather than each agent simply responding to prices on the basis of his own information, in a perfect foresight sequence economy each agent is required to have full information about the whole economy. In effect, each agent in the economy becomes the auctioneer. Indeed, each agent knows more than Walras's auctioneer, since he merely groped blindly to equilibrium, whereas our prescient agents calculate the path of prices over history. Of more interest, perhaps, are results which show that a full set of futures markets is not needed to replicate the Arrow–Debreu world: see Marimon (1987) for a survey and discussion of some of the important results.

We have seen the implications of time for Walrasian equilibrium. What of Cournot? The Cournot–Nash equilibrium is best conceived of as a one-shot game. What happens if firms compete over time? We shall examine the issues raised by competition over time to explore the concept of *subgame-perfect* equilibrium; for a fuller exposition, see Dixon (1988b). The basic idea of a subgame-perfect equilibrium is that at each point in time agents choose their best responses to each other, given that, in each subsequent period, they will continue to do so. The main use of this equilibrium concept has been to rule out non-credible threats, by which it is meant threats that it is not in the interest of the threatener to carry out (put another way, if the threatened agent called the bluff of the threatener, the threatener would not carry out the threat). The logic of subgame-perfect equilibrium rules out such non-credible threats by requiring agents to act in their best interest for each and subsequent periods. For example, I could threaten to kill you in a most unpleasant manner if you did not send me a £5 postal order. This is not a credible threat since, were you not to comply, it would not be in my interest to kill you (certain readers excepted). Suppose that the Cournot scenario is repeated for T periods. The 'subgame' for each period $t = 1, \ldots, T$ is simply the remainder of the game from period t through to T (for example, in period 5 of a ten-year game, the subgame consists of periods 5 through to 10). At each point in time t, we can imagine each Cournot duopolist choosing his outputs for the remaining periods (i.e. choosing outputs to produce in each period $s = t$, $t + 1, \ldots, T$). If the outputs chosen over the remaining periods by each firm are the best response to the other firm's choice, there is a Nash equilibrium in the period to subgame. Subgame perfection requires that the firms' strategies are a Nash equilibrium in each and every subgame. This rules out non-credible threats, since in effect it requires the firm to choose its strategy optimally at each stage of the game. When we arrive at the period when the non-credible threat needs to be carried out, the firm will not do this because it is not in its interest to do so.

In order to solve for a perfect equilibrium, agents need to 'work backwards'. In order to know what they will do in period $T - 1$, they need to work out what they will do in period T to evaluate the consequences of their choice of strategy in $T - 1$. They then proceed to work out what will happen in period $T - 1$ conditional on the choice of strategies in $T - 2$ and so on. In a perfect equilibrium, agents in effect become super-rational game theorists: in evaluating the consequences of their actions, each agent takes into account that future responses by all agents will be chosen optimally.

This equilibrium notion has been very popular in the last decade. However, it has a serious methodological paradox at its heart. If the players of the game are super-rational and solve the game, then the equilibrium will occur. However, in evaluating the equilibrium, the agents considered the possibility of taking non-equilibrium actions (i.e. actions off the equilibrium path) but, if agents were rational, then they would never take actions off the equilibrium path. If an agent were to move off the equilibrium path, then he could not be 'rational' in the sense required by the equilibrium concept. Indeed, what would his fellow players think of the player who deviated from the equilibrium path? It is as if the rationality of the players binds and constrains them to a certain course of action. Thus the equilibrium property P2 which defines equilibrium is in conflict with the notion of rationality underlying the equilibrium. Equilibrium is defined by comparison with a hypothetical deviation from equilibrium: yet no such deviation is consistent with the rationality of players.

There are of course ways of attempting to resolve this paradox: the players may be rational, but may make mistakes in choosing their actions (their hands might 'tremble'). However, the paradox remains and stems from the same source as the general problem with disequilibrium analysis that we noted in section 13.2. If agents deviate from equilibrium, then in some sense they could do better: they have made a mistake. A formal notion of economic rationality cannot explain such mistakes: as economists we cannot understand such mistakes.

To close this section on time and equilibrium, it is worth noting that in the case of an intertemporal equilibrium (e.g. the Arrow–Debreu world or a perfect equilibrium) the stability property P3 is redundant. In an intertemporal equilibrium, actions are made consistent across time. The question of how you get to equilibrium is not possible: you are always already there. In the case of a static equilibrium, you can imagine starting in a disequilibrium state and moving towards equilibrium. If equilibrium spreads across time, there is no possibility of a pocket or era of disequilibrium. This comment is still valid in adjustment models: there is an equilibrium adjustment path to a long-run steady state equilibrium.

13.5 Conclusion

In this chapter, some important equilibria have been looked at, and others have been ignored. What general lessons can be learned from the exercise? I will conclude with a few unguarded conclusions expressing my own feelings.

First, although there is a loosely defined equilibrium method employed in economics, there are many different types of equilibrium which embody different views of the world. It makes little or no sense to talk of 'the equilibrium concept in economics'. At most there is a family resemblance present.

Second, the equilibrium method plays a crucial role in the process of explanation in economics. Out of equilibrium, actions of agents become inconsistent, or plans cannot be realized, or agents do worse than they could. Mistakes are made. With a formal notion of rationality, economists cannot explain mistakes. In equilibrium, in contrast, the interactions of agents are brought together and made consistent, and in some sense their actions are the right ones to take. We can thus explain things by saying: 'if everyone does as well as they can, then this happens'. This puts a great constraint on economics. Because economists seek to explain, they seek to expand the equilibrium method to embrace more and more phenomena, real or imagined. Thus what is initially seen as a disequilibrium situation becomes a challenge to economists, who invent new equilibria to cover it (as in the case of 'disequilibrium' macroeconomics resting on fix-price equilibria). This paradox is particularly acute in game theory, where equilibrium is defined by hypothetical deviations from equilibrium which should not occur if agents are rational. The answer to the problem might seem obvious: replace a formal model of economic rationality with a substantive model of rationality. If we model the actual decision-making process, we can then explain why it might go wrong. Whilst this may well prove to be the way forward in future, at present it seems an unacceptable alternative to most: to economists there is no obvious model of substantive rationality that is consistent with economics as practised today (which is of course based on formal rationality). Alternatively, the spread of equilibrium may represent an expansion of our explanatory power, an advance of knowledge.

Third, different types of equilibria embody different visions of the world, and with the passing of time economists' perspectives change. Thus what economists view as the paradigmatic equilibrium has varied over time (as it may also vary geographically). Thus, recent years have seen a shift in interest from the Arrow–Debreu world of price-taking agents to a game-theoretic world of large or small agents strategically interacting within and across markets non-cooperatively. It will be interesting to see what comes next.

REFERENCES

Barro, R., and H. Grossman (1971) 'A general disequilibrium theory of income and employment', *American Economic Review* 61, 82–92.

Benassy, J. (1975) 'NeoKeynesian disequilibrium theory in a monetary economy', *Review of Economic Studies* 42, 503–23.

Cho, I. (1987) 'A refinement of sequential Equilibria', *Econometrica* 55, 1367–89.

Clower, R. (1965) 'The Keynesian counter-revolution: a theoretical appraisal', Reprinted in *Monetary Theory*. Ed. R. Clower, 1969, Harmondsworth: Penguin.

Cournot, A. (1838) *Recherches sur la Théorie Mathématique de la Richesse*. Trans. N. T. Bacon, 1960, London: Hafner.

Debreu, G. (1959) *Theory of Value*. New York: Wiley.

Dixon, H. (1987) 'Approximate Bertrand equilibria in a replicate economy', *Review of Economic Studies* 54, 47–62.

Dixon, H. (1988a) 'Bertrand–Edgeworth equilibria with discrete prices', Mimeo, University of Essex Discussion Papers.

Dixon, H. (1988b) 'Oligopoly theory made simple', in *Economics of Industrial Organisation*. Ed. Davies et al., Harlow: Longman, ch. 6.

Fischer, F. (1981) 'Stability, disequilibrium awareness, and the perception of new opportunities', *Econometrica* 49, 279–317.

Friedman, M. (1968) 'The role of monetary policy', *American Economic Review* 79, 1–18.

Hahn, F., and T. Negishi (1962) 'A theorem on non-tâtonnement stability', *Econometrica* 30, 463–9.

Jones, H. (1975) *Modern Theories of Economic Growth*. London: Nelson.

Kaldor, N. (1957) 'A model of economic growth', *Economic Journal* 591–624.

Keynes, J. M. (1936) *The General Theory of Employment, Interest, and Money*. London: Macmillan.

Leijonhufvud, A. (1968) *On Keynesian economics and the economics of Keynes*. Milton Keynes: Open University Press.

Malinvaud, E. (1977) *The Theory of Unemployment Reconsidered*. Oxford: Blackwell.

Marimon, R. (1987) 'Krep's "Three essays on capital markets". Almost ten years later', Discussion Paper No. 245, Minnesota University.

Marshall, A. (1890) *Principles of Economics*. London: Macmillan.

Modigliani, F., and P. Samuelson (1966) 'The Pasinetti paradox in neoclassical and more general models, *Review of Economic Studies* 76, 269–301.

Samuelson, P. (1948) 'The simple mathematics of income determination', in *Income, Employment and Policy*. New York: Norton.

Shackle, G. (1974) *Keynesian Kaleidics*. Edinburgh: Edinburgh University Press.

Shubik, M. (1985) *Strategy and Market Structure*. Cambridge: Cambridge University Press.

Spence, M. (1974): *Market Signalling*. Cambridge, Mass.: Harvard University Press.

Index

Index compiled by Jackie McDermott